BLADE OF THE IMMORTAL

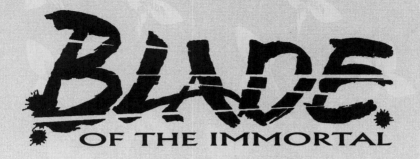

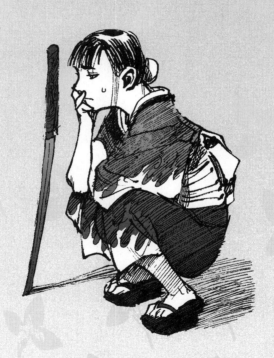

Dark Shadows

publisher
Mike Richardson

series editor
Rachel Penn

collection editor
Chris Warner

collection designer
Amy Arendts
& Darcy Hockett

**English-language version produced by
Studio Proteus for Dark Horse Comics, Inc.**

BLADE OF THE IMMORTAL Vol. 6: DARK SHADOWS
Blade of the Immortal © 1999, 2000 by Hiroaki Samura. All rights
reserved. First published in Japan in 1996 by Kodansha Ltd., Tokyo.
English translation rights arranged through Kodansha Ltd. New and
adapted artwork and text © 1999, 2000 Studio Proteus and Dark
Horse Comics, Inc. All other material © 2000 Dark Horse Comics, Inc.
All rights reserved. No portion of this publication may be reproduced,
in any form or by any means, without the express written permission
of the copyright holders. Names, characters, places, and incidents
featured in this publication either are the product of the author's
imagination or are used fictitiously. Any resemblance to actual persons
(living or dead), events, institutions, or locales, without satiric intent,
is coincidental. Dark Horse Comics® and the Dark Horse logo are
registered trademarks of Dark Horse Comics, Inc., registered in various
categories and countries. All rights reserved.

This book collects issues twenty-nine through
thirty-four of the Dark Horse comic-book series,
Blade of the Immortal.

Published by
Dark Horse Comics, Inc.
10956 SE Main Street
Milwaukie, OR 97222

www.darkhorse.com

To find a comics shop in your area, call the
Comic Shop Locator Service toll-free at 1-888-266-4226

First edition: September 2000
ISBN: 1-56971-469-X

1 3 5 7 9 10 8 6 4 2

Printed in Canada

BLADE
OF THE IMMORTAL

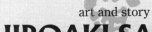

art and story
HIROAKI SAMURA

translation
Dana Lewis & Toren Smith

lettering and retouch
Tomoko Saito

Dark Shadows

DARK HORSE COMICS®

ABOUT THE TRANSLATION

The Swastika

The main character in *Blade of the Immortal*, Manji, has taken the "crux gammata" as both his name and his personal symbol. This symbol is also known as the *swastika*, a name derived from the Sanskrit *svastika* (meaning "welfare," from su — "well" + asti "he is"). As a symbol of prosperity and good fortune, the swastika was widely used throughout the ancient world (for example, appearing often on Mesopotamian coinage), including North and South America and has been used in Japan as a symbol of Buddhism since ancient times. To be precise, the symbol generally used by Japanese Buddhists is the *sauvastika*, which moves in a counterclockwise direction, and is called the *manji* in Japanese. The *sauvastika* generally stands for night, and often for magical practices. The *swastika*, whose arms point in a clockwise direction, is generally considered a solar symbol. It was this version (the *hakenkreuz*) that was perverted by the Nazis and used as their symbol. It is important that readers understand that the *swastika* has ancient and honorable origins and it is those that apply to this story, which takes place in the 18th century (ca. 1782-3). *There is no anti-Semitic or pro-Nazi meaning behind the use of the symbol in this story. Those meanings did not exist until after 1910.*

The Artwork

The creator of *Blade of the Immortal* requested that we make an effort to avoid mirror-imaging his artwork. Normally, all of our manga are first copied in a mirror-image in order to facilitate the left-to-right reading of the pages. However, Mr. Samura decided that he would rather see his pages reversed via the technique of cutting up the panels and re-pasting them in reverse order. While we feel that this often leads to problems in panel-to-panel continuity, we place primary importance on the wishes of the creator. Therefore, most of *Blade of the Immortal* has been produced using the "cut and paste" technique. There are, of course, some sequences where it was impossible to do this, and mirror-imaged panels or pages were used.

The Sound Effects & Dialogue

Since some of Mr. Samura's sound effects are integral parts of the artwork, we decided to leave those in their original Japanese. When it was crucial to the understanding of the panel that the sound effect be in English, however, Mr. Samura chose to redraw the panel. We hope readers will view the unretouched sound effects as essential portions of Mr. Samura's extraordinary artwork. In addition, Mr. Samura's treatment of dialogue is quite different from that featured in average samurai manga and is considered to be one of the things that has made *Blade* such a hit in Japan. Mr. Samura has mixed a variety of linguistic styles in this fantasy story, where some characters speak in the mannered style of old Japan, while others speak as if they were street-corner punks from a bad area of modern-day Tokyo. The anachronistic slang used by some of the characters in the English translation reflects the unusual mix of speech patterns from the original Japanese text.

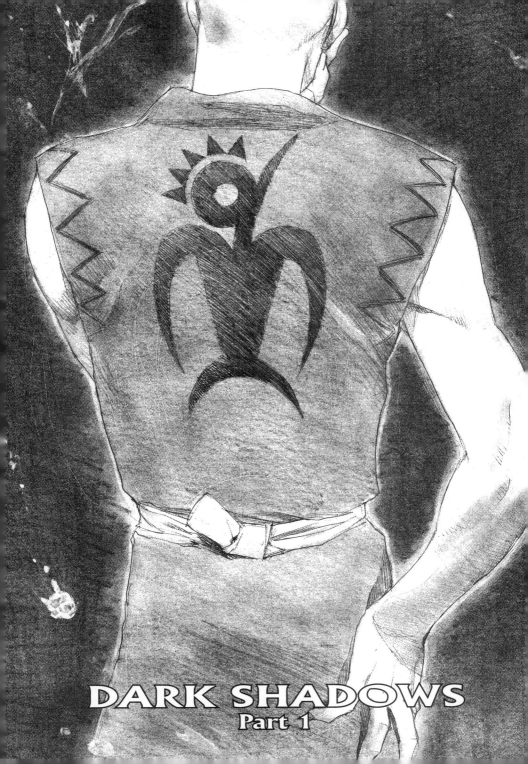

DARK SHADOWS
Part 1

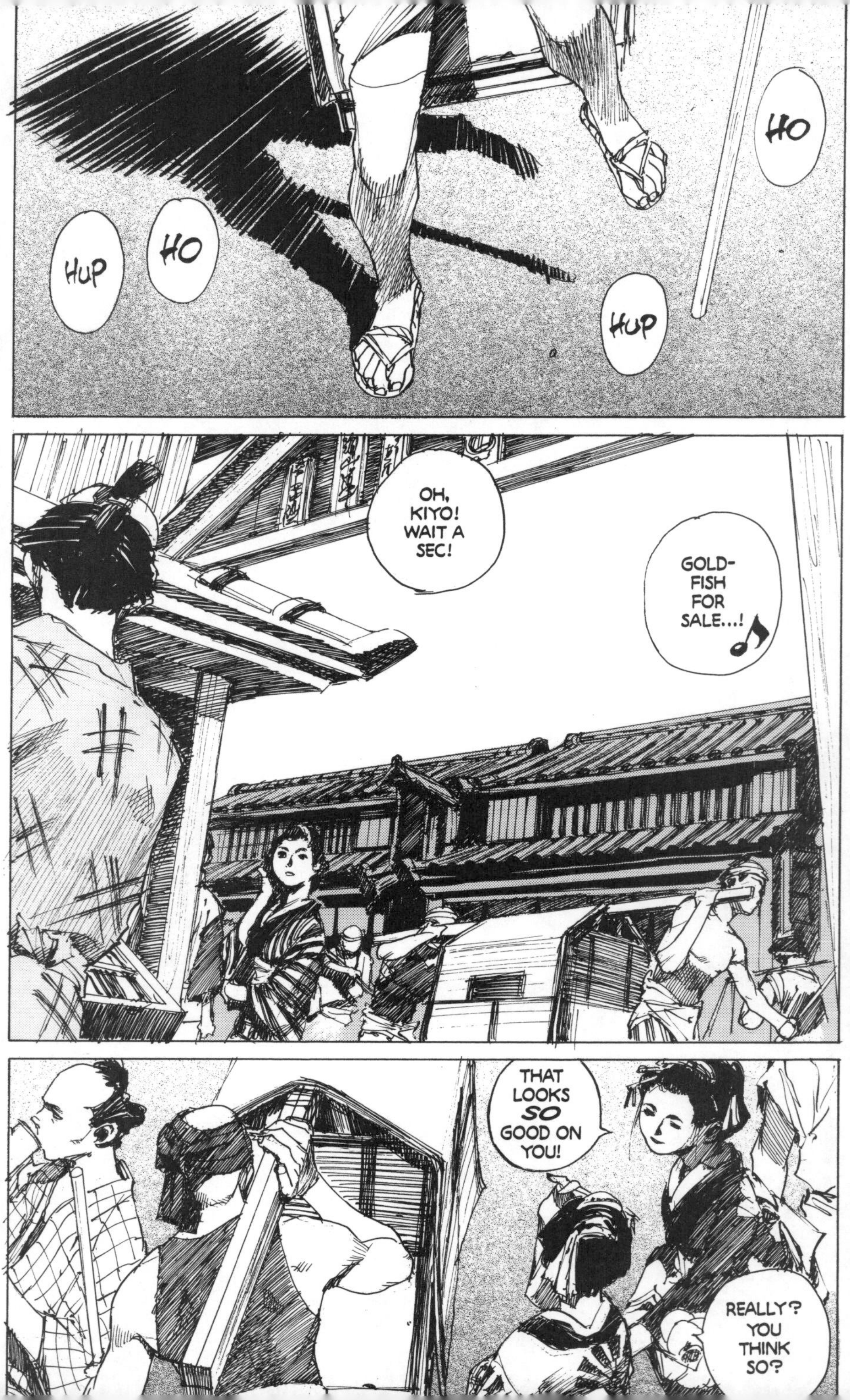
HUP
HO
HUP
HO
OH, KIYO! WAIT A SEC!
GOLD-FISH FOR SALE...! ♪
THAT LOOKS SO GOOD ON YOU!
REALLY? YOU THINK SO?

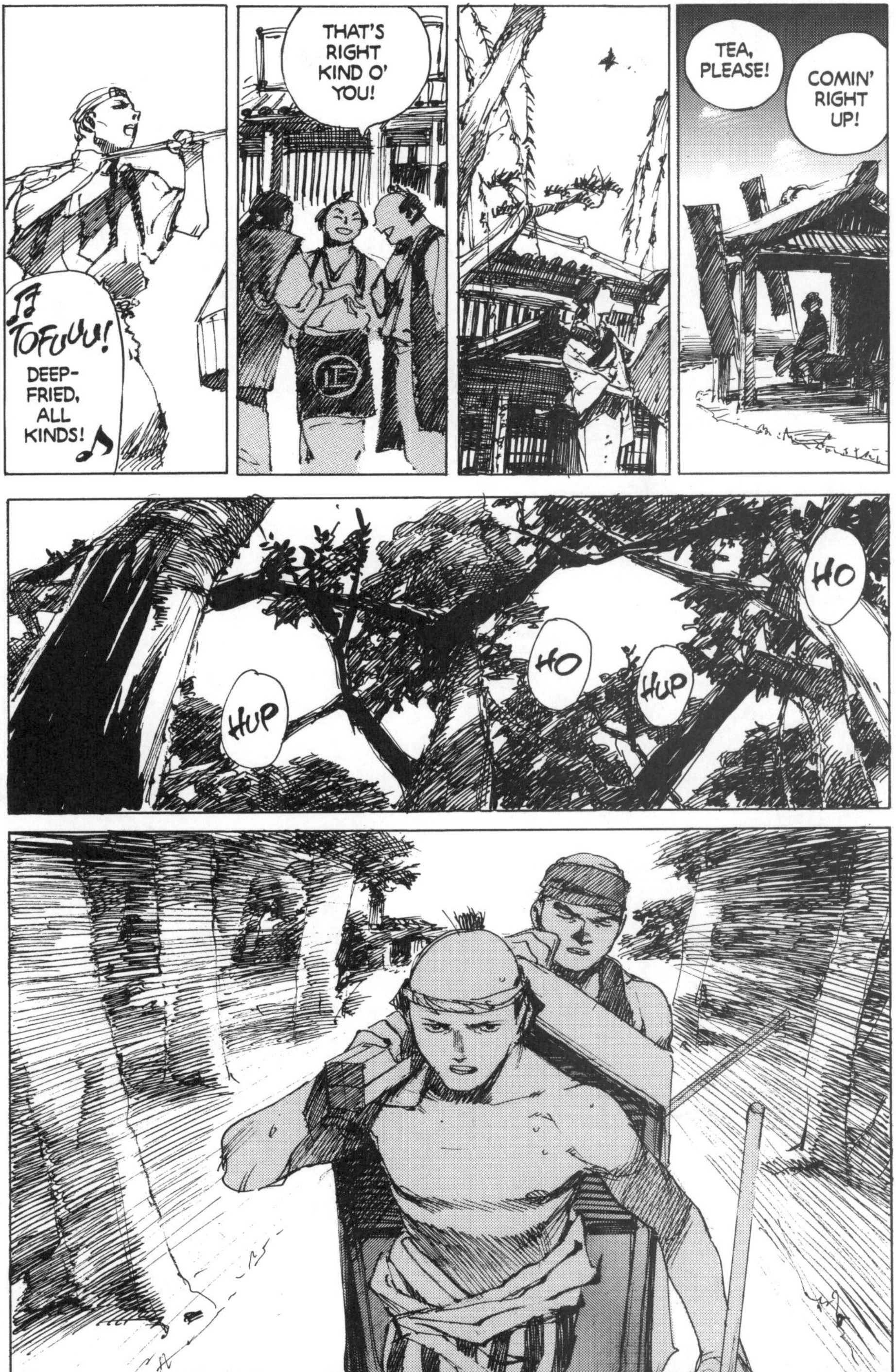
TOFUUU!
DEEP-FRIED, ALL KINDS!
THAT'S RIGHT KIND O' YOU!
TEA, PLEASE!
COMIN' RIGHT UP!
HUP
HO
HUP
HO

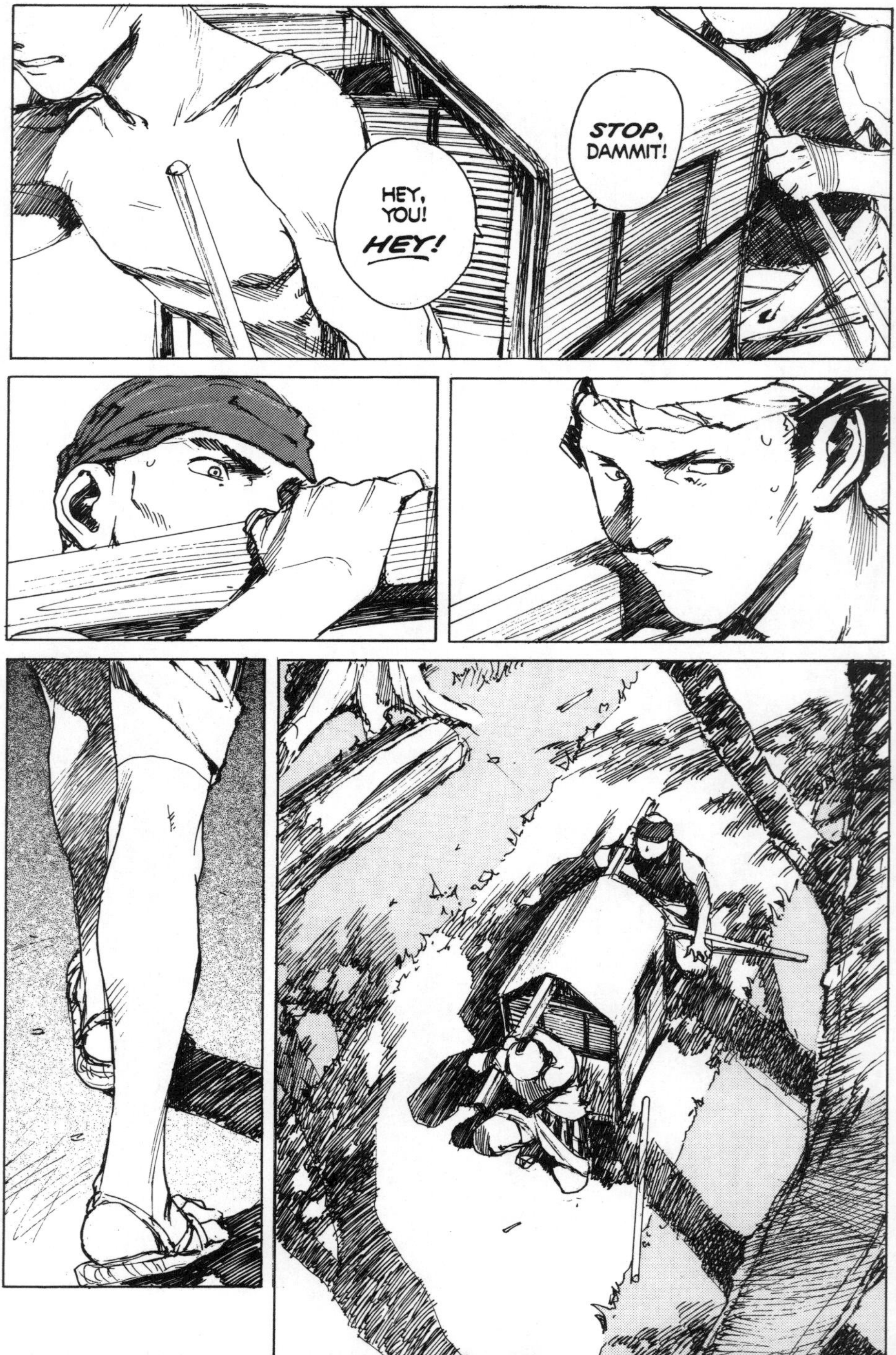
HEY, YOU! HEY!
STOP, DAMMIT!

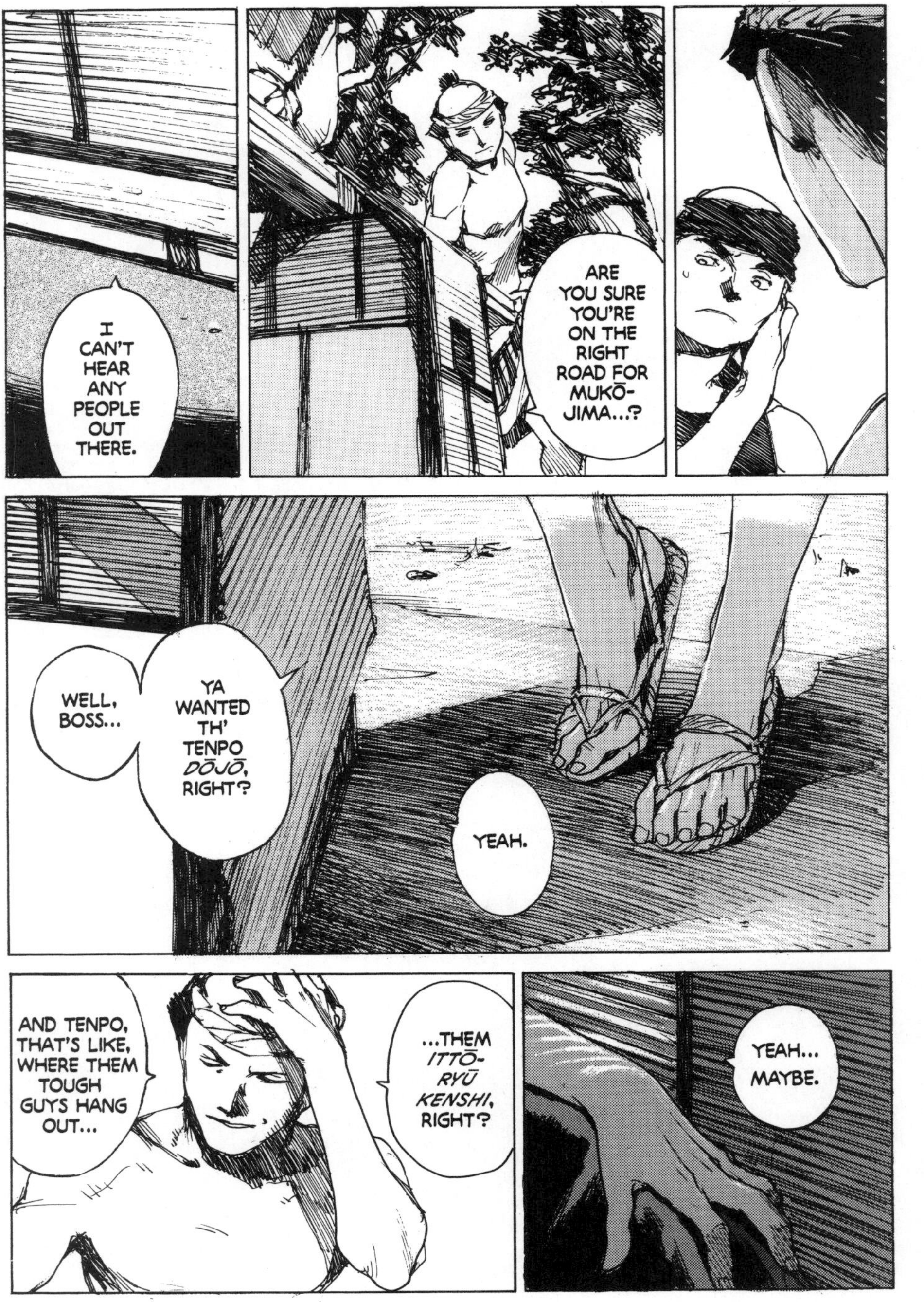
I CAN'T HEAR ANY PEOPLE OUT THERE.
ARE YOU SURE YOU'RE ON THE RIGHT ROAD FOR MUKŌ-JIMA...?
WELL, BOSS...
YA WANTED TH' TENPO *DŌJŌ*, RIGHT?
YEAH.
AND TENPO, THAT'S LIKE, WHERE THEM TOUGH GUYS HANG OUT...
...THEM *ITTŌ-RYŪ KENSHI*, RIGHT?
YEAH... MAYBE.

SO, IF YER HEADIN' FOR A PLACE LIKE THAT...

...WE FIGURED, Y'KNOW, MAYBE... YOU'RE ONE--

I FAIL TO SEE WHAT THIS HAS TO DO WITH YOUR JOB...?

WELL, NOTHING, BOSS. IT'S JUST, YA KNOW...

...IT'S LIKE, A BIG HONOR. EH?

YOU GUYS ARE COOL, MAN. ESPECIALLY NOWADAYS, WITH ALL THEM WIMPY SAMURAI AROUND...

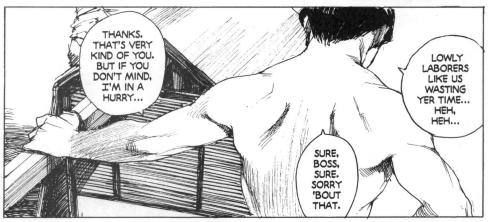

THANKS. THAT'S VERY KIND OF YOU. BUT IF YOU DON'T MIND, I'M IN A HURRY...

LOWLY LABORERS LIKE US WASTING YER TIME... HEH, HEH...

SURE, BOSS, SURE. SORRY 'BOUT THAT.

JUST LIE BACK AND ENJOY THE RIDE...

...AND IT'LL BE OVER BEFORE YA KNOW IT.

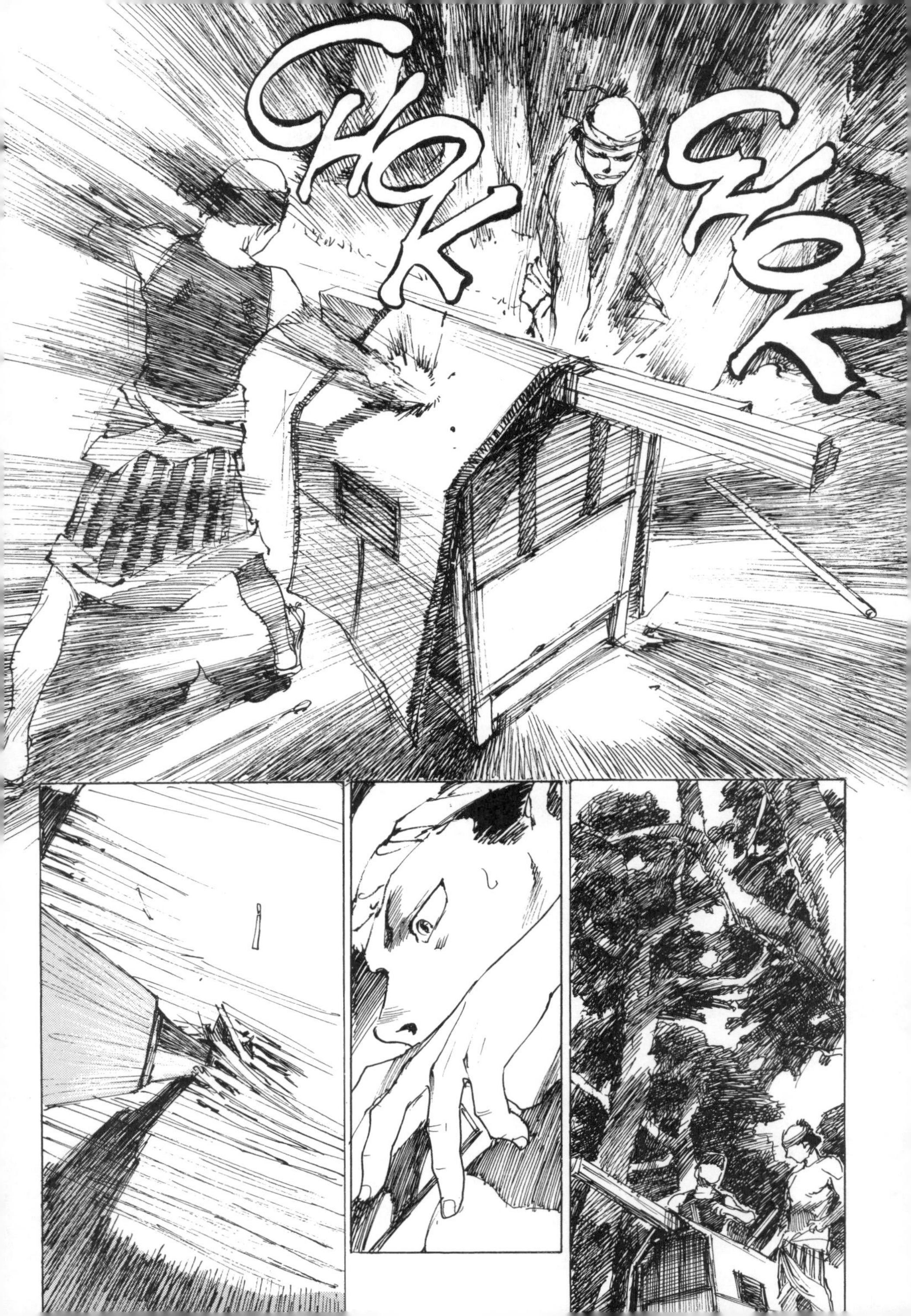
CHOK
CHOK

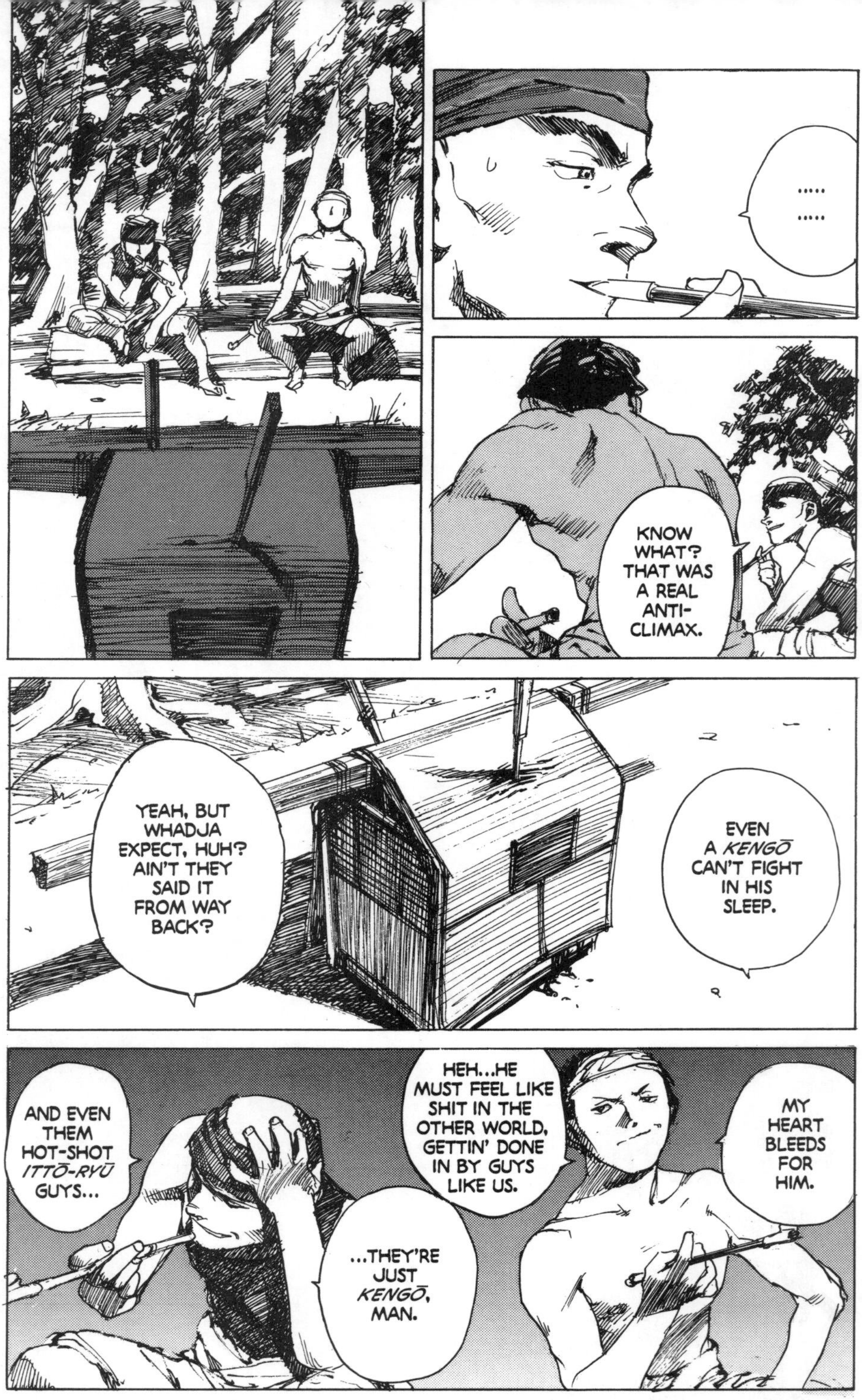
.....
.....
KNOW WHAT? THAT WAS A REAL ANTI-CLIMAX.
YEAH, BUT WHADJA EXPECT, HUH? AIN'T THEY SAID IT FROM WAY BACK?
EVEN A *KENGŌ* CAN'T FIGHT IN HIS SLEEP.
AND EVEN THEM HOT-SHOT *ITTŌ-RYŪ* GUYS...
HEH...HE MUST FEEL LIKE SHIT IN THE OTHER WORLD, GETTIN' DONE IN BY GUYS LIKE US.
...THEY'RE JUST *KENGŌ*, MAN.
MY HEART BLEEDS FOR HIM.

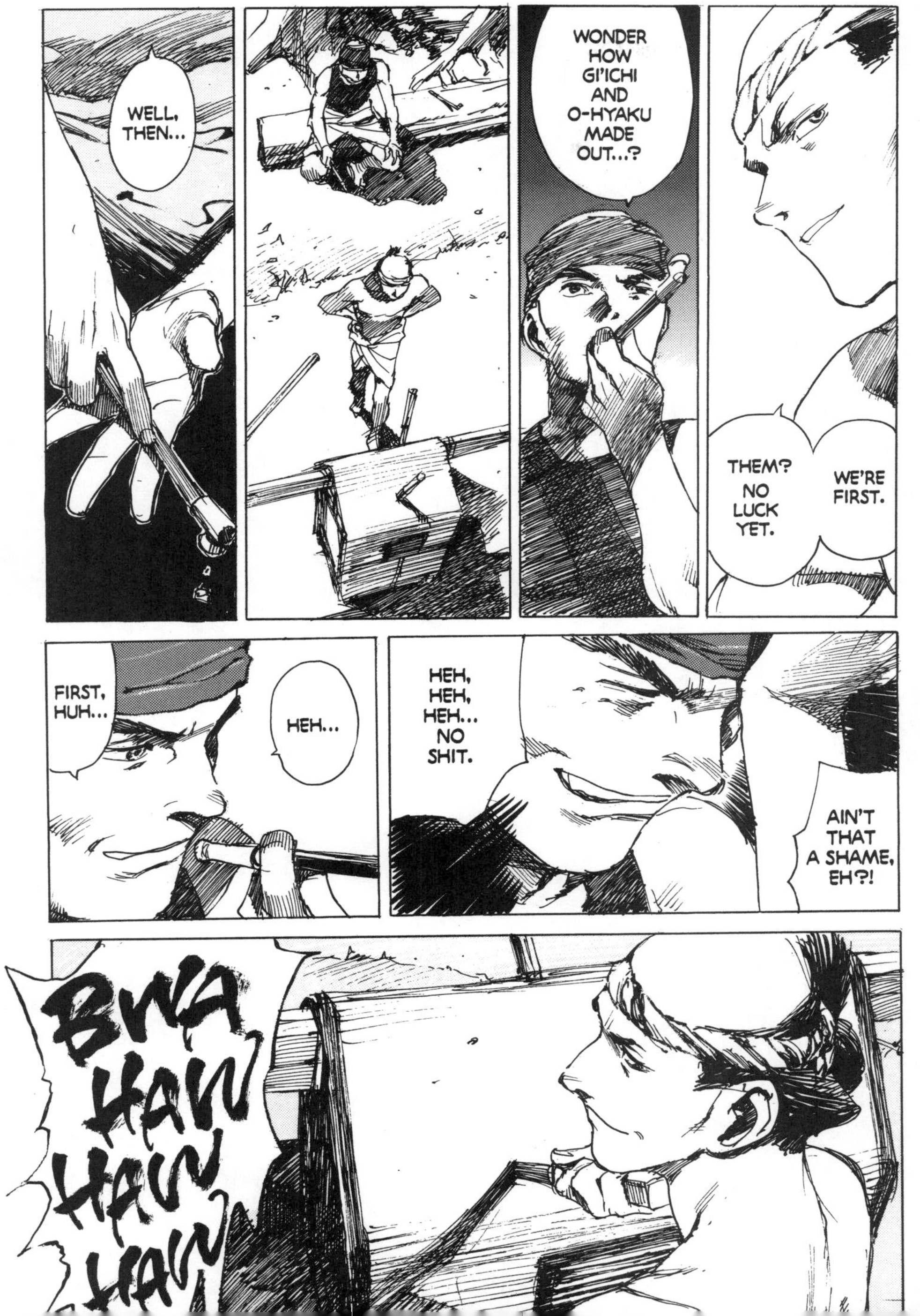
WELL, THEN...
WONDER HOW GI'ICHI AND O-HYAKU MADE OUT...?
THEM? NO LUCK YET.
WE'RE FIRST.
FIRST, HUH...
HEH...
HEH, HEH, HEH... NO SHIT.
AIN'T THAT A SHAME, EH?!
BWA HAW HAW HAW

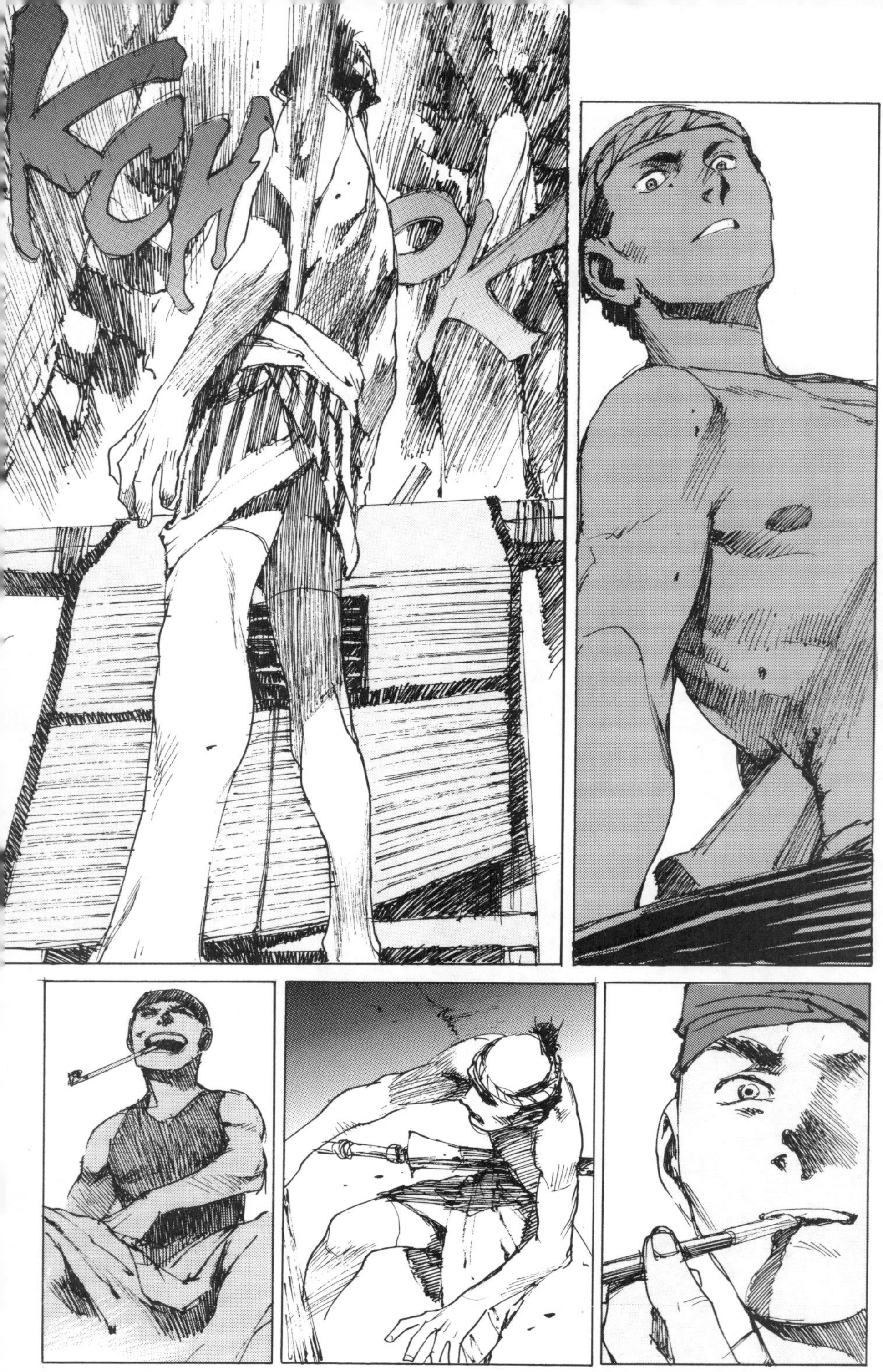
Kchok

....!

YOU KNOW, WE *ITTŌ-RYŪ* GUYS...

...WE'RE PRETTY MUCH JUST A BUNCH OF SCRUFFY WANDERERS. SO WE GOT TATTOO ARTISTS...

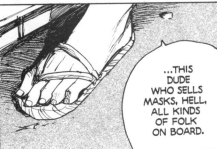

...THIS DUDE WHO SELLS MASKS, HELL, ALL KINDS OF FOLK ON BOARD.

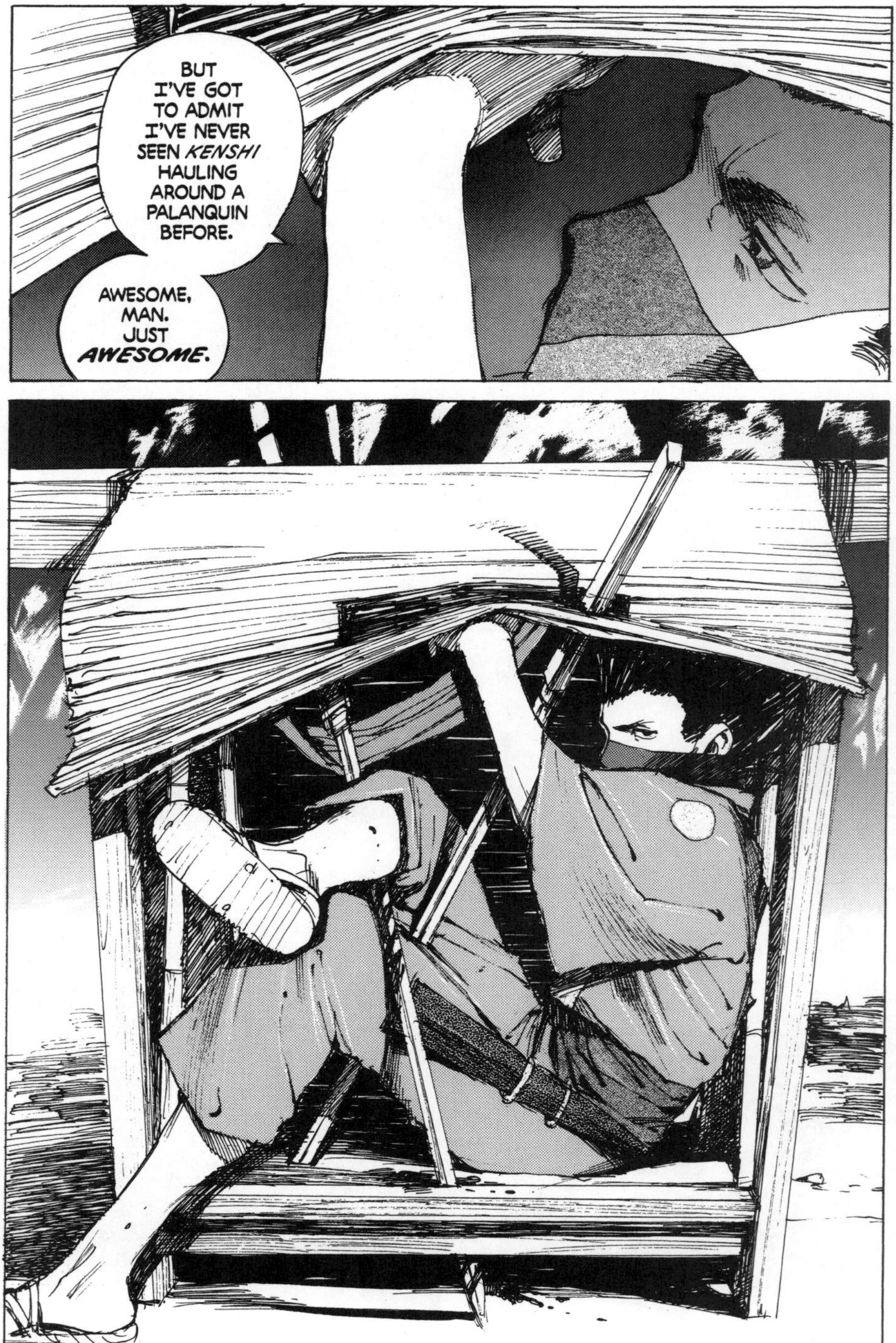
BUT I'VE GOT TO ADMIT I'VE NEVER SEEN *KENSHI* HAULING AROUND A PALANQUIN BEFORE.
AWESOME, MAN. JUST ***AWESOME***.

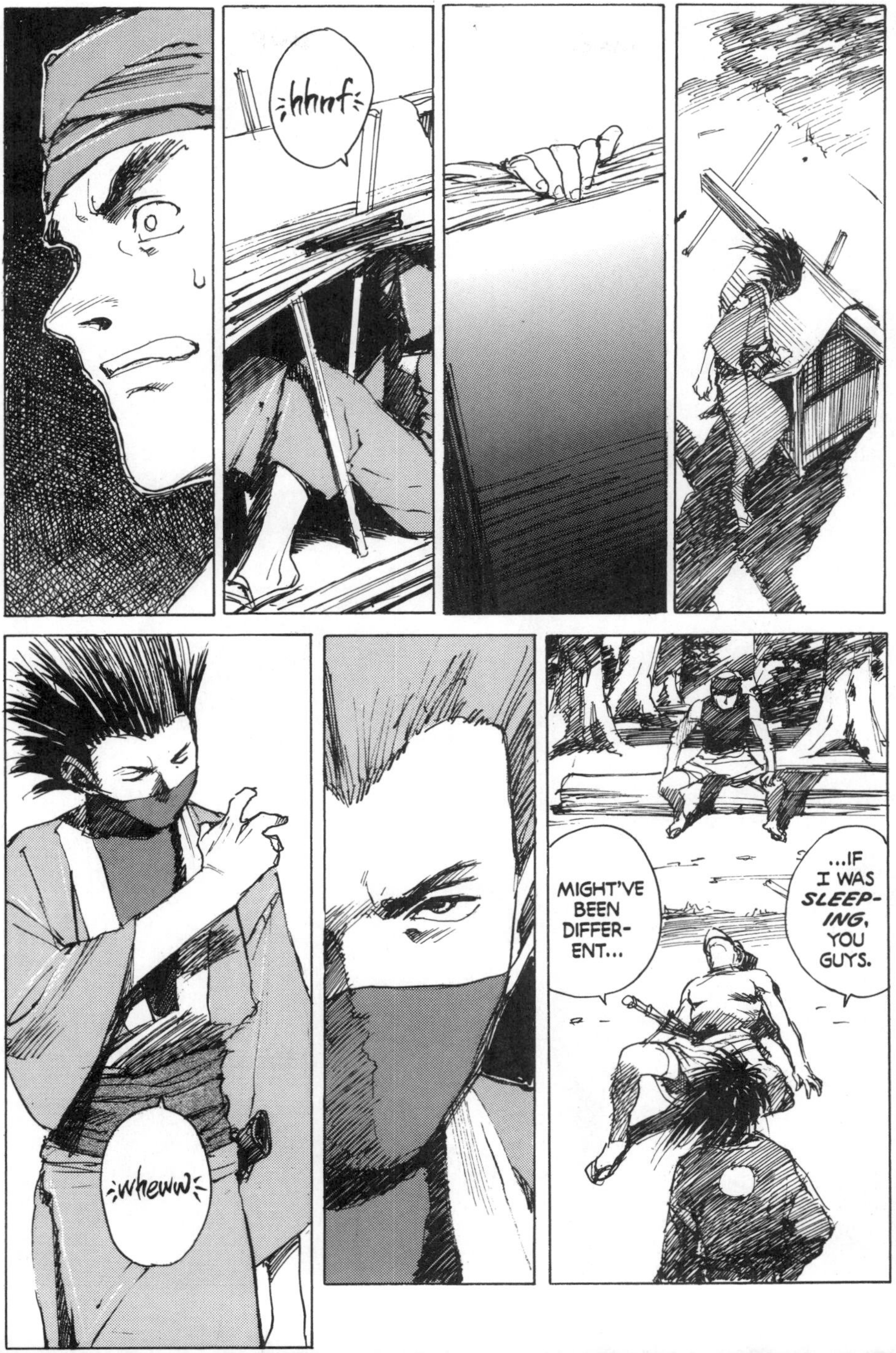
hhnf
wheww
MIGHT'VE BEEN DIFFER-ENT...
...IF I WAS SLEEP-ING, YOU GUYS.

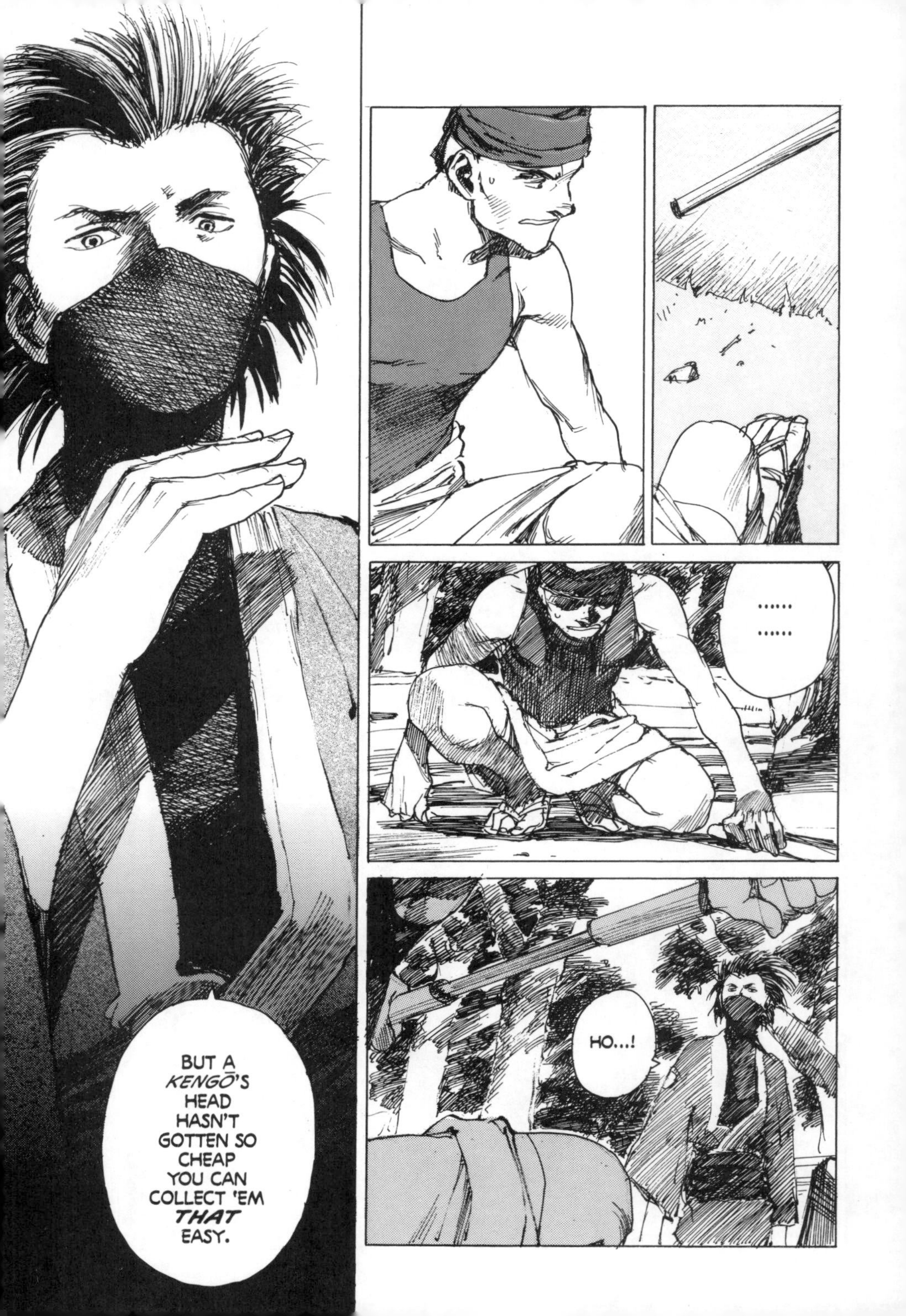
BUT A *KENGŌ*'S HEAD HASN'T GOTTEN SO CHEAP YOU CAN COLLECT 'EM ***THAT*** EASY.
......
......
HO...!

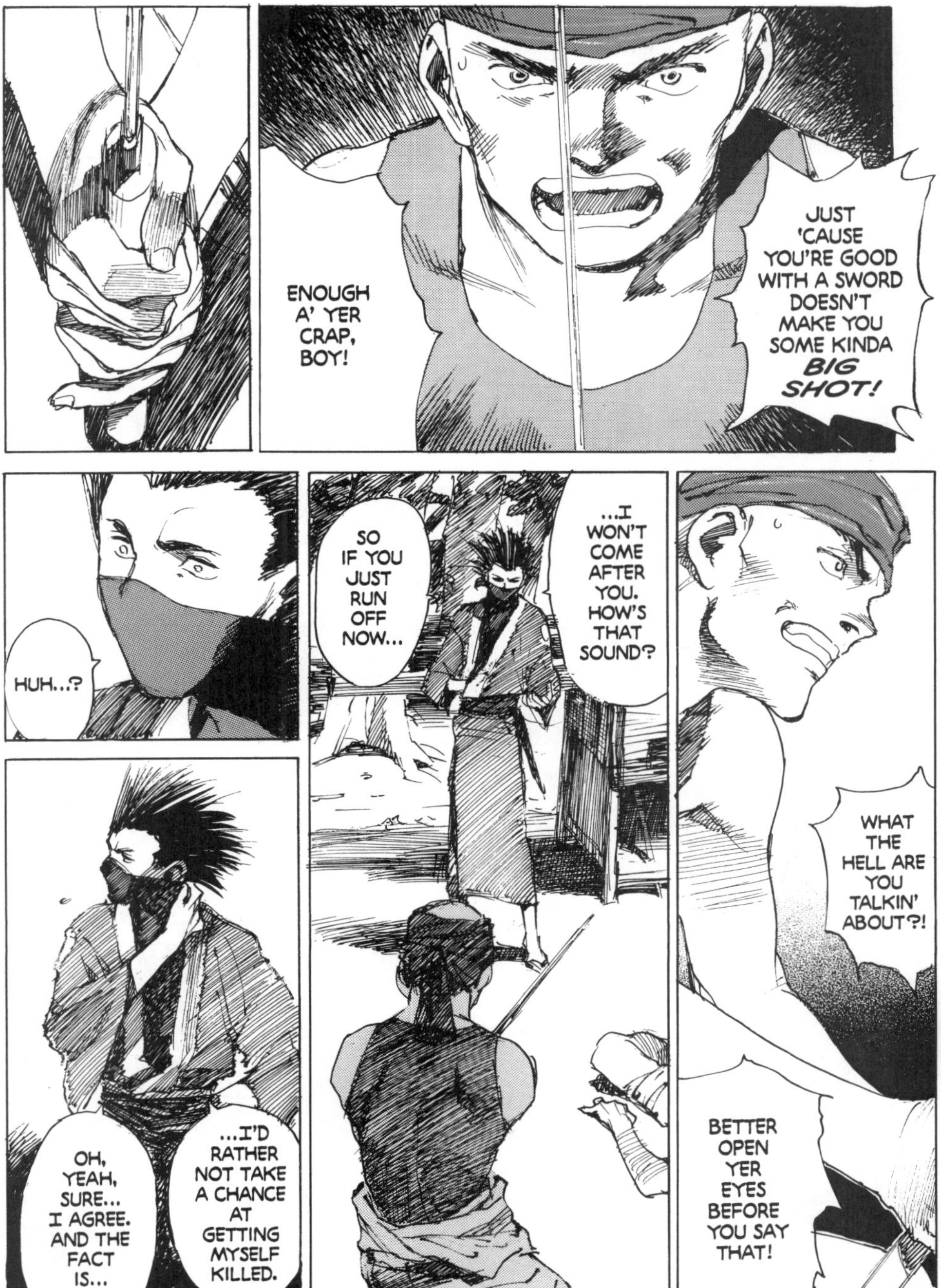
ENOUGH A' YER CRAP, BOY!
JUST 'CAUSE YOU'RE GOOD WITH A SWORD DOESN'T MAKE YOU SOME KINDA *BIG SHOT!*
HUH...?
OH, YEAH, SURE... I AGREE. AND THE FACT IS...
...I'D RATHER NOT TAKE A CHANCE AT GETTING MYSELF KILLED.
SO IF YOU JUST RUN OFF NOW...
...I WON'T COME AFTER YOU. HOW'S THAT SOUND?
WHAT THE HELL ARE YOU TALKIN' ABOUT?!
BETTER OPEN YER EYES BEFORE YOU SAY THAT!

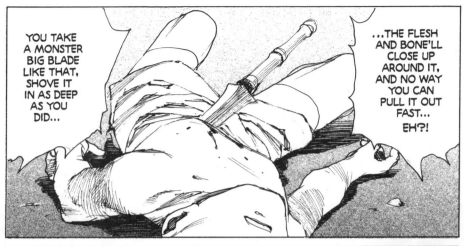

YOU TAKE A MONSTER BIG BLADE LIKE THAT, SHOVE IT IN AS DEEP AS YOU DID...

...THE FLESH AND BONE'LL CLOSE UP AROUND IT, AND NO WAY YOU CAN PULL IT OUT FAST... EH?!

?

SAY... NOW THAT YOU MENTION IT, THAT'S RIGHT.

HAH! A LOSER LIKE YOU COULDN'T EVEN MAKE *KENGŌ!*

PENCIL-NECKED *GEEK!!*

RRAAAH!!

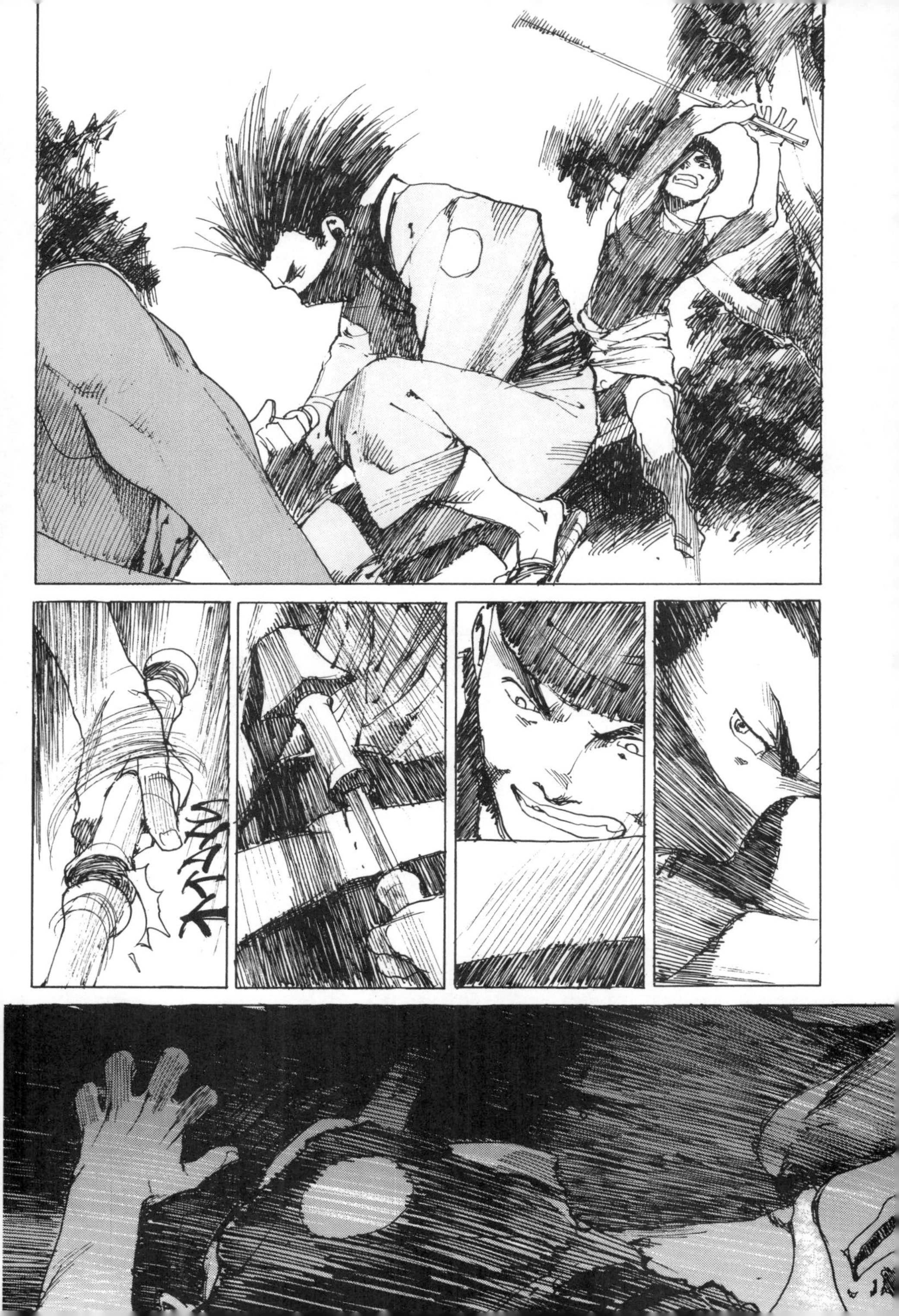
SMACK

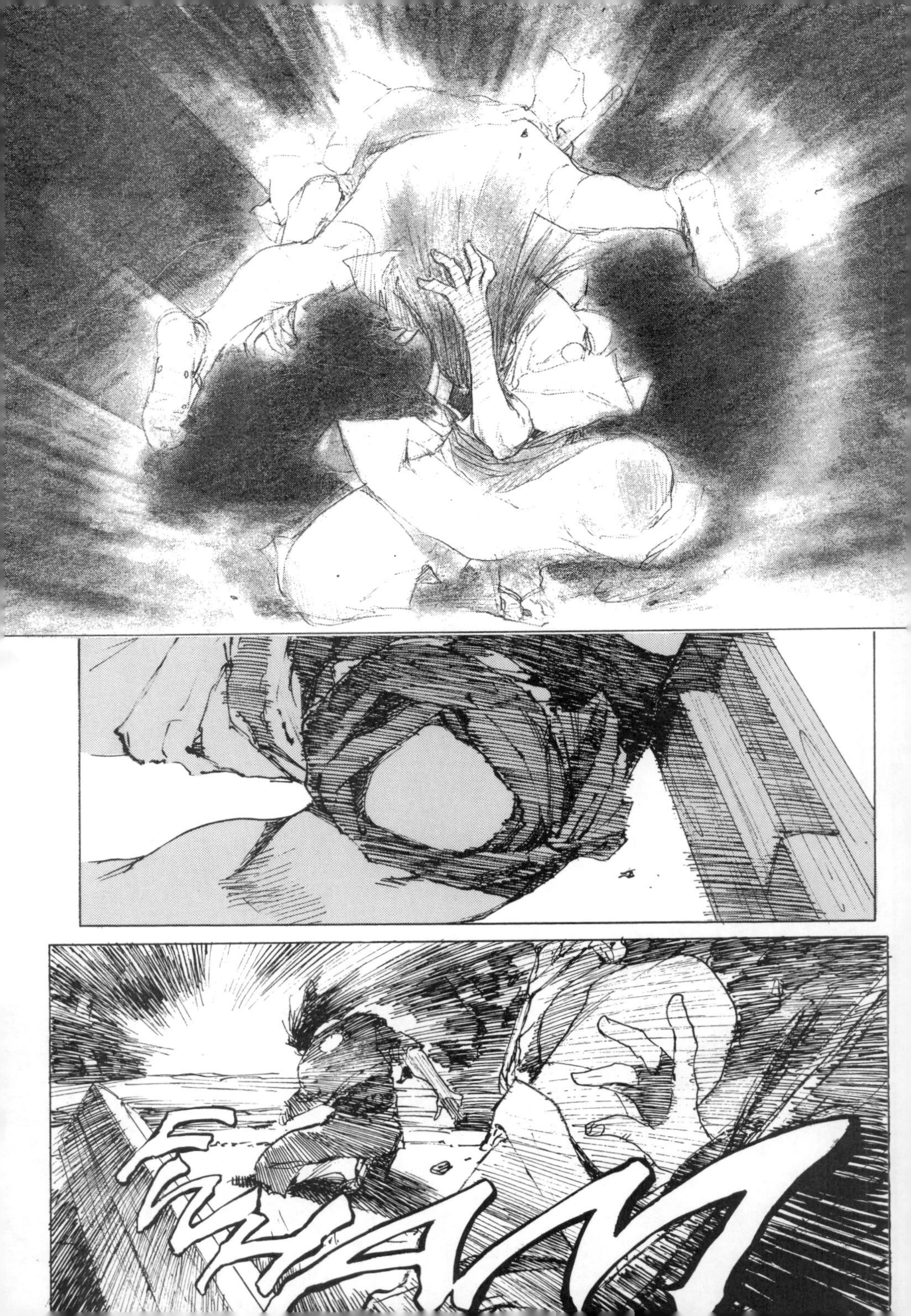

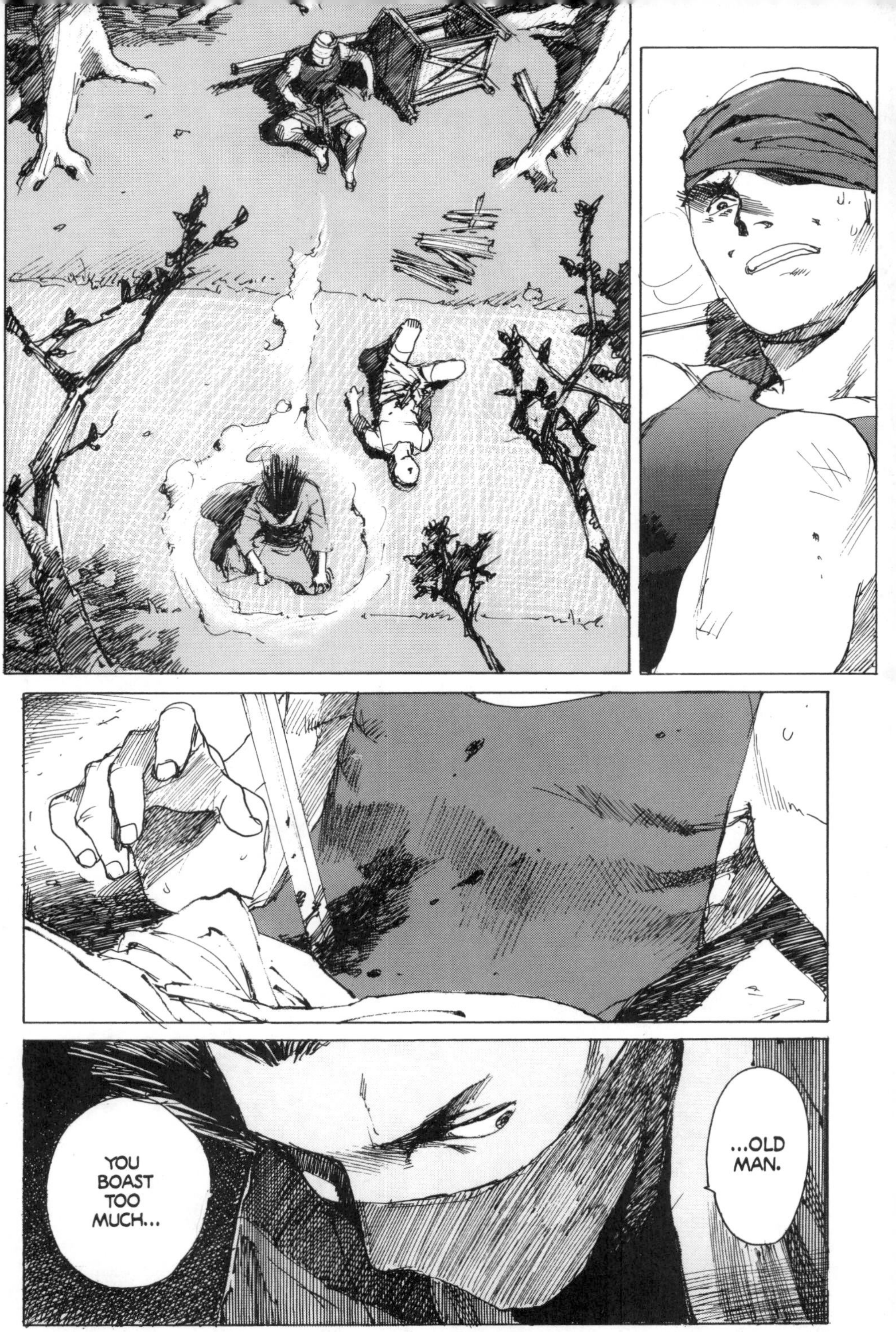
YOU BOAST TOO MUCH...
...OLD MAN.

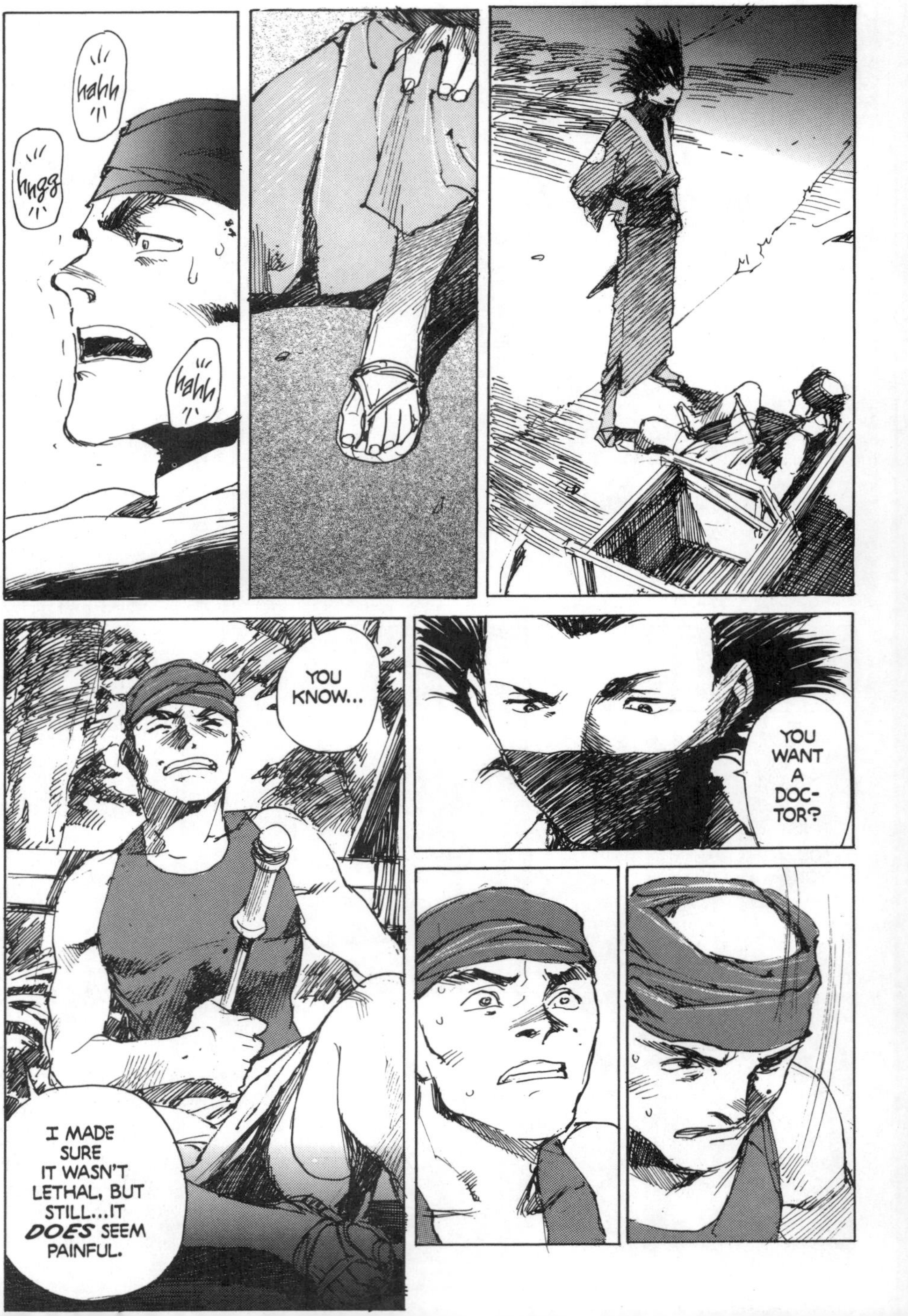
hahh
hngg
hahh
YOU KNOW...
YOU WANT A DOC-TOR?
I MADE SURE IT WASN'T LETHAL, BUT STILL...IT DOES SEEM PAINFUL.

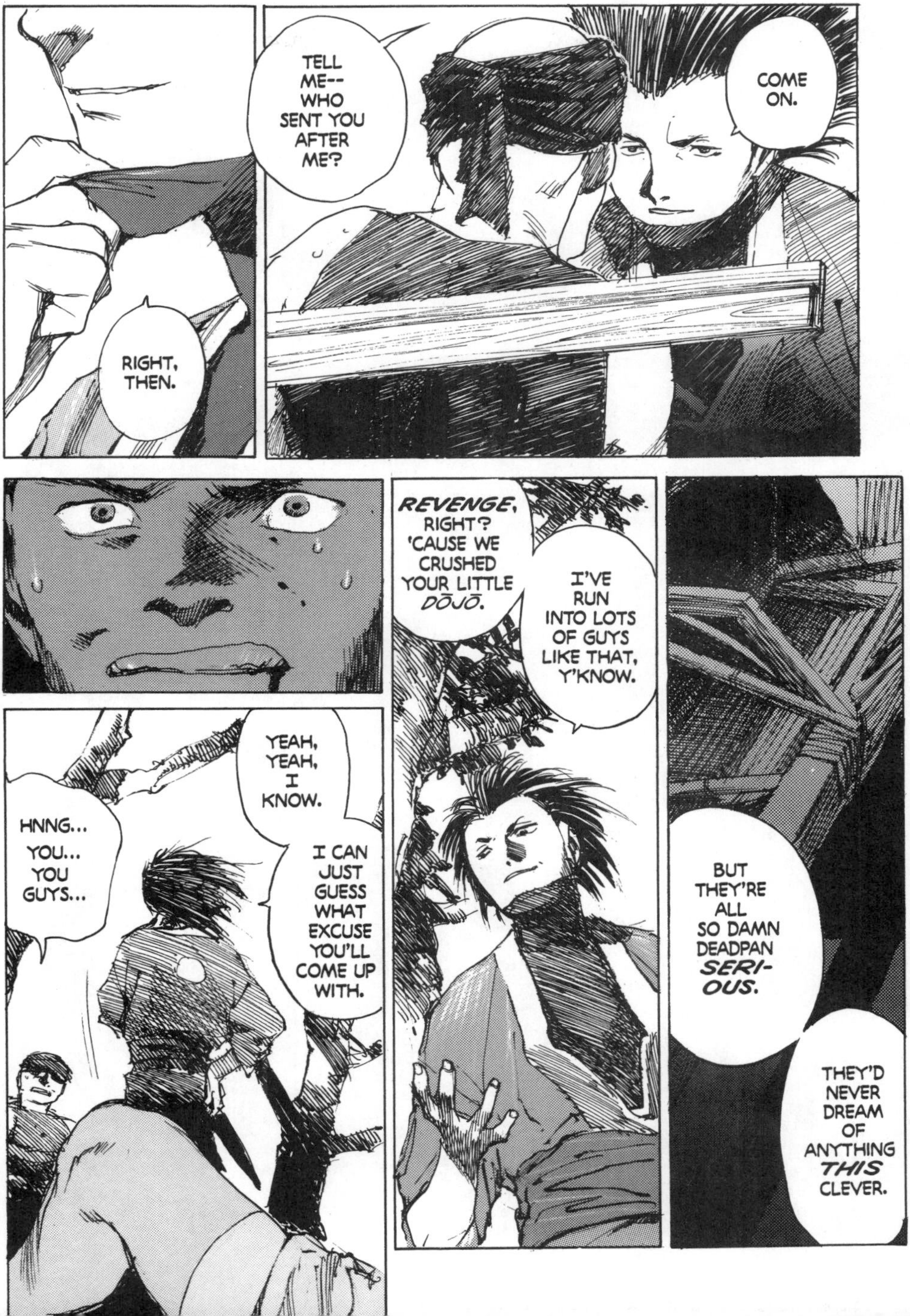
RIGHT, THEN.
TELL ME-- WHO SENT YOU AFTER ME?
COME ON.
REVENGE, RIGHT? 'CAUSE WE CRUSHED YOUR LITTLE DŌJŌ.
I'VE RUN INTO LOTS OF GUYS LIKE THAT, Y'KNOW.
BUT THEY'RE ALL SO DAMN DEADPAN SERI-OUS.
THEY'D NEVER DREAM OF ANYTHING THIS CLEVER.
HNNG... YOU... YOU GUYS...
YEAH, YEAH, I KNOW.
I CAN JUST GUESS WHAT EXCUSE YOU'LL COME UP WITH.

YOU KNOW... IF YOU DON'T GET YOURSELF PATCHED UP, YOU'LL BLEED TO DEATH.

ANSWER ME, AND I'LL DRAG YOUR SORRY ASS TO A DOCTOR. SO...?

hahh

hahh

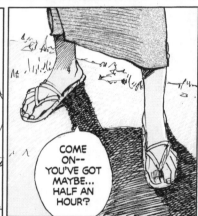

COME ON-- YOU'VE GOT MAYBE... HALF AN HOUR?

......

......

MM?

hahh

hahh

hahh

HNG!

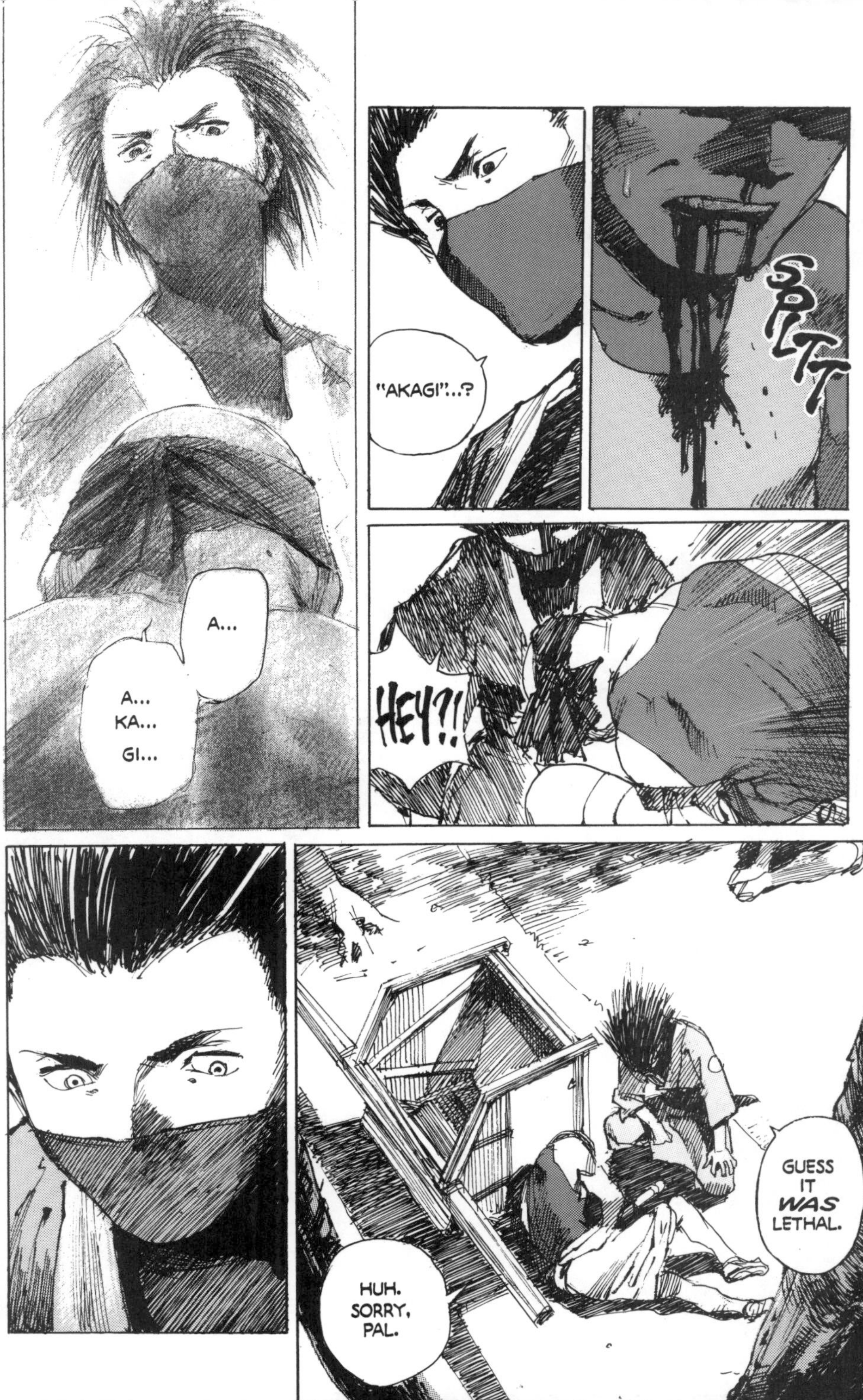
A...
A... KA... GI...
"AKAGI"..?
SPLTT
HEY?!
GUESS IT WAS LETHAL.
HUH. SORRY, PAL.

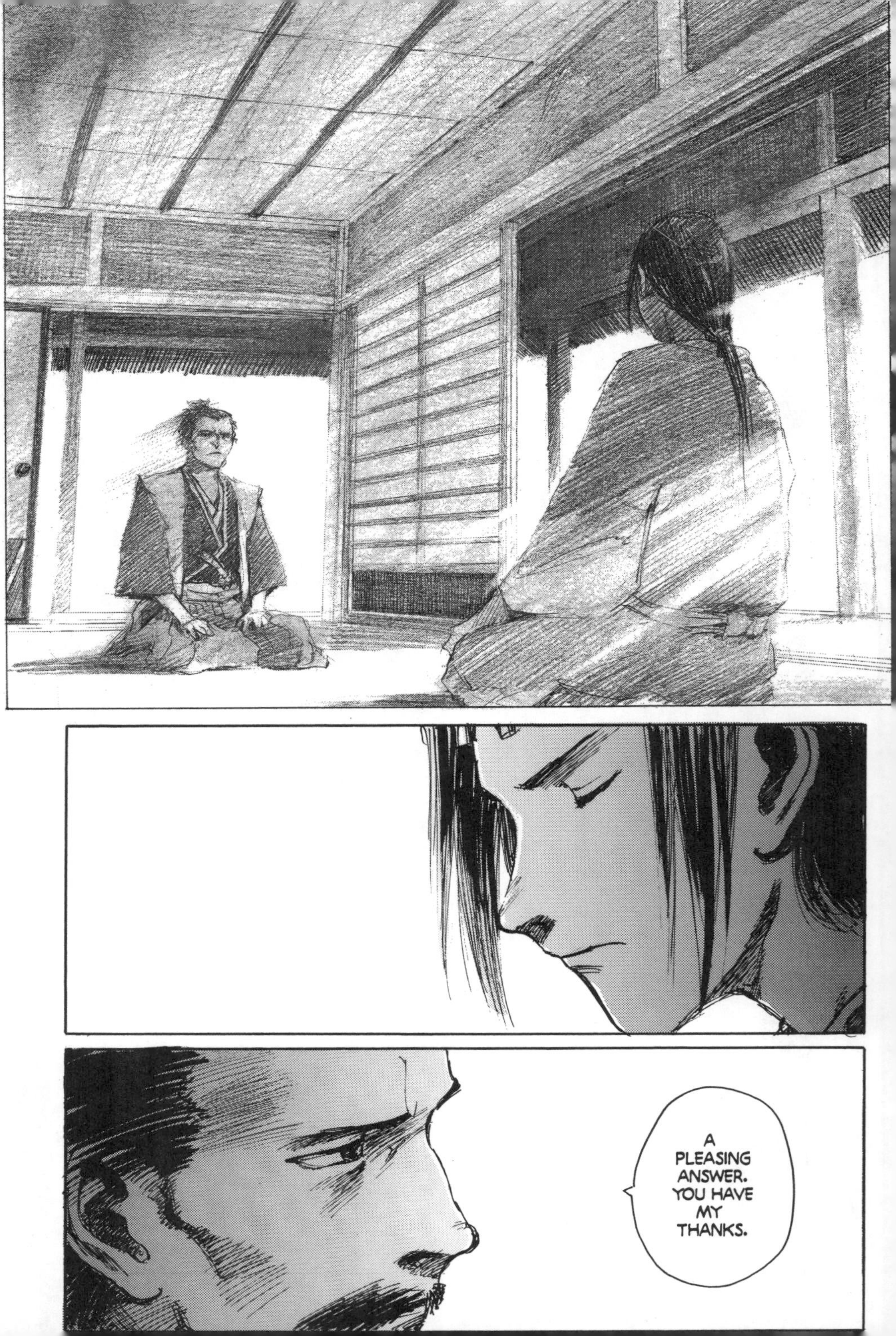
A PLEASING ANSWER. YOU HAVE MY THANKS.

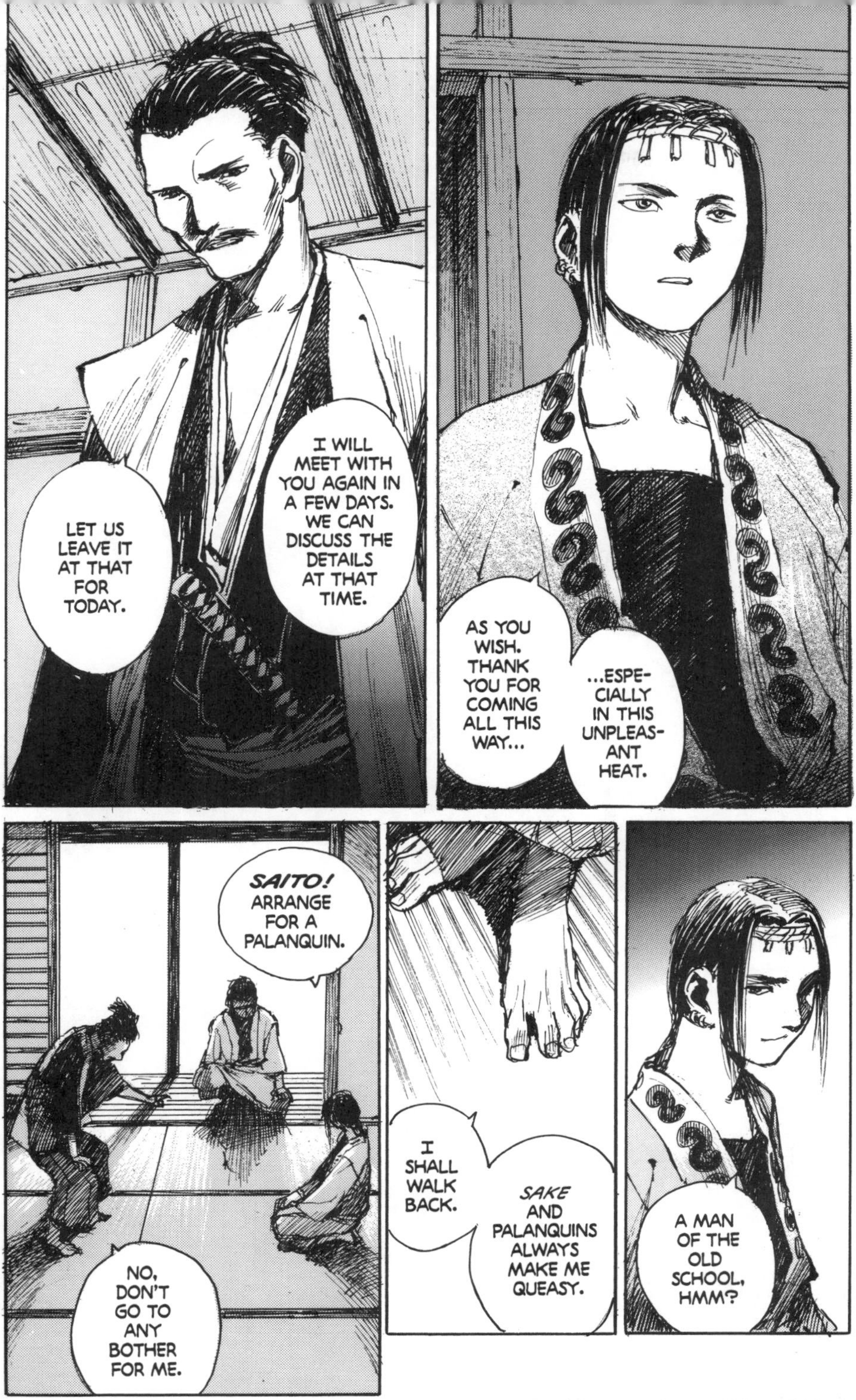
LET US LEAVE IT AT THAT FOR TODAY.
I WILL MEET WITH YOU AGAIN IN A FEW DAYS. WE CAN DISCUSS THE DETAILS AT THAT TIME.
AS YOU WISH. THANK YOU FOR COMING ALL THIS WAY...
...ESPE-CIALLY IN THIS UNPLEAS-ANT HEAT.
SAITO! ARRANGE FOR A PALANQUIN.
NO, DON'T GO TO ANY BOTHER FOR ME.
I SHALL WALK BACK.
SAKE AND PALANQUINS ALWAYS MAKE ME QUEASY.
A MAN OF THE OLD SCHOOL, HMM?

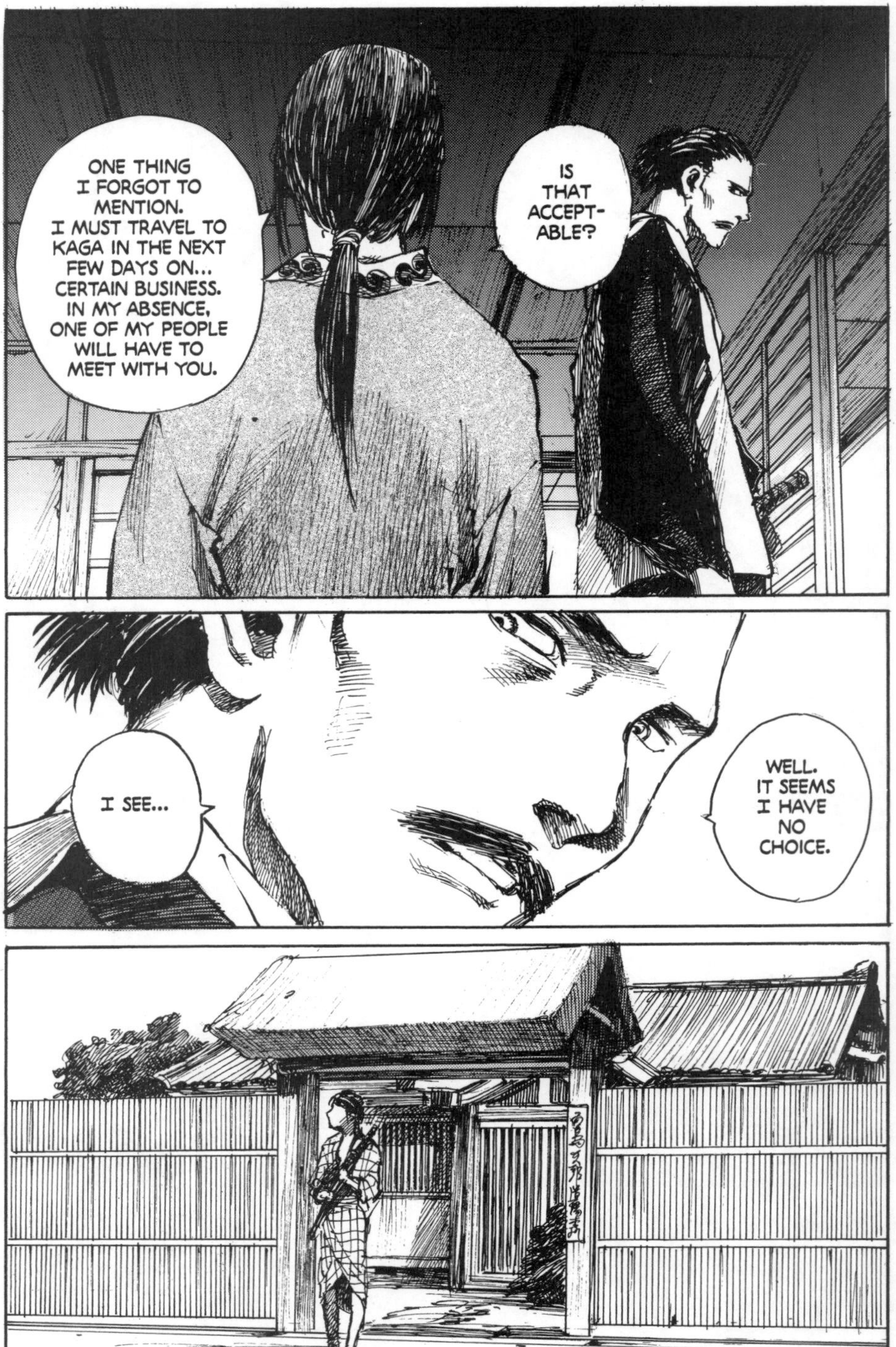
ONE THING I FORGOT TO MENTION. I MUST TRAVEL TO KAGA IN THE NEXT FEW DAYS ON... CERTAIN BUSINESS. IN MY ABSENCE, ONE OF MY PEOPLE WILL HAVE TO MEET WITH YOU.
IS THAT ACCEPT-ABLE?
I SEE...
WELL. IT SEEMS I HAVE NO CHOICE.

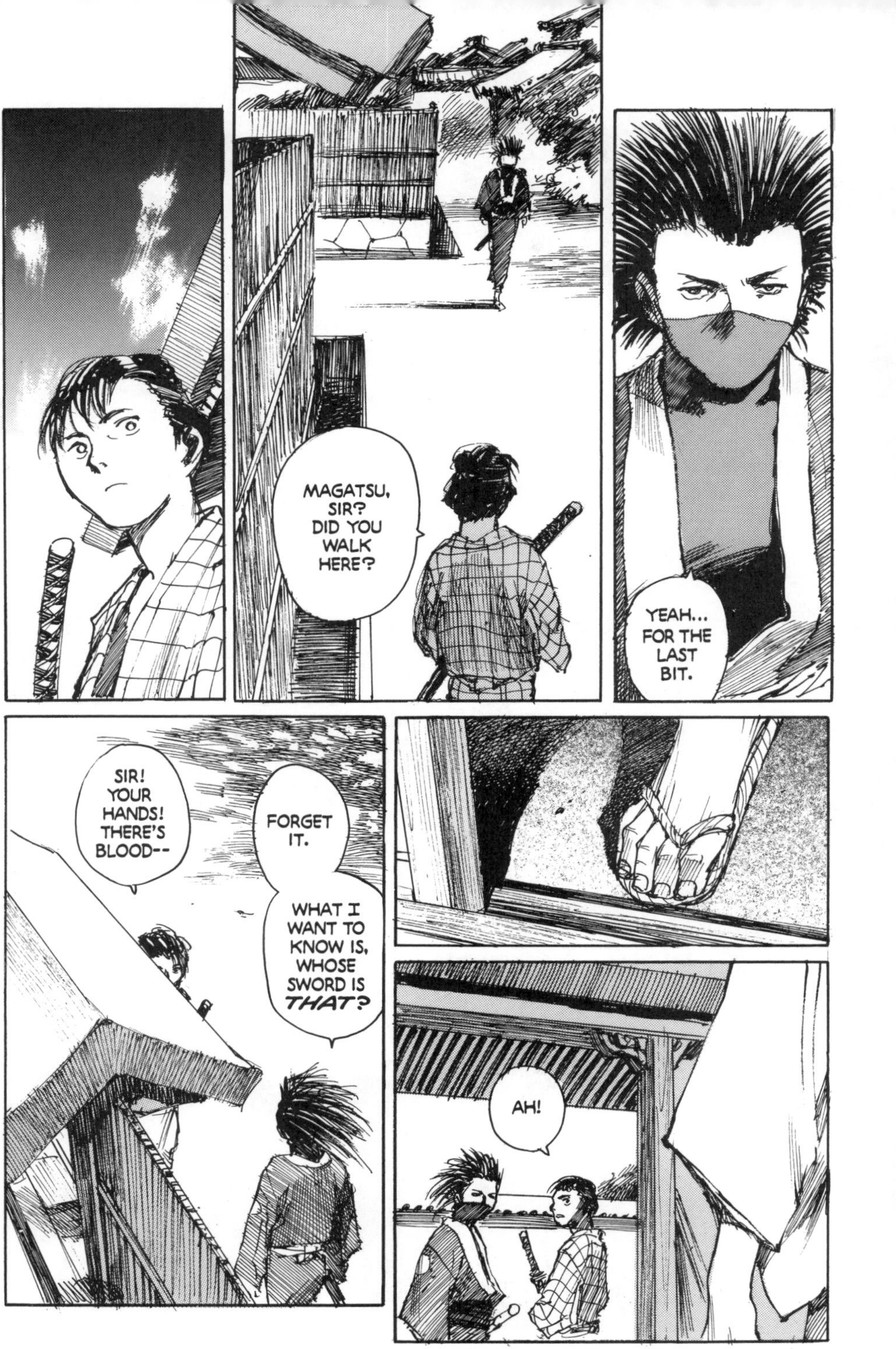
MAGATSU, SIR? DID YOU WALK HERE?
YEAH... FOR THE LAST BIT.
SIR! YOUR HANDS! THERE'S BLOOD--
FORGET IT.
WHAT I WANT TO KNOW IS, WHOSE SWORD IS *THAT*?
AH!

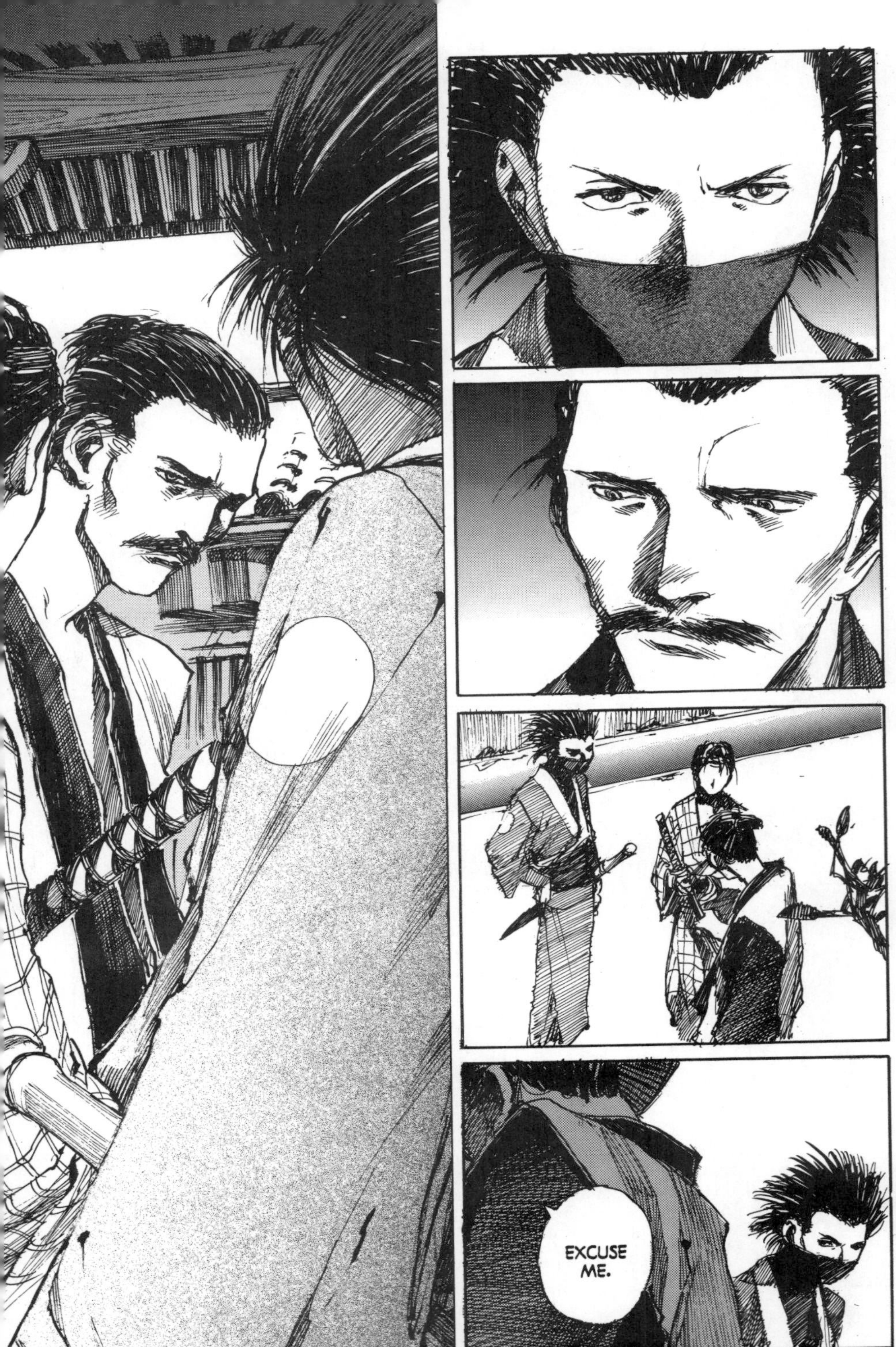
EXCUSE ME.

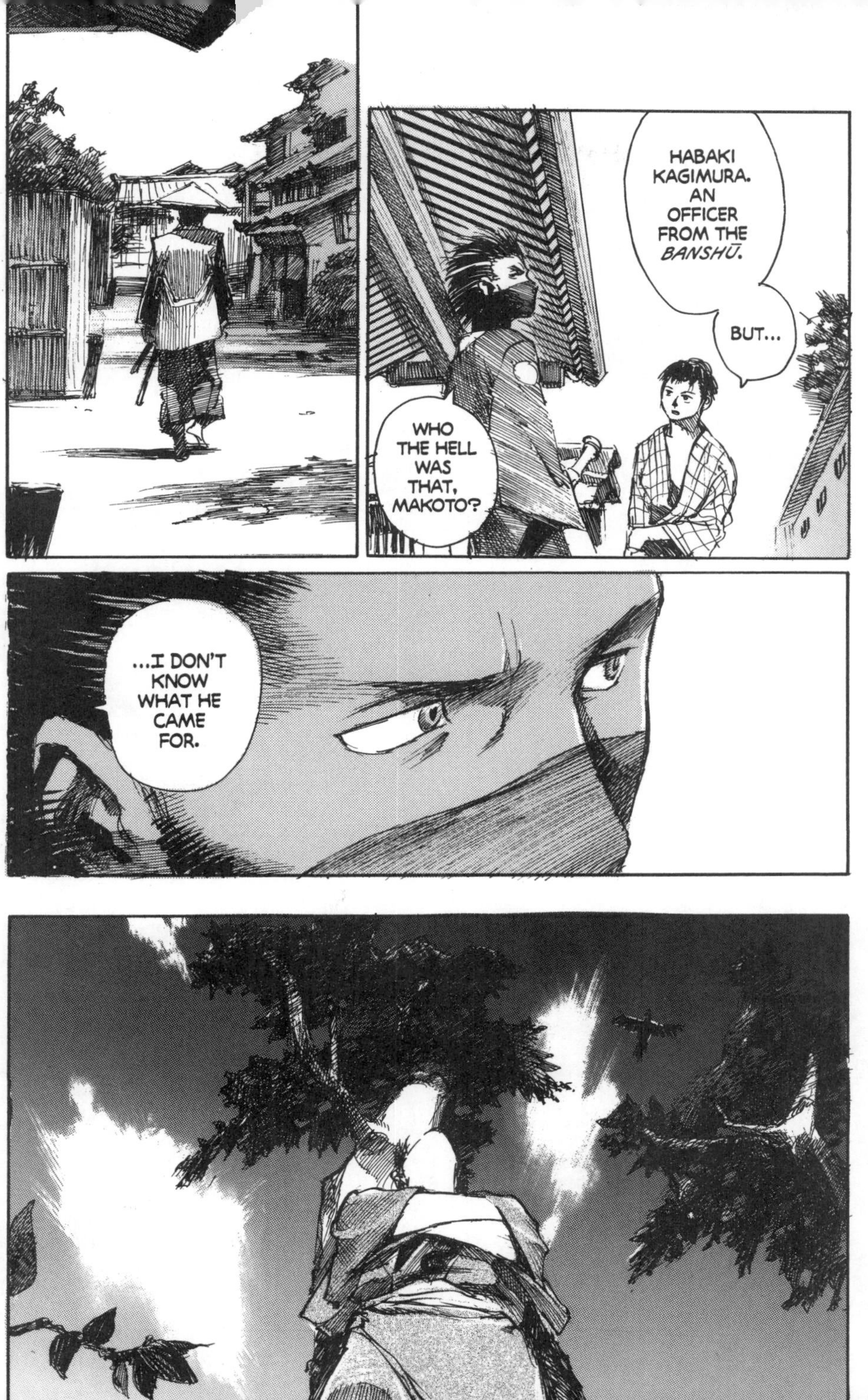
WHO THE HELL WAS THAT, MAKOTO?
HABAKI KAGIMURA. AN OFFICER FROM THE *BANSHŪ*.
BUT...
...I DON'T KNOW WHAT HE CAME FOR.

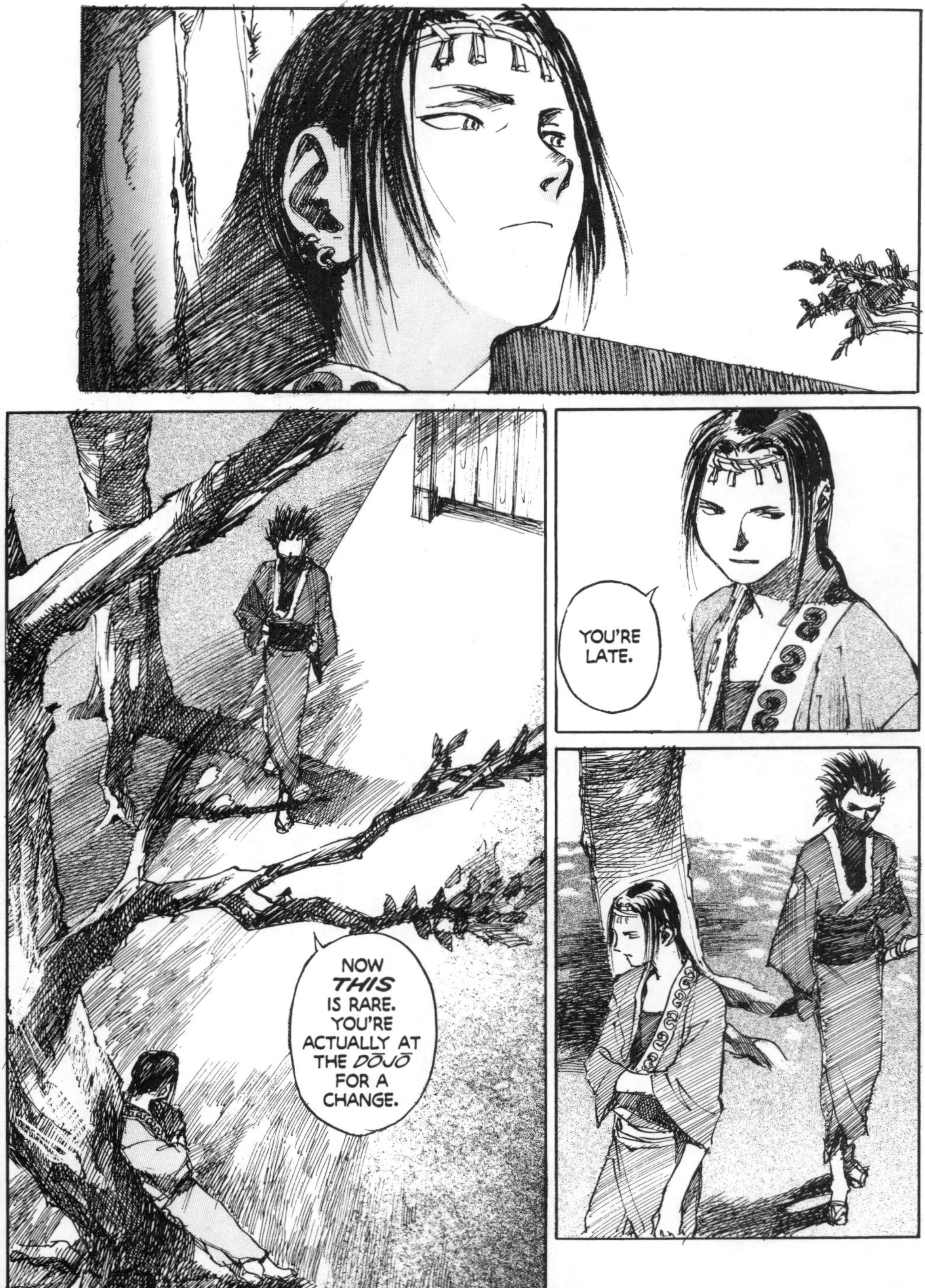
NOW *THIS* IS RARE. YOU'RE ACTUALLY AT THE *DŌJŌ* FOR A CHANGE.
YOU'RE LATE.

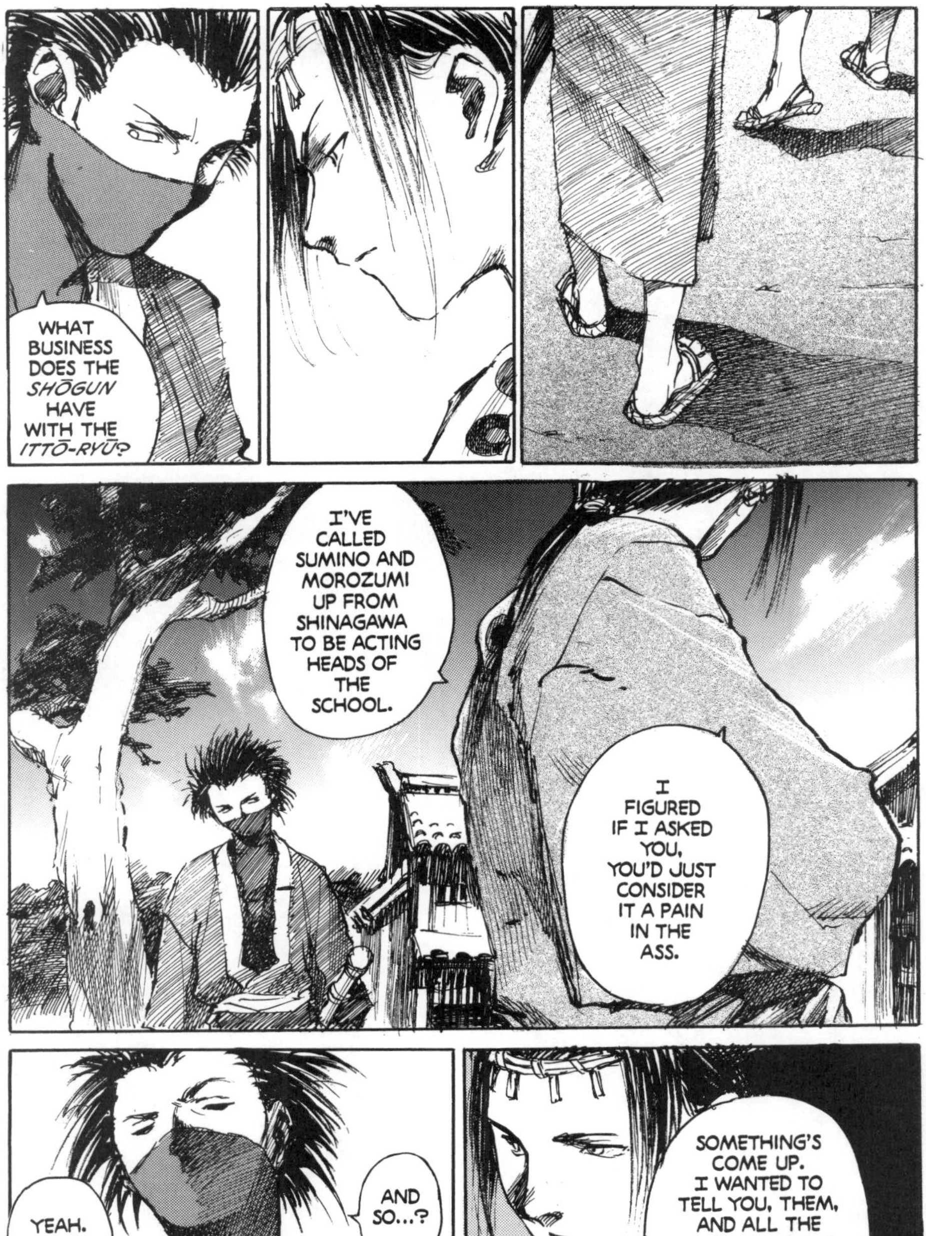
WHAT BUSINESS DOES THE *SHŌGUN* HAVE WITH THE *ITTŌ-RYŪ*?
I'VE CALLED SUMINO AND MOROZUMI UP FROM SHINAGAWA TO BE ACTING HEADS OF THE SCHOOL.
I FIGURED IF I ASKED YOU, YOU'D JUST CONSIDER IT A PAIN IN THE ASS.
YEAH. PRETTY MUCH.
AND SO...?
SOMETHING'S COME UP. I WANTED TO TELL YOU, THEM, AND ALL THE MEN WHO HAVE BEEN WITH ME FROM THE BEGINNING...

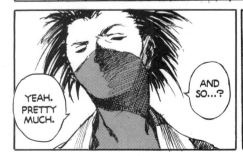

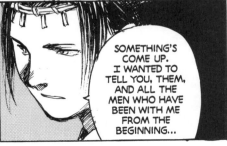

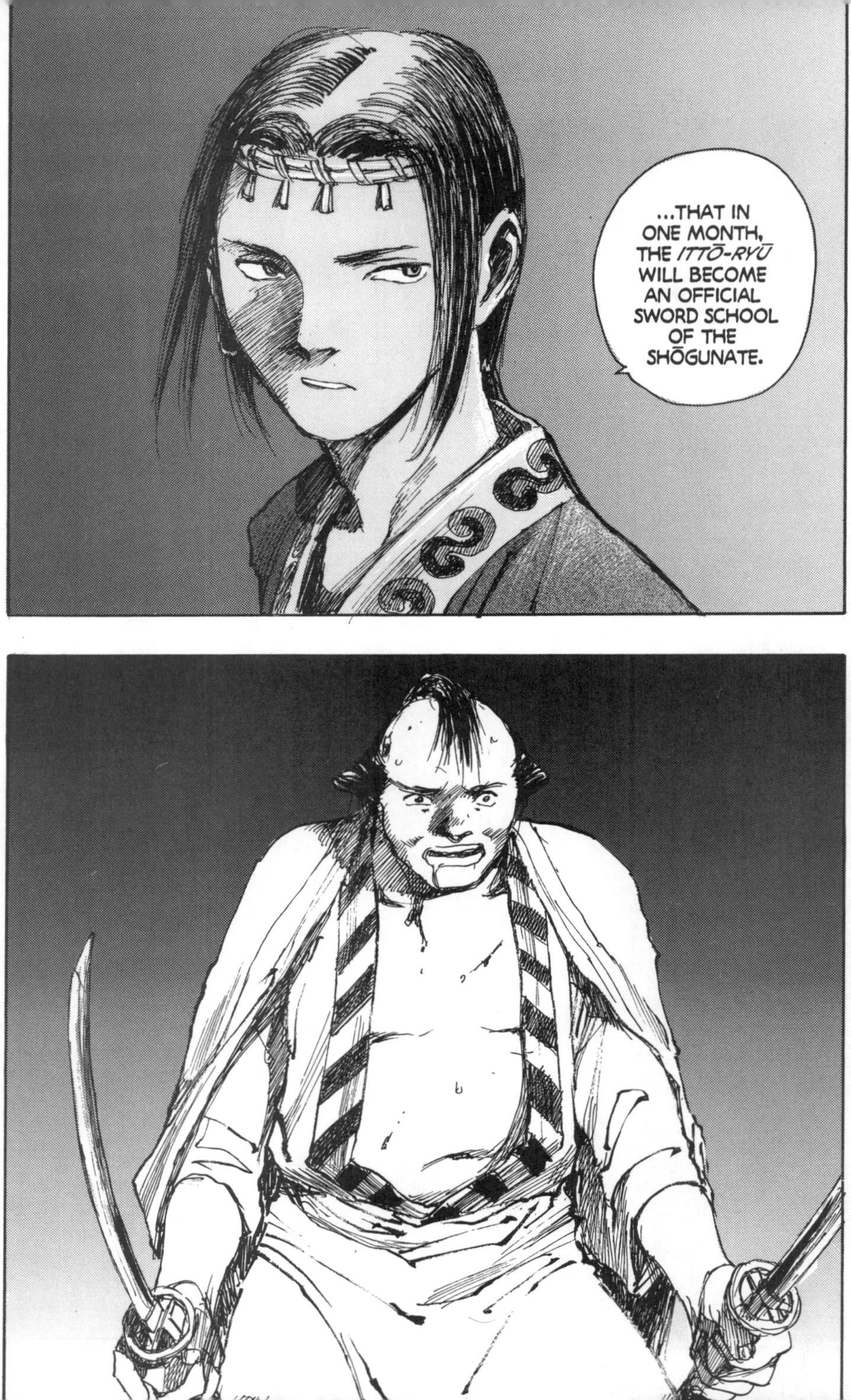
...THAT IN ONE MONTH, THE *ITTŌ-RYŪ* WILL BECOME AN OFFICIAL SWORD SCHOOL OF THE SHŌGUNATE.

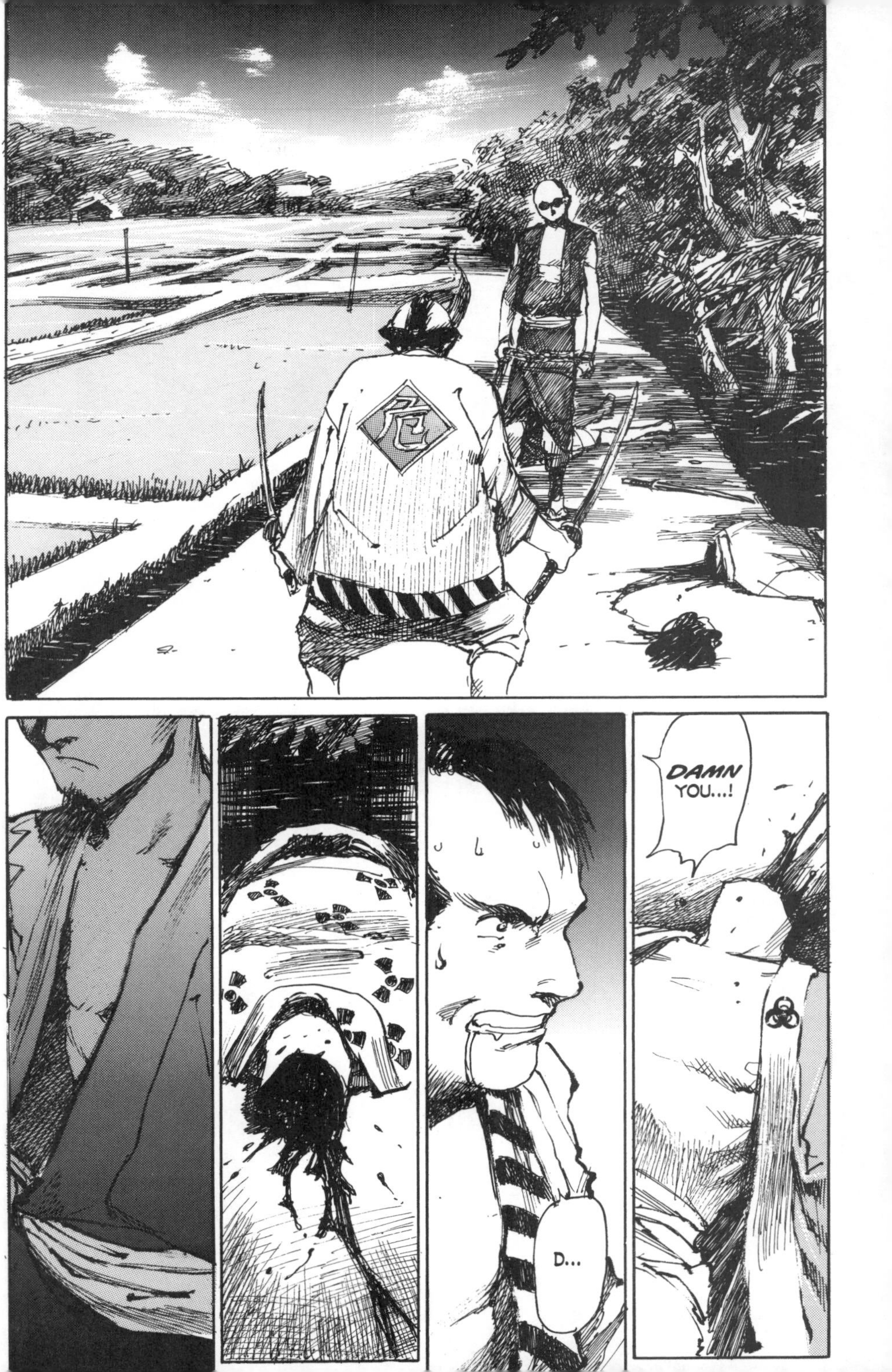
D...
DAMN YOU...!

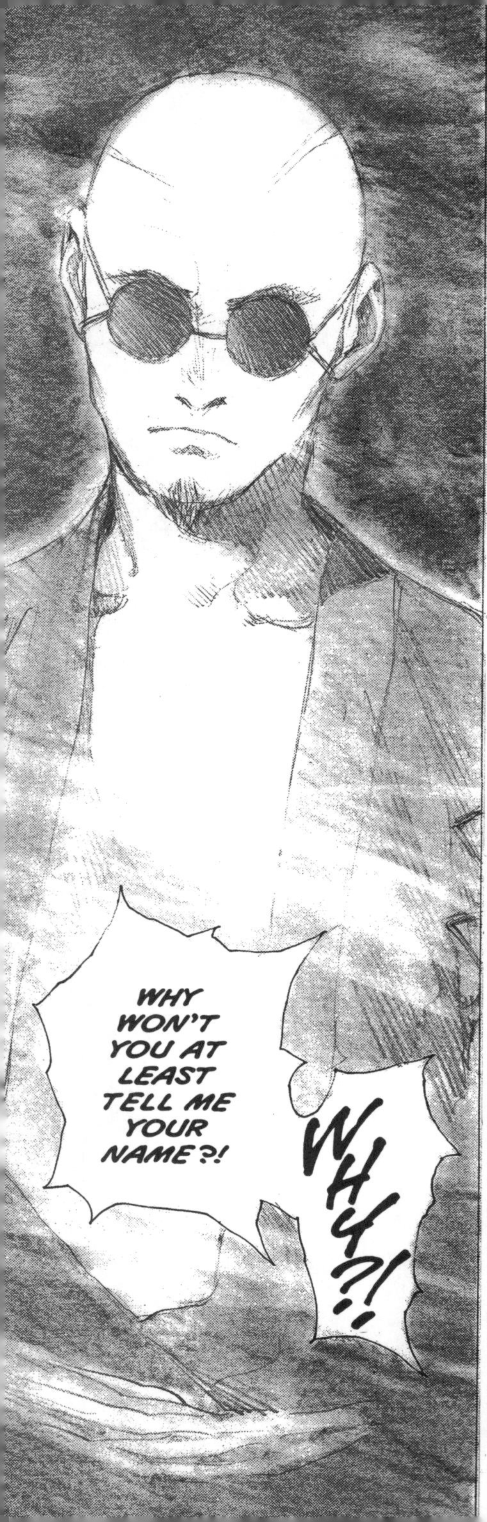
WHY WON'T YOU AT LEAST TELL ME YOUR NAME?!
WHY?!!

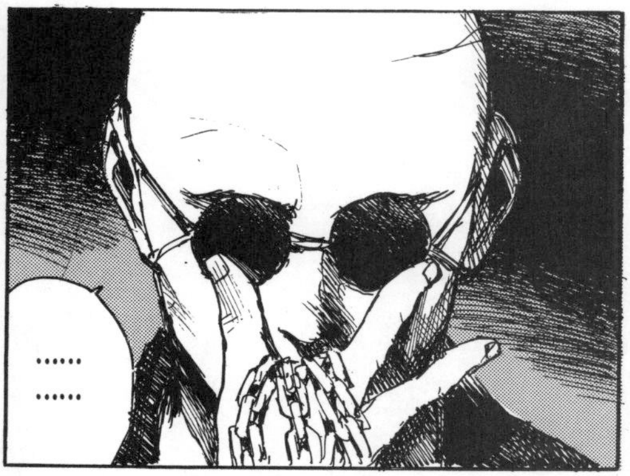
......
......

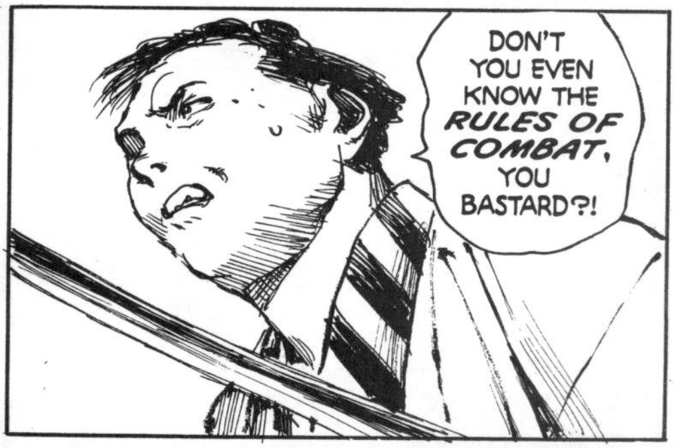
DON'T YOU EVEN KNOW THE *RULES OF COMBAT*, YOU BASTARD?!

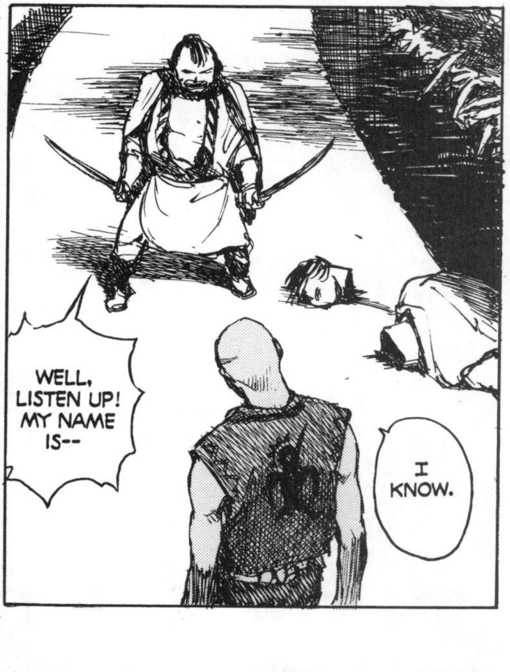
WELL, LISTEN UP! MY NAME IS--
I KNOW.

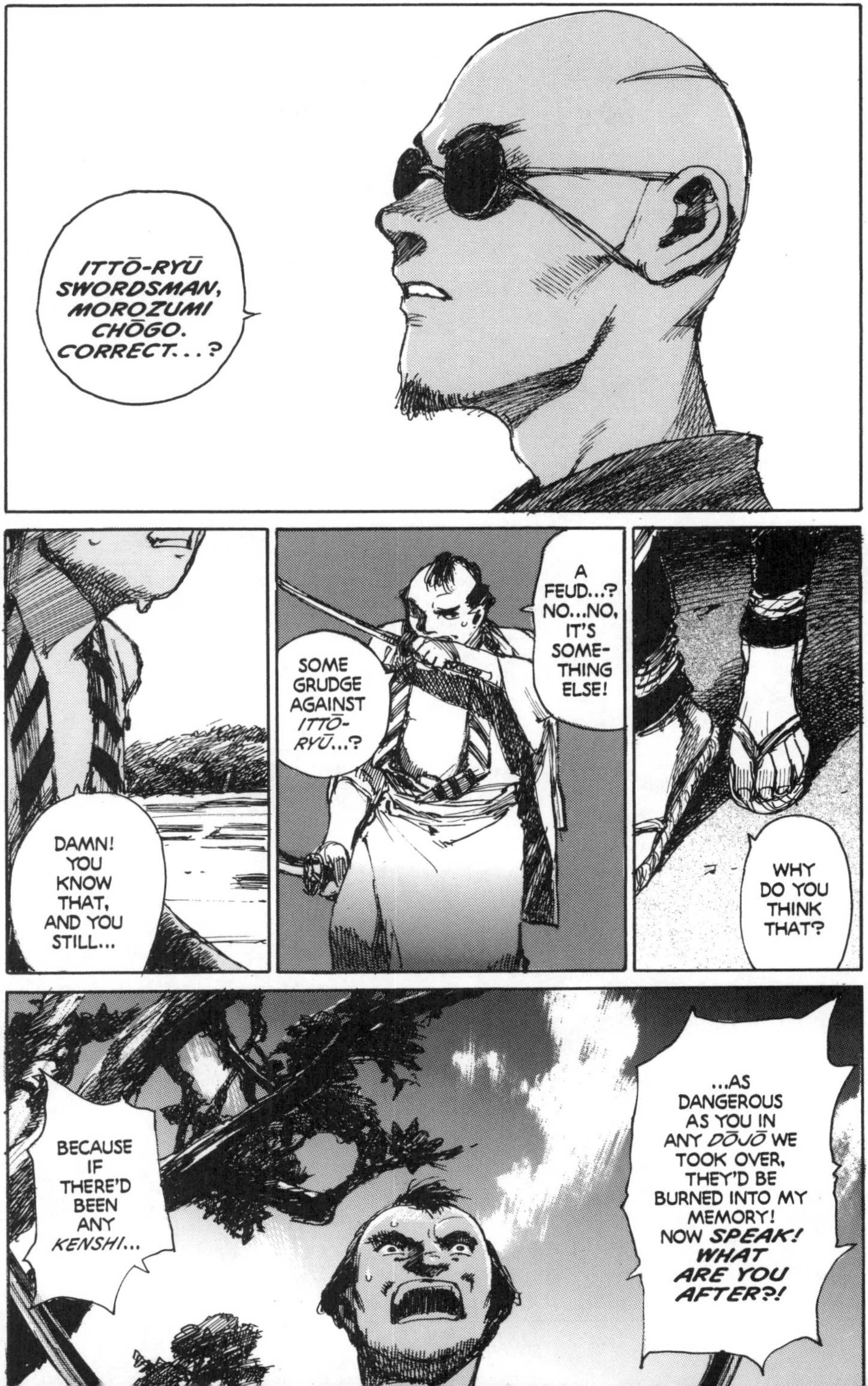
ITTŌ-RYŪ SWORDSMAN, MOROZUMI CHŌGO. CORRECT...?
DAMN! YOU KNOW THAT, AND YOU STILL...
SOME GRUDGE AGAINST ITTŌ-RYŪ...?
A FEUD...? NO...NO, IT'S SOME-THING ELSE!
WHY DO YOU THINK THAT?
BECAUSE IF THERE'D BEEN ANY KENSHI...
...AS DANGEROUS AS YOU IN ANY DŌJŌ WE TOOK OVER, THEY'D BE BURNED INTO MY MEMORY! NOW SPEAK! WHAT ARE YOU AFTER?!

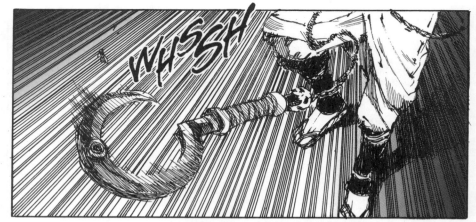

WHSSH

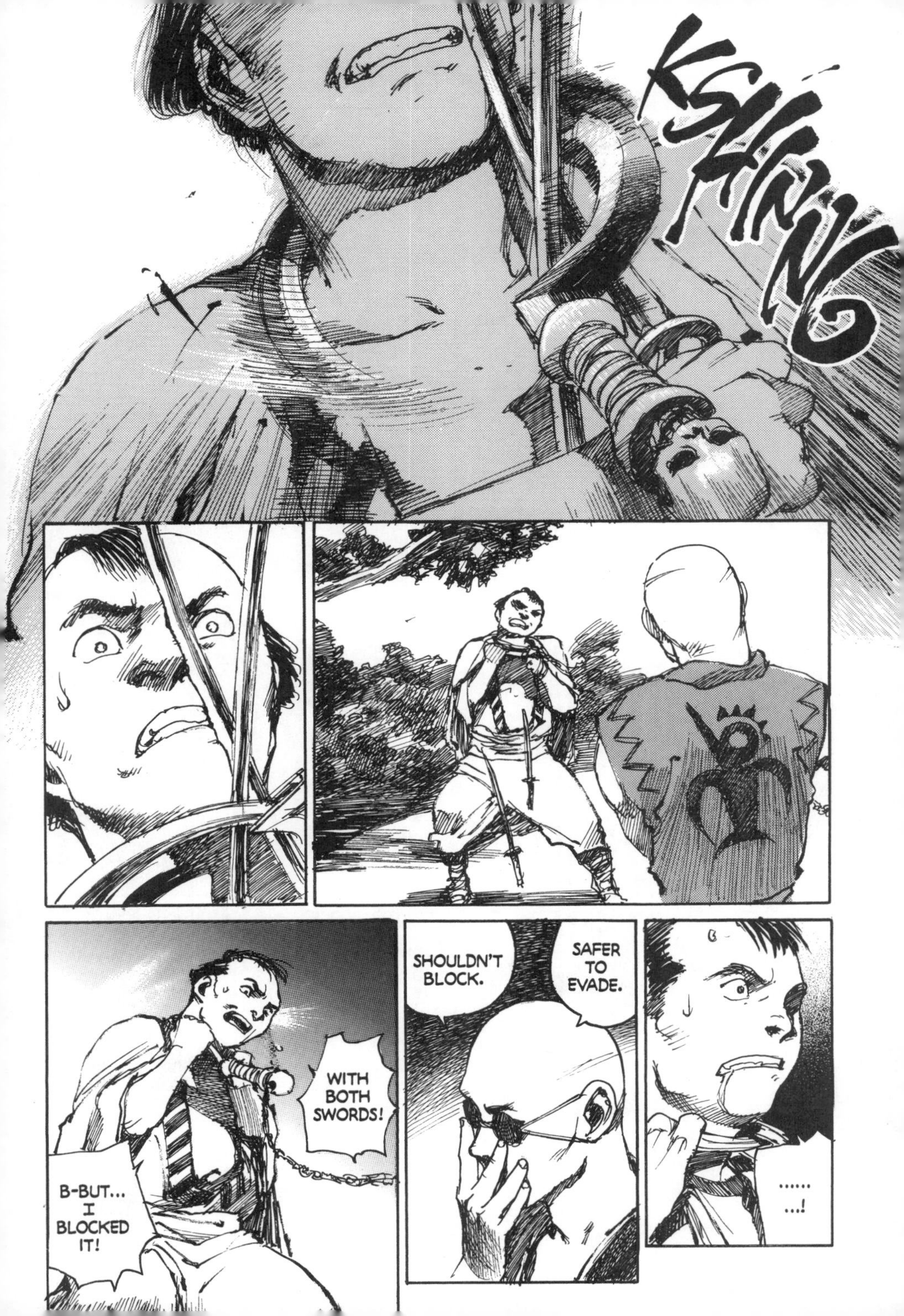
KSHINNG
WITH BOTH SWORDS!
B-BUT... I BLOCKED IT!
SHOULDN'T BLOCK.
SAFER TO EVADE.
....!

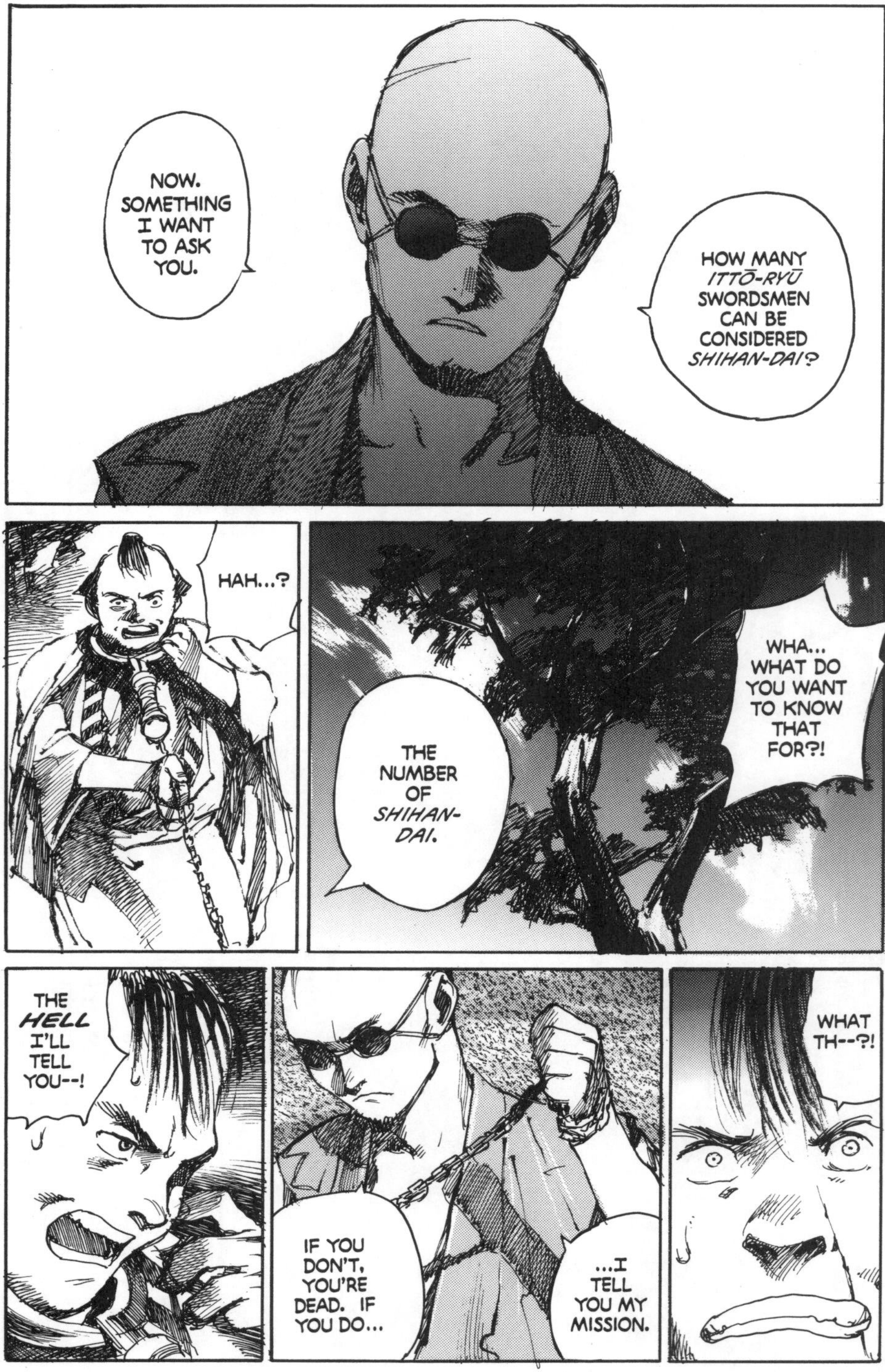
NOW. SOMETHING I WANT TO ASK YOU.
HOW MANY *ITTŌ-RYŪ* SWORDSMEN CAN BE CONSIDERED *SHIHAN-DAI*?
HAH...?
THE NUMBER OF *SHIHAN-DAI*.
WHA... WHAT DO YOU WANT TO KNOW THAT FOR?!
THE ***HELL*** I'LL TELL YOU--!
IF YOU DON'T, YOU'RE DEAD. IF YOU DO...
...I TELL YOU MY MISSION.
WHAT TH--?!

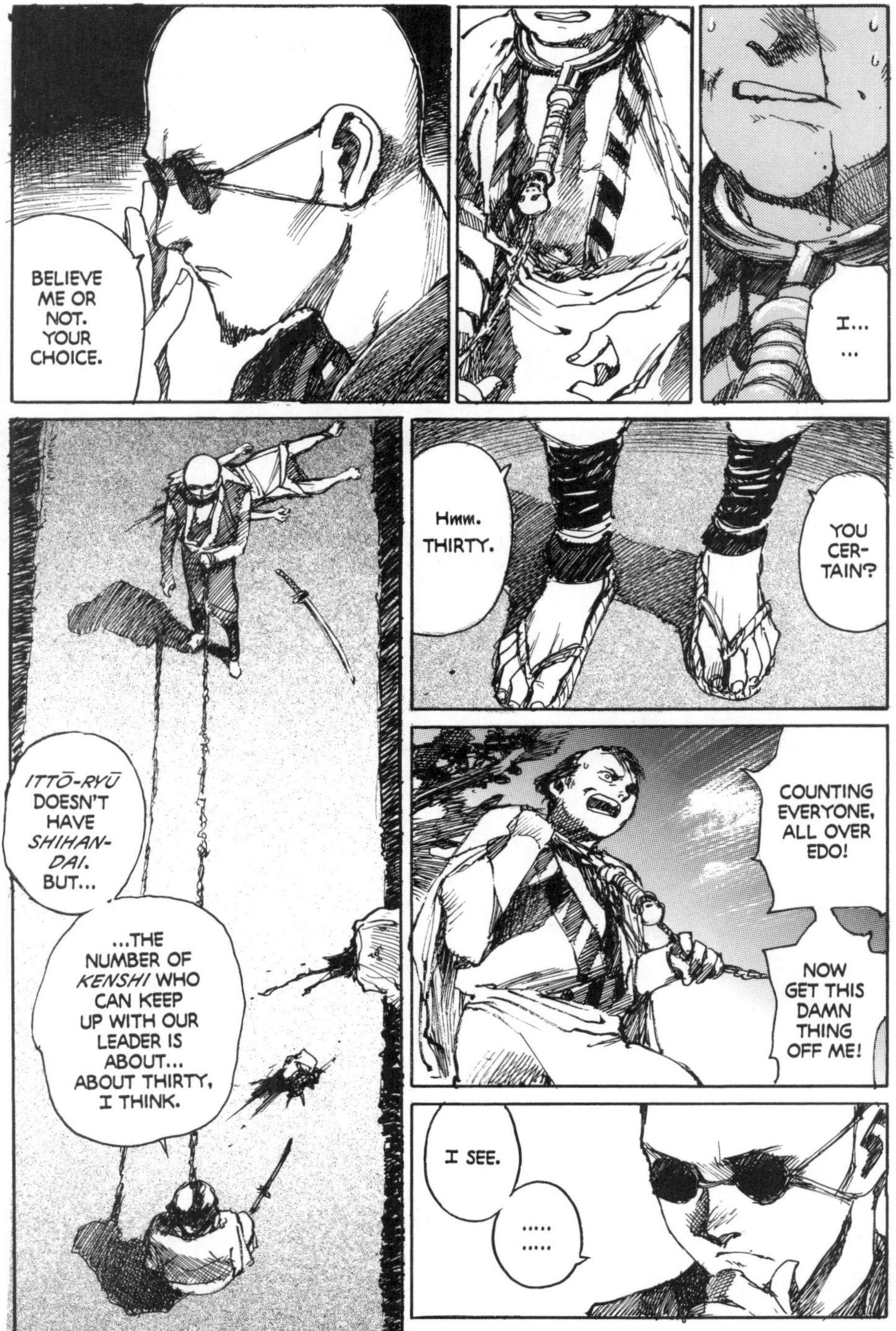
BELIEVE ME OR NOT. YOUR CHOICE.
I... ...
Hmm. THIRTY.
YOU CER- TAIN?
ITTŌ-RYŪ DOESN'T HAVE *SHIHAN-DAI*. BUT...
...THE NUMBER OF *KENSHI* WHO CAN KEEP UP WITH OUR LEADER IS ABOUT... ABOUT THIRTY, I THINK.
COUNTING EVERYONE, ALL OVER EDO!
NOW GET THIS DAMN THING OFF ME!
I SEE.
....

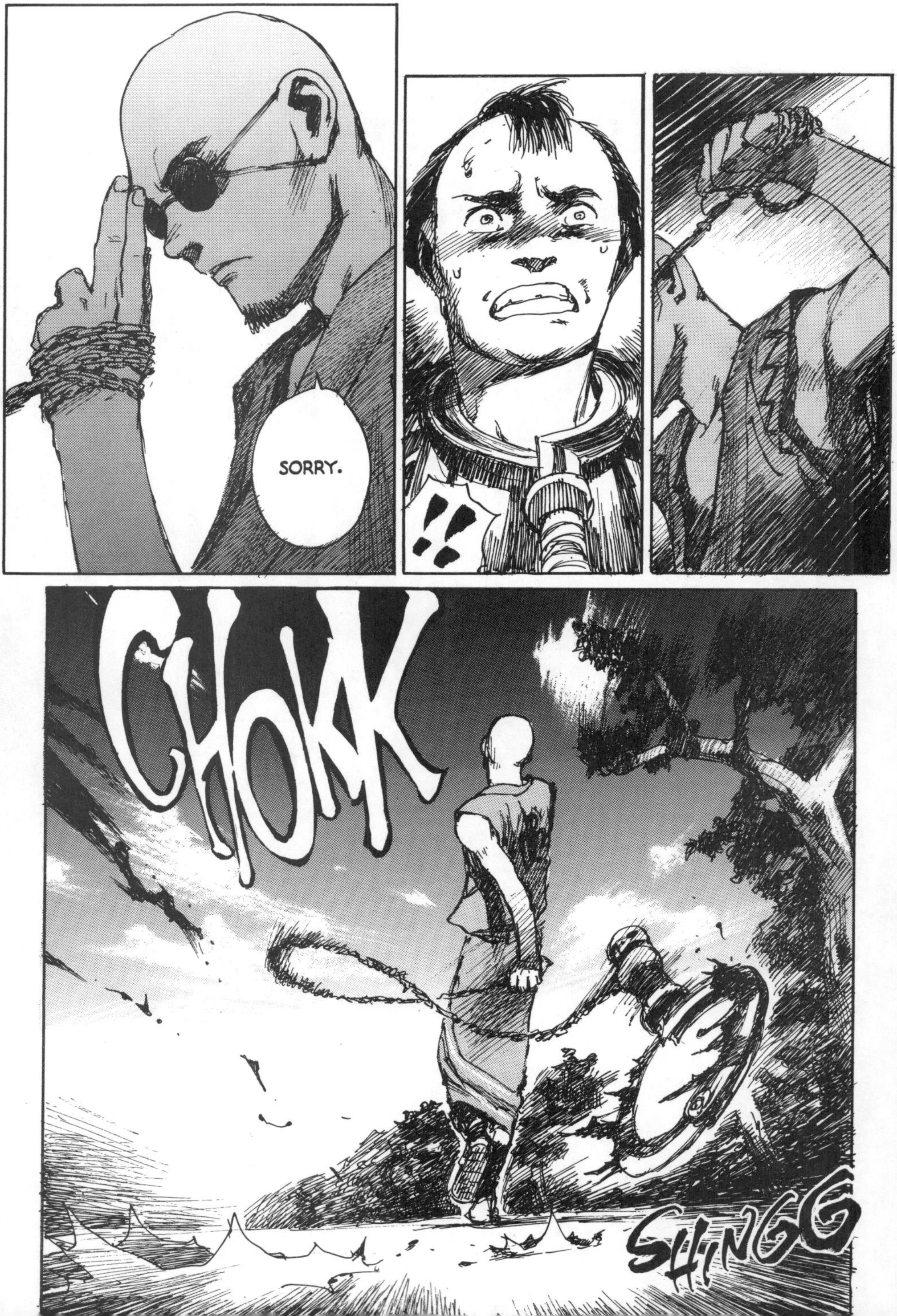
SORRY.
!!
CHOKK
SHINGG

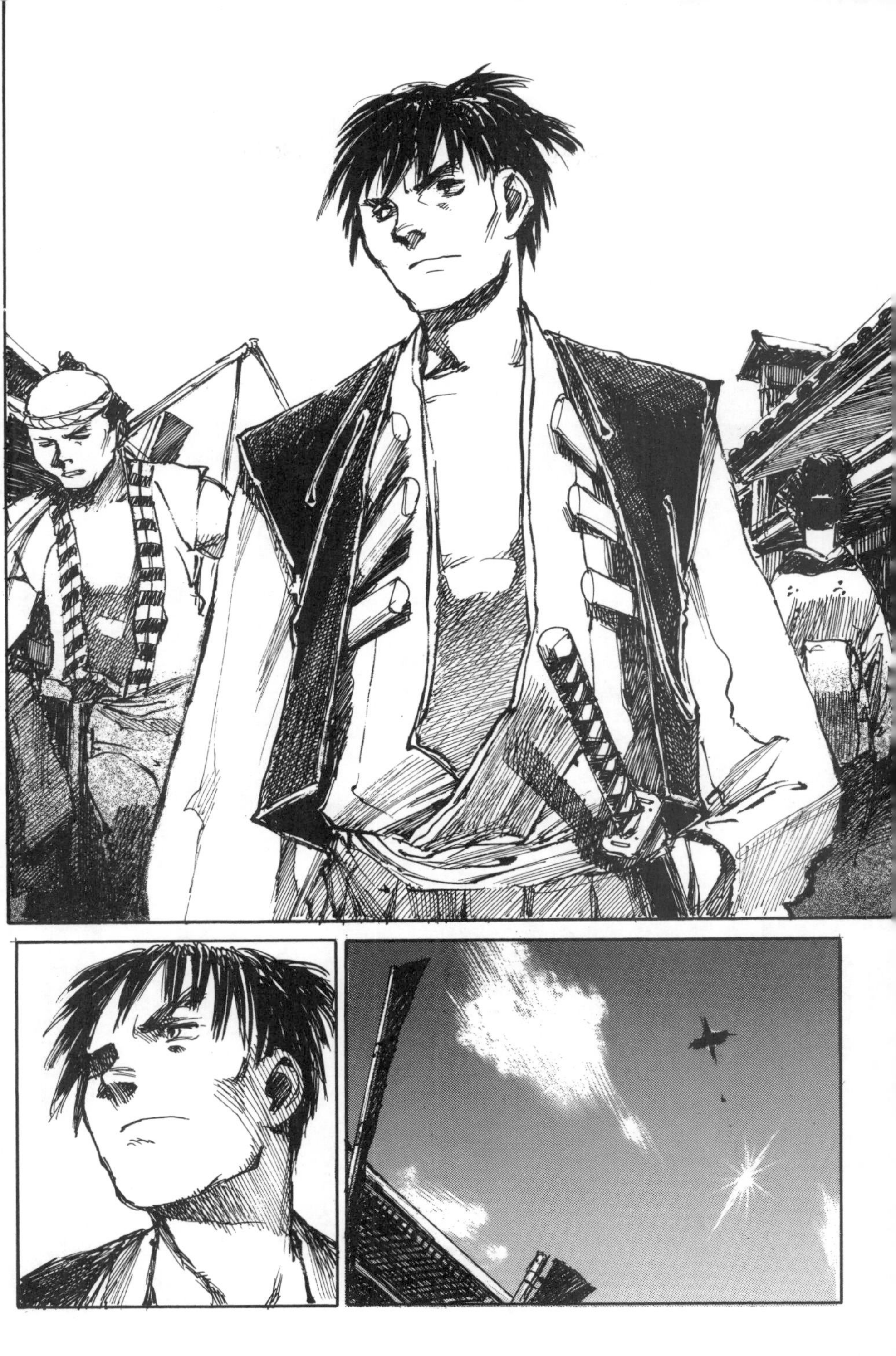

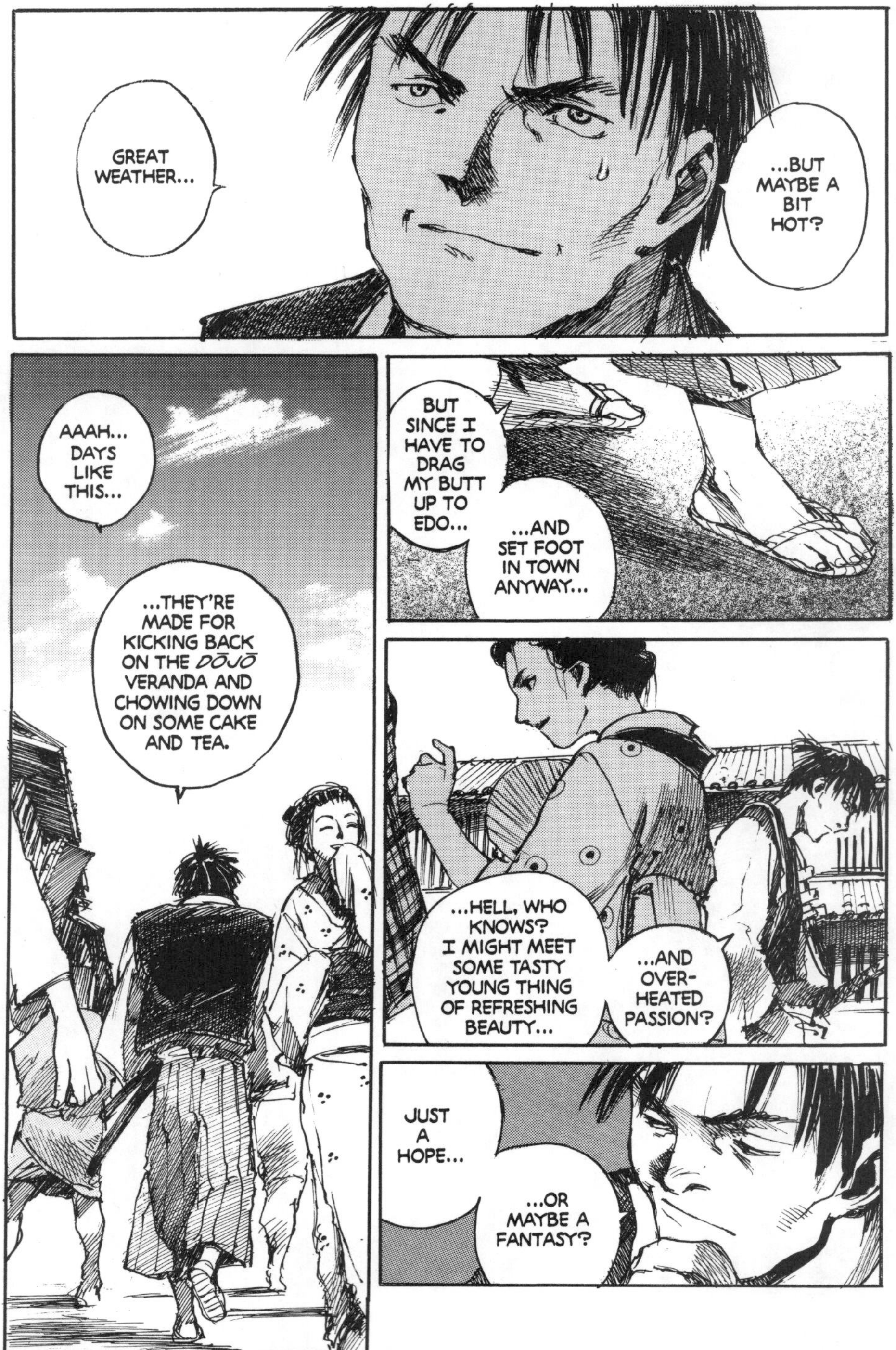
GREAT WEATHER...
...BUT MAYBE A BIT HOT?
AAAH... DAYS LIKE THIS...
...THEY'RE MADE FOR KICKING BACK ON THE *DŌJŌ* VERANDA AND CHOWING DOWN ON SOME CAKE AND TEA.
BUT SINCE I HAVE TO DRAG MY BUTT UP TO EDO...
...AND SET FOOT IN TOWN ANYWAY...
...HELL, WHO KNOWS? I MIGHT MEET SOME TASTY YOUNG THING OF REFRESHING BEAUTY...
...AND OVER-HEATED PASSION?
JUST A HOPE...
...OR MAYBE A FANTASY?

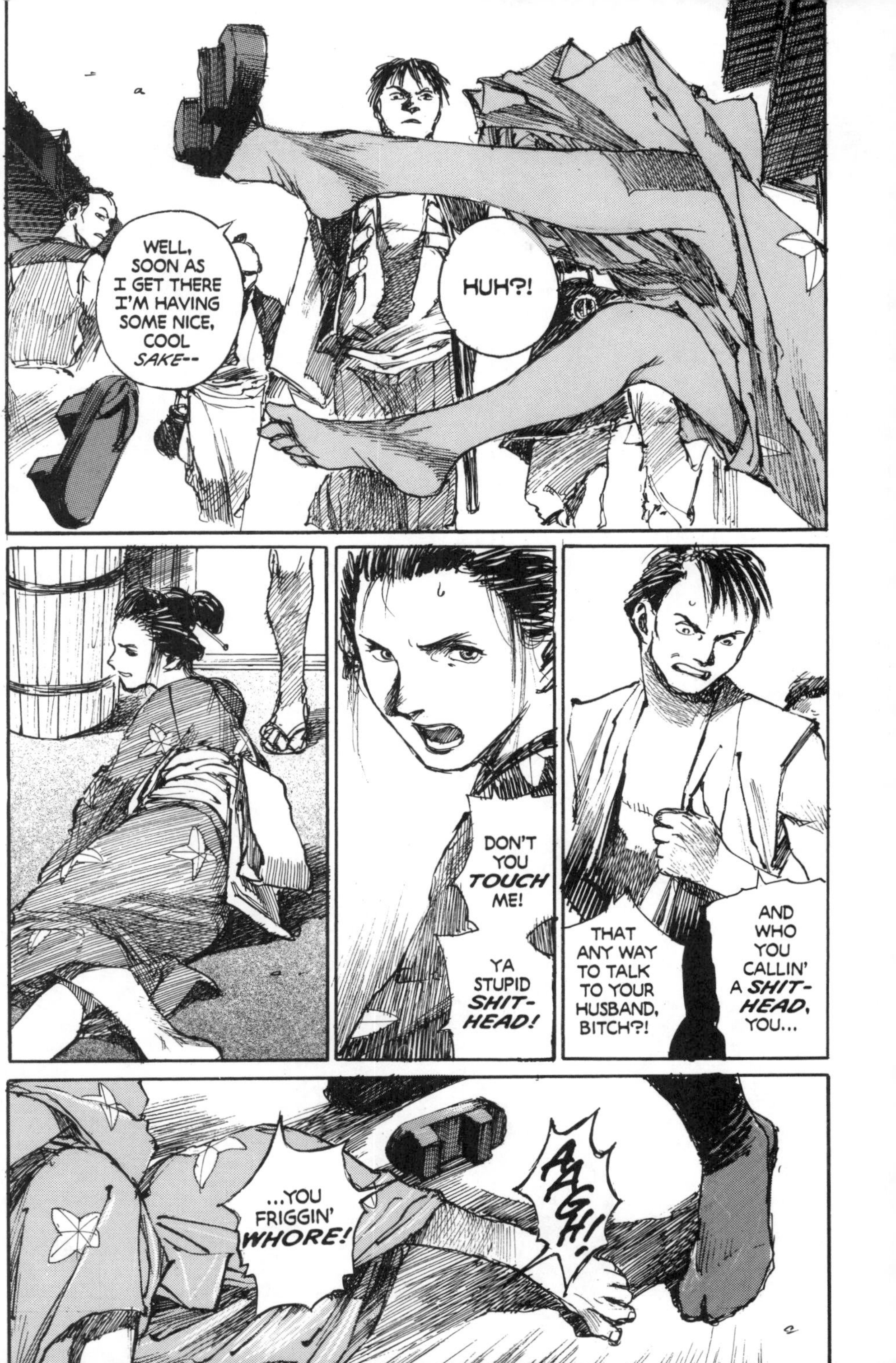
WELL, SOON AS I GET THERE I'M HAVING SOME NICE, COOL *SAKE*--
HUH?!
DON'T YOU ***TOUCH*** ME!
YA STUPID ***SHIT-HEAD!***
THAT ANY WAY TO TALK TO YOUR HUSBAND, BITCH?!
AND WHO YOU CALLIN' A ***SHIT-HEAD,*** YOU...
...YOU FRIGGIN' ***WHORE!***
AAAGH!!

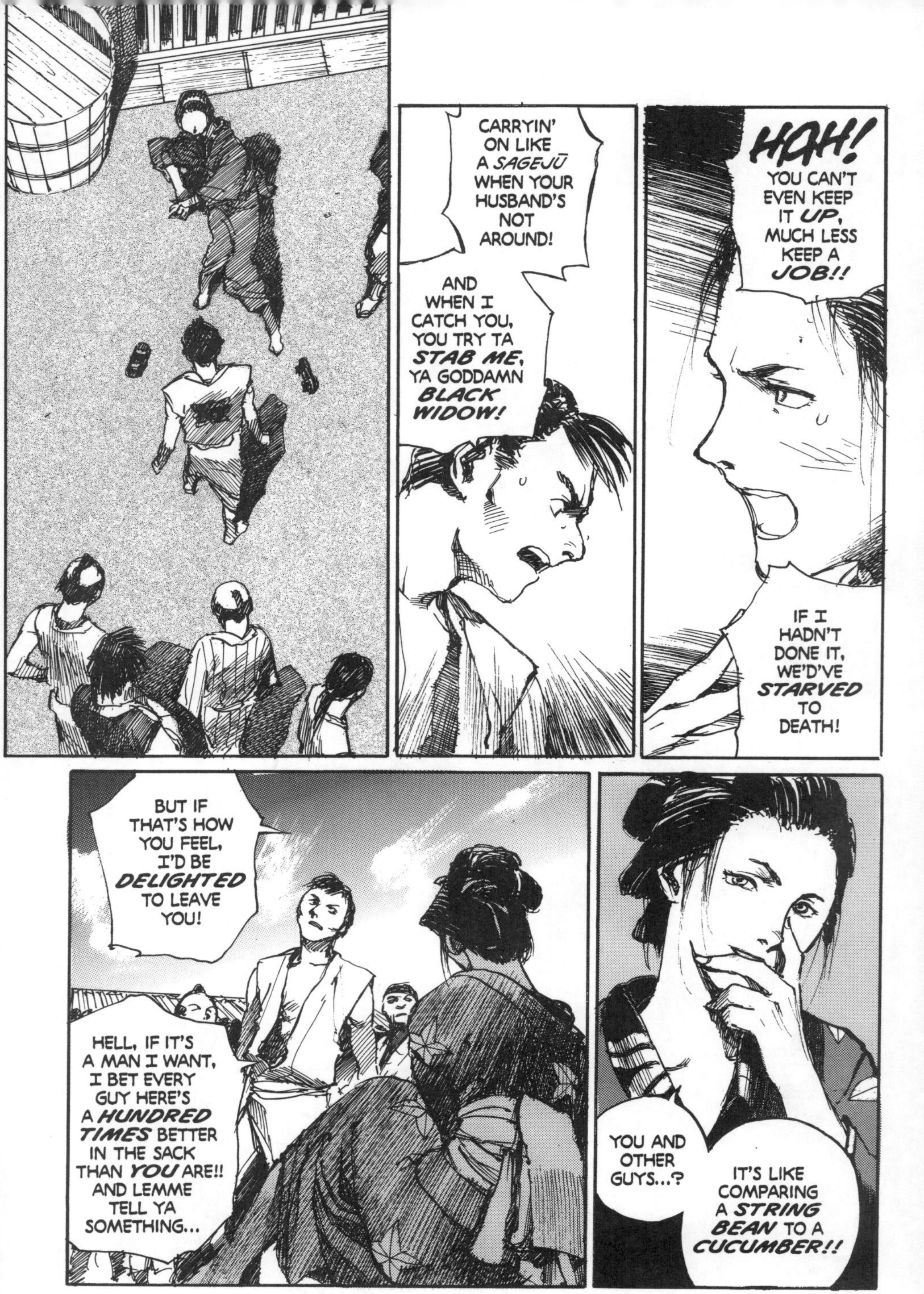
CARRYIN' ON LIKE A SAGEJŪ WHEN YOUR HUSBAND'S NOT AROUND!
AND WHEN I CATCH YOU, YOU TRY TA STAB ME, YA GODDAMN BLACK WIDOW!
HOH!
YOU CAN'T EVEN KEEP IT UP, MUCH LESS KEEP A JOB!!
IF I HADN'T DONE IT, WE'D'VE STARVED TO DEATH!
BUT IF THAT'S HOW YOU FEEL, I'D BE DELIGHTED TO LEAVE YOU!
HELL, IF IT'S A MAN I WANT, I BET EVERY GUY HERE'S A HUNDRED TIMES BETTER IN THE SACK THAN YOU ARE!! AND LEMME TELL YA SOMETHING...
YOU AND OTHER GUYS...?
IT'S LIKE COMPARING A STRING BEAN TO A CUCUMBER!!

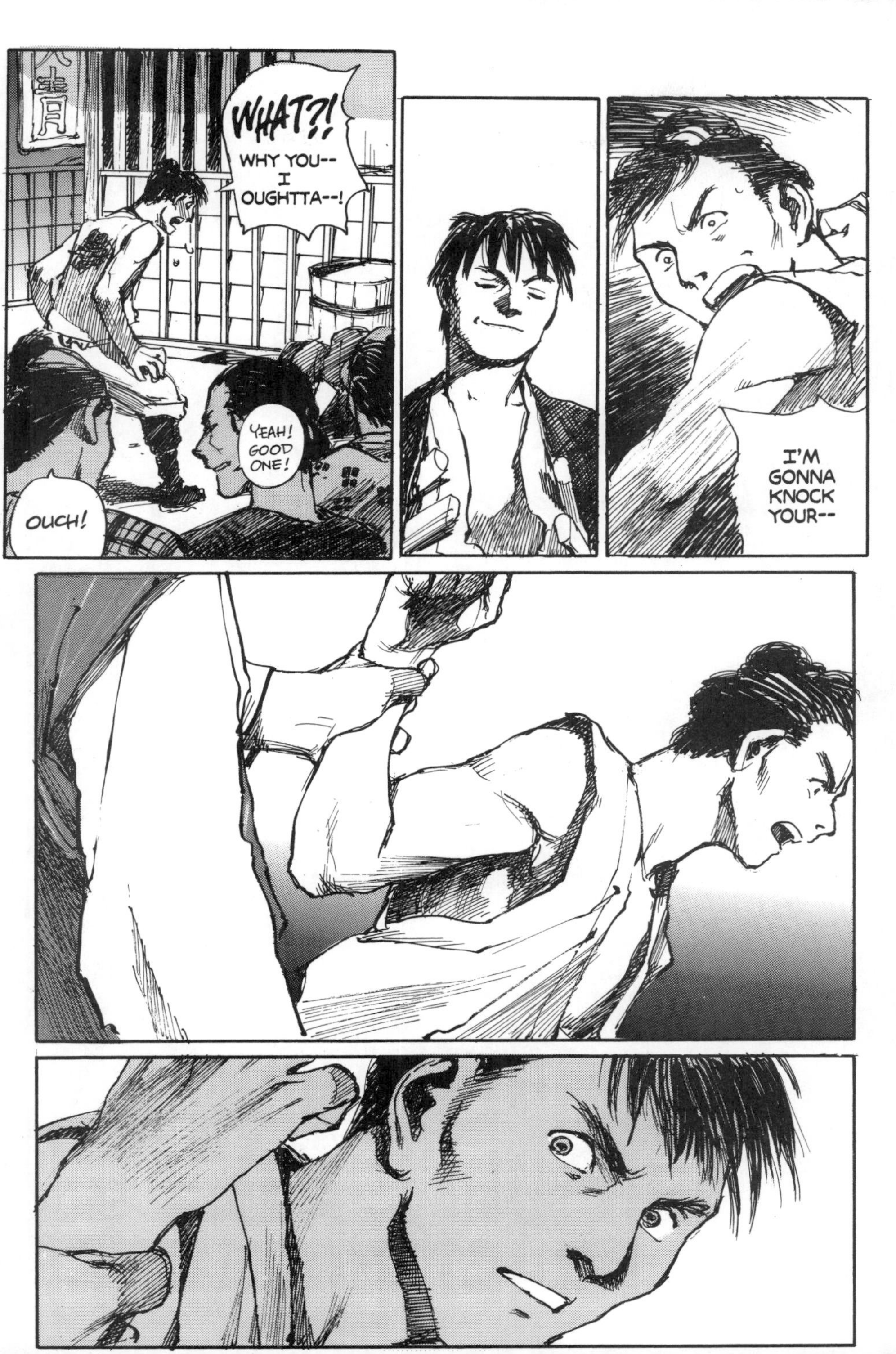
WHAT?!
WHY YOU-- I OUGHTTA--!
YEAH! GOOD ONE!
OUCH!
I'M GONNA KNOCK YOUR--

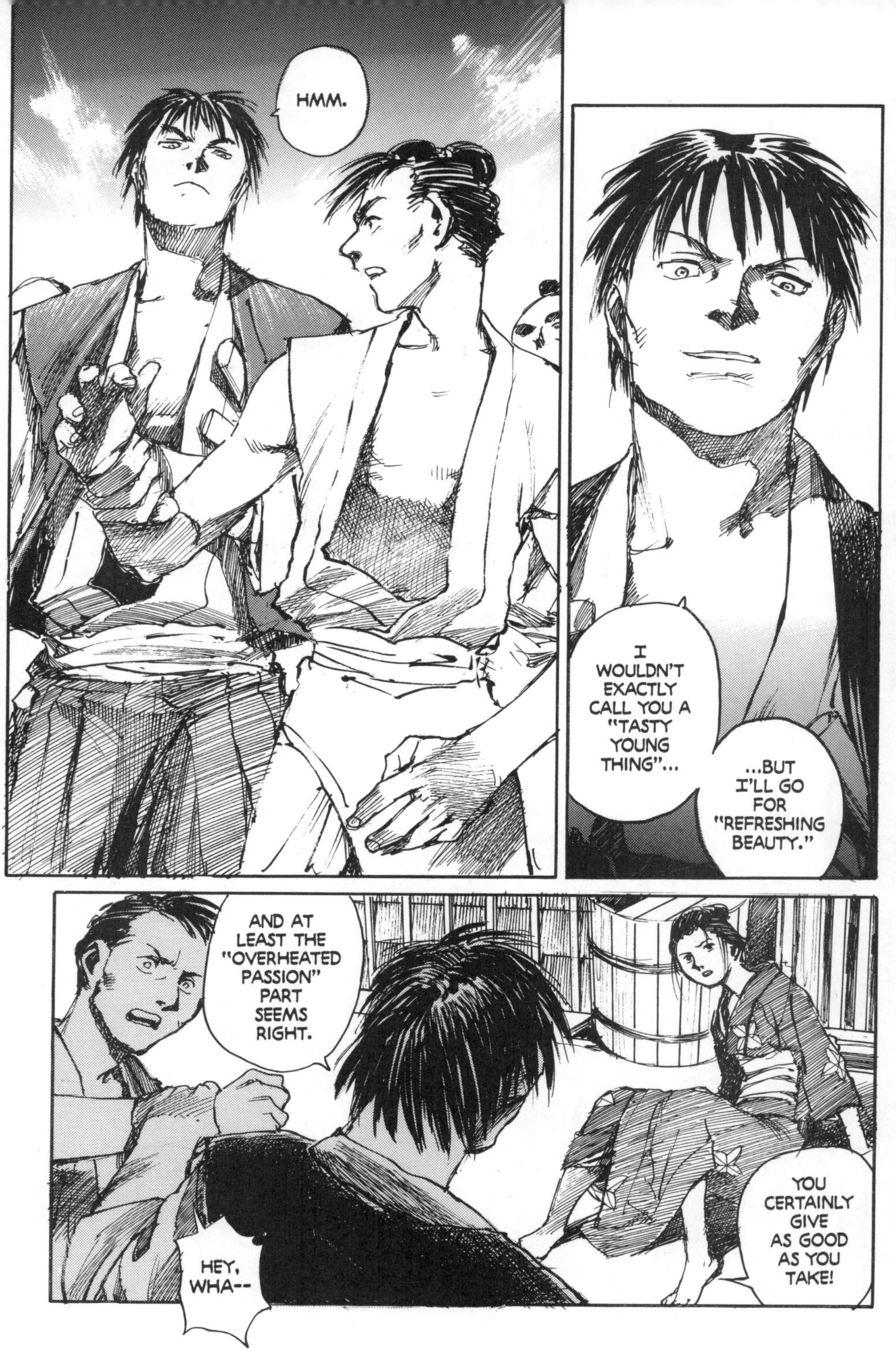
HMM.
I WOULDN'T EXACTLY CALL YOU A "TASTY YOUNG THING"...
...BUT I'LL GO FOR "REFRESHING BEAUTY."
AND AT LEAST THE "OVERHEATED PASSION" PART SEEMS RIGHT.
HEY, WHA--
YOU CERTAINLY GIVE AS GOOD AS YOU TAKE!

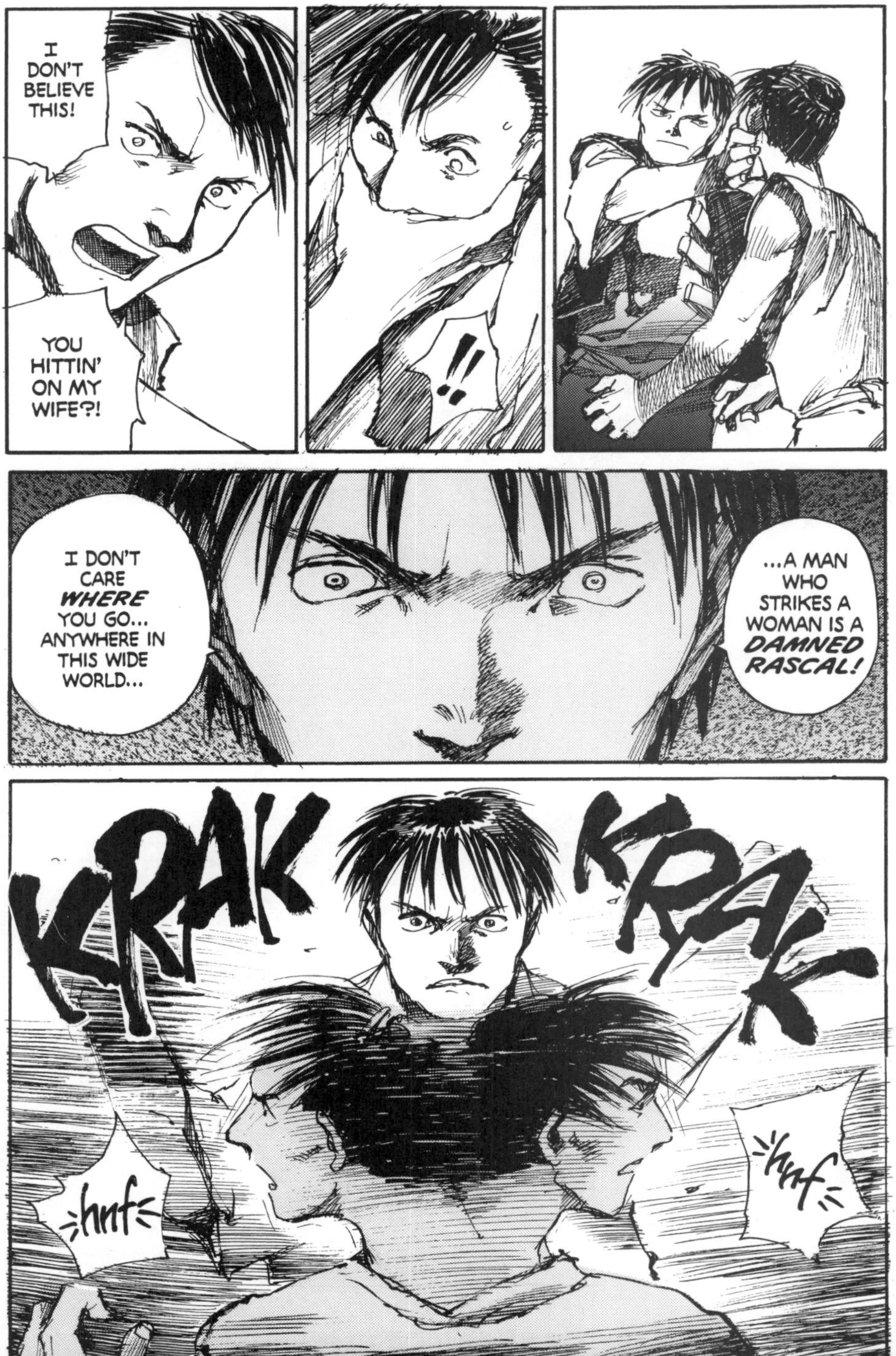
I DON'T BELIEVE THIS!
YOU HITTIN' ON MY WIFE?!
!!
I DON'T CARE *WHERE* YOU GO... ANYWHERE IN THIS WIDE WORLD...
...A MAN WHO STRIKES A WOMAN IS A *DAMNED RASCAL!*
KRAK
KRAK
hnf
hnf

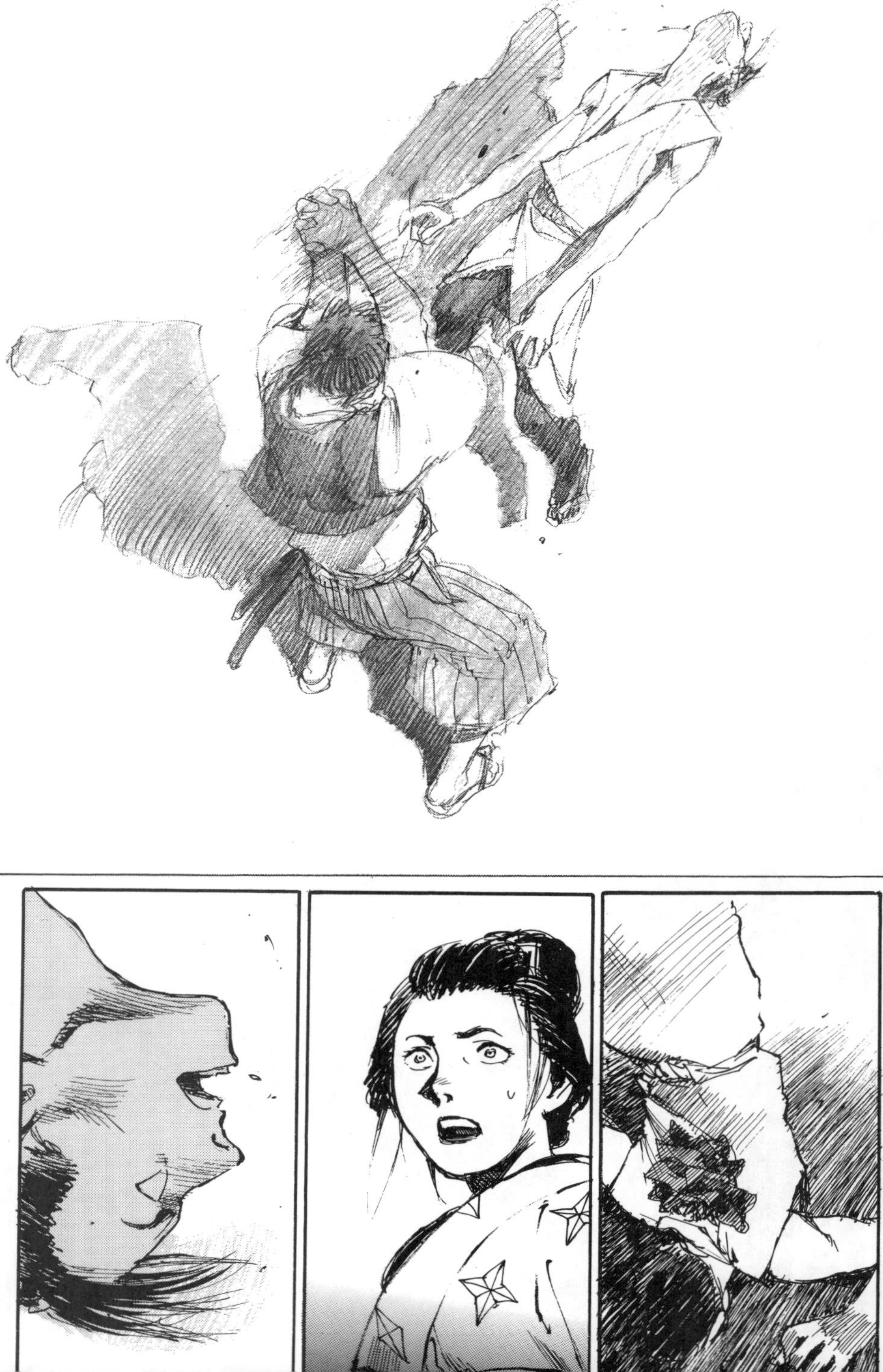

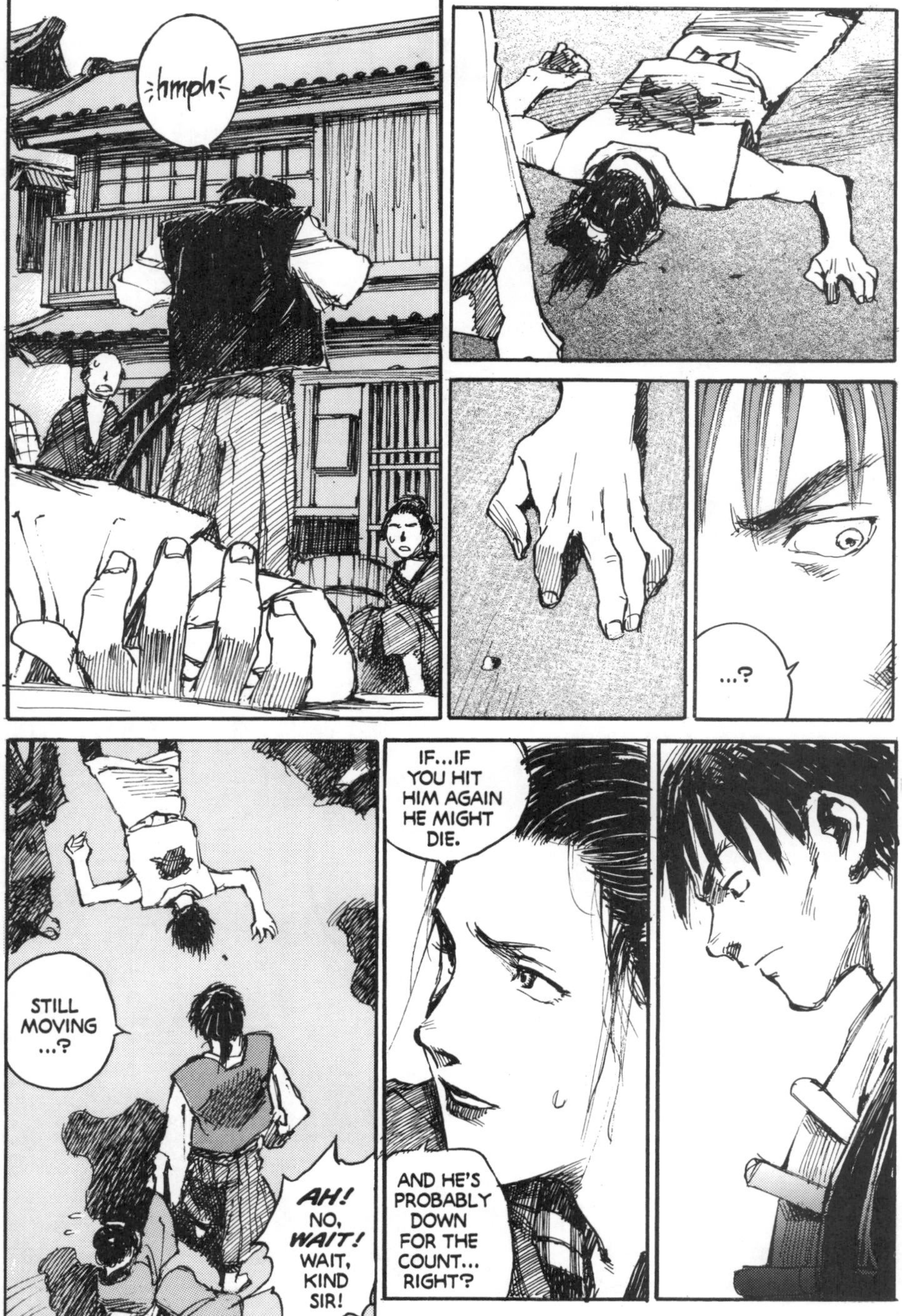
hmph
...?
STILL MOVING ...?
AH! NO, WAIT! WAIT, KIND SIR!
IF...IF YOU HIT HIM AGAIN HE MIGHT DIE.
AND HE'S PROBABLY DOWN FOR THE COUNT... RIGHT?

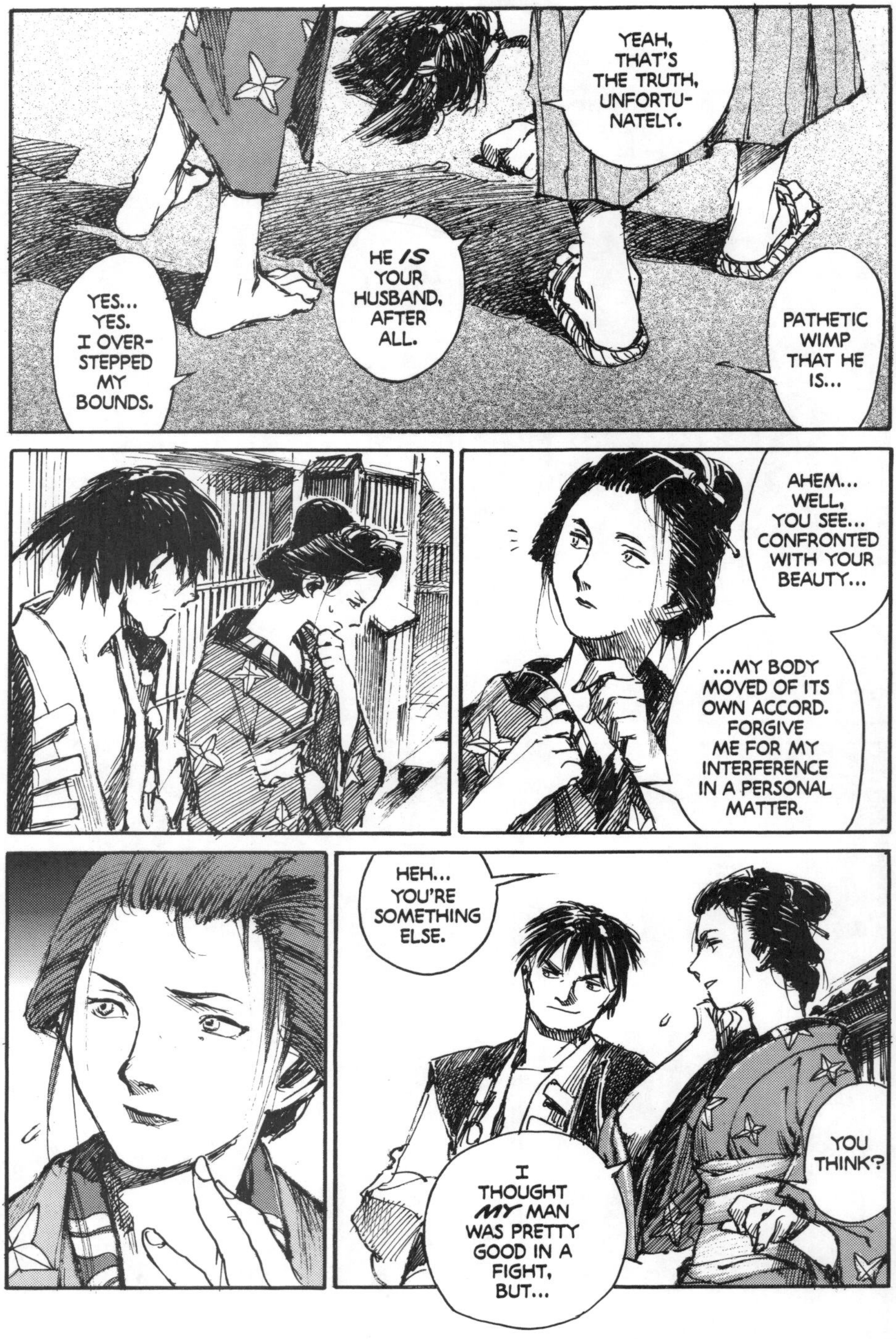
HE *IS* YOUR HUSBAND, AFTER ALL.
YEAH, THAT'S THE TRUTH, UNFORTUNATELY.
PATHETIC WIMP THAT HE IS...
YES... YES. I OVER-STEPPED MY BOUNDS.
AHEM... WELL, YOU SEE... CONFRONTED WITH YOUR BEAUTY...
...MY BODY MOVED OF ITS OWN ACCORD. FORGIVE ME FOR MY INTERFERENCE IN A PERSONAL MATTER.
HEH... YOU'RE SOMETHING ELSE.
I THOUGHT *MY* MAN WAS PRETTY GOOD IN A FIGHT, BUT...
YOU THINK?

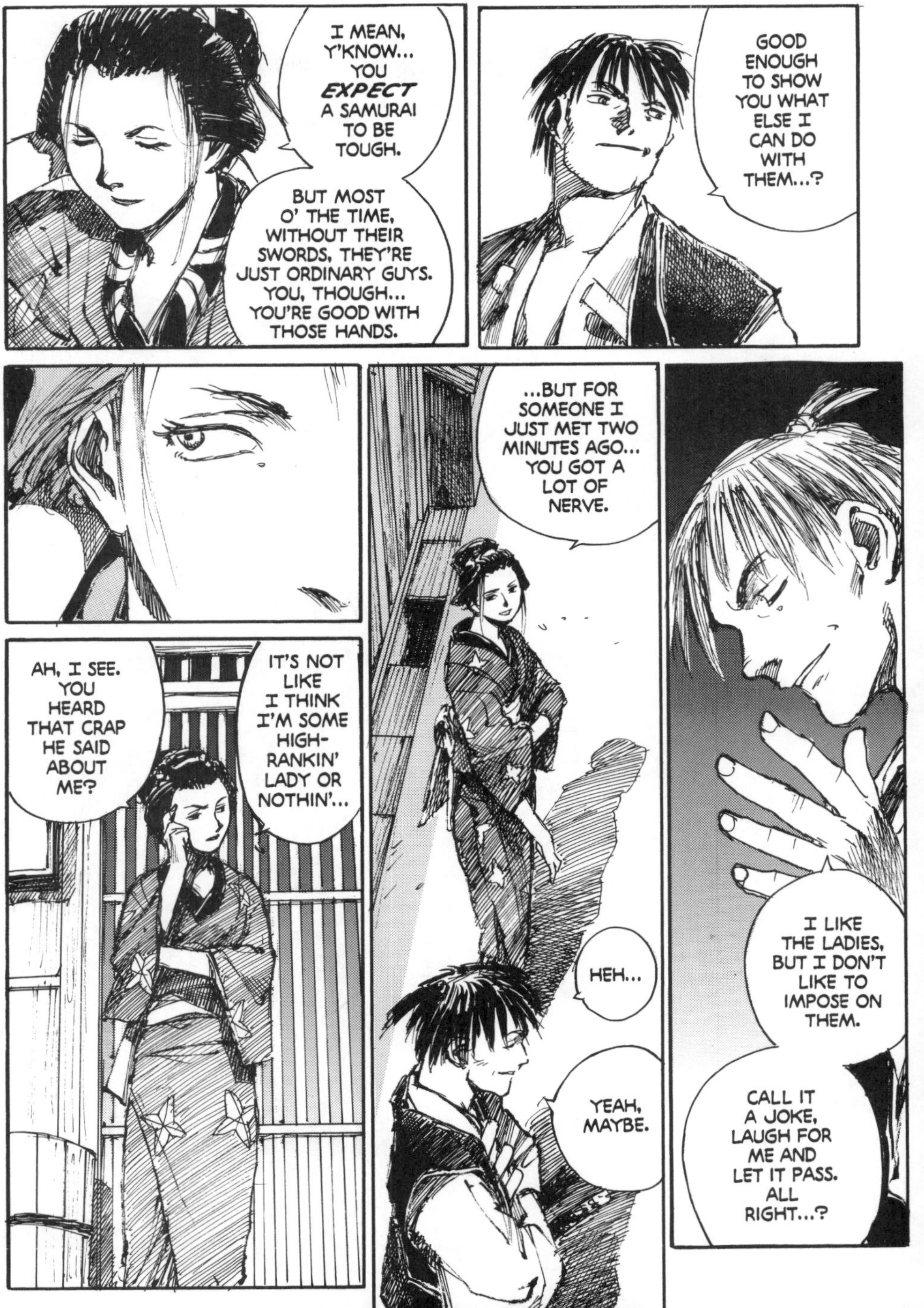
I MEAN, Y'KNOW... YOU *EXPECT* A SAMURAI TO BE TOUGH.
BUT MOST O' THE TIME, WITHOUT THEIR SWORDS, THEY'RE JUST ORDINARY GUYS. YOU, THOUGH... YOU'RE GOOD WITH THOSE HANDS.
GOOD ENOUGH TO SHOW YOU WHAT ELSE I CAN DO WITH THEM...?
AH, I SEE. YOU HEARD THAT CRAP HE SAID ABOUT ME?
IT'S NOT LIKE I THINK I'M SOME HIGH-RANKIN' LADY OR NOTHIN'...
...BUT FOR SOMEONE I JUST MET TWO MINUTES AGO... YOU GOT A LOT OF NERVE.
HEH...
YEAH, MAYBE.
I LIKE THE LADIES, BUT I DON'T LIKE TO IMPOSE ON THEM.
CALL IT A JOKE, LAUGH FOR ME AND LET IT PASS. ALL RIGHT...?

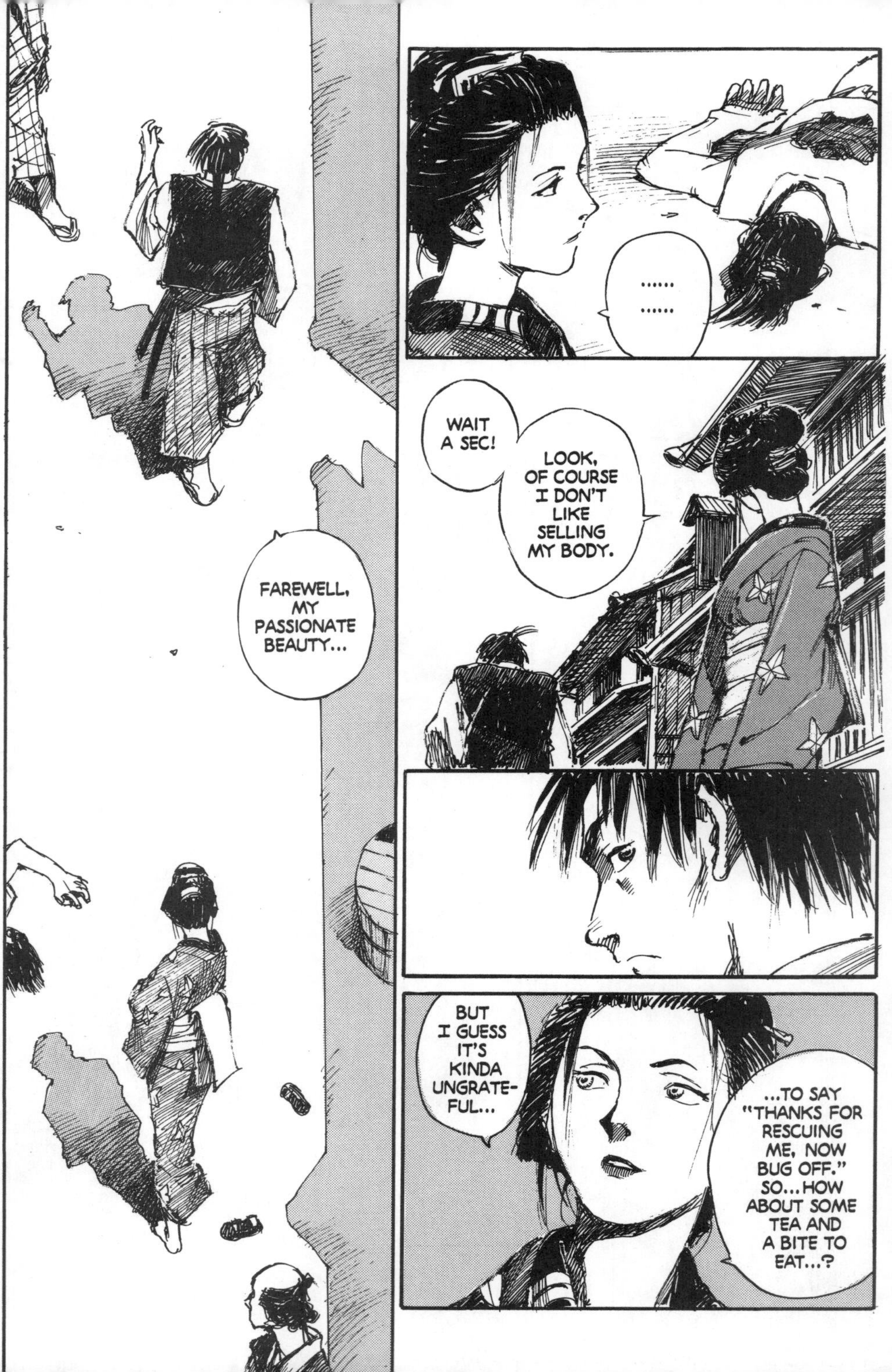
FAREWELL, MY PASSIONATE BEAUTY...
......
......
WAIT A SEC!
LOOK, OF COURSE I DON'T LIKE SELLING MY BODY.
BUT I GUESS IT'S KINDA UNGRATE-FUL...
...TO SAY "THANKS FOR RESCUING ME, NOW BUG OFF." SO...HOW ABOUT SOME TEA AND A BITE TO EAT...?

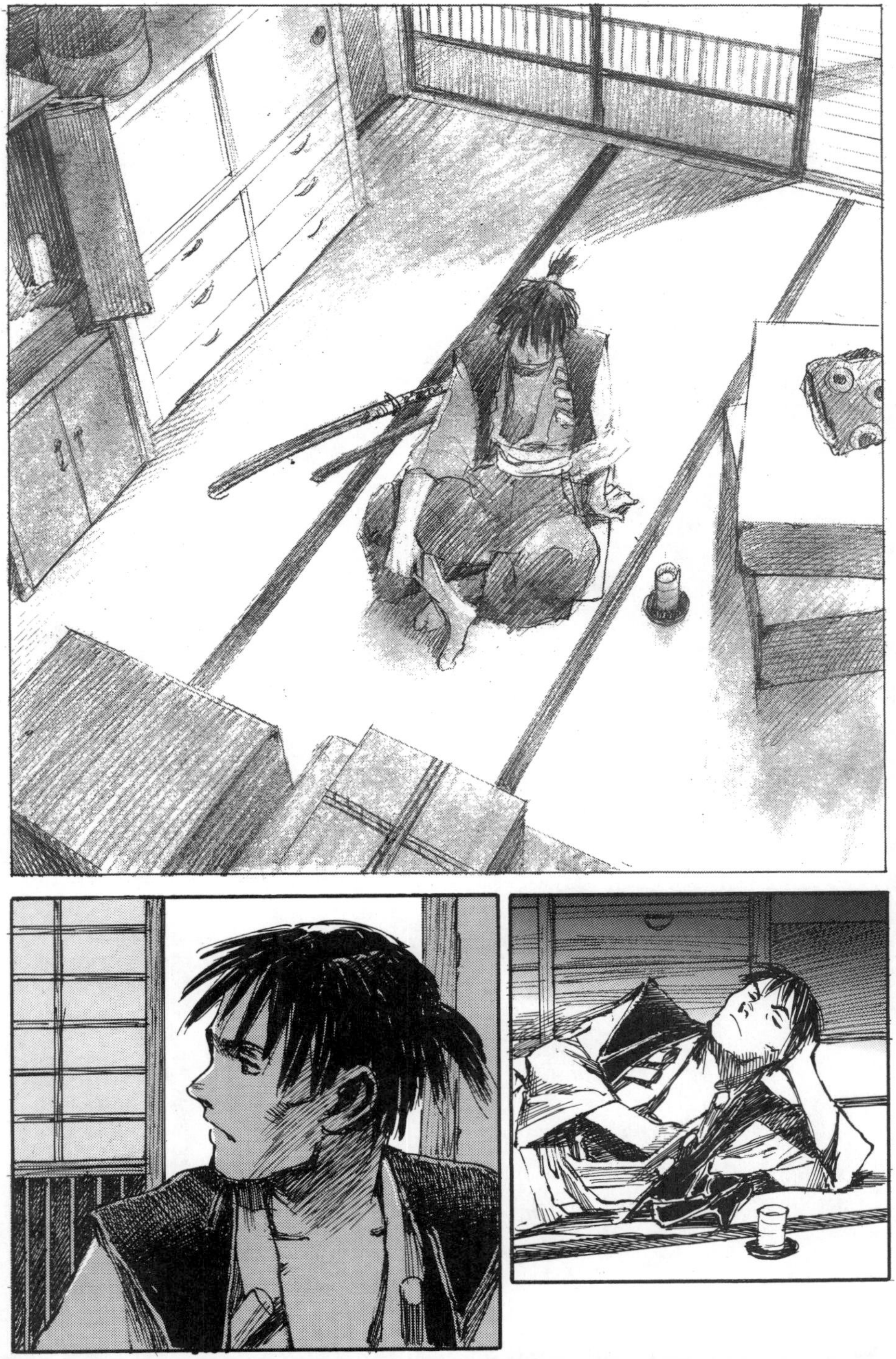

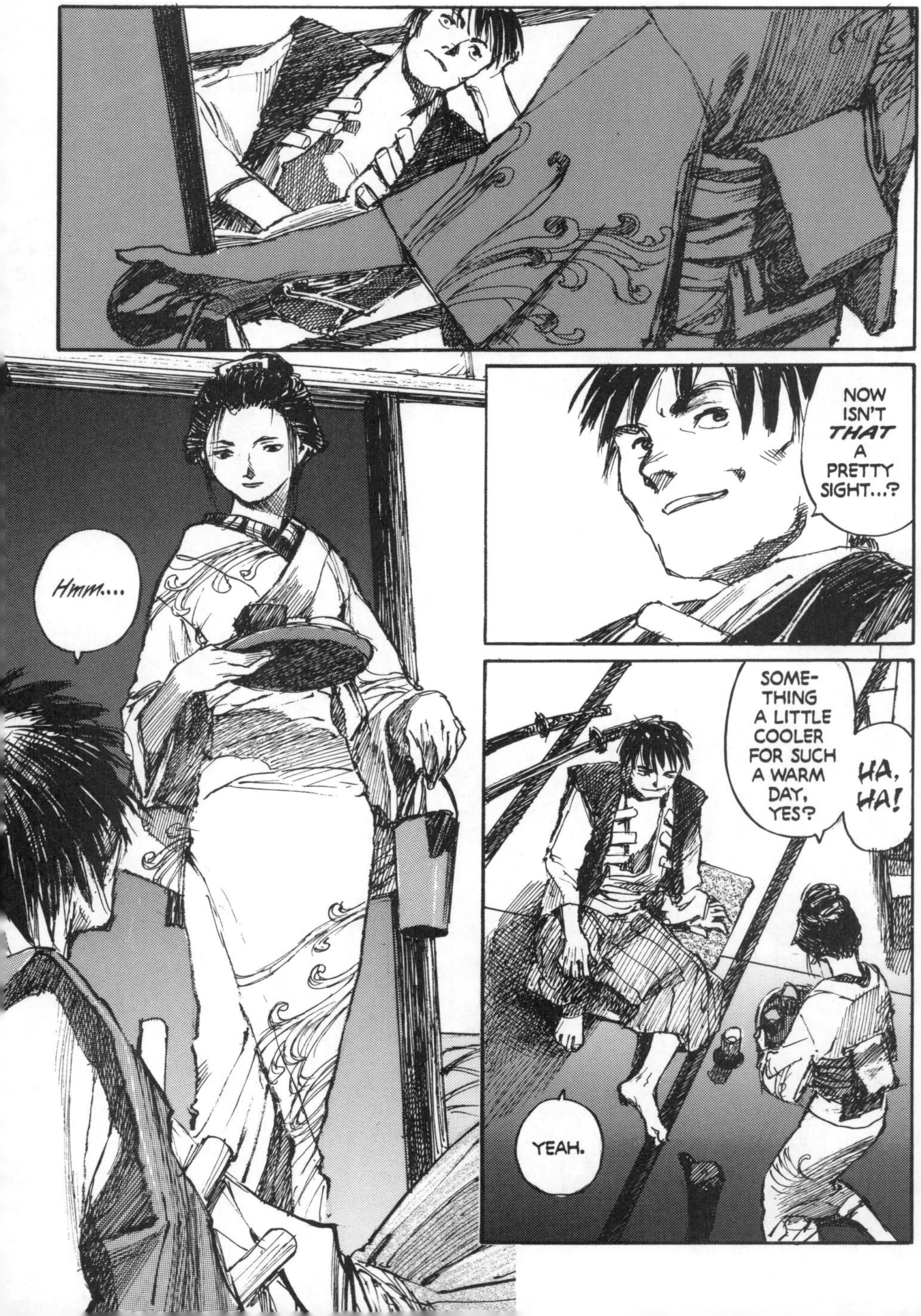
Hmm....
NOW ISN'T *THAT* A PRETTY SIGHT...?
SOME-THING A LITTLE COOLER FOR SUCH A WARM DAY, YES?
HA, HA!
YEAH.

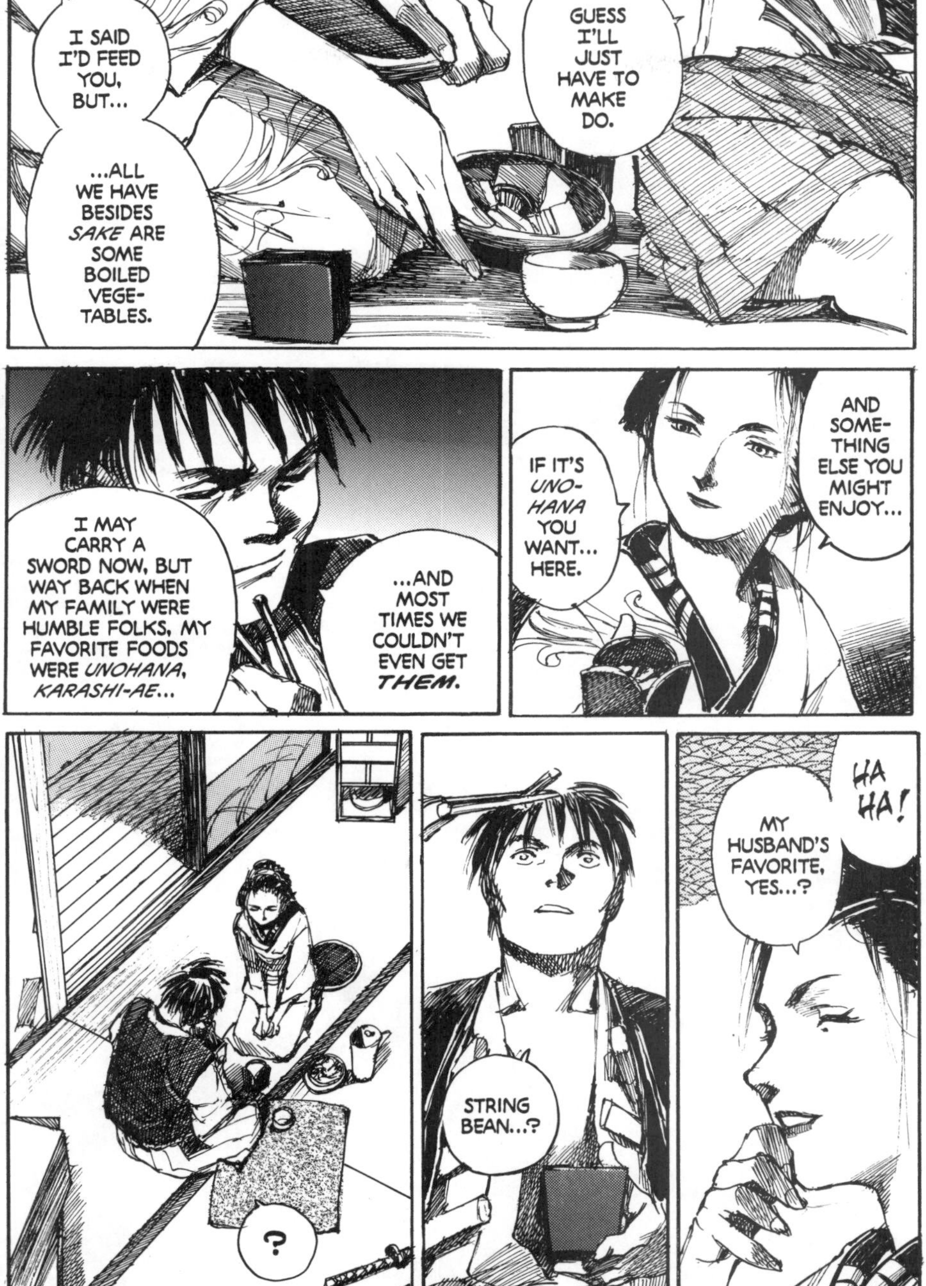
I SAID I'D FEED YOU, BUT...
...ALL WE HAVE BESIDES *SAKE* ARE SOME BOILED VEGE-TABLES.
GUESS I'LL JUST HAVE TO MAKE DO.
I MAY CARRY A SWORD NOW, BUT WAY BACK WHEN MY FAMILY WERE HUMBLE FOLKS, MY FAVORITE FOODS WERE *UNOHANA, KARASHI-AE*...
...AND MOST TIMES WE COULDN'T EVEN GET ***THEM***.
IF IT'S *UNO-HANA* YOU WANT... HERE.
AND SOME-THING ELSE YOU MIGHT ENJOY...
?
STRING BEAN...?
HA HA!
MY HUSBAND'S FAVORITE, YES...?

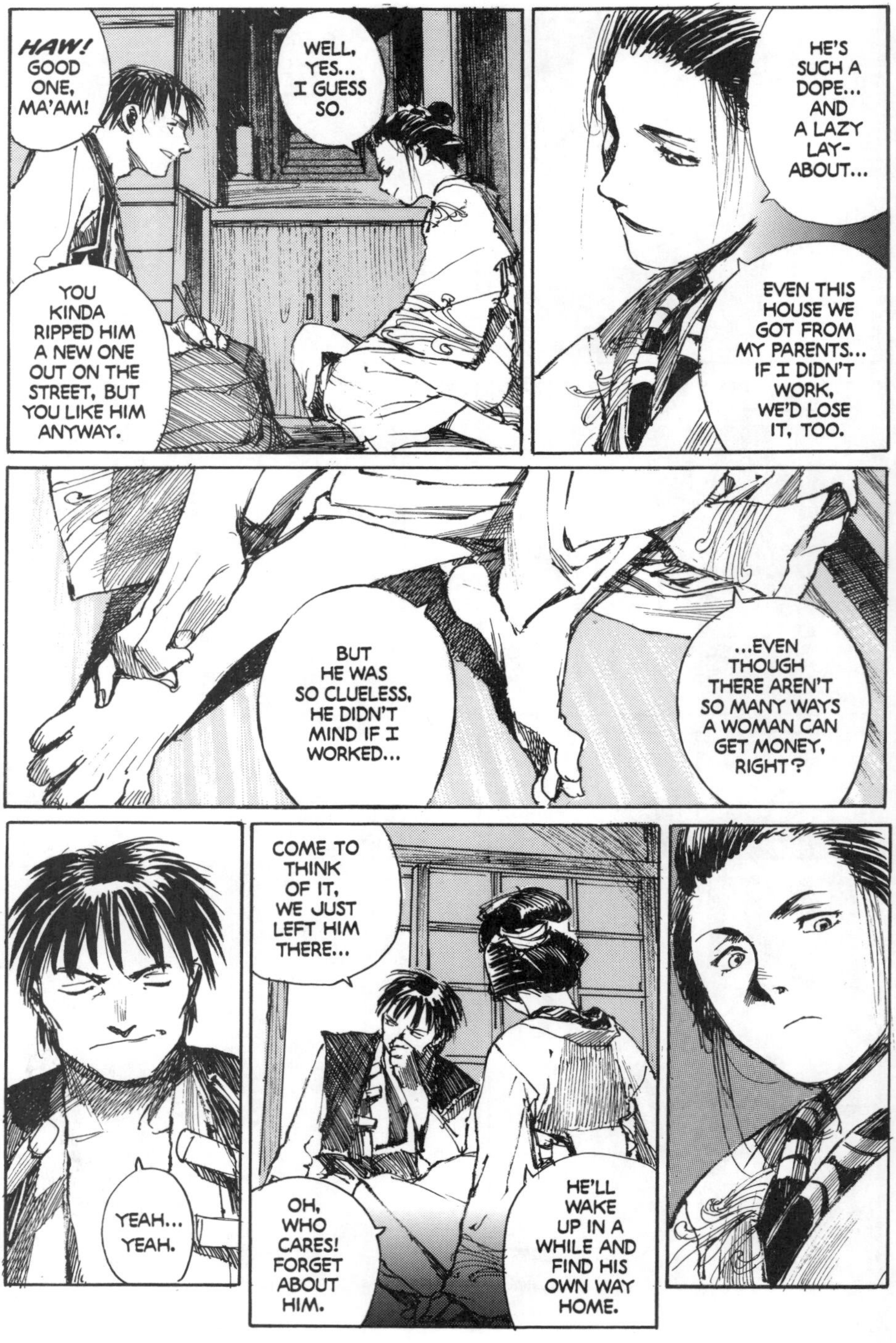
HAW! GOOD ONE, MA'AM!
WELL, YES... I GUESS SO.
YOU KINDA RIPPED HIM A NEW ONE OUT ON THE STREET, BUT YOU LIKE HIM ANYWAY.
HE'S SUCH A DOPE... AND A LAZY LAY-ABOUT...
EVEN THIS HOUSE WE GOT FROM MY PARENTS... IF I DIDN'T WORK, WE'D LOSE IT, TOO.
BUT HE WAS SO CLUELESS, HE DIDN'T MIND IF I WORKED...
...EVEN THOUGH THERE AREN'T SO MANY WAYS A WOMAN CAN GET MONEY, RIGHT?
YEAH... YEAH.
COME TO THINK OF IT, WE JUST LEFT HIM THERE...
OH, WHO CARES! FORGET ABOUT HIM.
HE'LL WAKE UP IN A WHILE AND FIND HIS OWN WAY HOME.

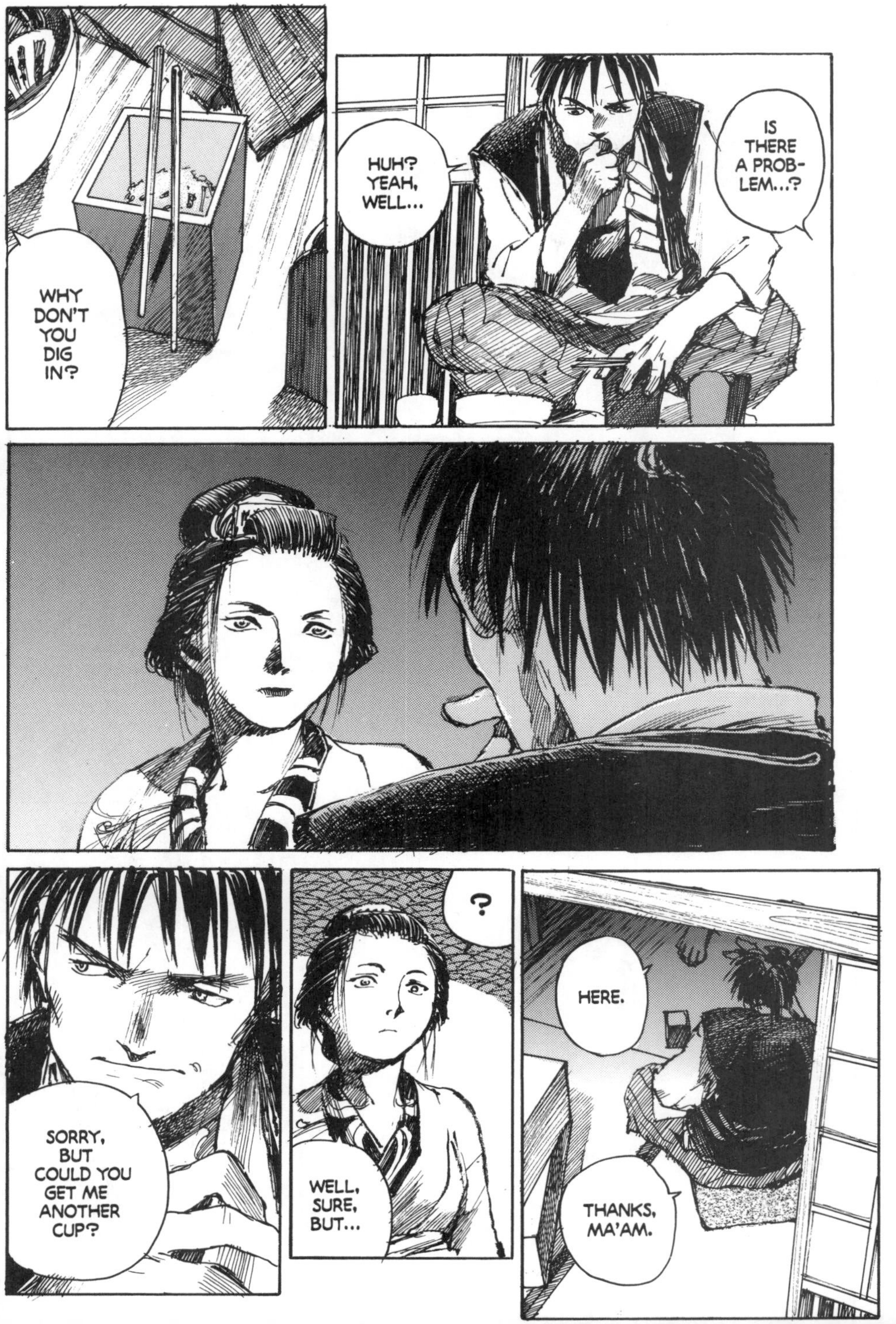
WHY DON'T YOU DIG IN?
IS THERE A PROB-LEM...?
HUH? YEAH, WELL...
SORRY, BUT COULD YOU GET ME ANOTHER CUP?
?
WELL, SURE, BUT...
HERE.
THANKS, MA'AM.

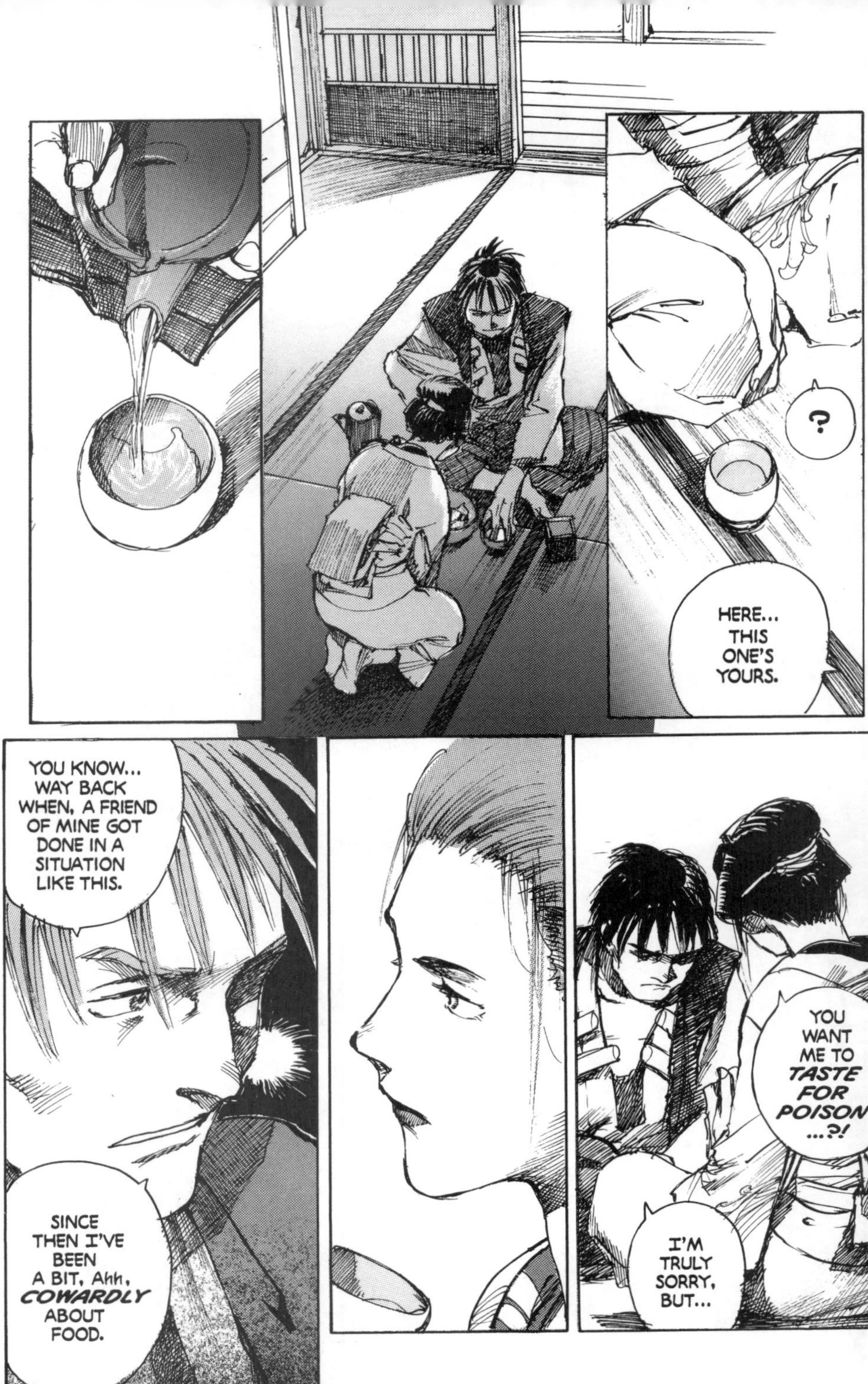
?
HERE... THIS ONE'S YOURS.
YOU KNOW... WAY BACK WHEN, A FRIEND OF MINE GOT DONE IN A SITUATION LIKE THIS.
SINCE THEN I'VE BEEN A BIT, Ahh, COWARDLY ABOUT FOOD.
YOU WANT ME TO TASTE FOR POISON ...?!
I'M TRULY SORRY, BUT...

OKAY!
FINE!

I MEAN, IT'S JUST *TOO* STUPID FOR YOU TO MISS OUT ON MY COOKING BECAUSE OF SOMETHING LIKE *THAT*.

OKAY THEN! LOOK... WATCH CLOSELY, NOW!

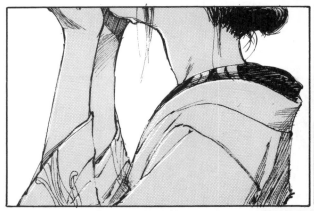

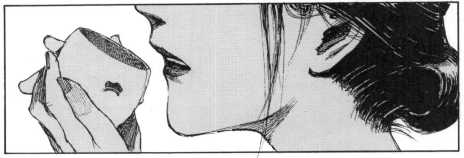

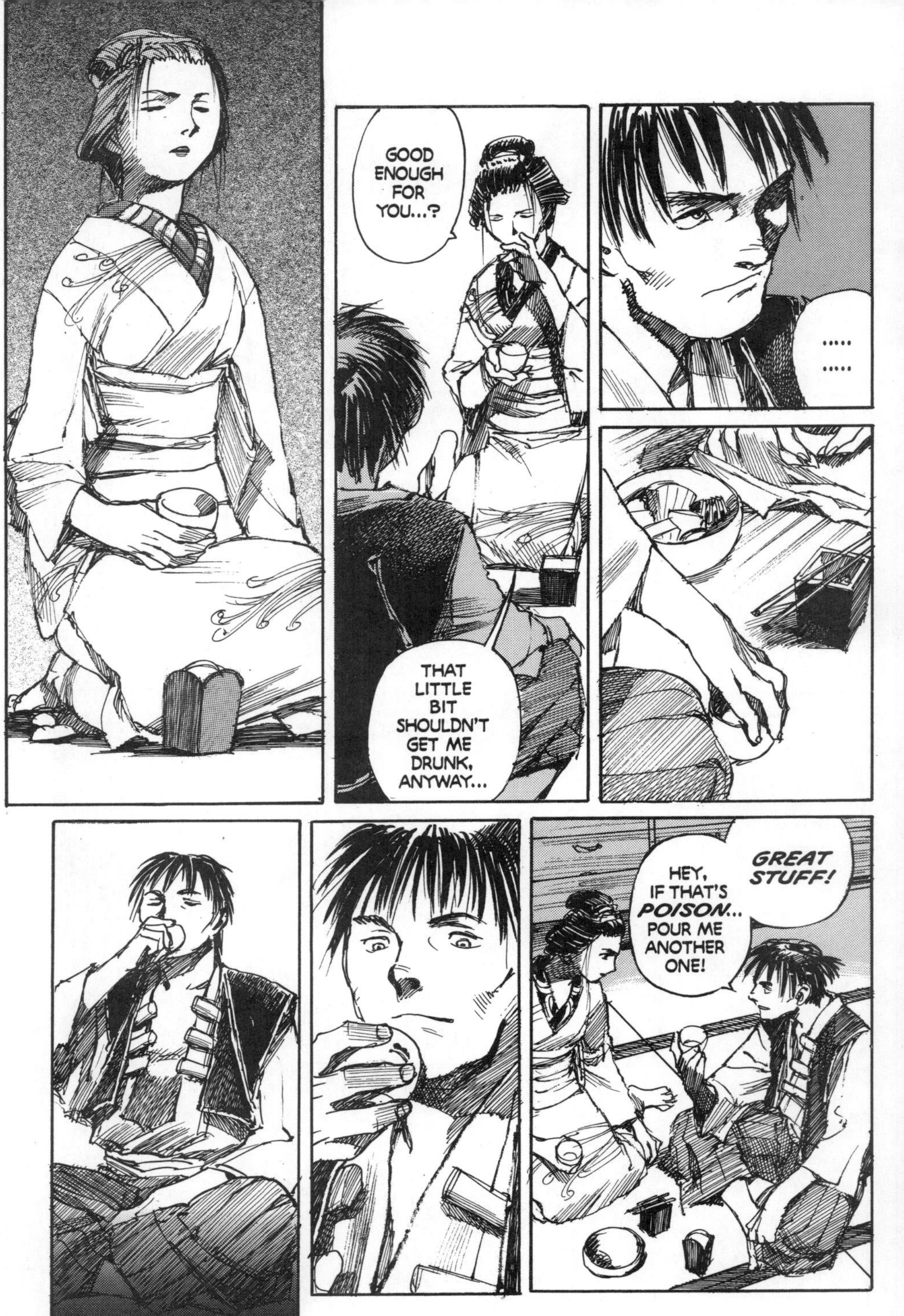
GOOD ENOUGH FOR YOU...?
THAT LITTLE BIT SHOULDN'T GET ME DRUNK, ANYWAY...
.....
.....
HEY, IF THAT'S POISON... POUR ME ANOTHER ONE!
GREAT STUFF!

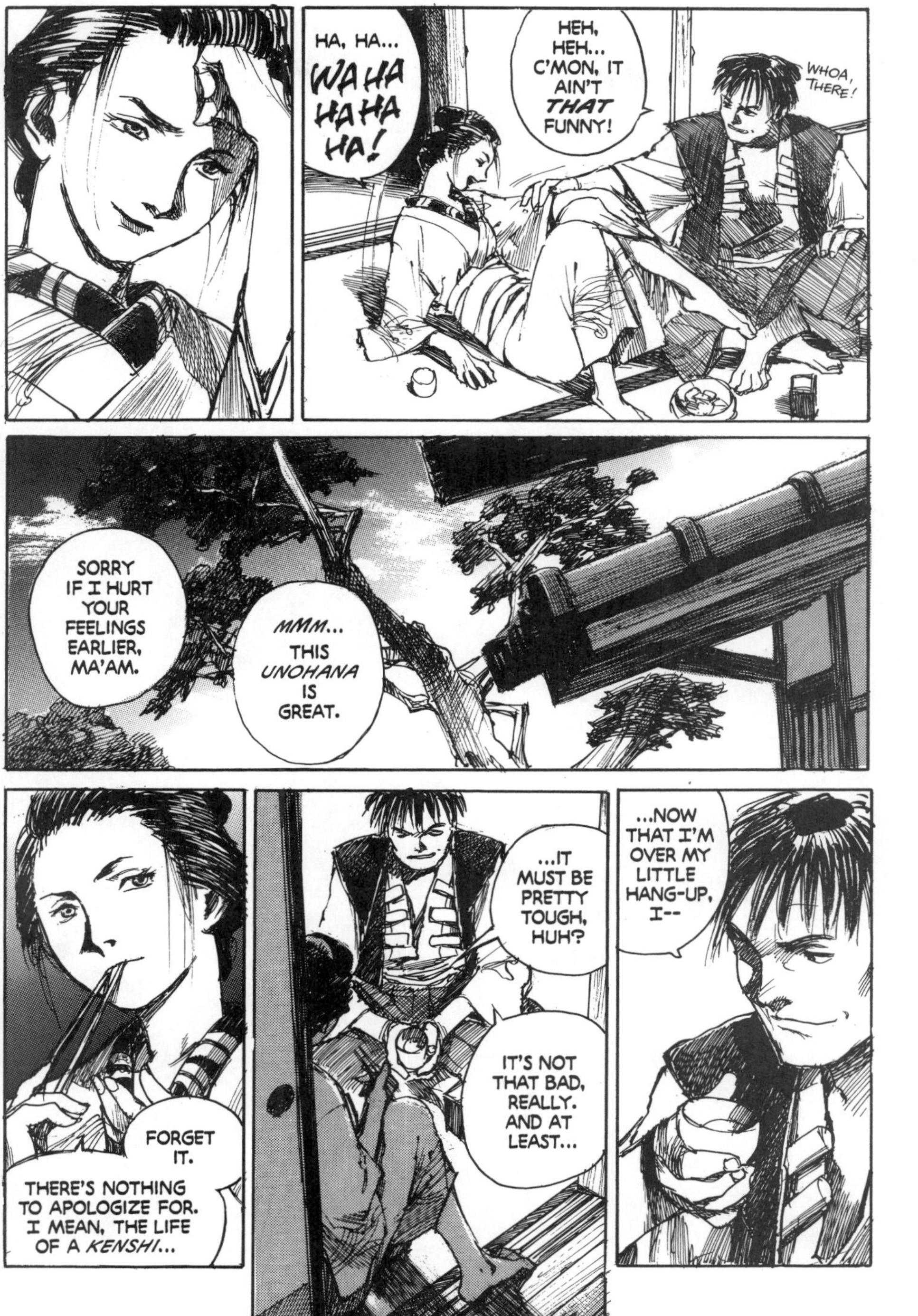
HA, HA...
WA HA HA HA HA!
HEH, HEH... C'MON, IT AIN'T THAT FUNNY!
WHOA, THERE!
SORRY IF I HURT YOUR FEELINGS EARLIER, MA'AM.
MMM... THIS UNOHANA IS GREAT.
FORGET IT.
THERE'S NOTHING TO APOLOGIZE FOR. I MEAN, THE LIFE OF A KENSHI...
...IT MUST BE PRETTY TOUGH, HUH?
IT'S NOT THAT BAD, REALLY. AND AT LEAST...
...NOW THAT I'M OVER MY LITTLE HANG-UP, I--

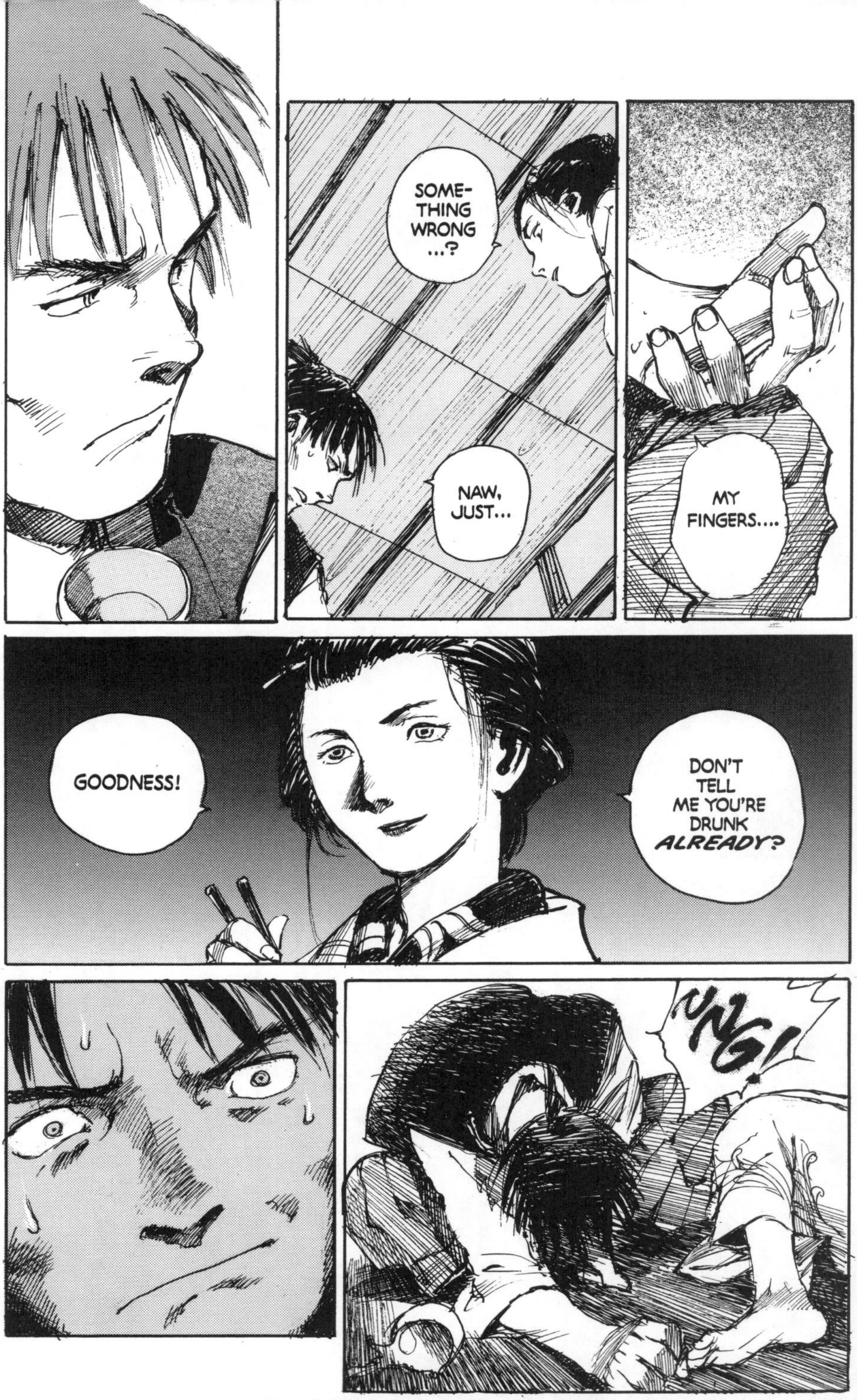
SOME-THING WRONG ...?
NAW, JUST...
MY FINGERS....
GOODNESS!
DON'T TELL ME YOU'RE DRUNK *ALREADY?*
UNG!

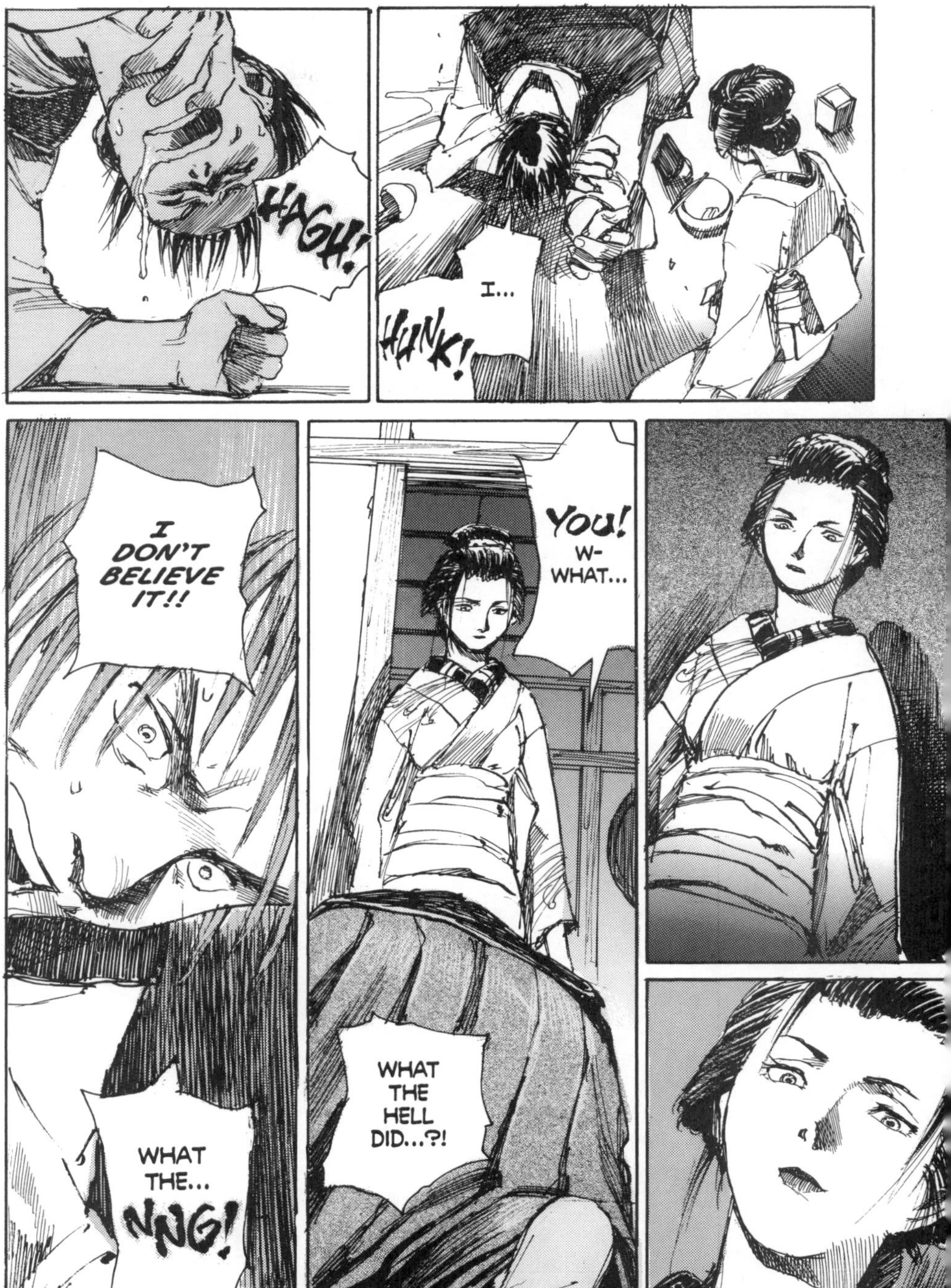
HAGH!
I...
HUNK!
I DON'T BELIEVE IT!!
YOU!
W-WHAT...
WHAT THE...
NNG!
WHAT THE HELL DID...?!

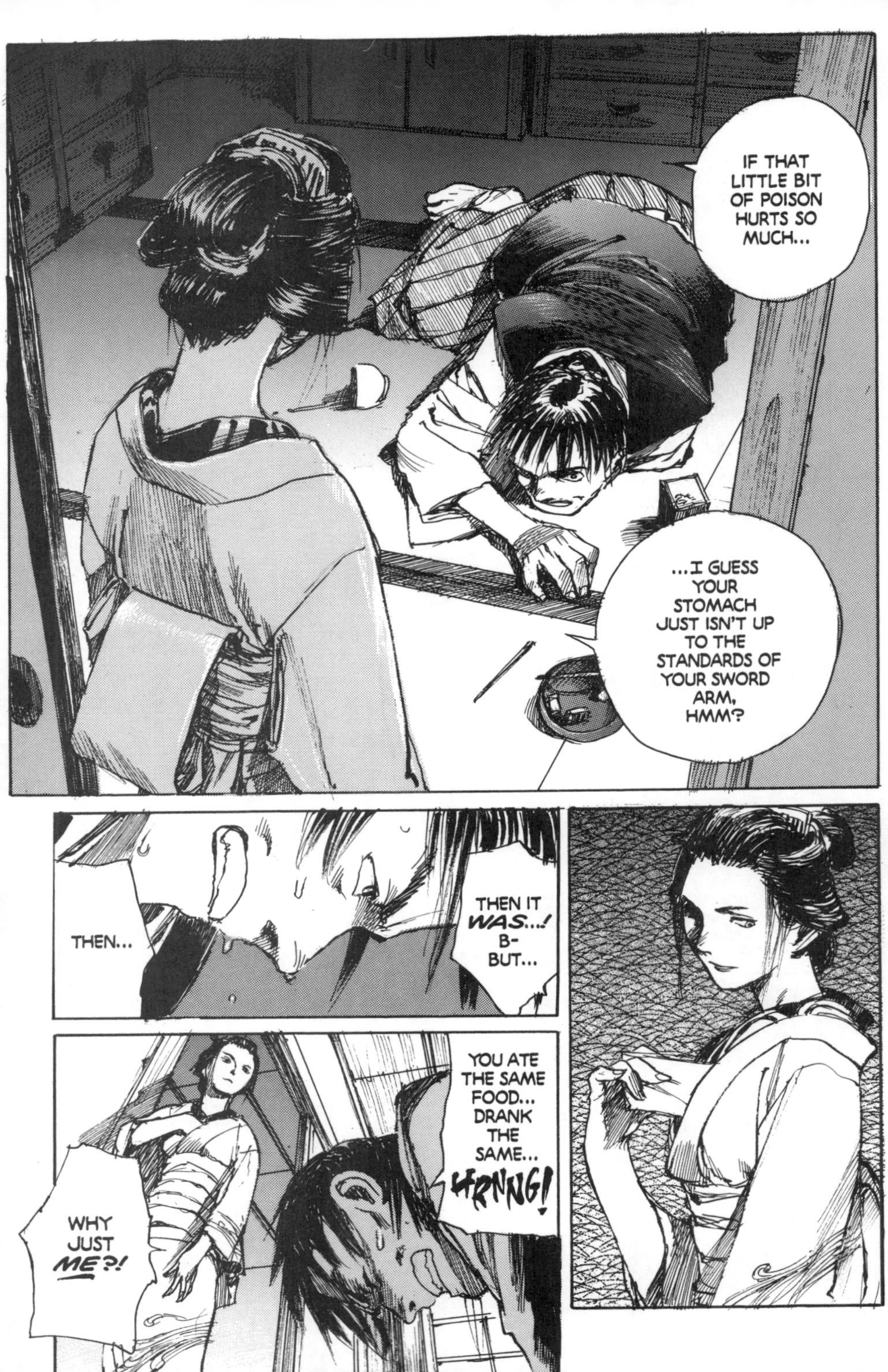
IF THAT LITTLE BIT OF POISON HURTS SO MUCH...
...I GUESS YOUR STOMACH JUST ISN'T UP TO THE STANDARDS OF YOUR SWORD ARM, HMM?
THEN...
THEN IT WAS...! B-BUT...
YOU ATE THE SAME FOOD... DRANK THE SAME...
HRNNG!
WHY JUST ME?!

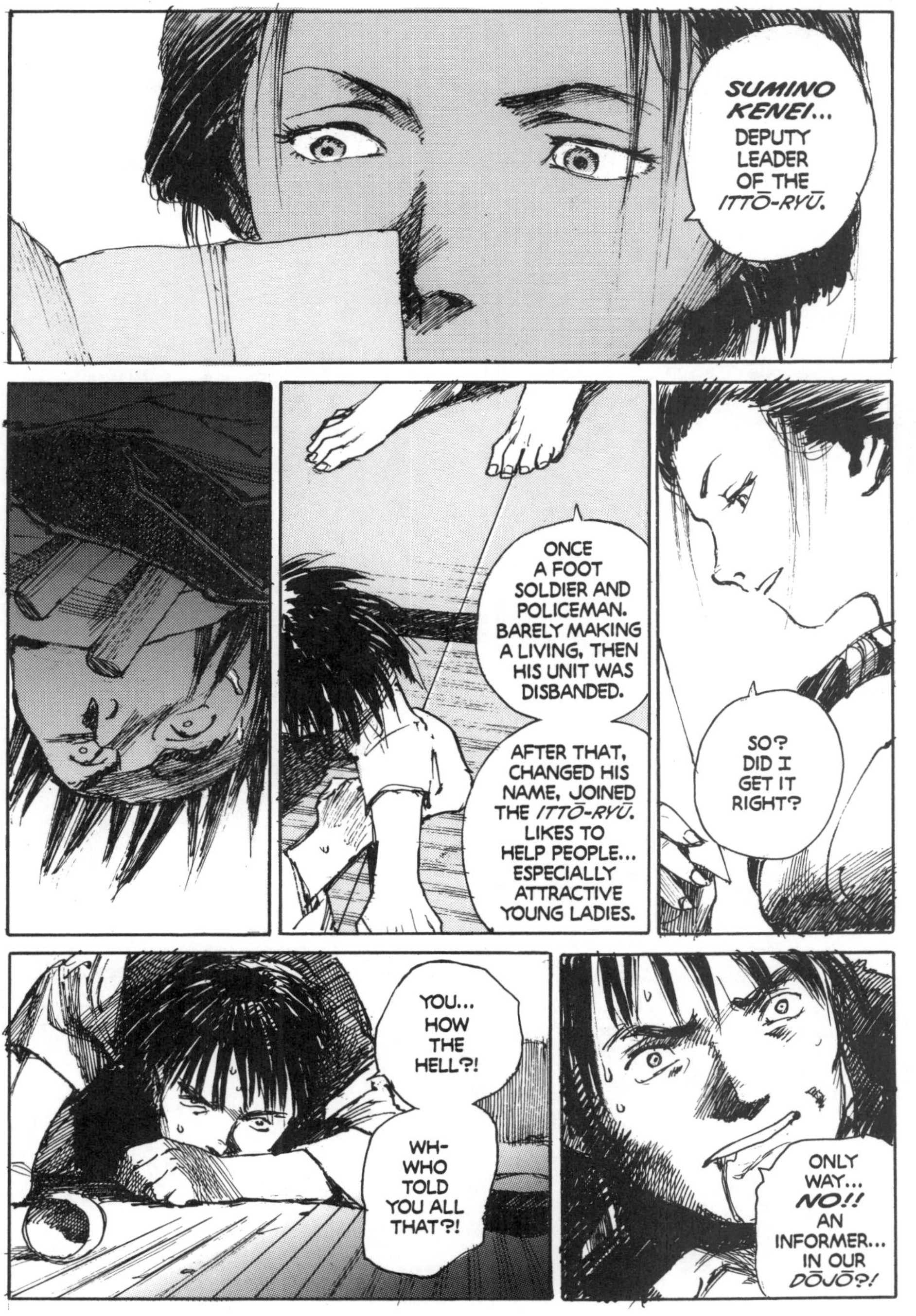
SUMINO KENEI... DEPUTY LEADER OF THE ITTŌ-RYŪ.
ONCE A FOOT SOLDIER AND POLICEMAN. BARELY MAKING A LIVING, THEN HIS UNIT WAS DISBANDED.
AFTER THAT, CHANGED HIS NAME, JOINED THE ITTŌ-RYŪ. LIKES TO HELP PEOPLE... ESPECIALLY ATTRACTIVE YOUNG LADIES.
SO? DID I GET IT RIGHT?
YOU... HOW THE HELL?!
WH-WHO TOLD YOU ALL THAT?!
ONLY WAY... NO!! AN INFORMER... IN OUR DŌJŌ?!

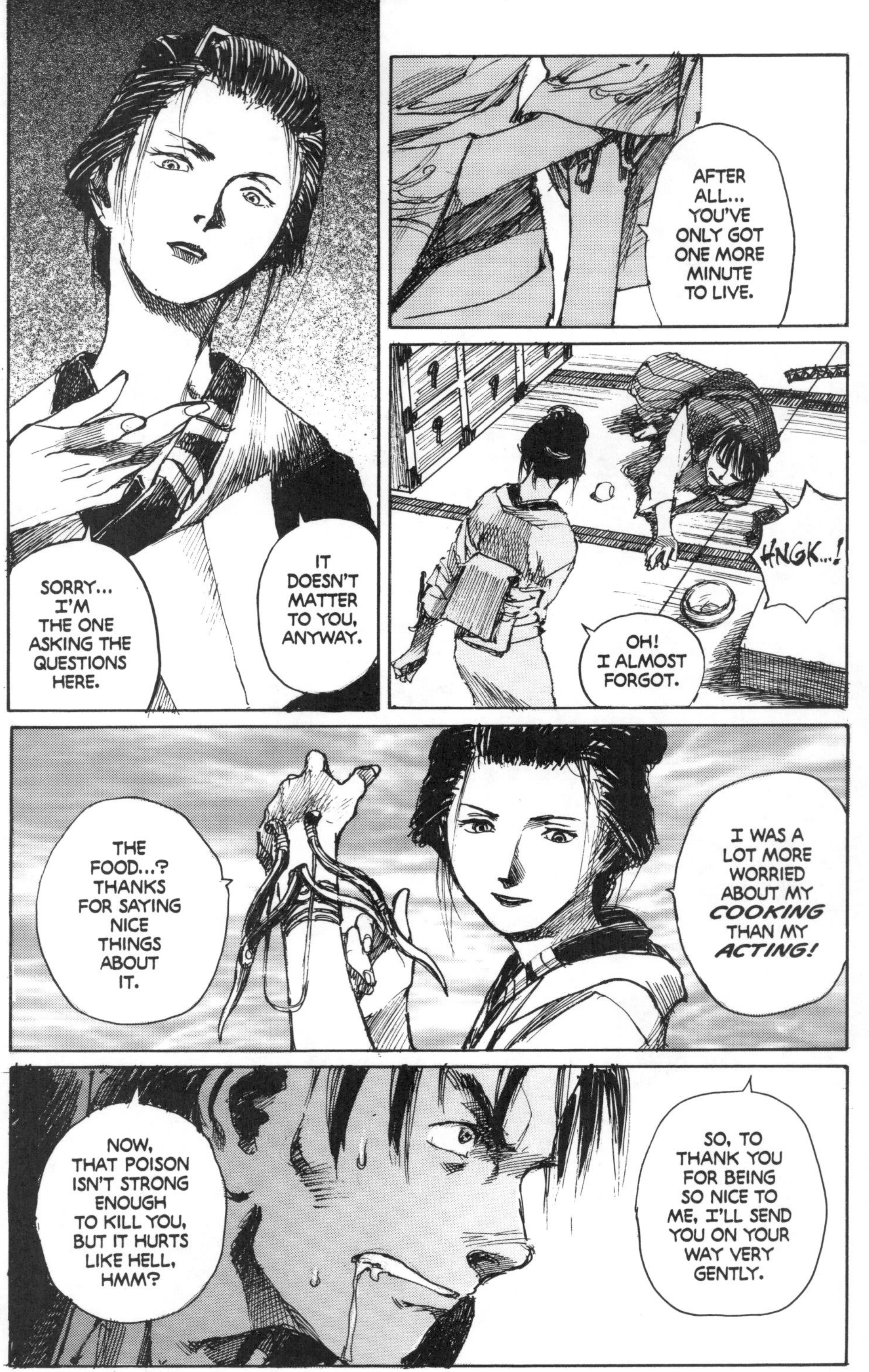
SORRY... I'M THE ONE ASKING THE QUESTIONS HERE.
IT DOESN'T MATTER TO YOU, ANYWAY.
AFTER ALL... YOU'VE ONLY GOT ONE MORE MINUTE TO LIVE.
HNGK...!
OH! I ALMOST FORGOT.
THE FOOD...? THANKS FOR SAYING NICE THINGS ABOUT IT.
I WAS A LOT MORE WORRIED ABOUT MY *COOKING* THAN MY *ACTING!*
NOW, THAT POISON ISN'T STRONG ENOUGH TO KILL YOU, BUT IT HURTS LIKE HELL, HMM?
SO, TO THANK YOU FOR BEING SO NICE TO ME, I'LL SEND YOU ON YOUR WAY VERY GENTLY.

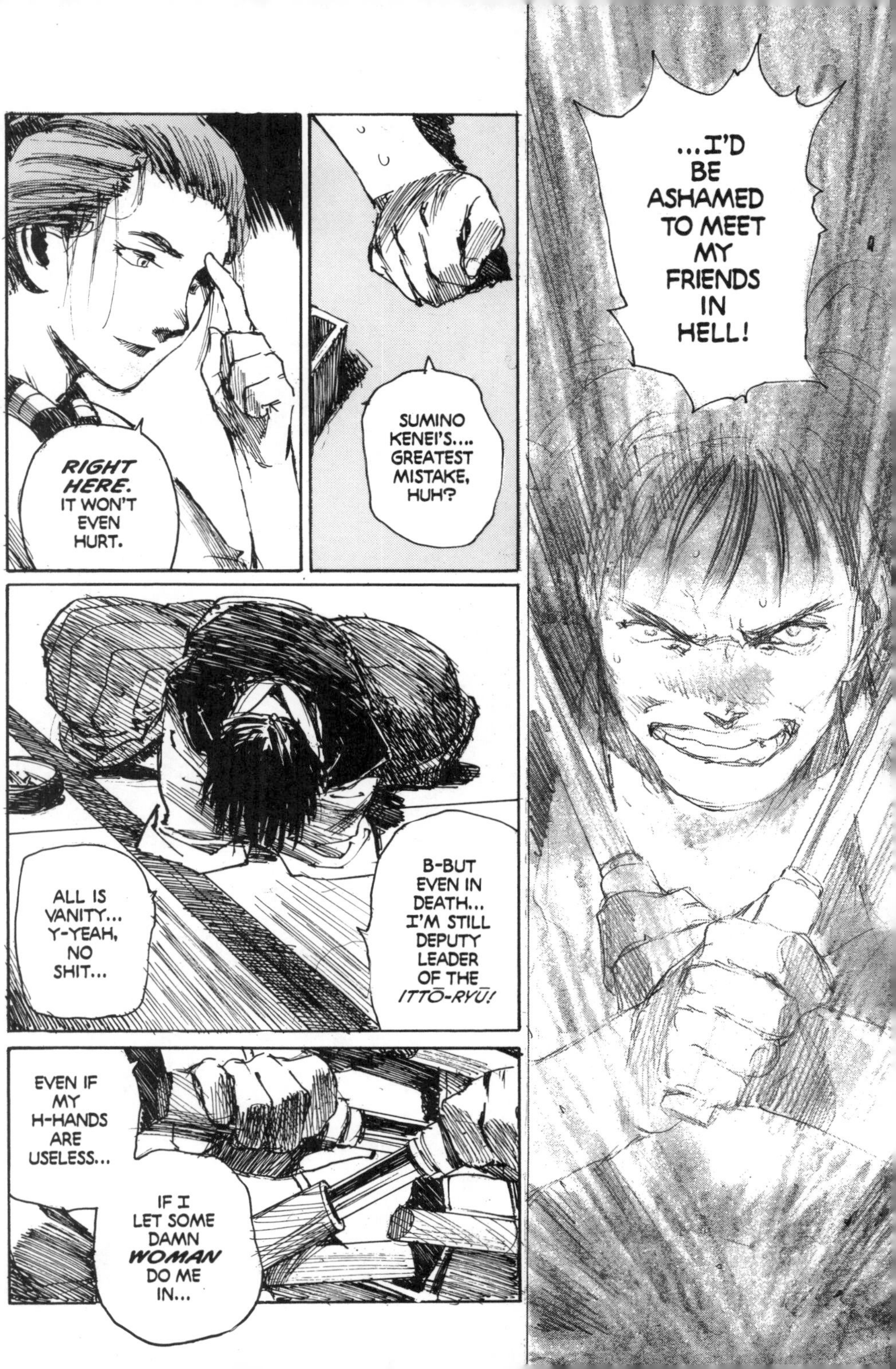
RIGHT HERE. IT WON'T EVEN HURT.
SUMINO KENEI'S.... GREATEST MISTAKE, HUH?
ALL IS VANITY... Y-YEAH, NO SHIT...
B-BUT EVEN IN DEATH... I'M STILL DEPUTY LEADER OF THE *ITTŌ-RYŪ!*
EVEN IF MY H-HANDS ARE USELESS...
IF I LET SOME DAMN ***WOMAN*** DO ME IN...
...I'D BE ASHAMED TO MEET MY FRIENDS IN HELL!

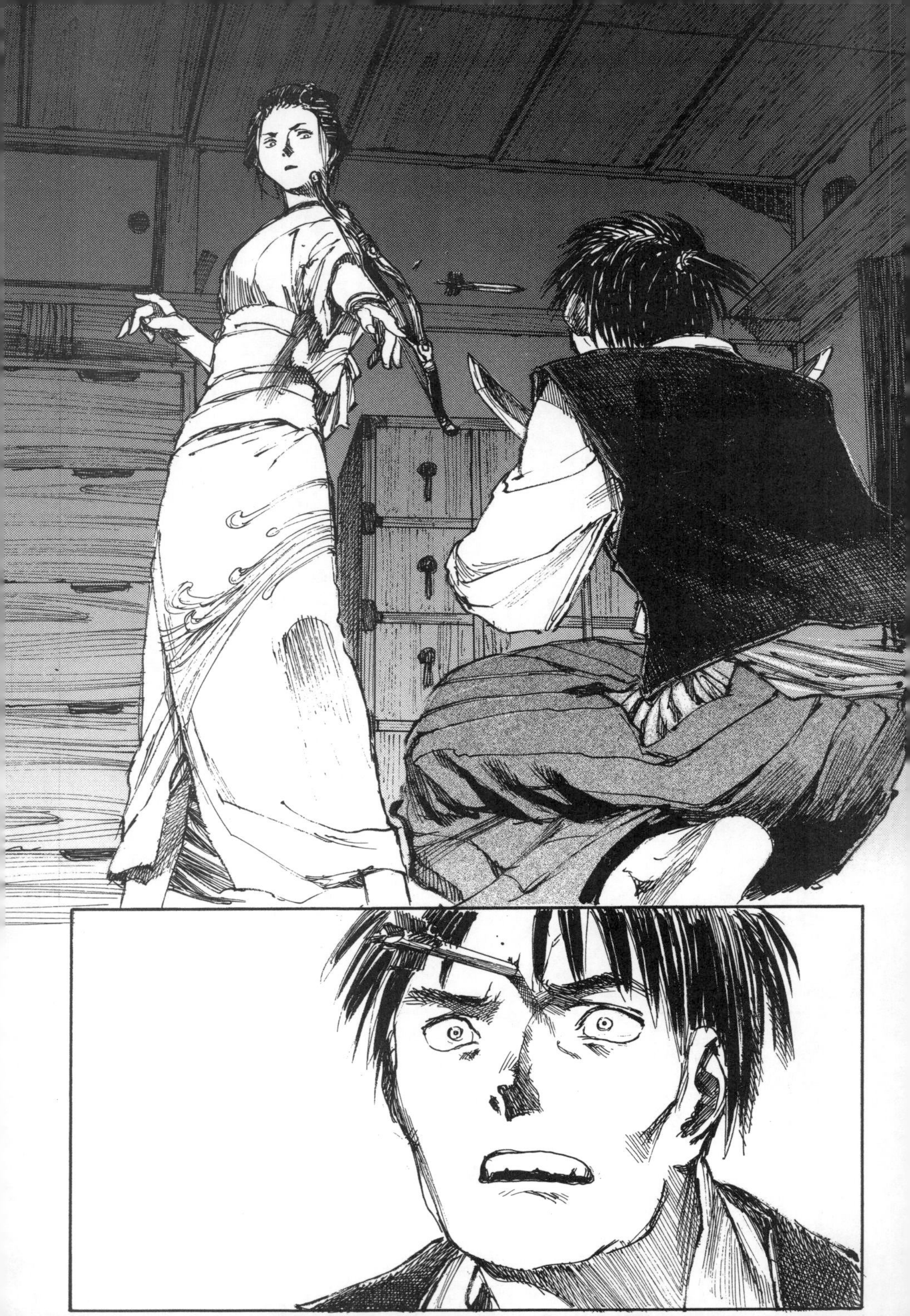

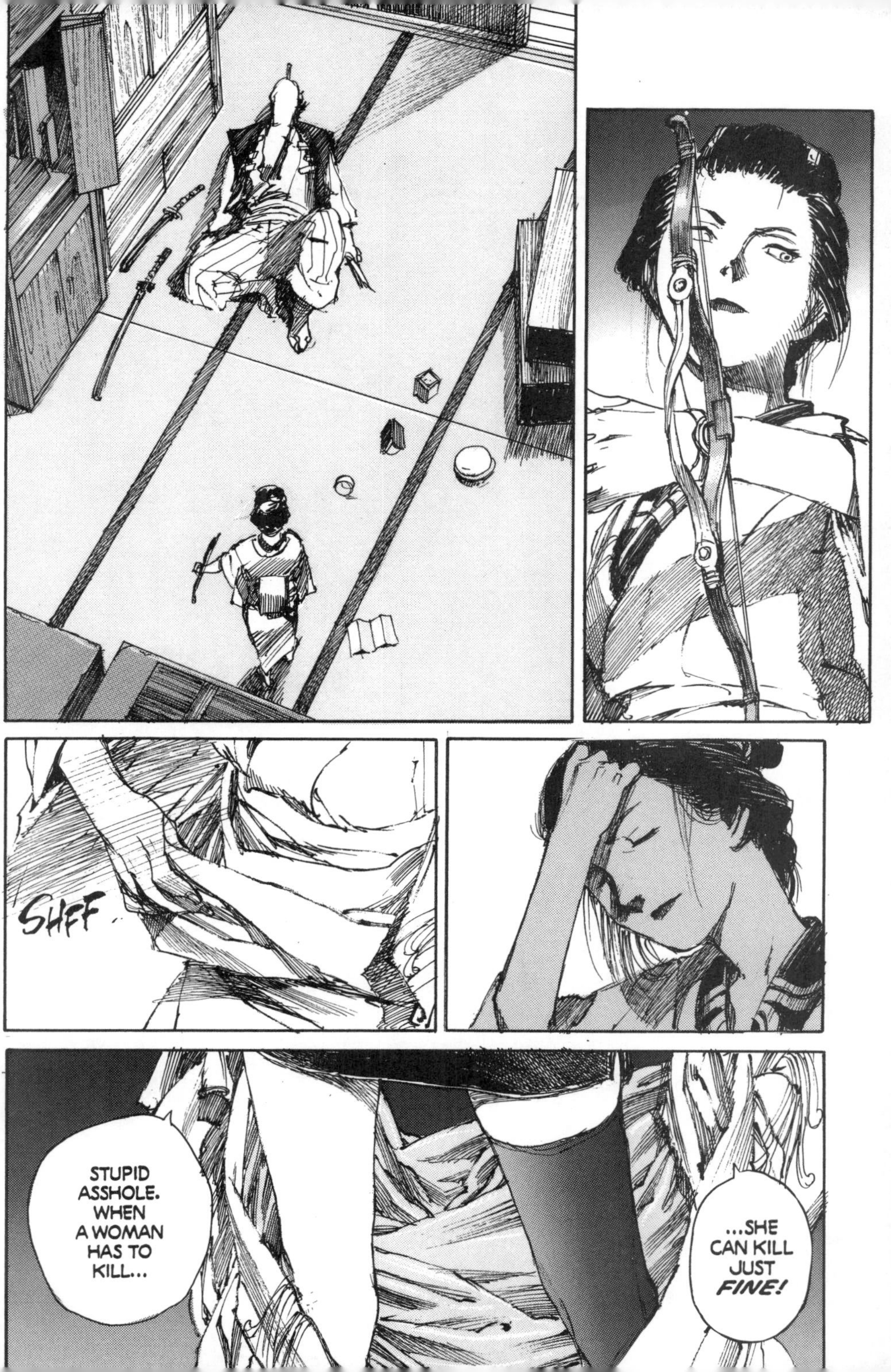
SHFF
STUPID ASSHOLE. WHEN A WOMAN HAS TO KILL...
...SHE CAN KILL JUST FINE!

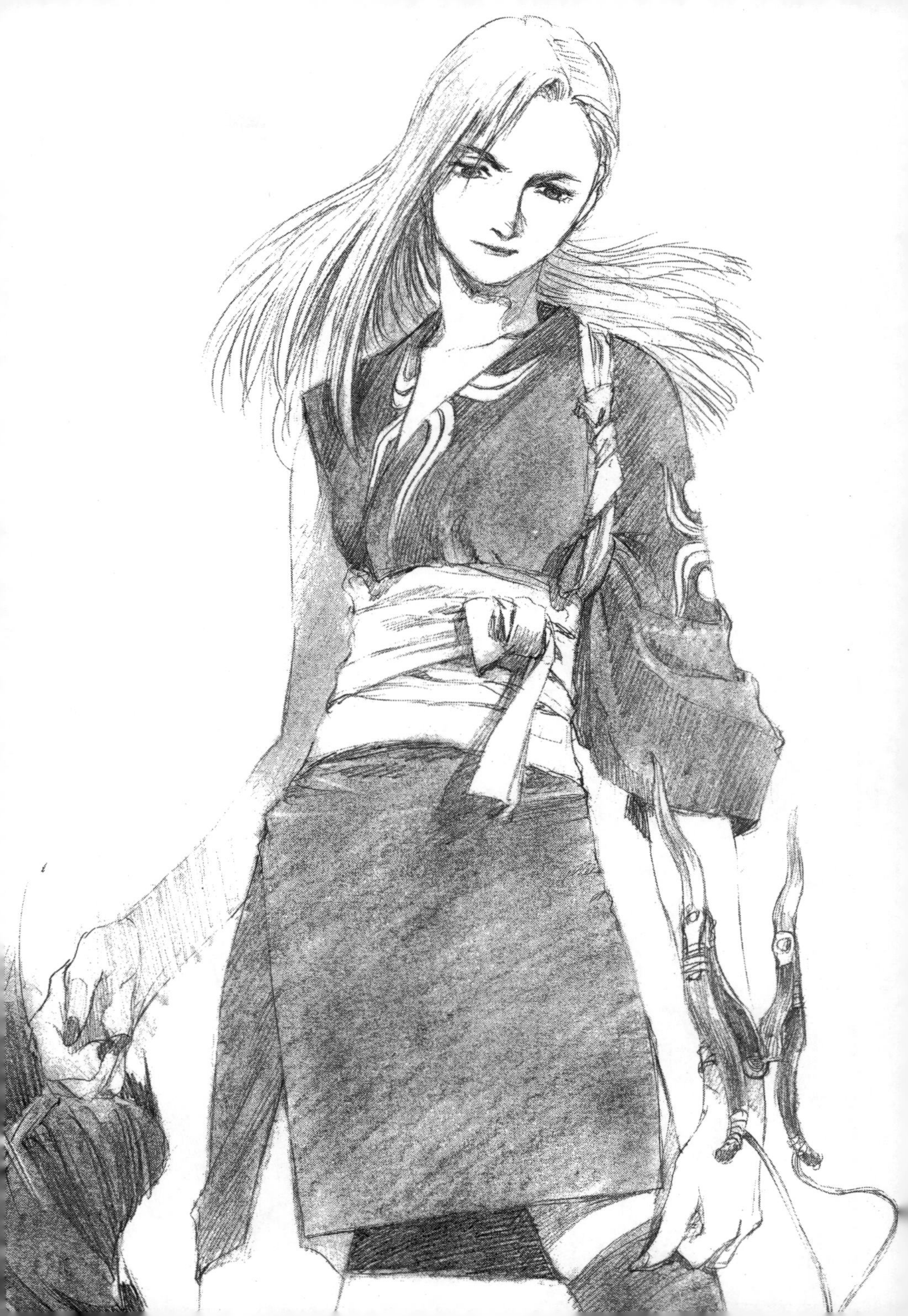

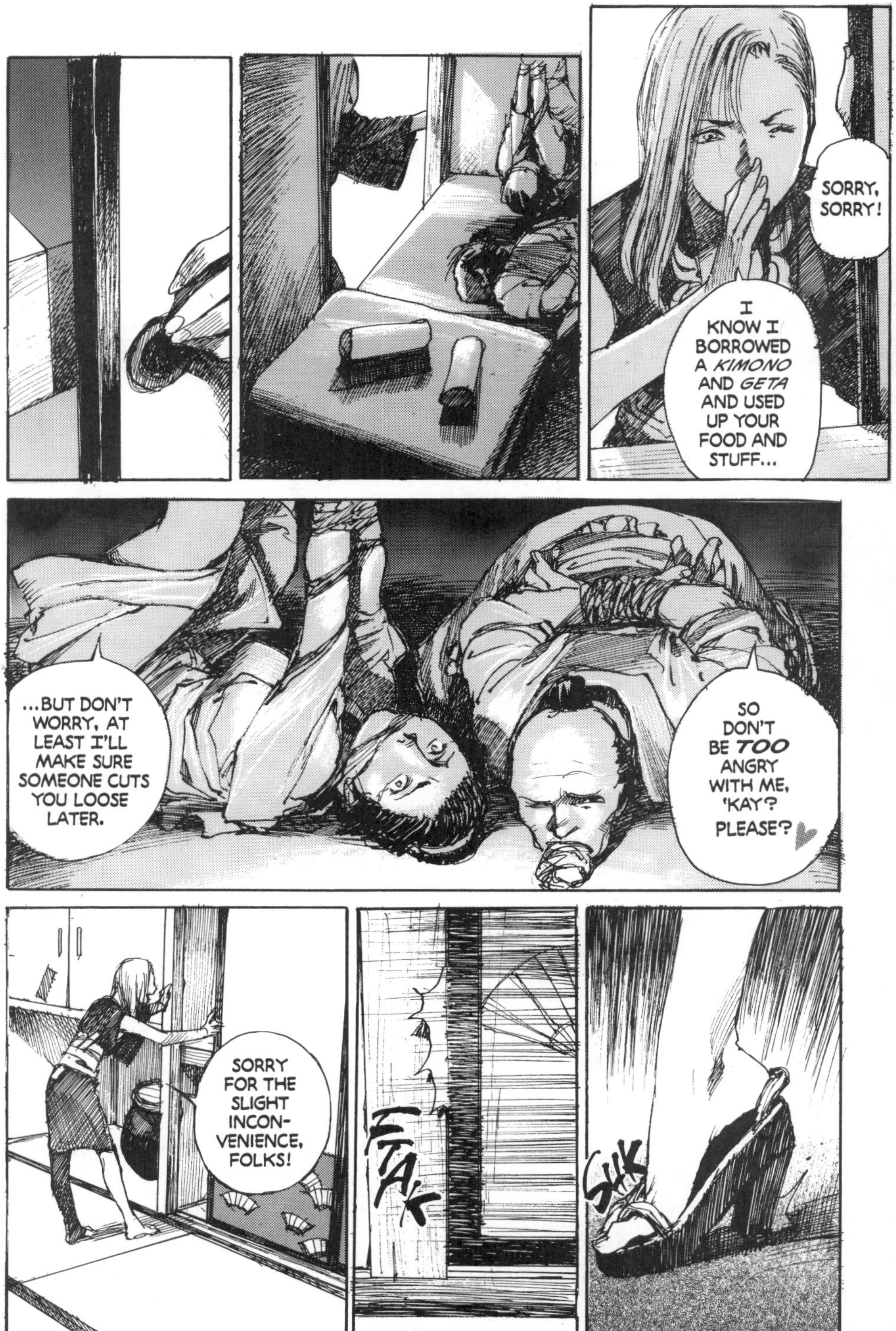

SORRY, SORRY!
I KNOW I BORROWED A *KIMONO* AND *GETA* AND USED UP YOUR FOOD AND STUFF...
...BUT DON'T WORRY, AT LEAST I'LL MAKE SURE SOMEONE CUTS YOU LOOSE LATER.
SO DON'T BE *TOO* ANGRY WITH ME, 'KAY? PLEASE?
SORRY FOR THE SLIGHT INCON-VENIENCE, FOLKS!
FTAK
SLIK

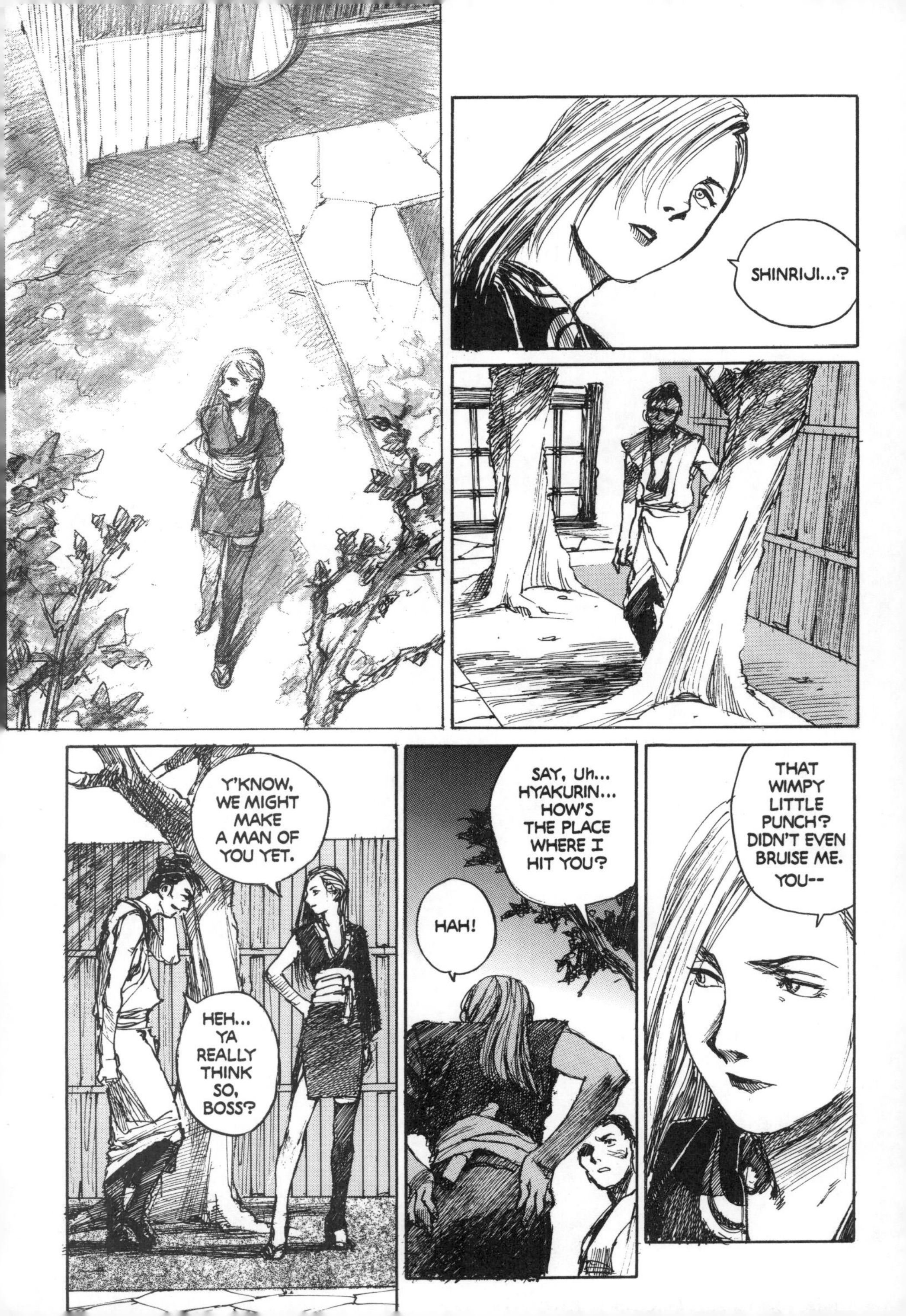
SHINRIJI...?
Y'KNOW, WE MIGHT MAKE A MAN OF YOU YET.
HEH... YA REALLY THINK SO, BOSS?
SAY, Uh... HYAKURIN... HOW'S THE PLACE WHERE I HIT YOU?
HAH!
THAT WIMPY LITTLE PUNCH? DIDN'T EVEN BRUISE ME.
YOU--

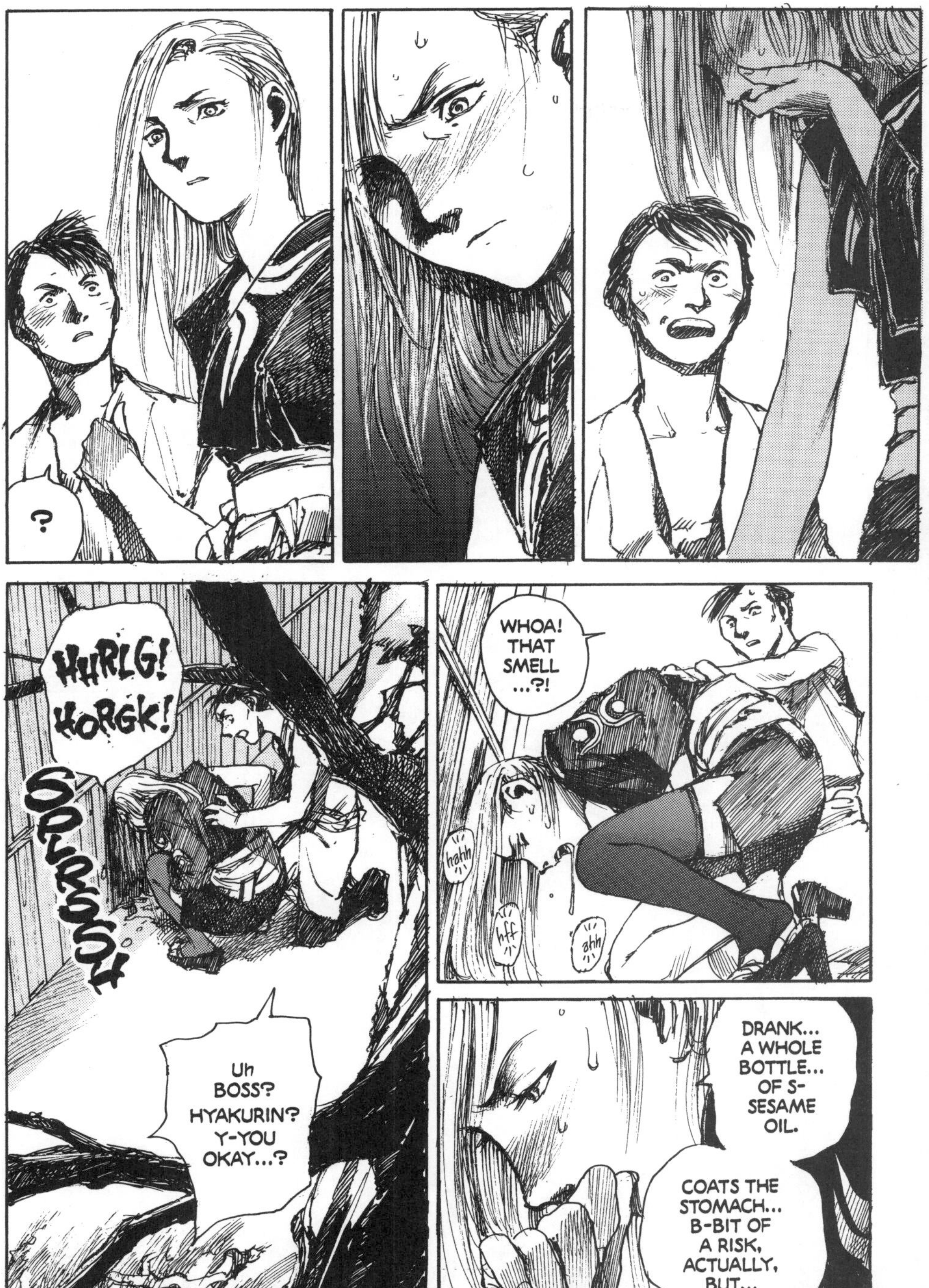
?
HURLG! HORGK!
SPLURSSH
Uh BOSS? HYAKURIN? Y-YOU OKAY...?
WHOA! THAT SMELL ...?!
hahh
hff
ahh
DRANK... A WHOLE BOTTLE... OF S-SESAME OIL.
COATS THE STOMACH... B-BIT OF A RISK, ACTUALLY, BUT...

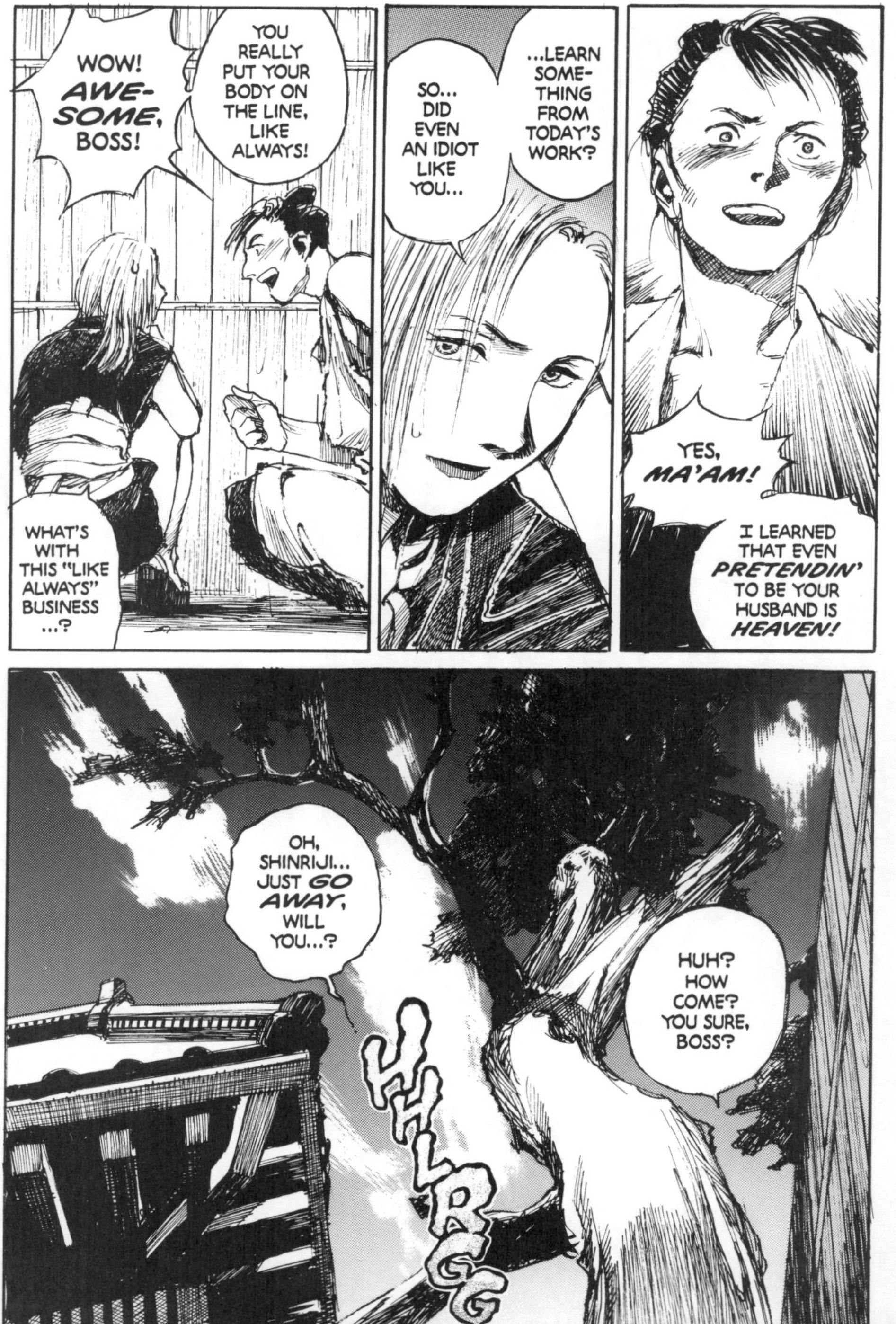
WOW! AWE-SOME, BOSS!
YOU REALLY PUT YOUR BODY ON THE LINE, LIKE ALWAYS!
WHAT'S WITH THIS "LIKE ALWAYS" BUSINESS ...?
SO... DID EVEN AN IDIOT LIKE YOU...
...LEARN SOME-THING FROM TODAY'S WORK?
YES, MA'AM!
I LEARNED THAT EVEN PRETENDIN' TO BE YOUR HUSBAND IS HEAVEN!
OH, SHINRIJI... JUST GO AWAY, WILL YOU...?
HUH? HOW COME? YOU SURE, BOSS?
HHLRGG

DARK SHADOWS
Part 2

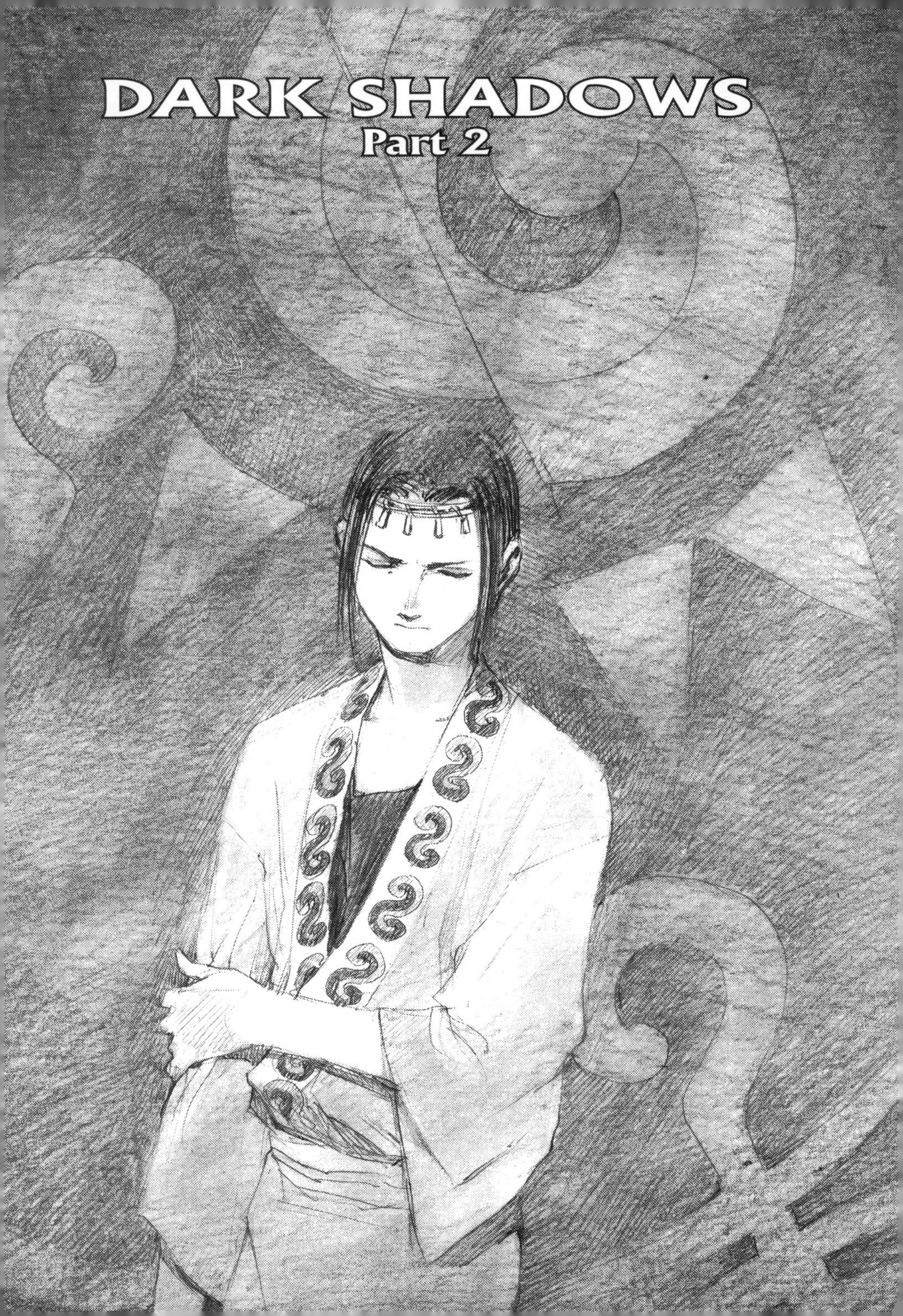

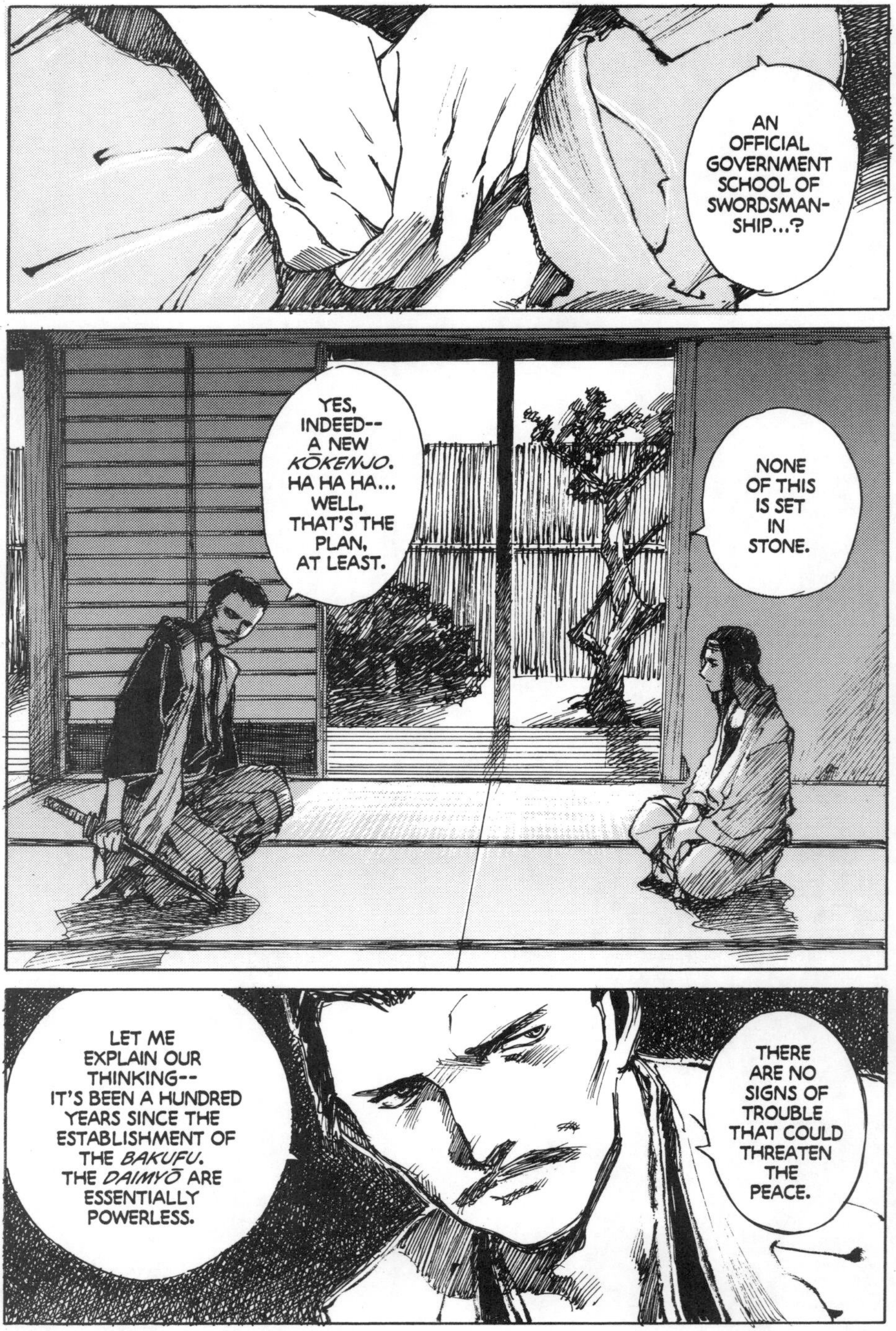
AN OFFICIAL GOVERNMENT SCHOOL OF SWORDSMAN-SHIP...?
YES, INDEED-- A NEW *KŌKENJO*. HA HA HA... WELL, THAT'S THE PLAN, AT LEAST.
NONE OF THIS IS SET IN STONE.
LET ME EXPLAIN OUR THINKING-- IT'S BEEN A HUNDRED YEARS SINCE THE ESTABLISHMENT OF THE *BAKUFU*. THE *DAIMYŌ* ARE ESSENTIALLY POWERLESS.
THERE ARE NO SIGNS OF TROUBLE THAT COULD THREATEN THE PEACE.

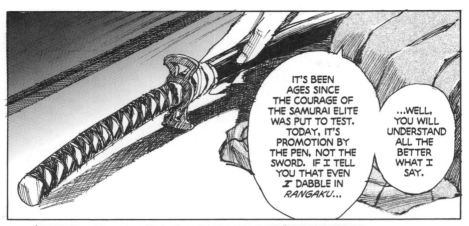

IT'S BEEN AGES SINCE THE COURAGE OF THE SAMURAI ELITE WAS PUT TO TEST. TODAY, IT'S PROMOTION BY THE PEN, NOT THE SWORD. IF I TELL YOU THAT EVEN *I* DABBLE IN *RANGAKU*...

...WELL, YOU WILL UNDERSTAND ALL THE BETTER WHAT I SAY.

ALL THAT IS BAD ENOUGH... BUT TODAY MANY OF THESE RASCALS DON'T EVEN ASPIRE TO SCHOLAR-SHIP!

FLUTTERING ABOUT IN SILK ROBES, CARRYING ONLY CEREMONIAL *HOSOMI* AT THEIR WAISTS.

THROWING THEMSELVES INTO *KO-UTA* AND *SHAMISEN* MUSIC...IN TRUTH, THERE ARE SAMURAI NOW WHO STRIVE TO PROMOTE THEMSELVES...

...BY SUCH FRIVOLITY **ALONE!**

SLOTH AND DECA-DENCE... *THAT'S* WHAT IT IS!

ANOTSU KAGEHISA...

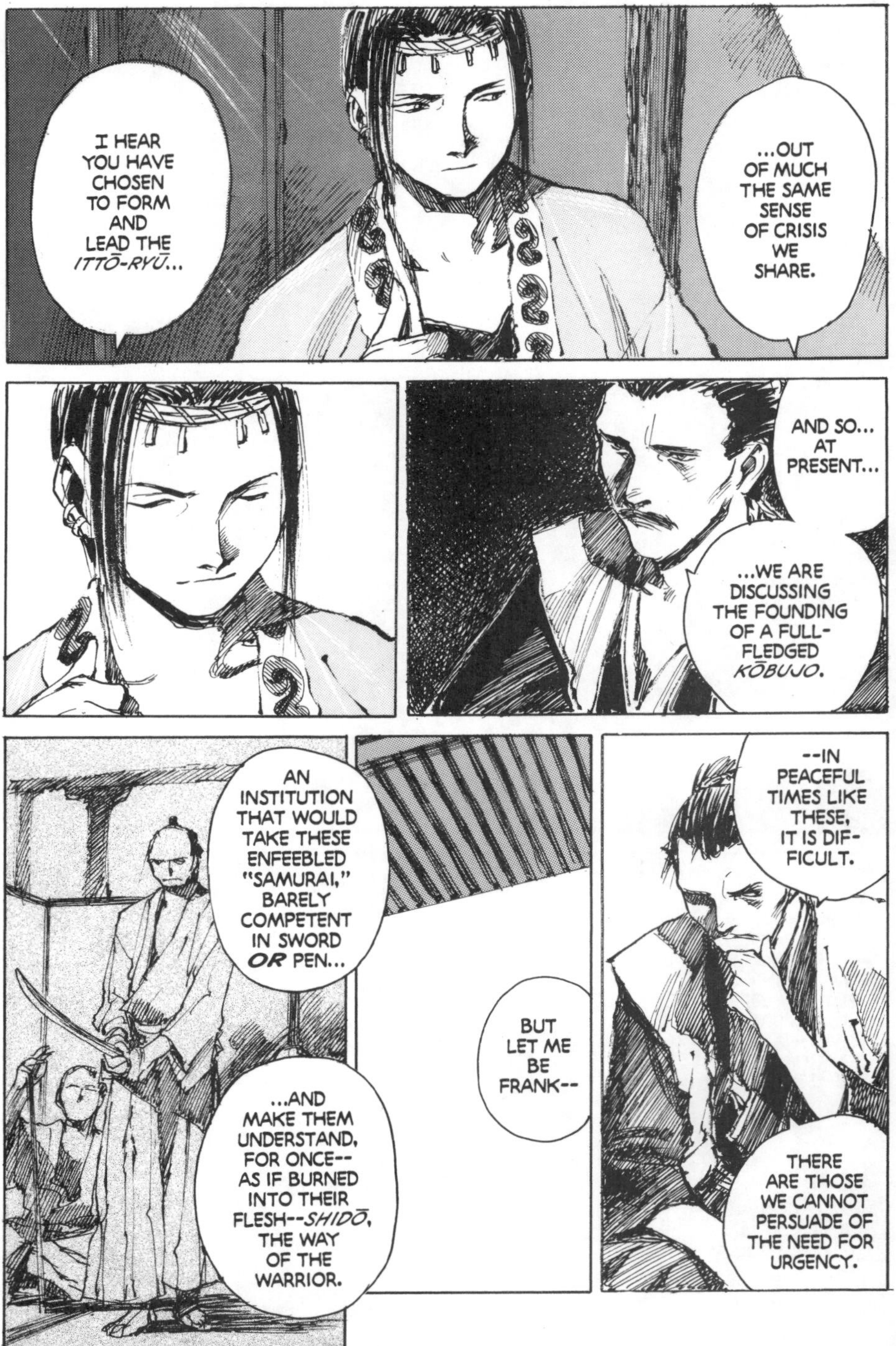
I HEAR YOU HAVE CHOSEN TO FORM AND LEAD THE *ITTŌ-RYŪ*...
...OUT OF MUCH THE SAME SENSE OF CRISIS WE SHARE.
AND SO... AT PRESENT...
...WE ARE DISCUSSING THE FOUNDING OF A FULL-FLEDGED *KŌBUJO*.
AN INSTITUTION THAT WOULD TAKE THESE ENFEEBLED "SAMURAI," BARELY COMPETENT IN SWORD ***OR*** PEN...
...AND MAKE THEM UNDERSTAND, FOR ONCE-- AS IF BURNED INTO THEIR FLESH--*SHIDŌ*, THE WAY OF THE WARRIOR.
BUT LET ME BE FRANK--
--IN PEACEFUL TIMES LIKE THESE, IT IS DIFFICULT.
THERE ARE THOSE WE CANNOT PERSUADE OF THE NEED FOR URGENCY.

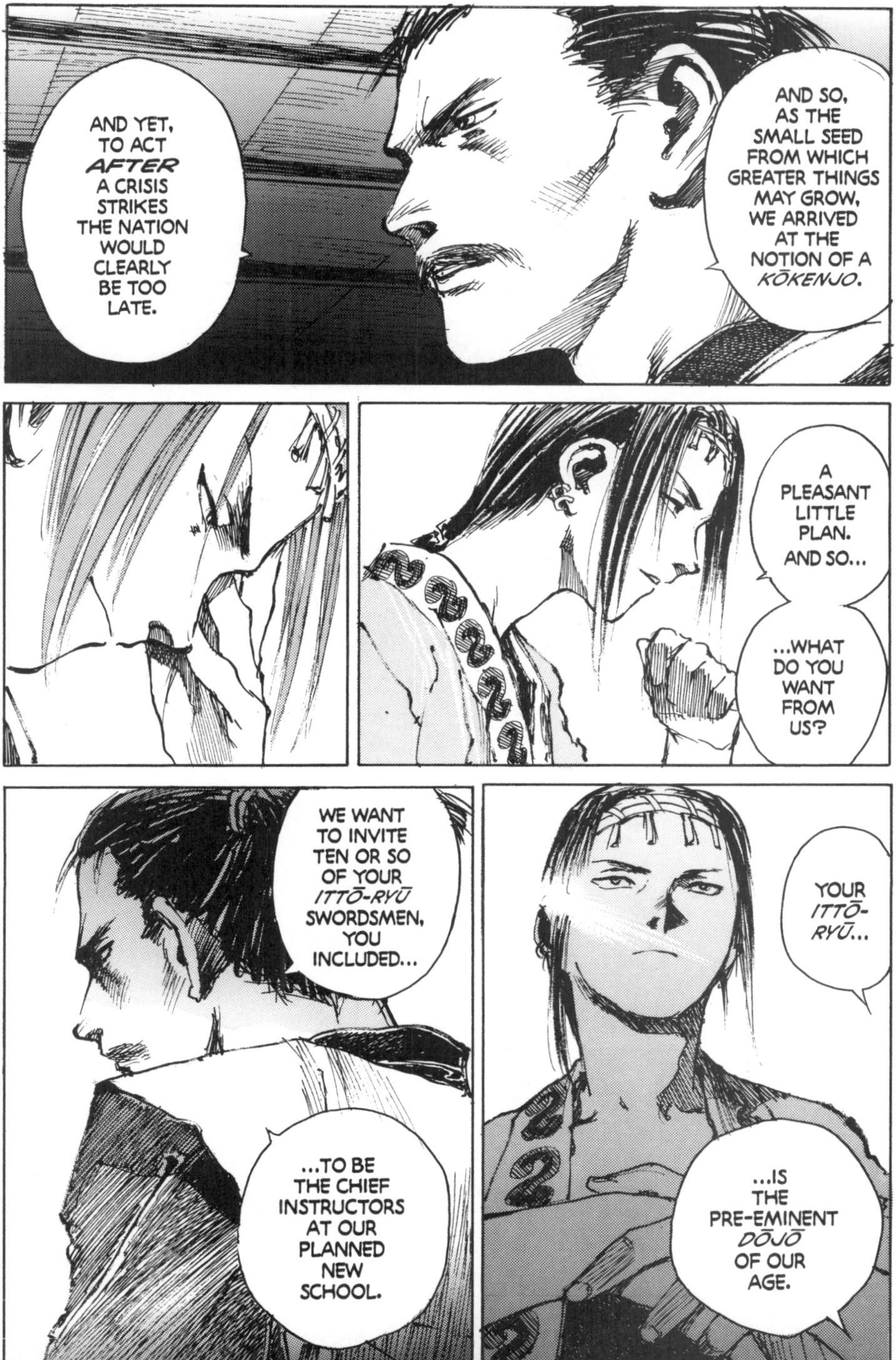
AND YET, TO ACT *AFTER* A CRISIS STRIKES THE NATION WOULD CLEARLY BE TOO LATE.
AND SO, AS THE SMALL SEED FROM WHICH GREATER THINGS MAY GROW, WE ARRIVED AT THE NOTION OF A *KŌKENJO*.
A PLEASANT LITTLE PLAN. AND SO...
...WHAT DO YOU WANT FROM US?
WE WANT TO INVITE TEN OR SO OF YOUR *ITTŌ-RYŪ* SWORDSMEN, YOU INCLUDED...
...TO BE THE CHIEF INSTRUCTORS AT OUR PLANNED NEW SCHOOL.
YOUR *ITTŌ-RYŪ*...
...IS THE PRE-EMINENT *DŌJŌ* OF OUR AGE.

YOUR OFFER BRINGS HONOR TO OUR SCHOOL.

BUT TO BE HONEST, I LACK CONFIDENCE THAT WE ARE UP TO THE TASK.

YES, THE *ITTŌ-RYŪ* IS UNIQUE. THAT'S TRUE.

"THE SWORD EXCUSES ALL." THAT IS THE CREDO OUR SCHOOL PURSUES.

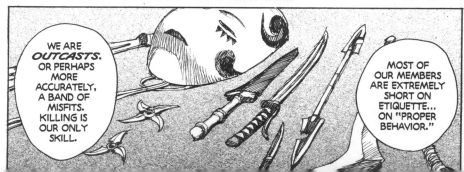

WE ARE *OUTCASTS*. OR PERHAPS MORE ACCURATELY, A BAND OF MISFITS. KILLING IS OUR ONLY SKILL.

MOST OF OUR MEMBERS ARE EXTREMELY SHORT ON ETIQUETTE... ON "PROPER BEHAVIOR."

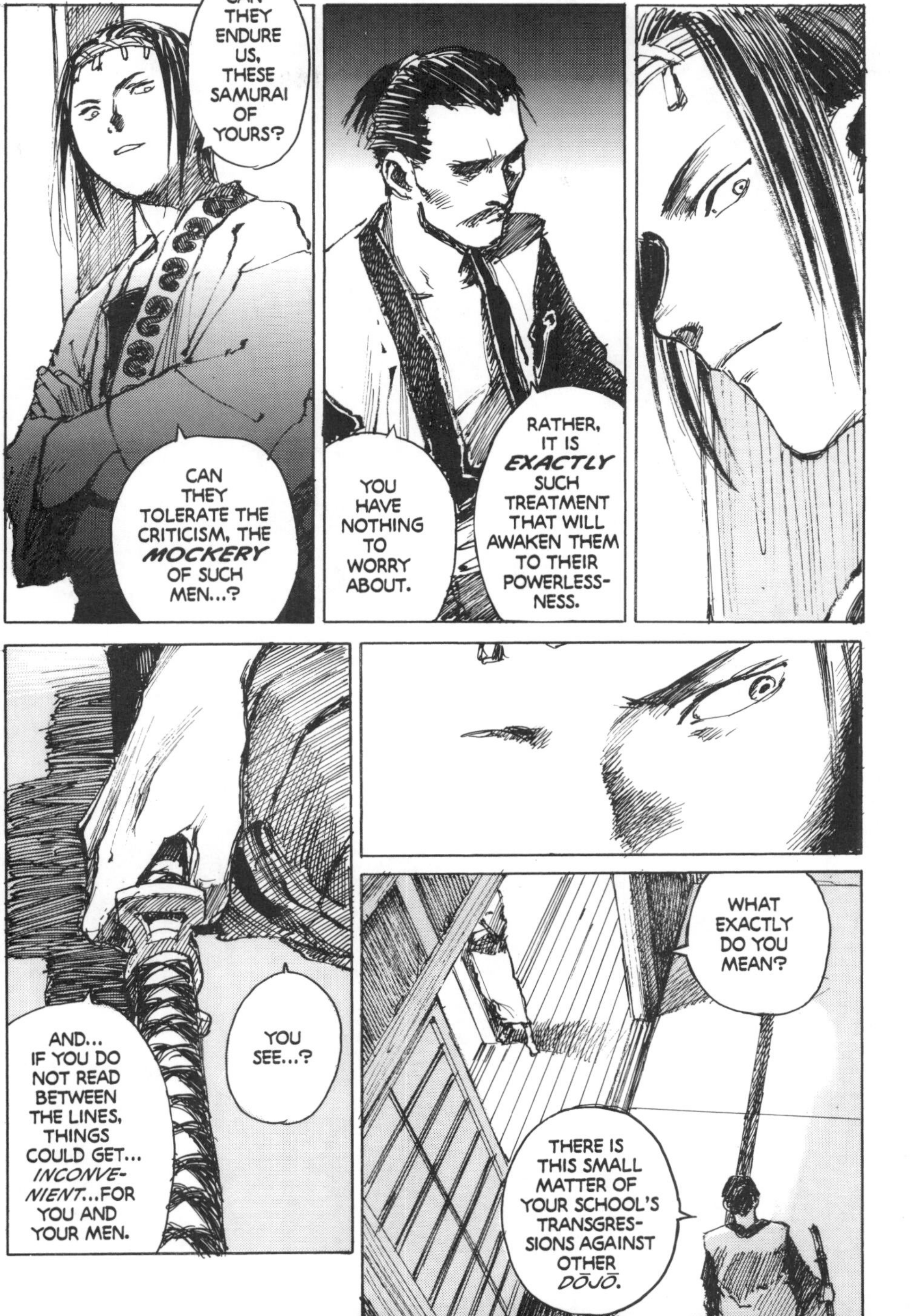
CAN THEY ENDURE US, THESE SAMURAI OF YOURS?
CAN THEY TOLERATE THE CRITICISM, THE *MOCKERY* OF SUCH MEN...?
YOU HAVE NOTHING TO WORRY ABOUT.
RATHER, IT IS *EXACTLY* SUCH TREATMENT THAT WILL AWAKEN THEM TO THEIR POWERLESS-NESS.
YOU SEE...?
AND... IF YOU DO NOT READ BETWEEN THE LINES, THINGS COULD GET... *INCONVE-NIENT*...FOR YOU AND YOUR MEN.
WHAT EXACTLY DO YOU MEAN?
THERE IS THIS SMALL MATTER OF YOUR SCHOOL'S TRANSGRES-SIONS AGAINST OTHER *DŌJŌ*.

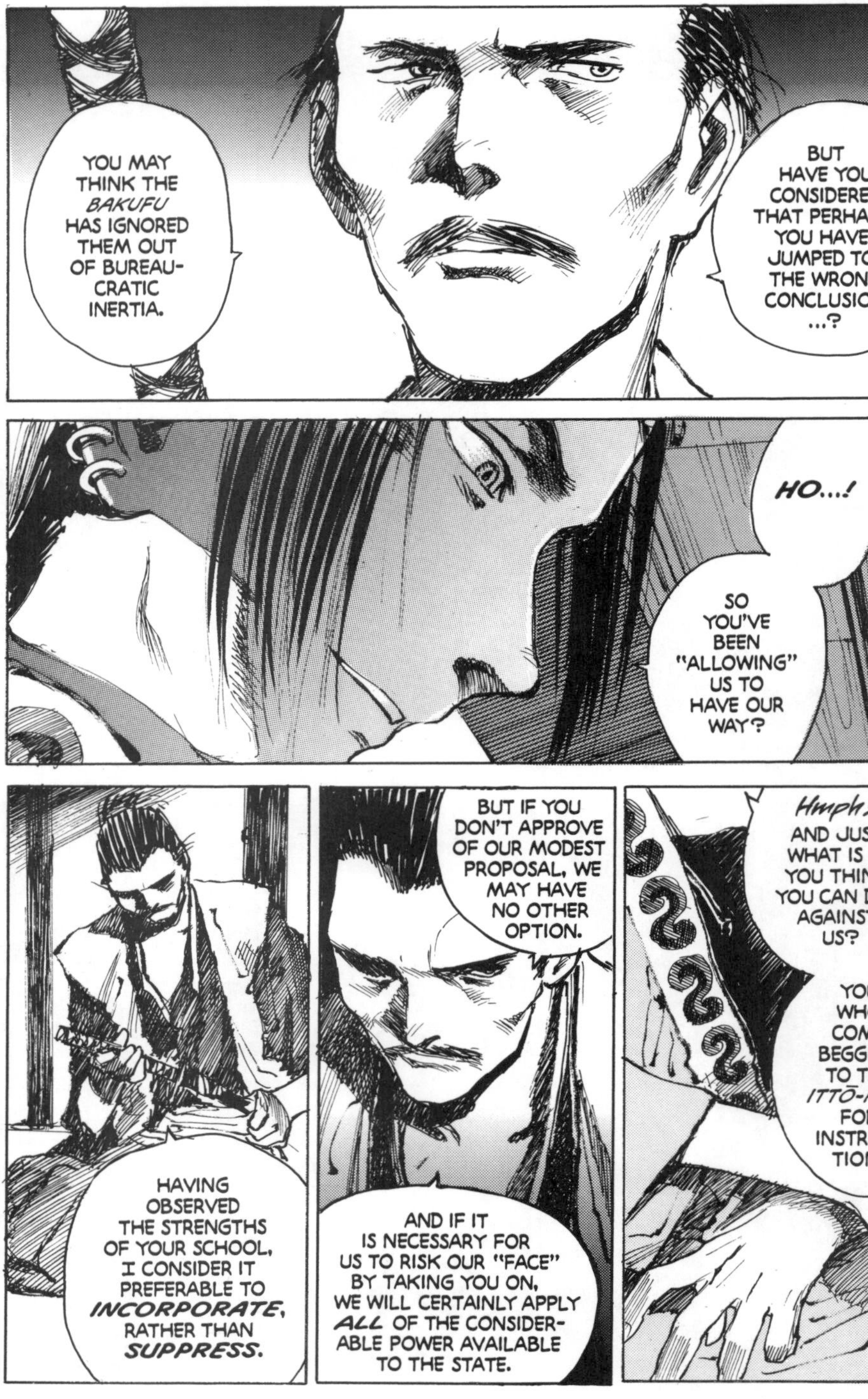
YOU MAY THINK THE *BAKUFU* HAS IGNORED THEM OUT OF BUREAU-CRATIC INERTIA.
BUT HAVE YOU CONSIDERED THAT PERHAPS YOU HAVE JUMPED TO THE WRONG CONCLUSION ...?
HO...!
SO YOU'VE BEEN "ALLOWING" US TO HAVE OUR WAY?
HAVING OBSERVED THE STRENGTHS OF YOUR SCHOOL, I CONSIDER IT PREFERABLE TO *INCORPORATE*, RATHER THAN *SUPPRESS*.
BUT IF YOU DON'T APPROVE OF OUR MODEST PROPOSAL, WE MAY HAVE NO OTHER OPTION.
AND IF IT IS NECESSARY FOR US TO RISK OUR "FACE" BY TAKING YOU ON, WE WILL CERTAINLY APPLY *ALL* OF THE CONSIDER-ABLE POWER AVAILABLE TO THE STATE.
Hmph! AND JUST WHAT IS IT YOU THINK YOU CAN DO AGAINST US?
YOU WHO COME BEGGING TO THE *ITTŌ-RYŪ* FOR INSTRUC-TION!

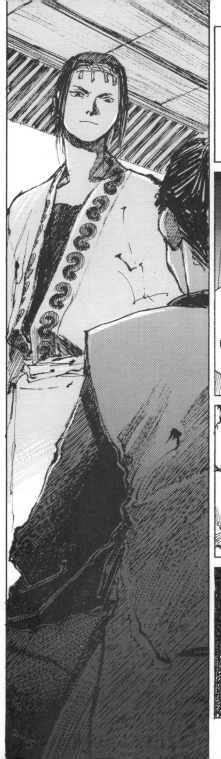

VERY WELL, LORD HABAKI.

HAVE NO FEAR.

MY MIND WAS MADE UP...

...LONG, LONG AGO.

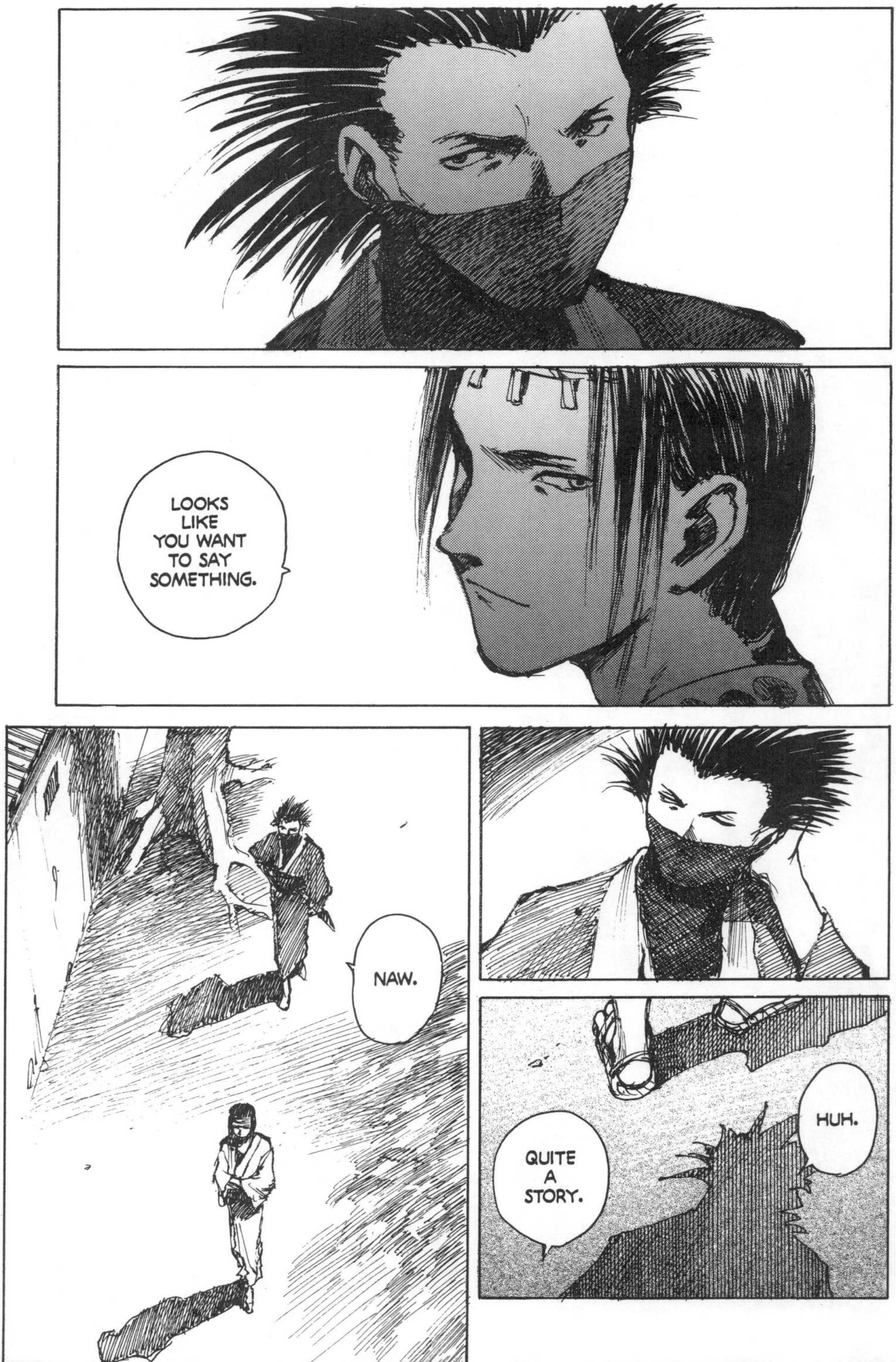
LOOKS LIKE YOU WANT TO SAY SOMETHING.
NAW.
HUH.
QUITE A STORY.

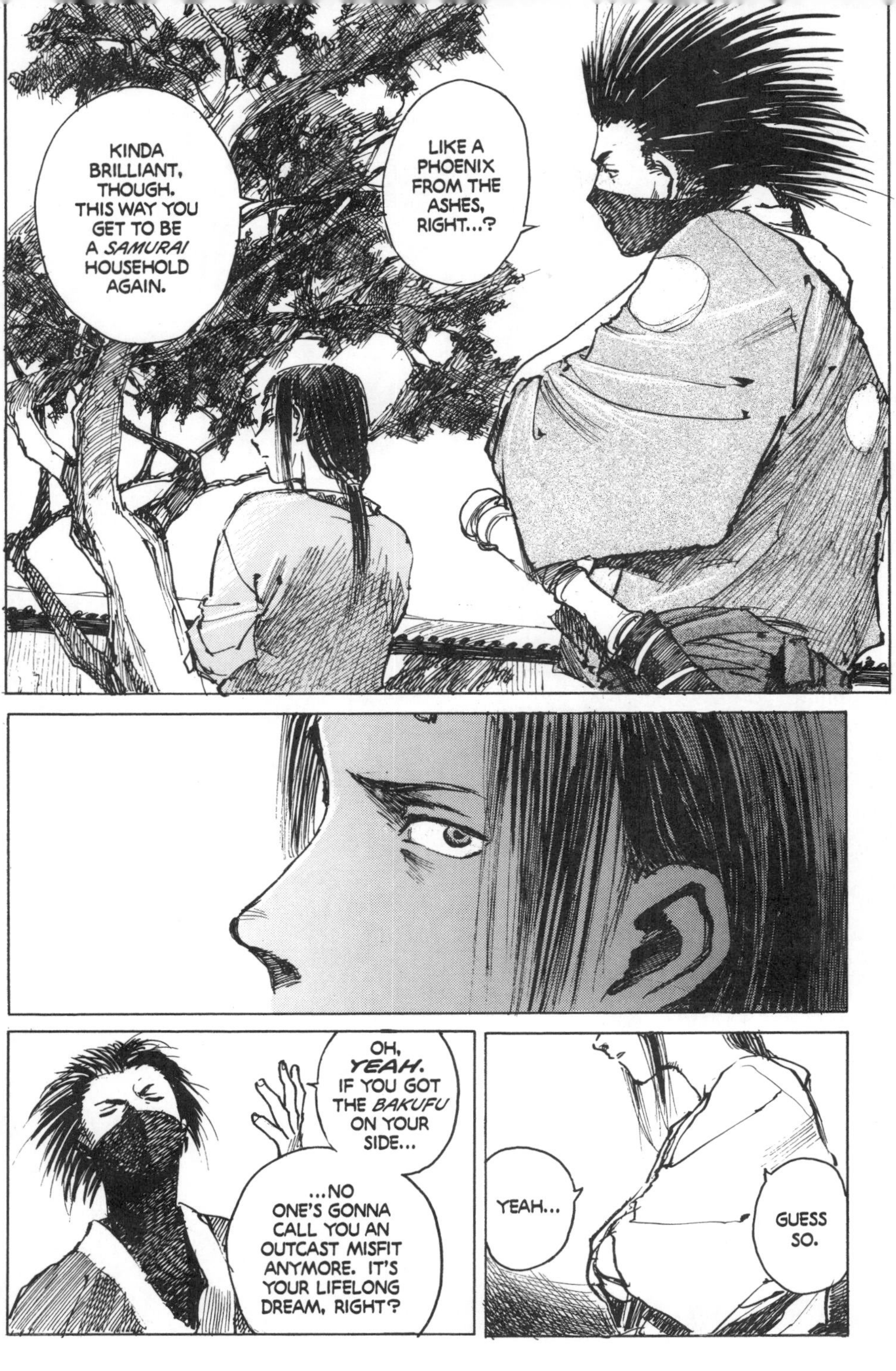
KINDA BRILLIANT, THOUGH. THIS WAY YOU GET TO BE A *SAMURAI* HOUSEHOLD AGAIN.
LIKE A PHOENIX FROM THE ASHES, RIGHT...?
OH, *YEAH.* IF YOU GOT THE *BAKUFU* ON YOUR SIDE...
...NO ONE'S GONNA CALL YOU AN OUTCAST MISFIT ANYMORE. IT'S YOUR LIFELONG DREAM, RIGHT?
YEAH...
GUESS SO.

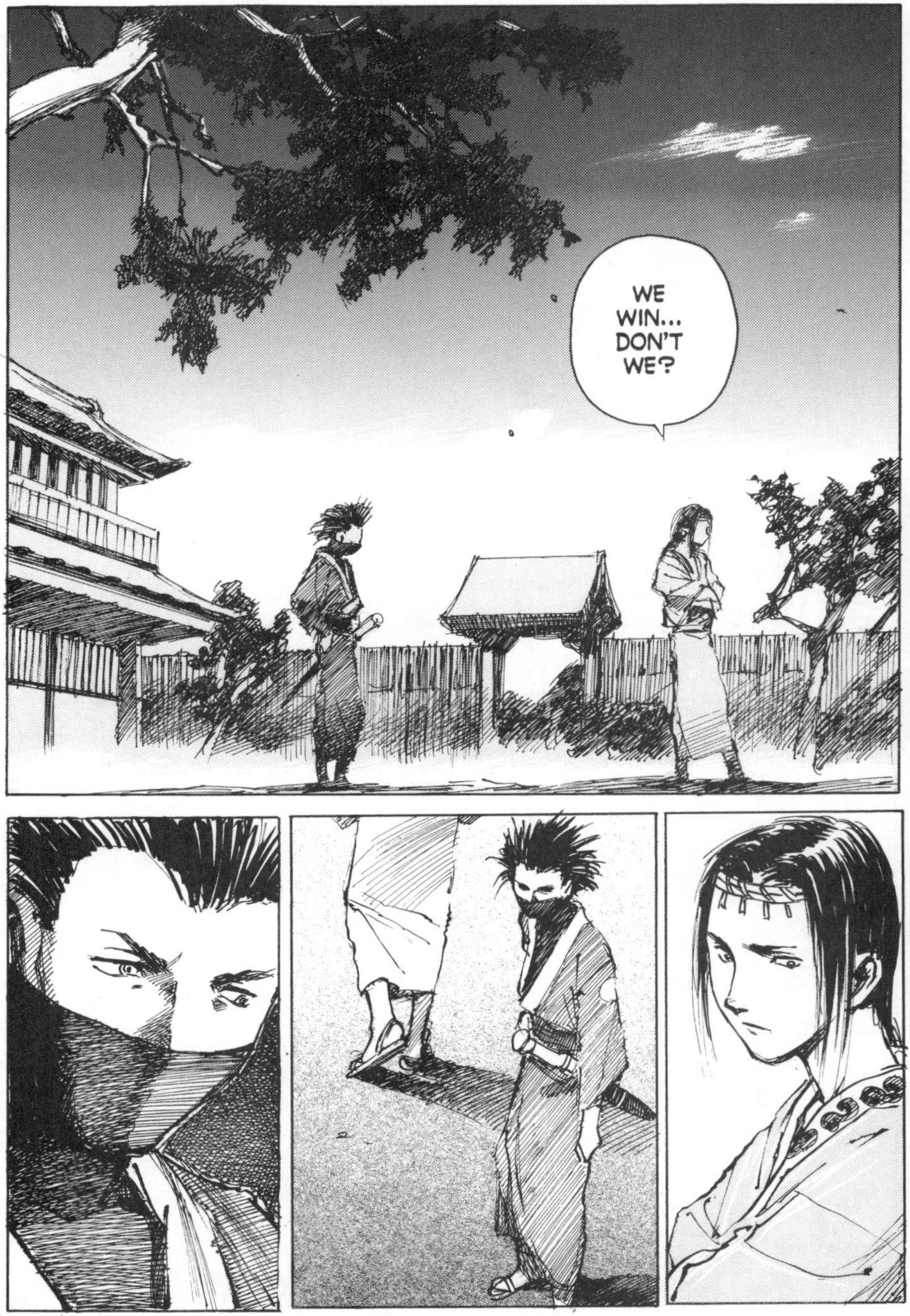
WE WIN... DON'T WE?

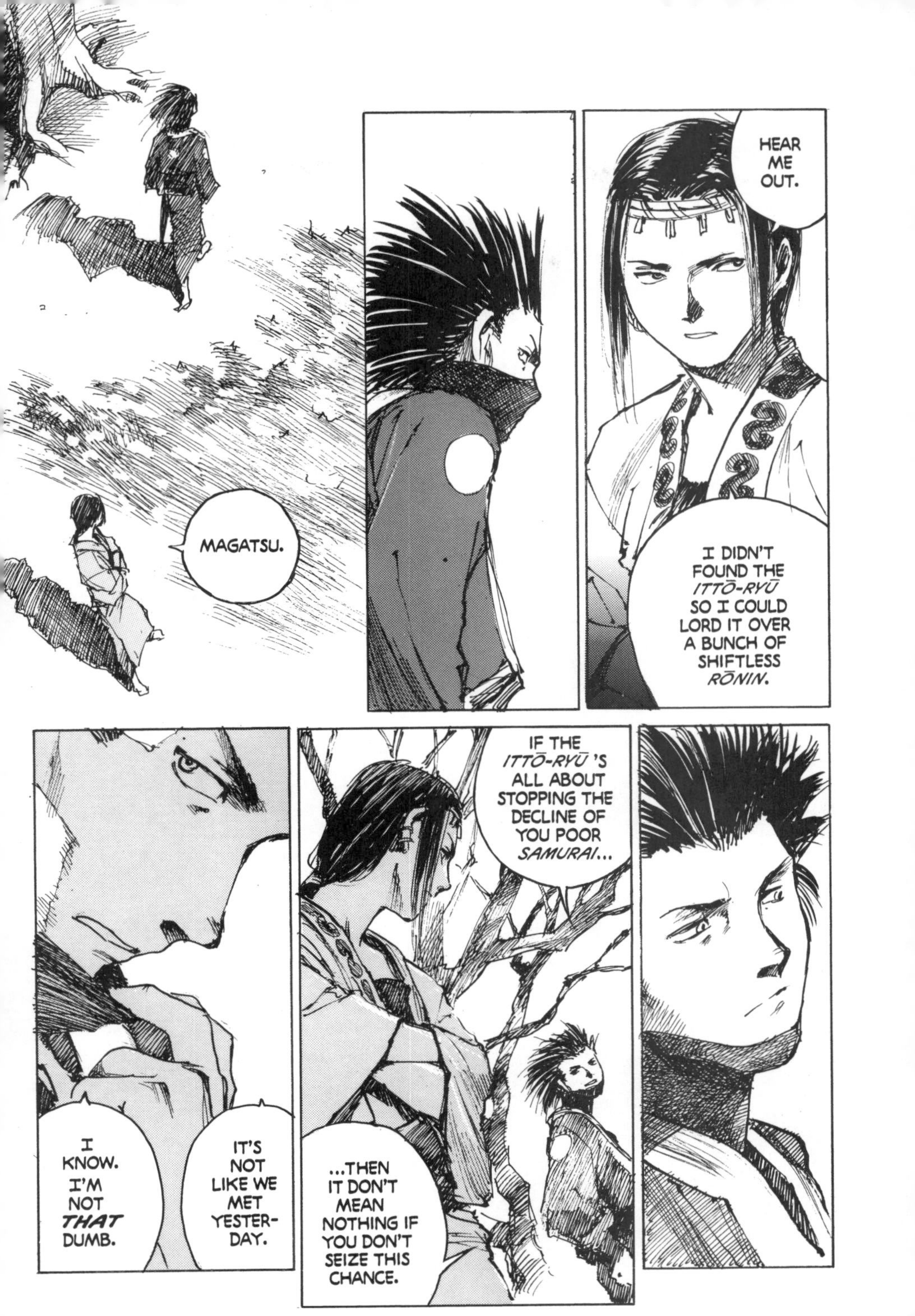
MAGATSU.
HEAR ME OUT.
I DIDN'T FOUND THE *ITTŌ-RYŪ* SO I COULD LORD IT OVER A BUNCH OF SHIFTLESS *RŌNIN*.
I KNOW. I'M NOT *THAT* DUMB.
IT'S NOT LIKE WE MET YESTER-DAY.
IF THE *ITTŌ-RYŪ*'S ALL ABOUT STOPPING THE DECLINE OF YOU POOR *SAMURAI*...
...THEN IT DON'T MEAN NOTHING IF YOU DON'T SEIZE THIS CHANCE.

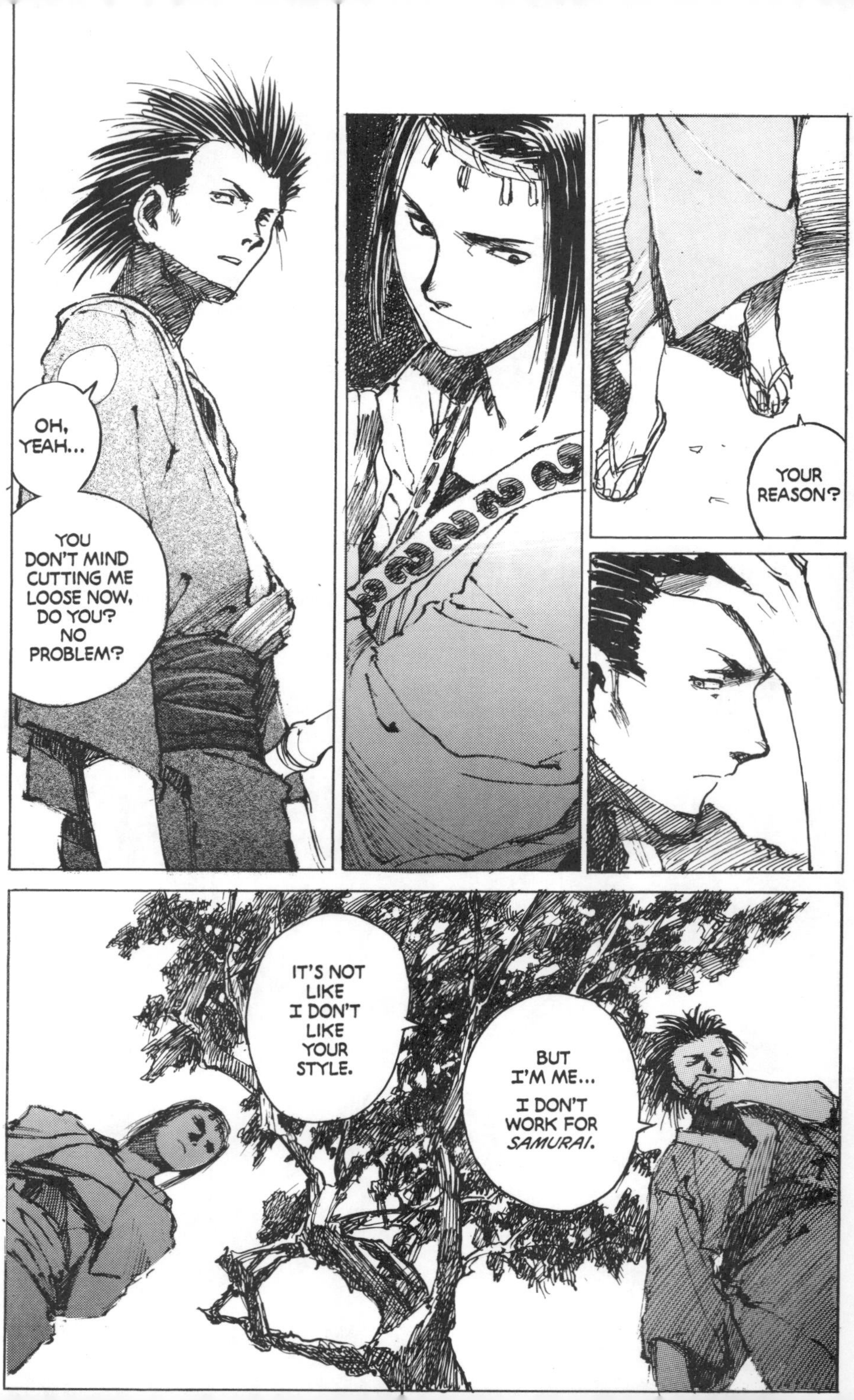
OH, YEAH...
YOU DON'T MIND CUTTING ME LOOSE NOW, DO YOU? NO PROBLEM?
YOUR REASON?
IT'S NOT LIKE I DON'T LIKE YOUR STYLE.
BUT I'M ME... I DON'T WORK FOR *SAMURAI*.

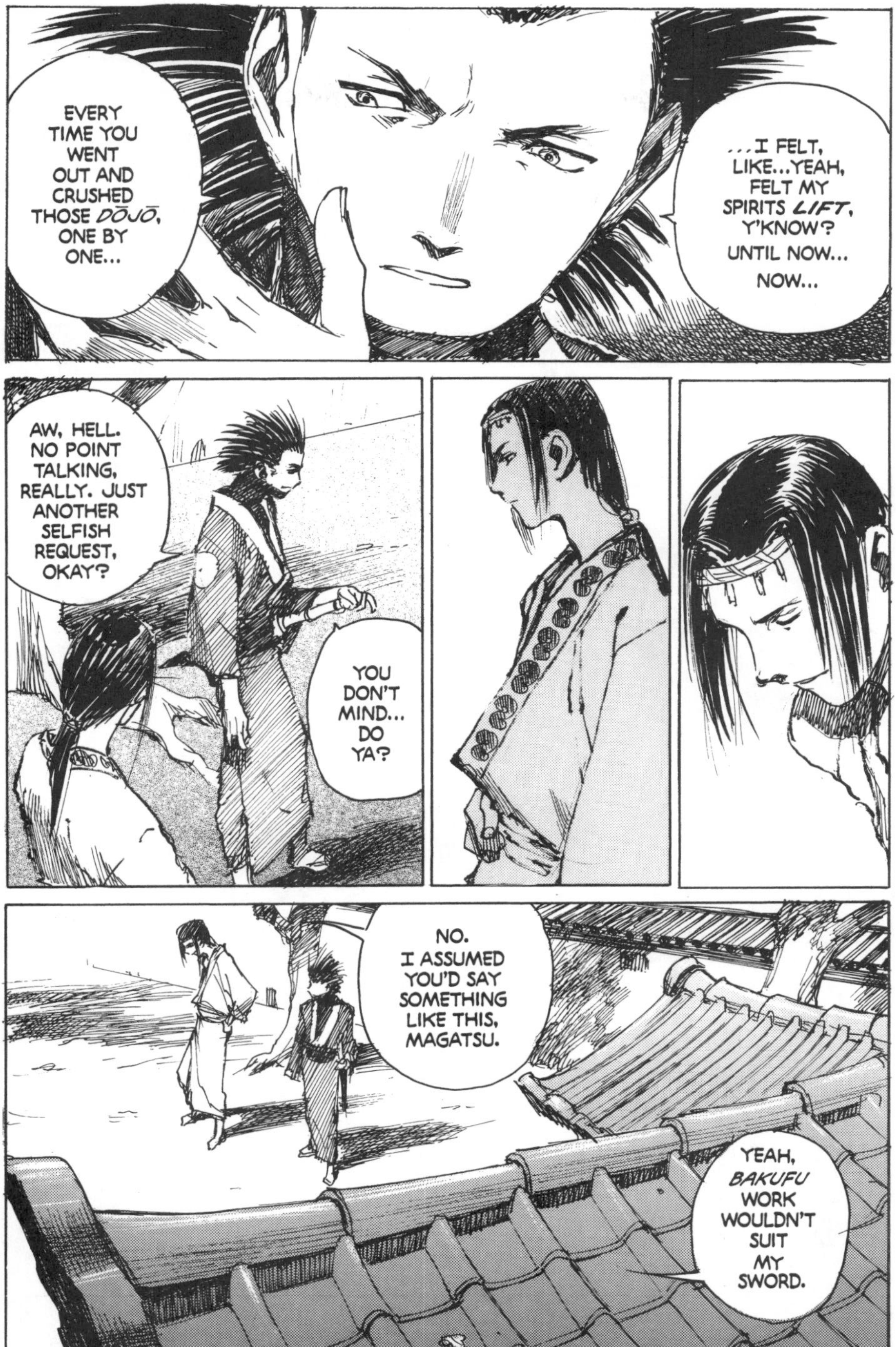
EVERY TIME YOU WENT OUT AND CRUSHED THOSE *DŌJŌ*, ONE BY ONE...
...I FELT, LIKE...YEAH, FELT MY SPIRITS *LIFT*, Y'KNOW? UNTIL NOW...
NOW...
AW, HELL. NO POINT TALKING, REALLY. JUST ANOTHER SELFISH REQUEST, OKAY?
YOU DON'T MIND... DO YA?
NO. I ASSUMED YOU'D SAY SOMETHING LIKE THIS, MAGATSU.
YEAH, *BAKUFU* WORK WOULDN'T SUIT MY SWORD.

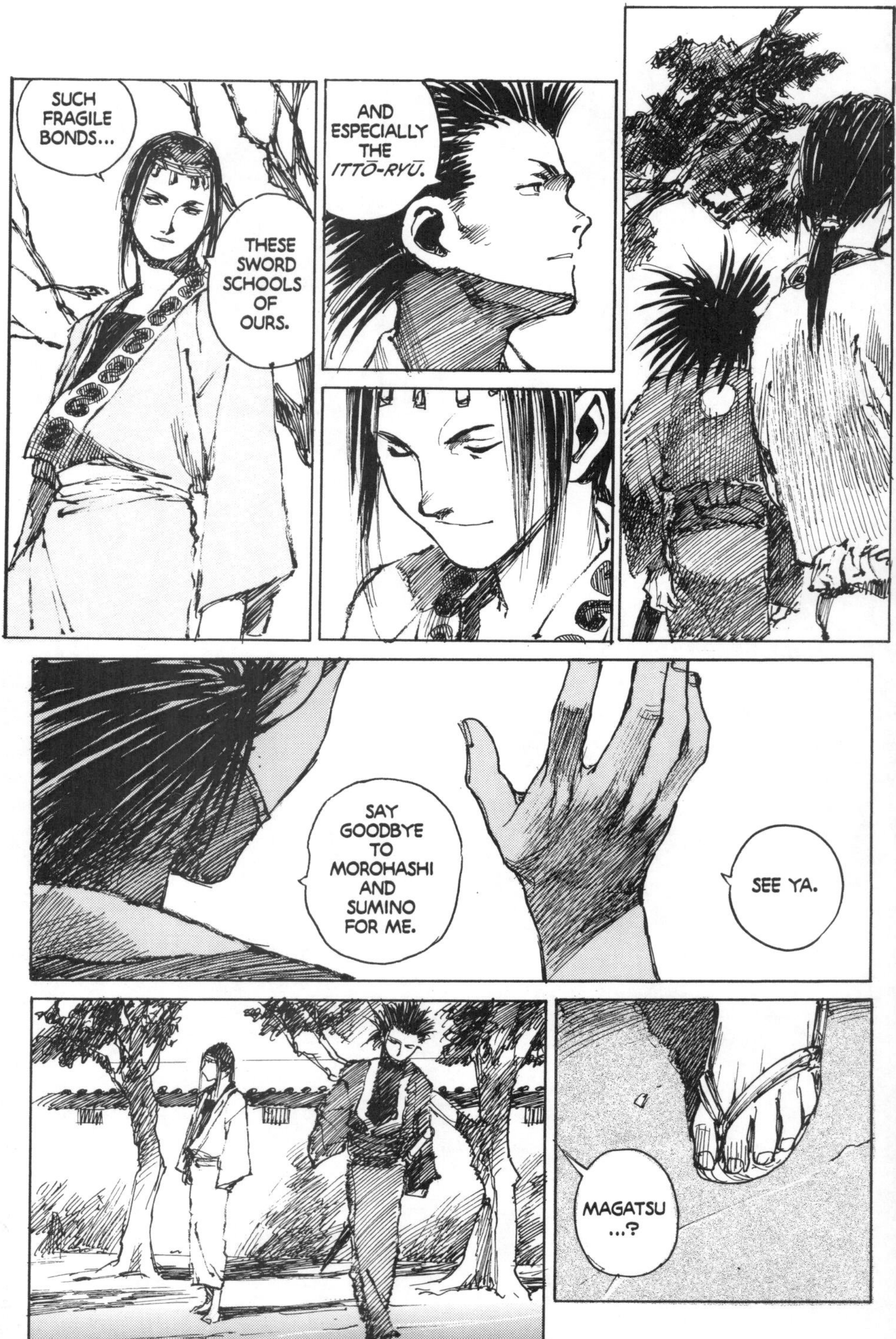
SUCH FRAGILE BONDS...
THESE SWORD SCHOOLS OF OURS.
AND ESPECIALLY THE *ITTŌ-RYŪ*.
SAY GOODBYE TO MOROHASHI AND SUMINO FOR ME.
SEE YA.
MAGATSU ...?

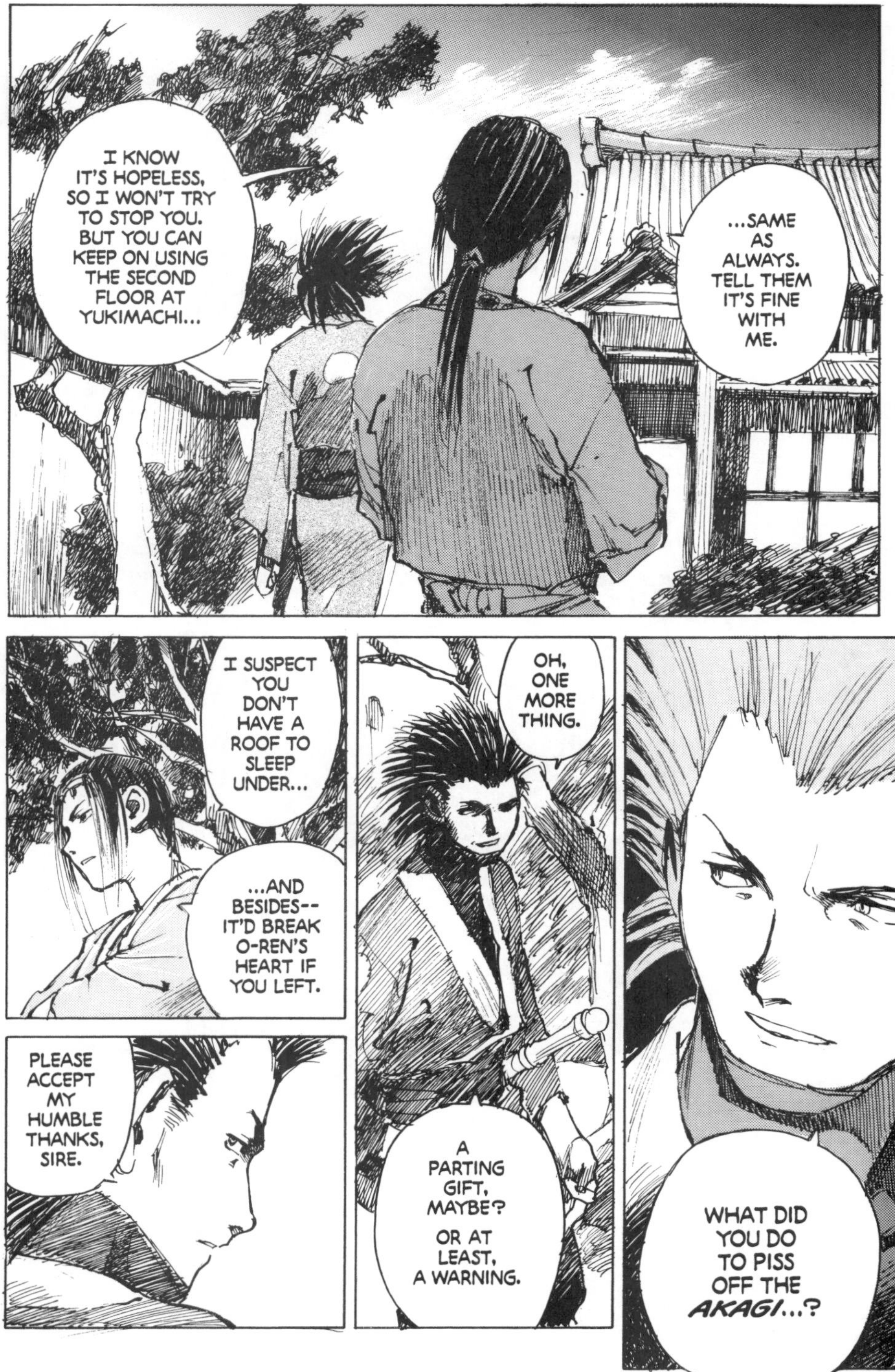
I KNOW IT'S HOPELESS, SO I WON'T TRY TO STOP YOU. BUT YOU CAN KEEP ON USING THE SECOND FLOOR AT YUKIMACHI...
...SAME AS ALWAYS. TELL THEM IT'S FINE WITH ME.
I SUSPECT YOU DON'T HAVE A ROOF TO SLEEP UNDER...
...AND BESIDES-- IT'D BREAK O-REN'S HEART IF YOU LEFT.
PLEASE ACCEPT MY HUMBLE THANKS, SIRE.
OH, ONE MORE THING.
A PARTING GIFT, MAYBE?
OR AT LEAST, A WARNING.
WHAT DID YOU DO TO PISS OFF THE *AKAGI*...?

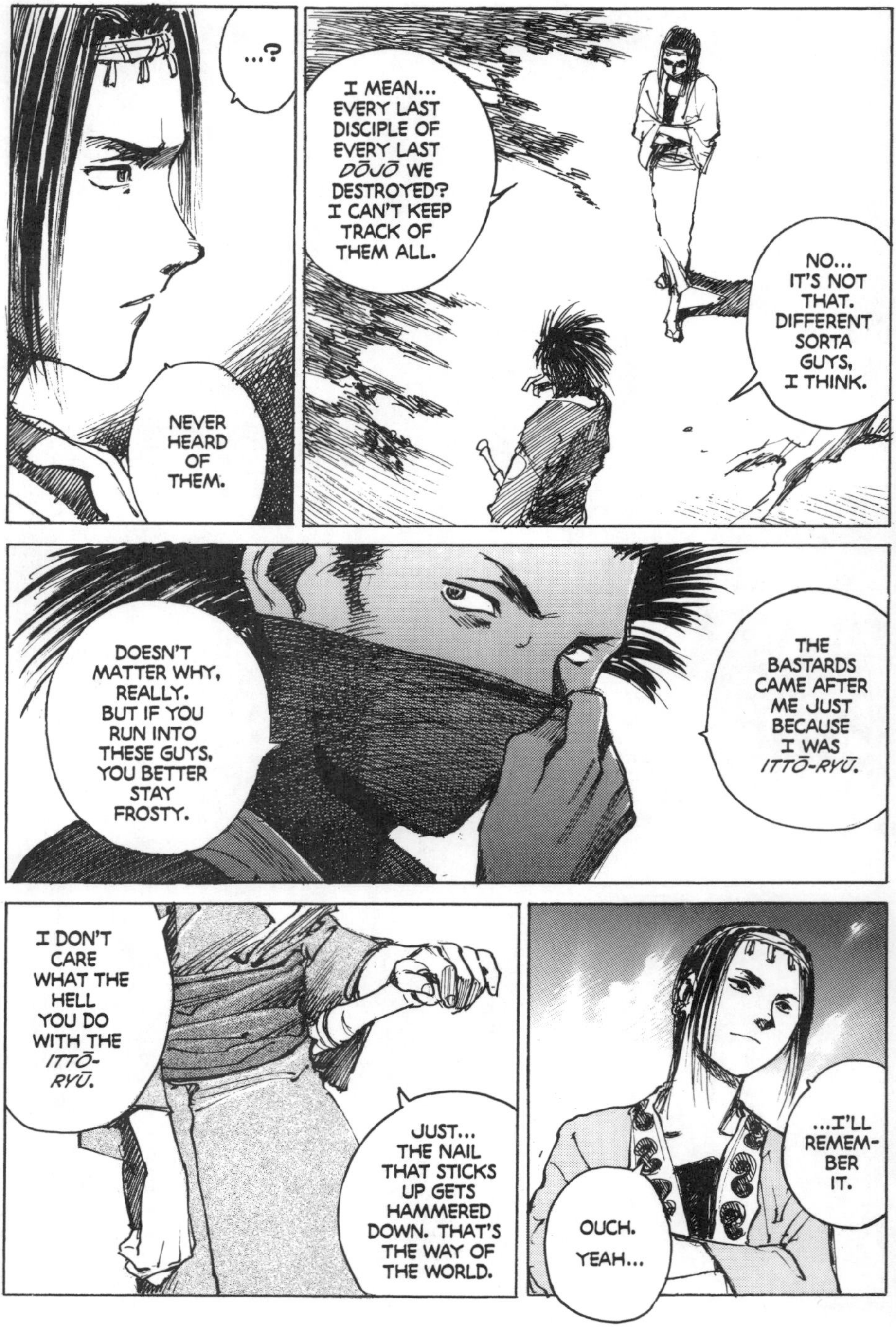
...?
NEVER HEARD OF THEM.
I MEAN... EVERY LAST DISCIPLE OF EVERY LAST *DŌJŌ* WE DESTROYED? I CAN'T KEEP TRACK OF THEM ALL.
NO... IT'S NOT THAT. DIFFERENT SORTA GUYS, I THINK.
THE BASTARDS CAME AFTER ME JUST BECAUSE I WAS *ITTŌ-RYŪ*.
DOESN'T MATTER WHY, REALLY. BUT IF YOU RUN INTO THESE GUYS, YOU BETTER STAY FROSTY.
I DON'T CARE WHAT THE HELL YOU DO WITH THE *ITTŌ-RYŪ*.
JUST... THE NAIL THAT STICKS UP GETS HAMMERED DOWN. THAT'S THE WAY OF THE WORLD.
...I'LL REMEM-BER IT.
OUCH.
YEAH...

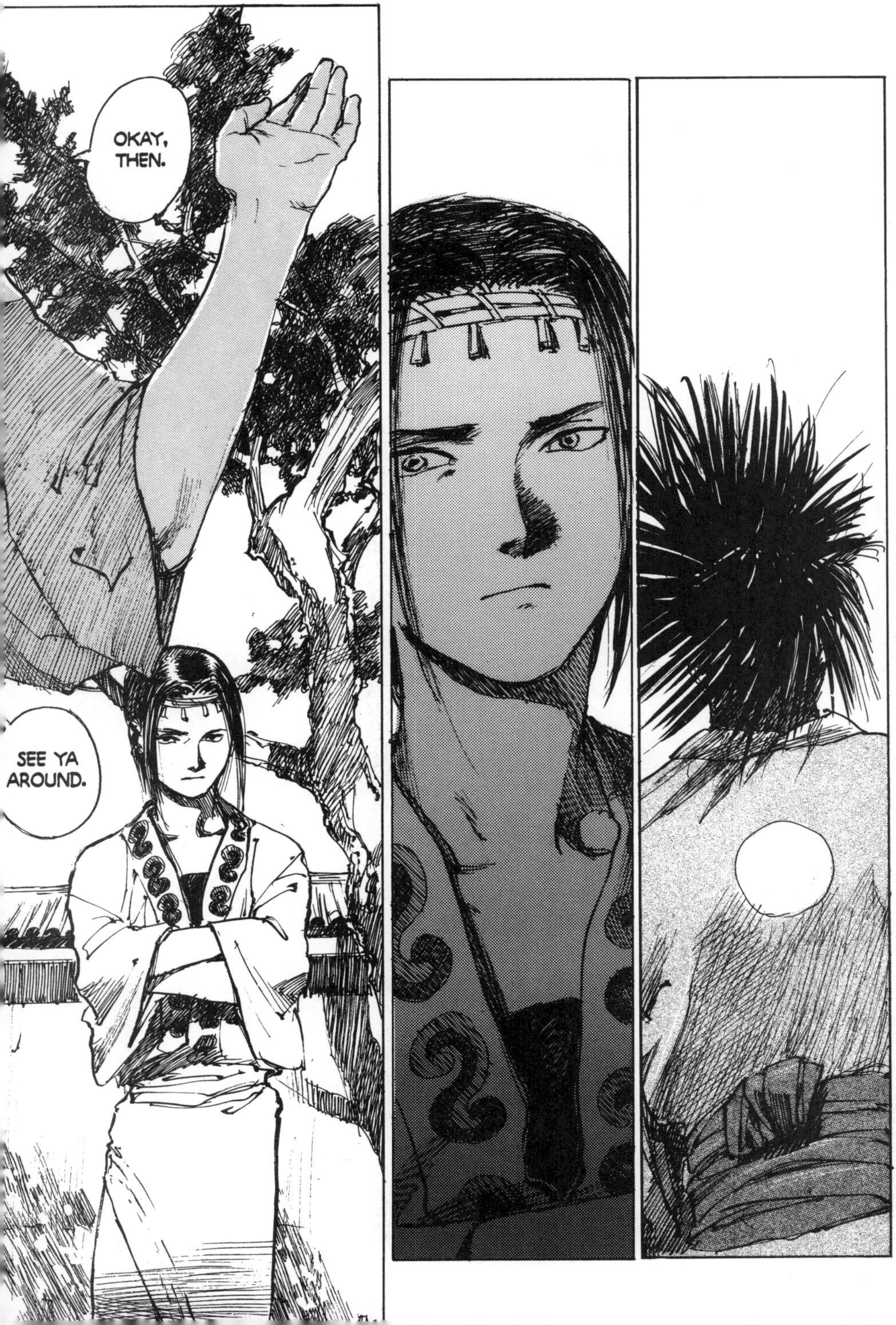
OKAY, THEN.
SEE YA AROUND.

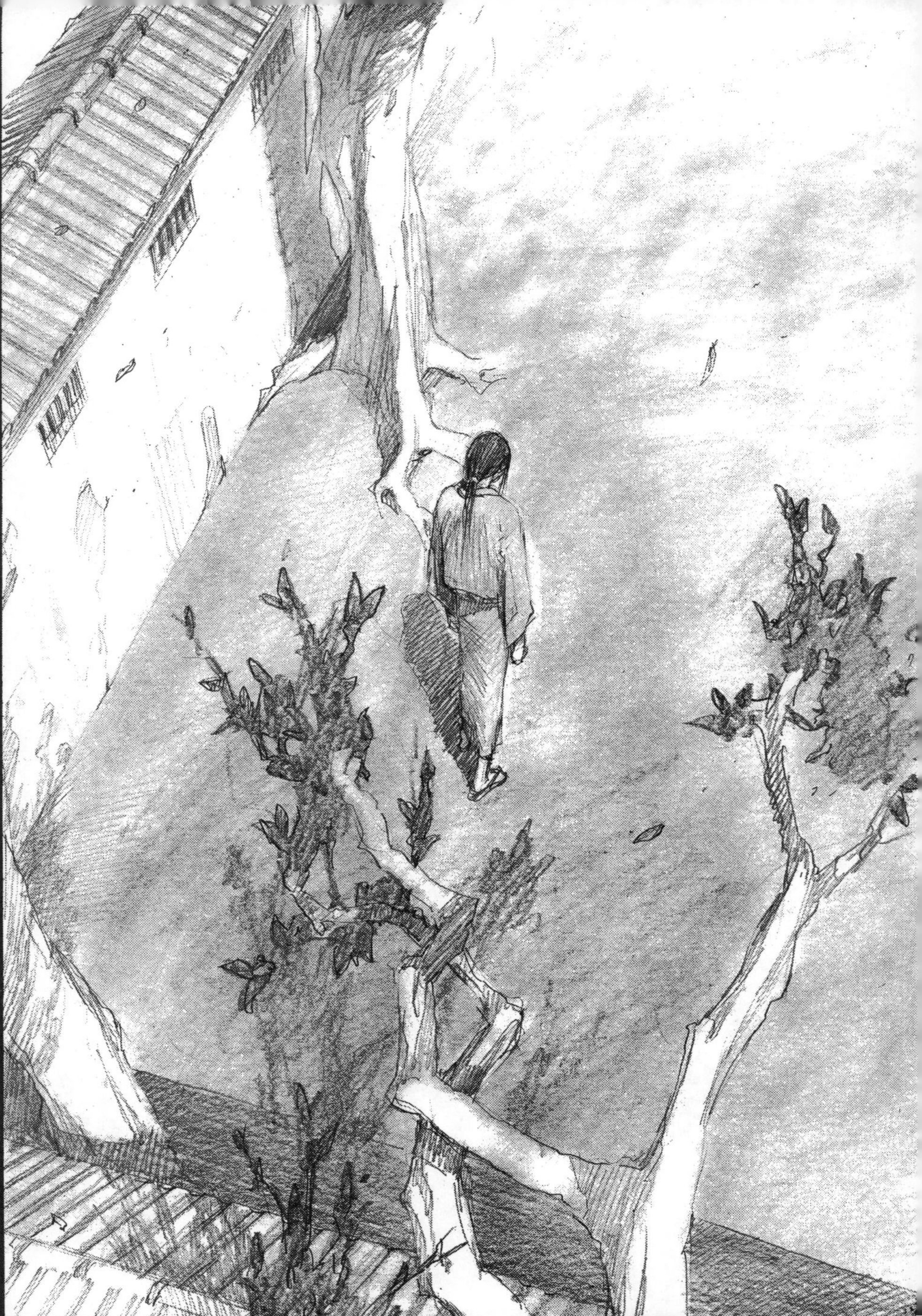

SO THAT'S THE STORY, ANYWAY. SAY...

...IS THIS REALLY ALL MY STUFF?

......
......

J- JUST WAIT A SEC!

B- BUT... *NO! WAIT!*

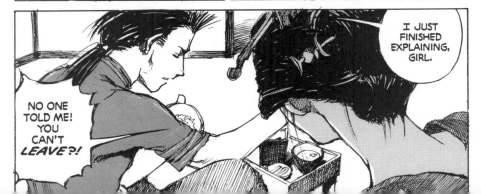

I JUST FINISHED EXPLAINING, GIRL.

NO ONE TOLD ME! YOU CAN'T *LEAVE?!*

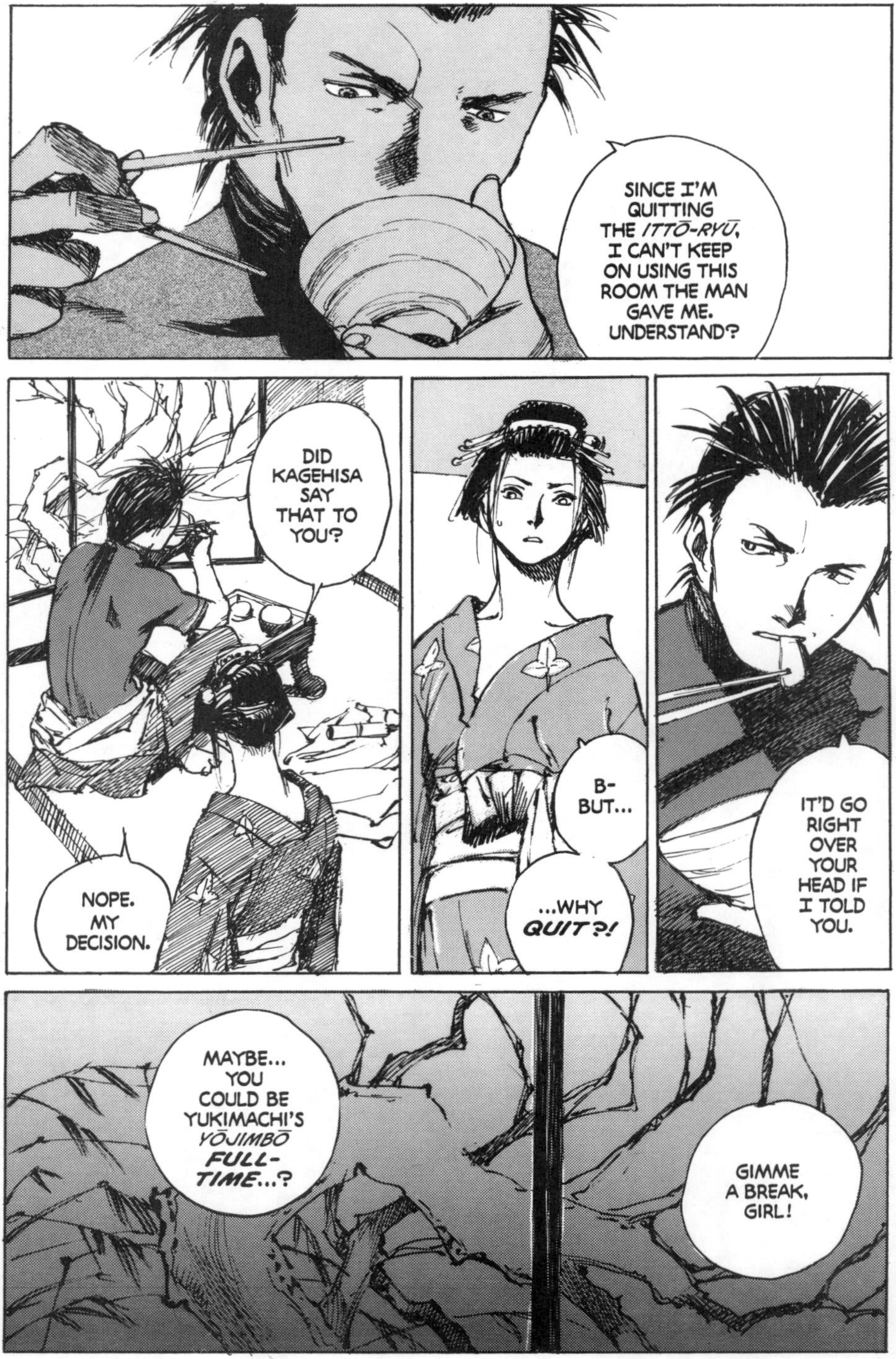
SINCE I'M QUITTING THE *ITTŌ-RYŪ*, I CAN'T KEEP ON USING THIS ROOM THE MAN GAVE ME. UNDERSTAND?
DID KAGEHISA SAY THAT TO YOU?
NOPE. MY DECISION.
B- BUT...
...WHY ***QUIT***?!
IT'D GO RIGHT OVER YOUR HEAD IF I TOLD YOU.
MAYBE... YOU COULD BE YUKIMACHI'S *YŌJIMBŌ* ***FULL-TIME***...?
GIMME A BREAK, GIRL!

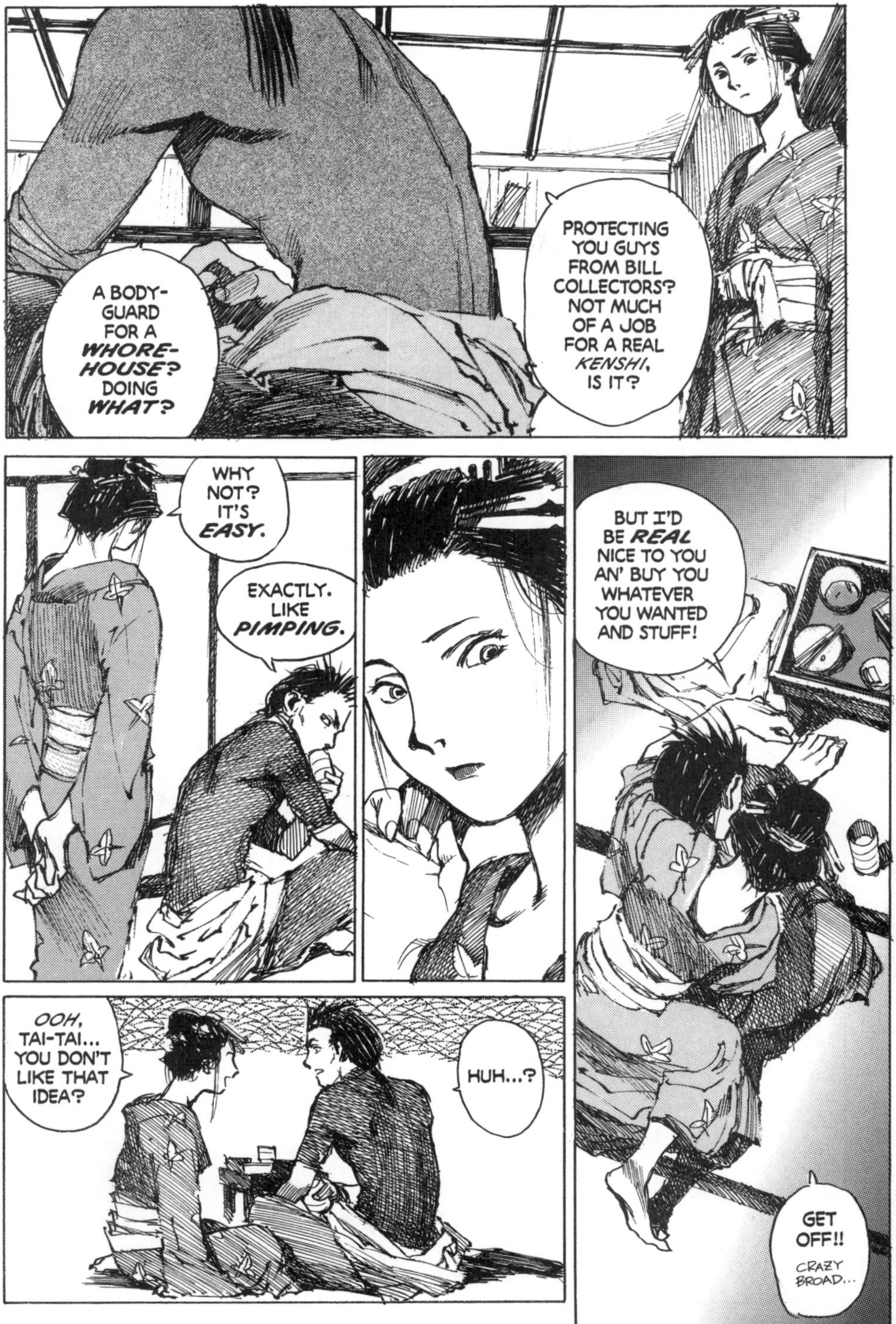
A BODY-GUARD FOR A *WHORE-HOUSE?* DOING *WHAT?*
PROTECTING YOU GUYS FROM BILL COLLECTORS? NOT MUCH OF A JOB FOR A REAL *KENSHI*, IS IT?
WHY NOT? IT'S *EASY*.
EXACTLY. LIKE *PIMPING*.
OOH, TAI-TAI... YOU DON'T LIKE THAT IDEA?
HUH...?
BUT I'D BE *REAL* NICE TO YOU AN' BUY YOU WHATEVER YOU WANTED AND STUFF!
GET OFF!!
CRAZY BROAD...

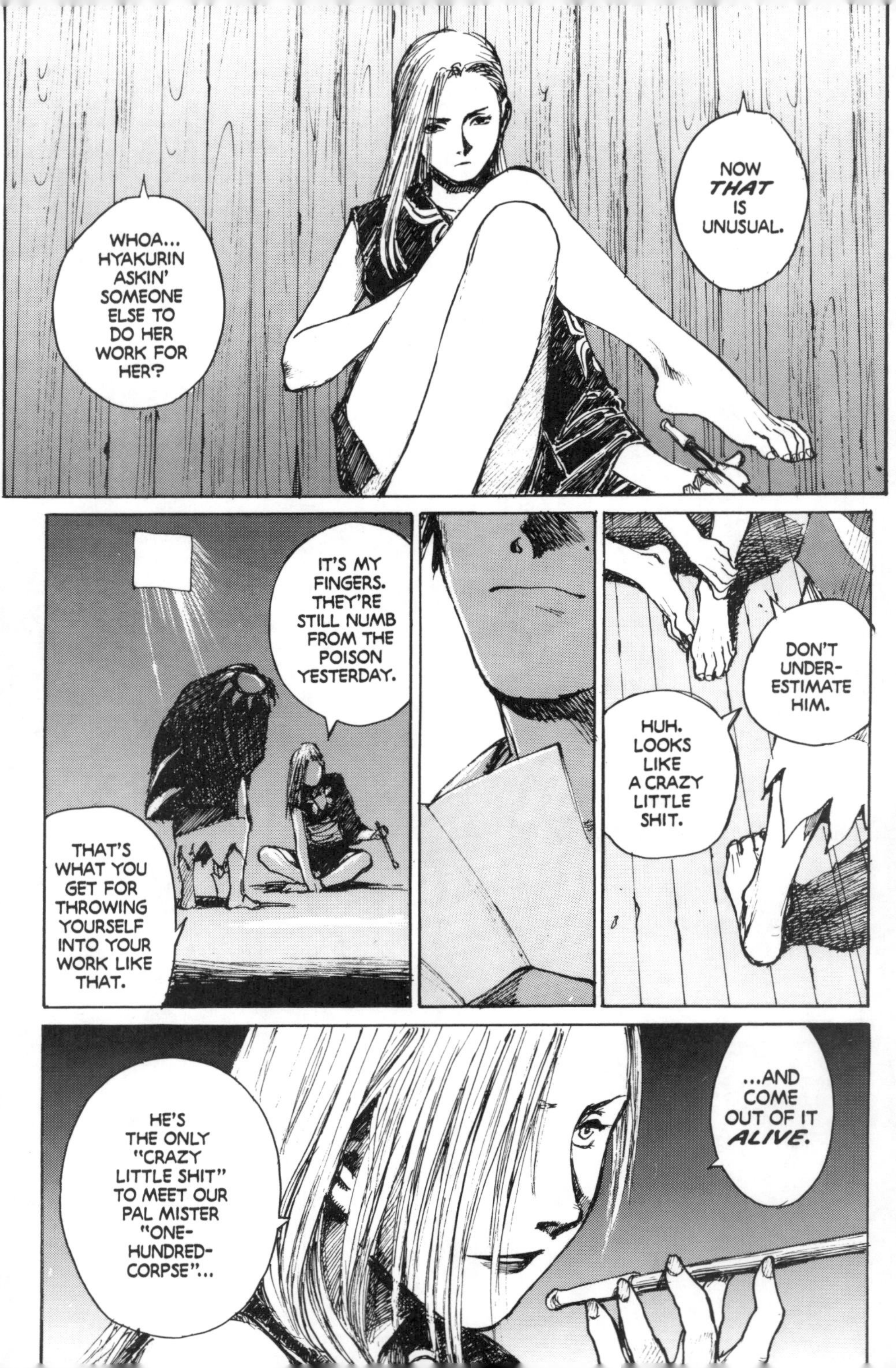
WHOA... HYAKURIN ASKIN' SOMEONE ELSE TO DO HER WORK FOR HER?
NOW *THAT* IS UNUSUAL.
IT'S MY FINGERS. THEY'RE STILL NUMB FROM THE POISON YESTERDAY.
THAT'S WHAT YOU GET FOR THROWING YOURSELF INTO YOUR WORK LIKE THAT.
HUH. LOOKS LIKE A CRAZY LITTLE SHIT.
DON'T UNDER-ESTIMATE HIM.
HE'S THE ONLY "CRAZY LITTLE SHIT" TO MEET OUR PAL MISTER "ONE-HUNDRED-CORPSE"...
...AND COME OUT OF IT *ALIVE*.

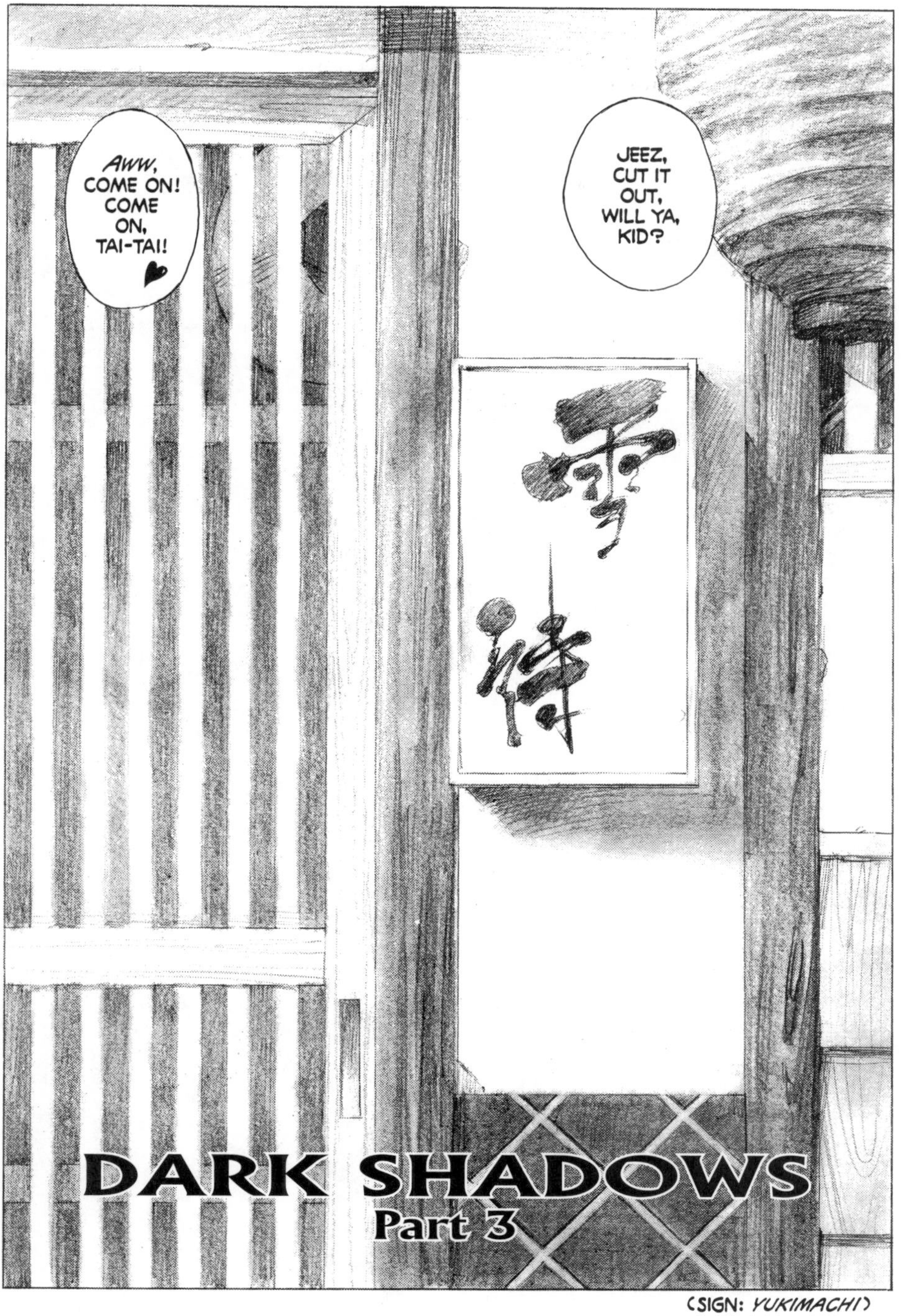
AWW, COME ON! COME ON, TAI-TAI! ♥
JEEZ, CUT IT OUT, WILL YA, KID?
DARK SHADOWS
Part 3

(SIGN: *YUKIMACHI*)

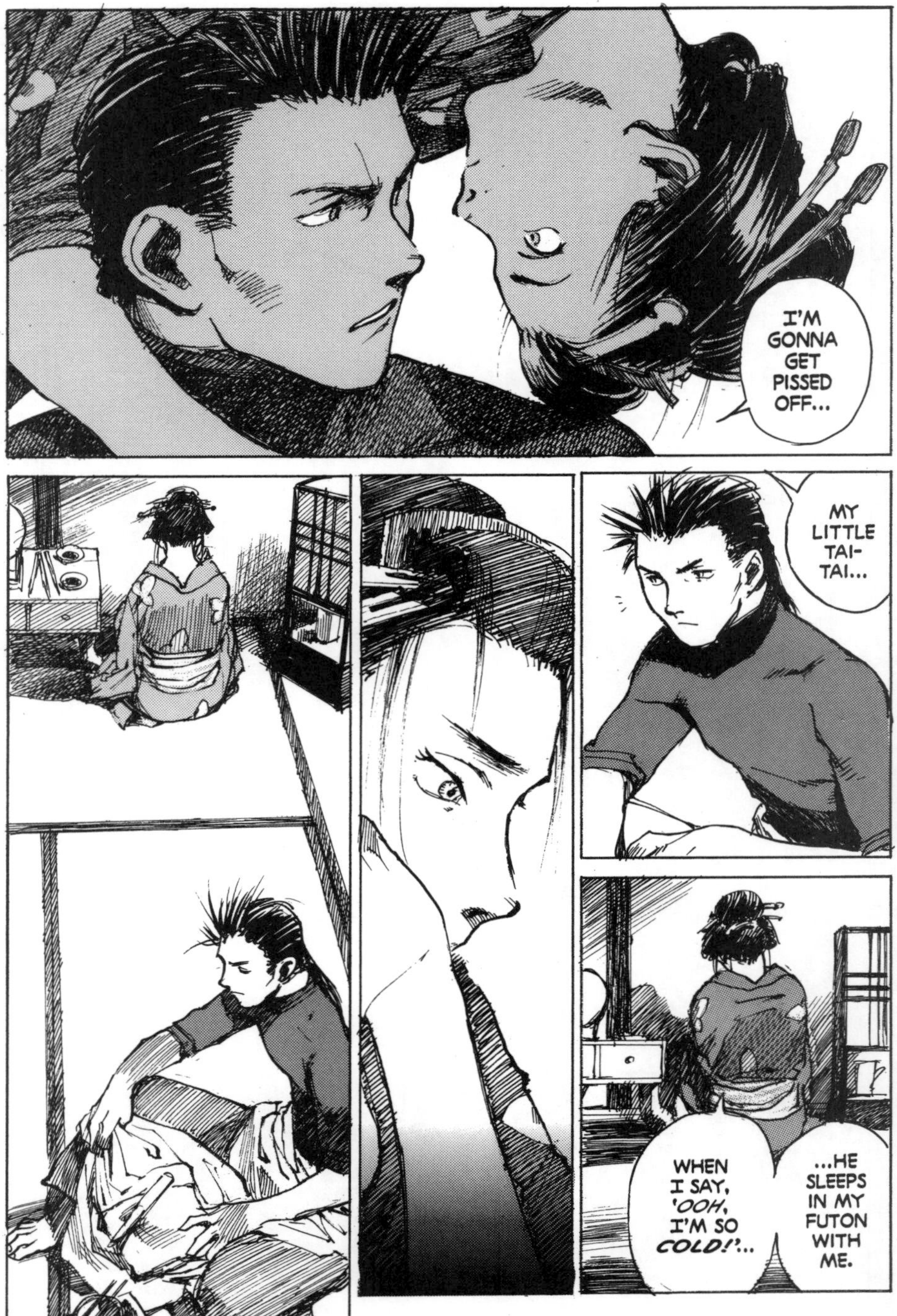
I'M GONNA GET PISSED OFF...
MY LITTLE TAI-TAI...
WHEN I SAY, '*OOH*, I'M SO ***COLD!***'...
...HE SLEEPS IN MY FUTON WITH ME.

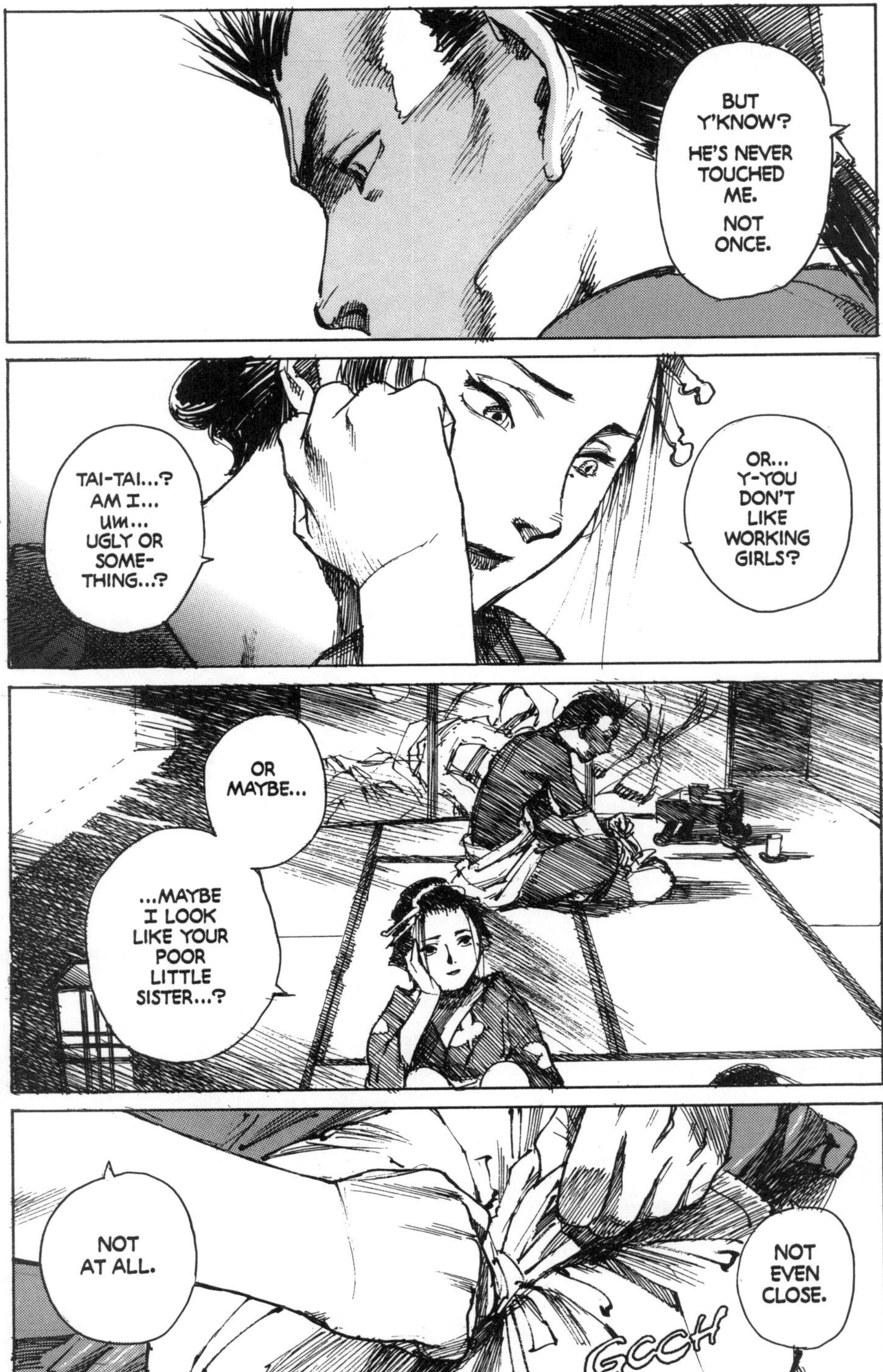
BUT Y'KNOW?
HE'S NEVER TOUCHED ME.
NOT ONCE.
TAI-TAI...? AM I... UM... UGLY OR SOME-THING...?
OR... Y-YOU DON'T LIKE WORKING GIRLS?
OR MAYBE...
...MAYBE I LOOK LIKE YOUR POOR LITTLE SISTER...?
NOT AT ALL.
NOT EVEN CLOSE.
GCCH

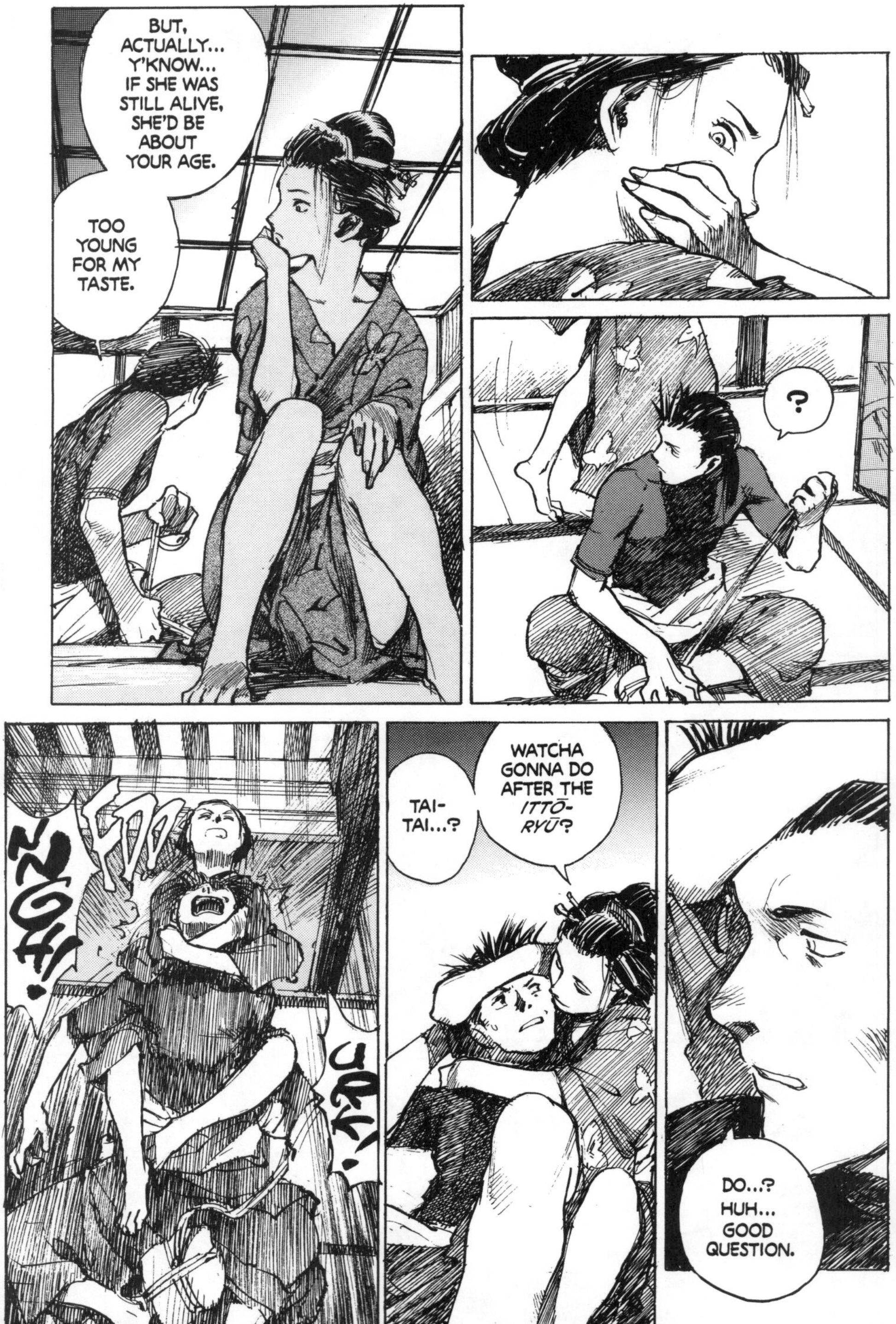
BUT, ACTUALLY... Y'KNOW... IF SHE WAS STILL ALIVE, SHE'D BE ABOUT YOUR AGE.
TOO YOUNG FOR MY TASTE.
?
NNGH!!
URK!
TAI-TAI...?
WATCHA GONNA DO AFTER THE *ITTŌ-RYŪ*?
DO...? HUH... GOOD QUESTION.

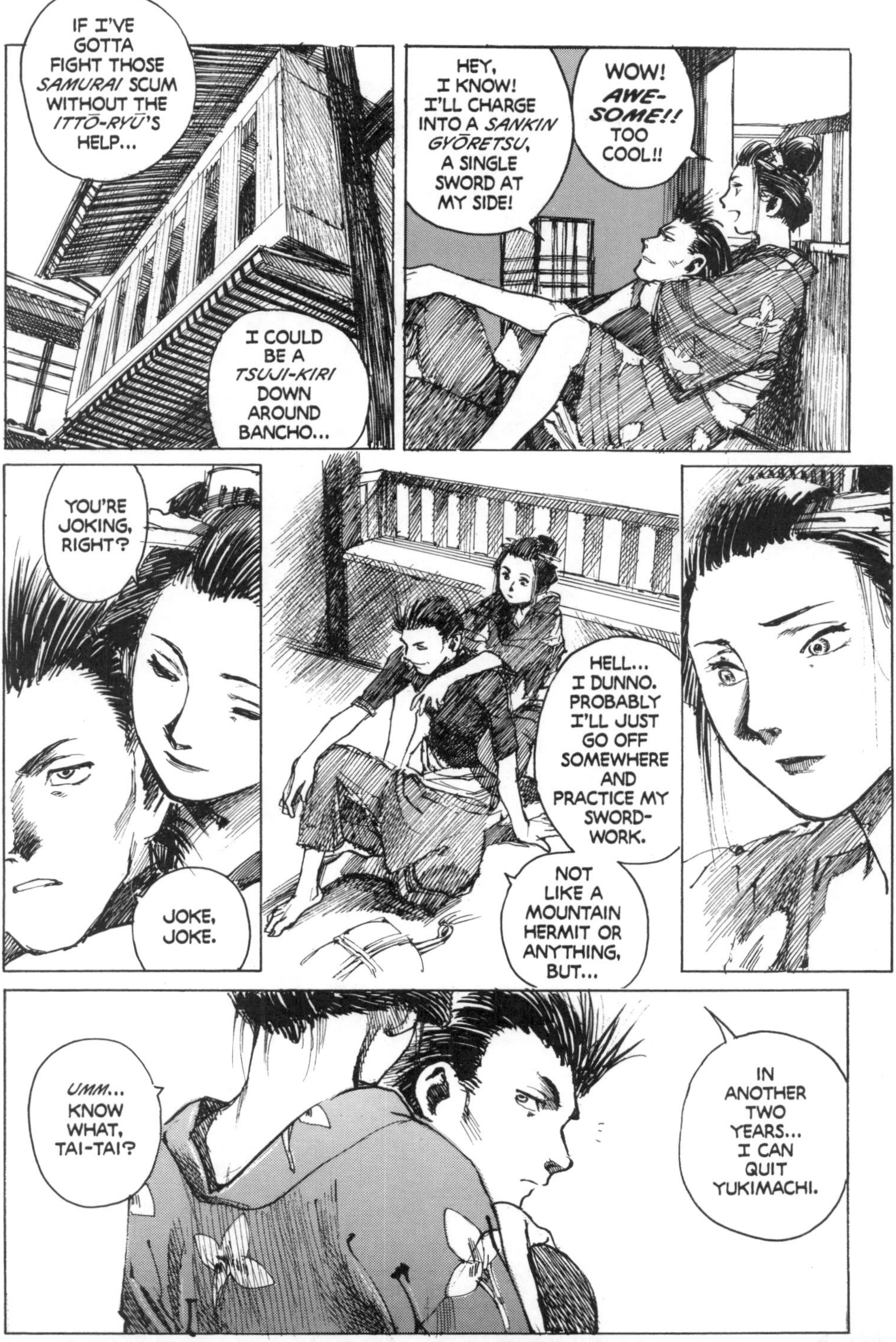
IF I'VE GOTTA FIGHT THOSE *SAMURAI* SCUM WITHOUT THE *ITTŌ-RYŪ*'S HELP...
I COULD BE A *TSUJI-KIRI* DOWN AROUND BANCHO...
HEY, I KNOW! I'LL CHARGE INTO A *SANKIN GYŌRETSU*, A SINGLE SWORD AT MY SIDE!
WOW! ***AWE-SOME!!*** TOO COOL!!
YOU'RE JOKING, RIGHT?
JOKE, JOKE.
HELL... I DUNNO. PROBABLY I'LL JUST GO OFF SOMEWHERE AND PRACTICE MY SWORD-WORK.
NOT LIKE A MOUNTAIN HERMIT OR ANYTHING, BUT...
UMM... KNOW WHAT, TAI-TAI?
IN ANOTHER TWO YEARS... I CAN QUIT YUKIMACHI.

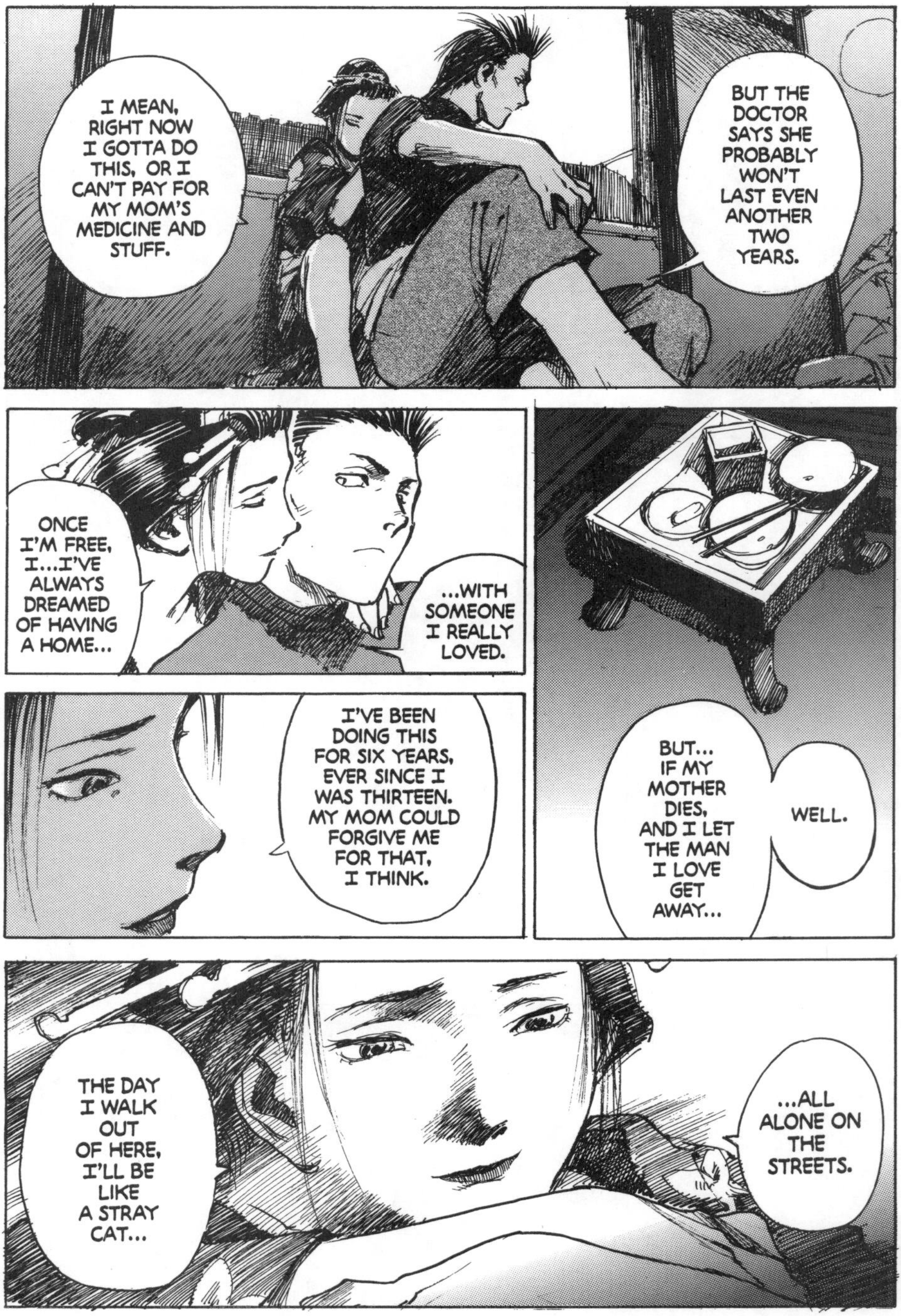
I MEAN, RIGHT NOW I GOTTA DO THIS, OR I CAN'T PAY FOR MY MOM'S MEDICINE AND STUFF.
BUT THE DOCTOR SAYS SHE PROBABLY WON'T LAST EVEN ANOTHER TWO YEARS.
ONCE I'M FREE, I...I'VE ALWAYS DREAMED OF HAVING A HOME...
...WITH SOMEONE I REALLY LOVED.
I'VE BEEN DOING THIS FOR SIX YEARS, EVER SINCE I WAS THIRTEEN. MY MOM COULD FORGIVE ME FOR THAT, I THINK.
BUT... IF MY MOTHER DIES, AND I LET THE MAN I LOVE GET AWAY...
WELL.
THE DAY I WALK OUT OF HERE, I'LL BE LIKE A STRAY CAT...
...ALL ALONE ON THE STREETS.

O-REN...

HMM?

NO, IT'S OKAY, REALLY. I DON'T CARE IF YOU LEAVE ME.

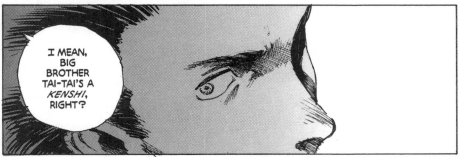

I MEAN, BIG BROTHER TAI-TAI'S A *KENSHI*, RIGHT?

SOMEONE WHO CAN GO OFF WHENEVER HE LIKES, JUST HIM AND HIS SWORD, LIVING FREE...

AN'... AN' SOME CLINGY WOMAN WHO D-DREAMS OF HAVING A LITTLE HOUSE SOME-WHERE...

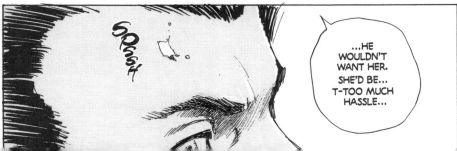

SPLASH

...HE WOULDN'T WANT HER. SHE'D BE... T-TOO MUCH HASSLE...

YOU'RE ALWAYS SAYING HOW YOU HATE *BUSHI*... ALWAYS...

BUT YOU CAN'T THROW AWAY YOUR SWORD. YOU...YOU S-STUPID *FOOL*...

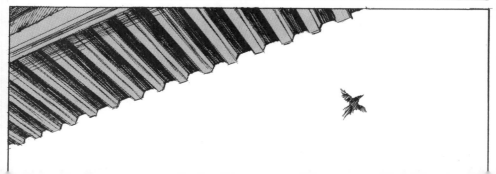

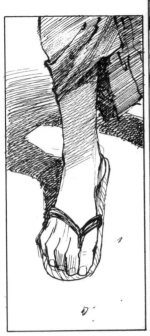

TAI-
TAI...?

HN?

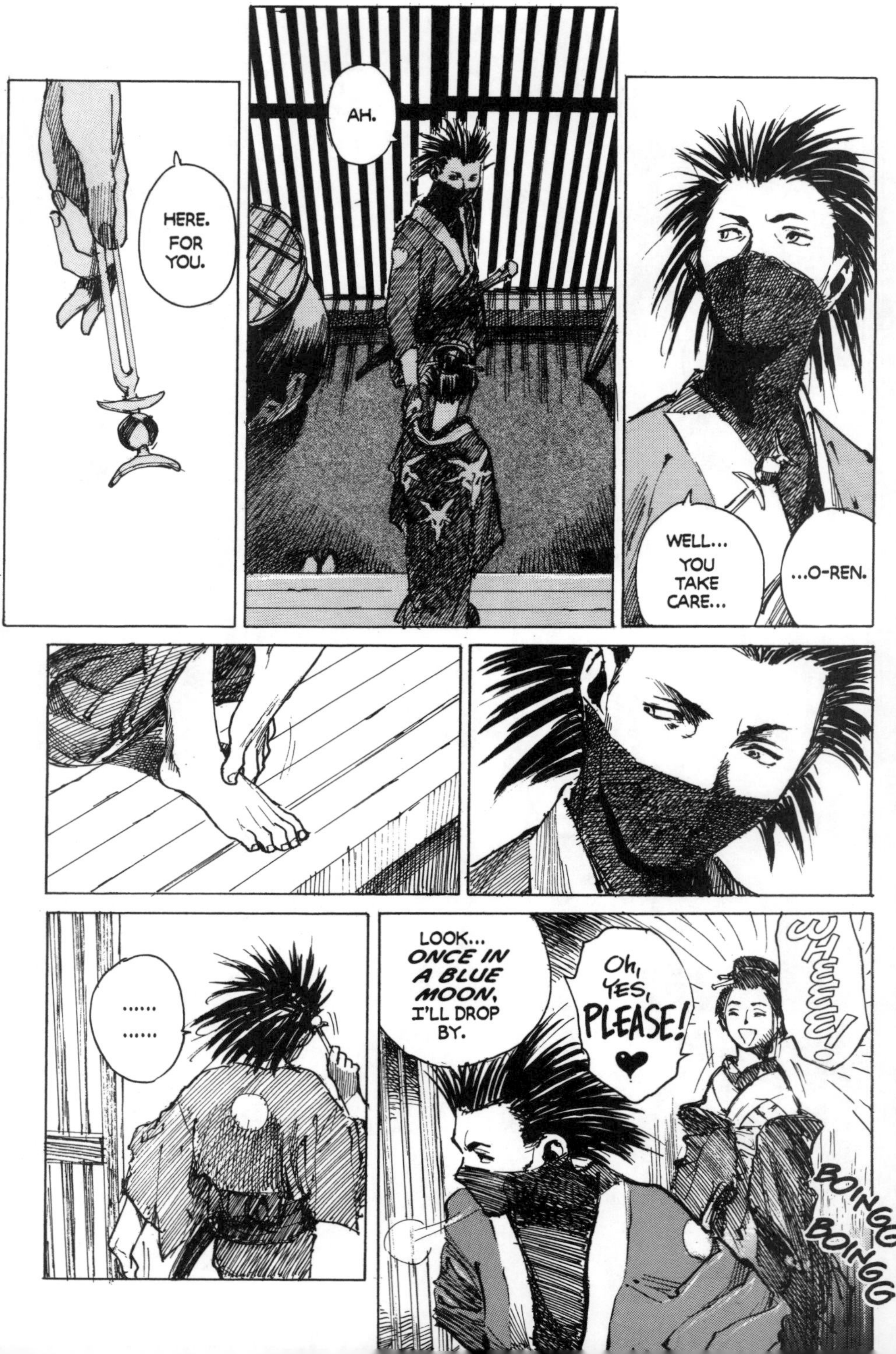
HERE. FOR YOU.
AH.
WELL... YOU TAKE CARE...
...O-REN.
....
LOOK... ONCE IN A BLUE MOON, I'LL DROP BY.
Oh, YES, PLEASE! ♥
WHEEEEE!
BOINGG BOINGG

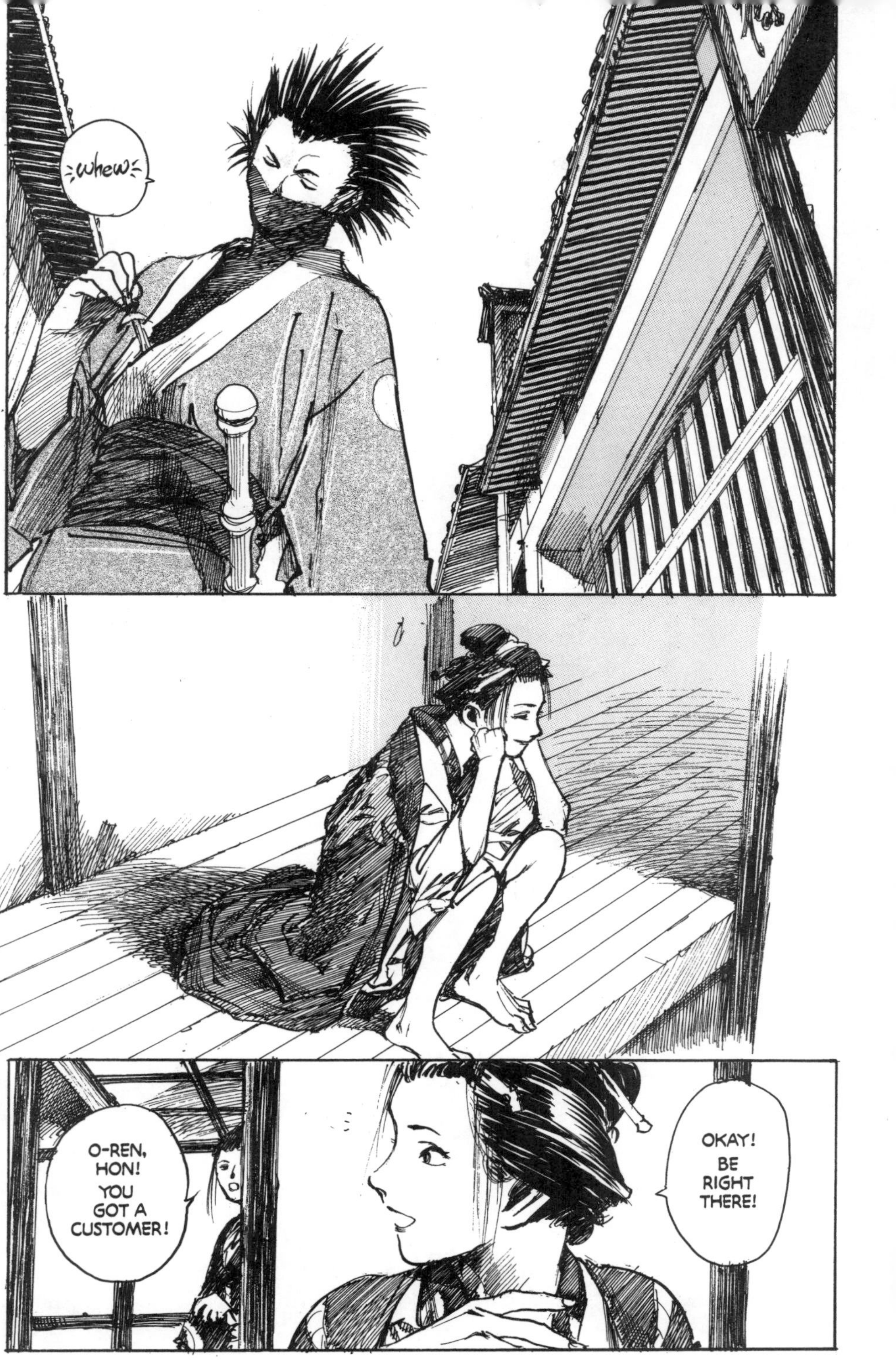
whew
OKAY! BE RIGHT THERE!
O-REN, HON! YOU GOT A CUSTOMER!

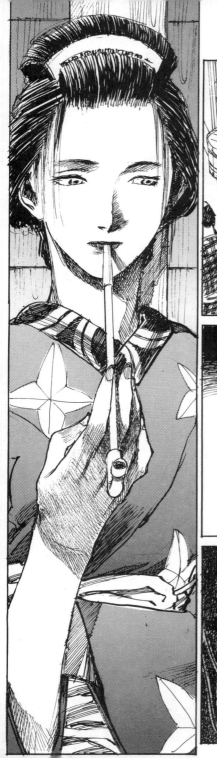

TOOK YOUR DAMN TIME.

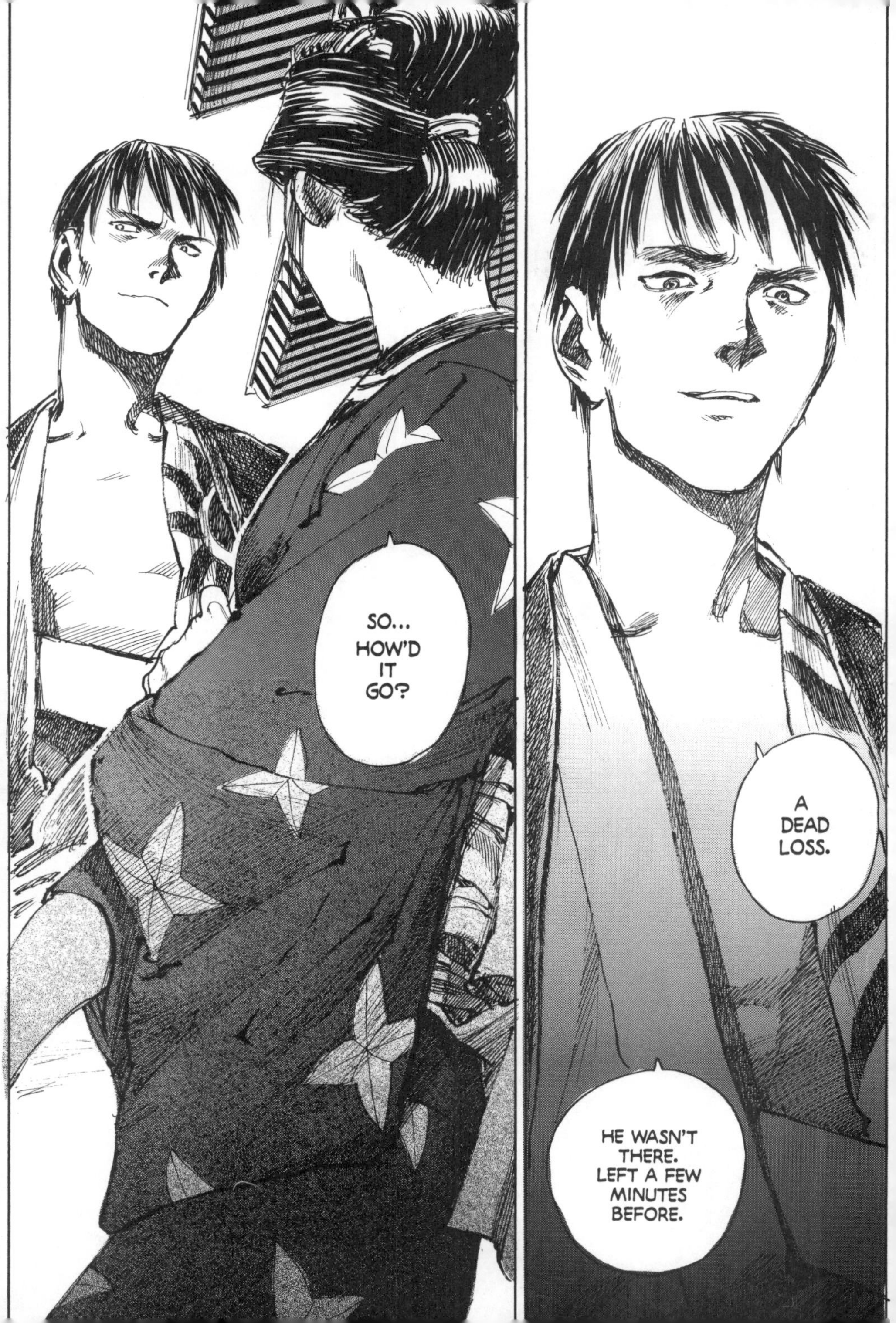
SO... HOW'D IT GO?
A DEAD LOSS.
HE WASN'T THERE. LEFT A FEW MINUTES BEFORE.

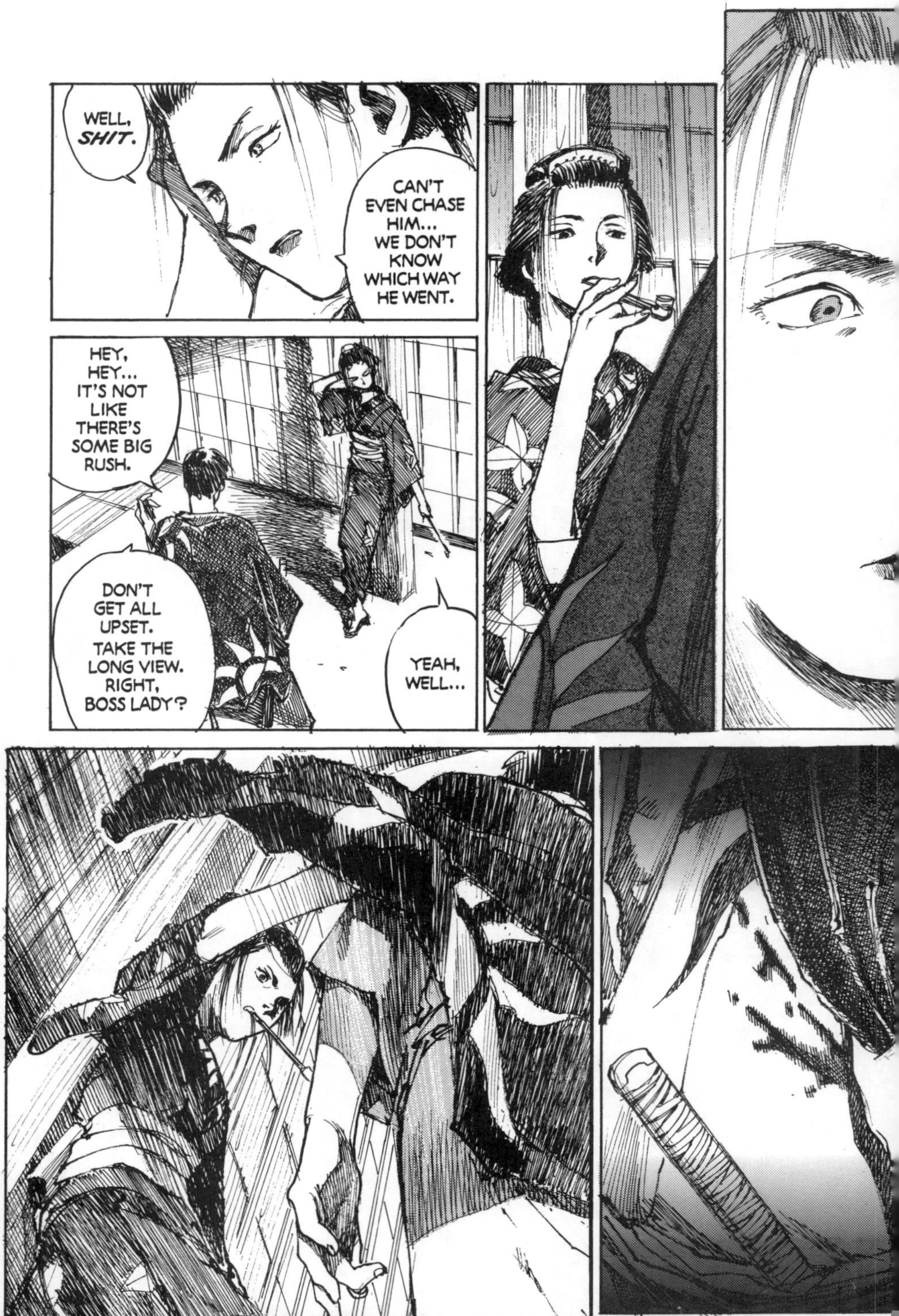
WELL, *SHIT*.
CAN'T EVEN CHASE HIM... WE DON'T KNOW WHICH WAY HE WENT.
HEY, HEY... IT'S NOT LIKE THERE'S SOME BIG RUSH.
DON'T GET ALL UPSET. TAKE THE LONG VIEW. RIGHT, BOSS LADY?
YEAH, WELL...

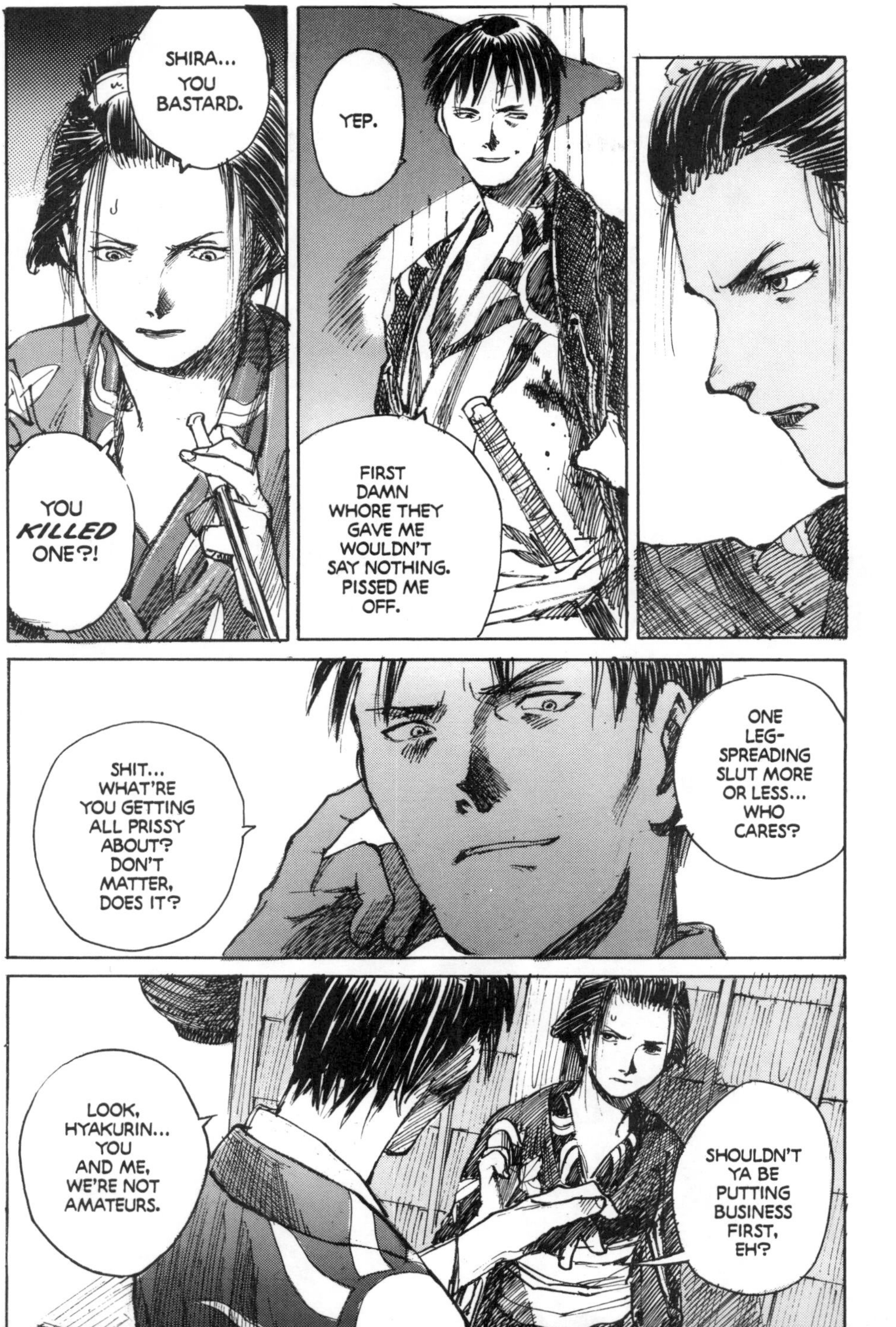
SHIRA... YOU BASTARD.
YOU *KILLED* ONE?!
YEP.
FIRST DAMN WHORE THEY GAVE ME WOULDN'T SAY NOTHING. PISSED ME OFF.
SHIT... WHAT'RE YOU GETTING ALL PRISSY ABOUT? DON'T MATTER, DOES IT?
ONE LEG-SPREADING SLUT MORE OR LESS... WHO CARES?
LOOK, HYAKURIN... YOU AND ME, WE'RE NOT AMATEURS.
SHOULDN'T YA BE PUTTING BUSINESS FIRST, EH?

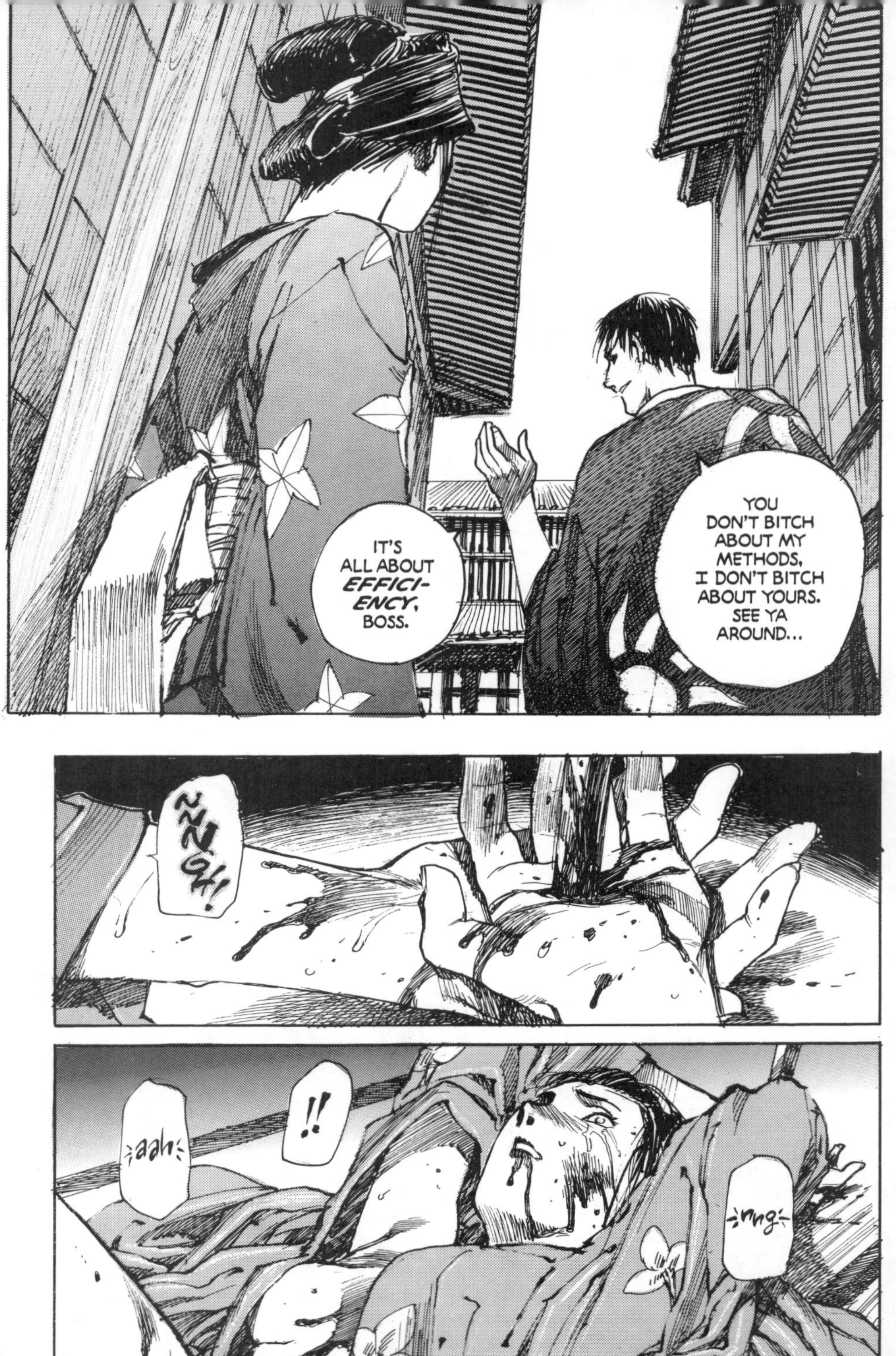
IT'S ALL ABOUT EFFICIENCY, BOSS.
YOU DON'T BITCH ABOUT MY METHODS, I DON'T BITCH ABOUT YOURS. SEE YA AROUND...
NNNGH!
aah
!!
nng

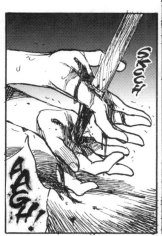

SKOOR

AAGH!!

-hahh-

aahh...

!!

T--
....

TAI...

T-
TAI...

TAI...

tai...

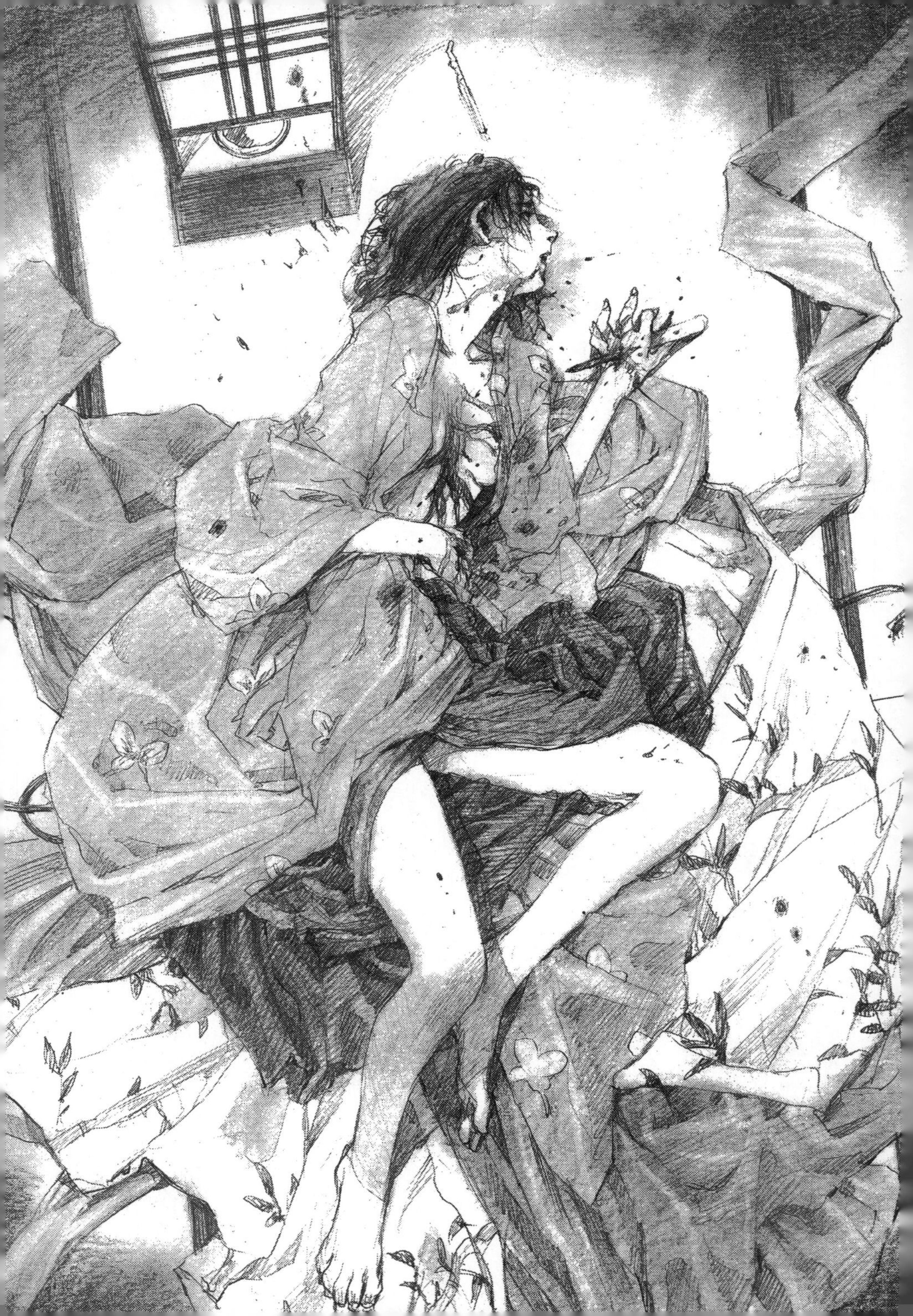

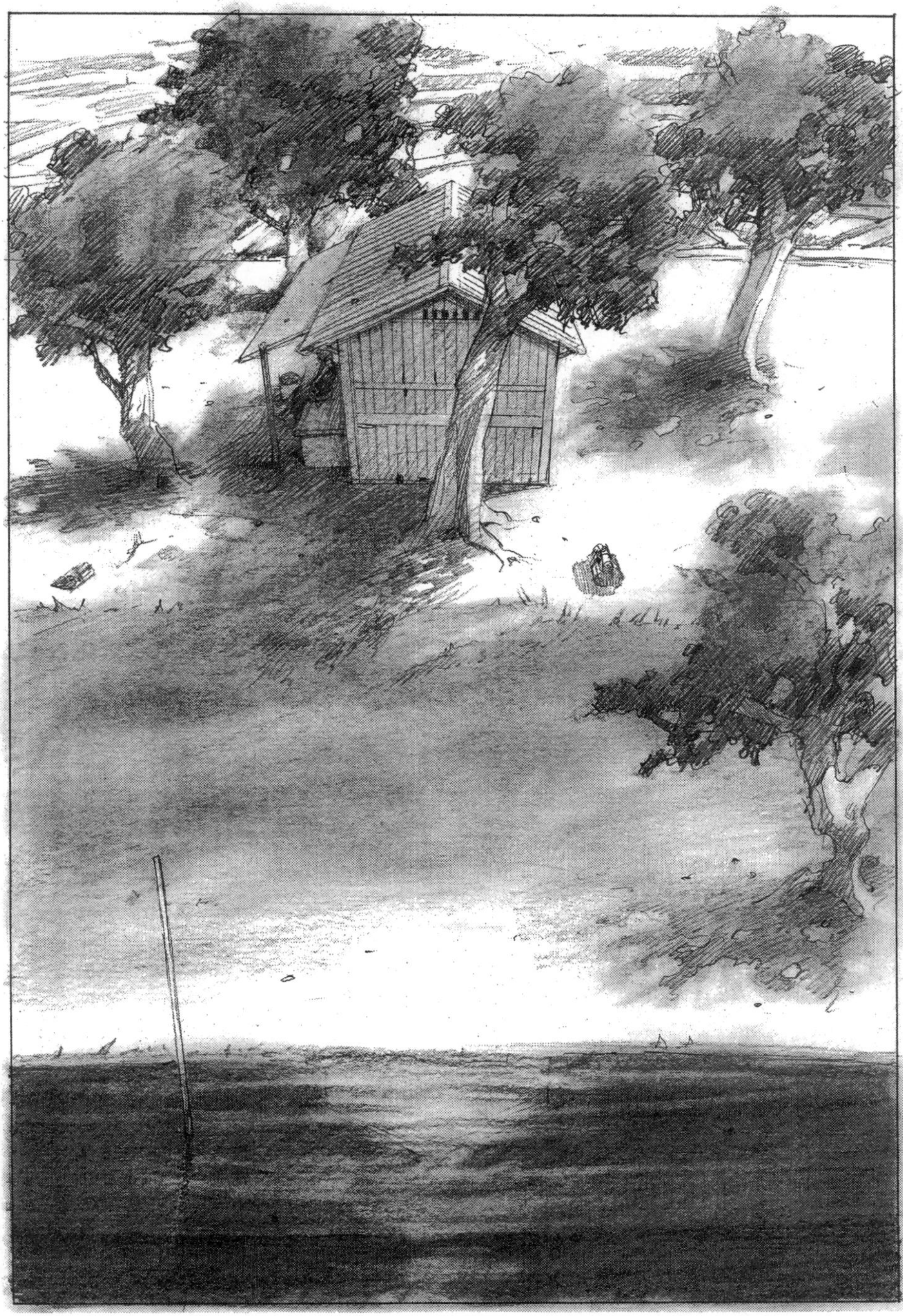

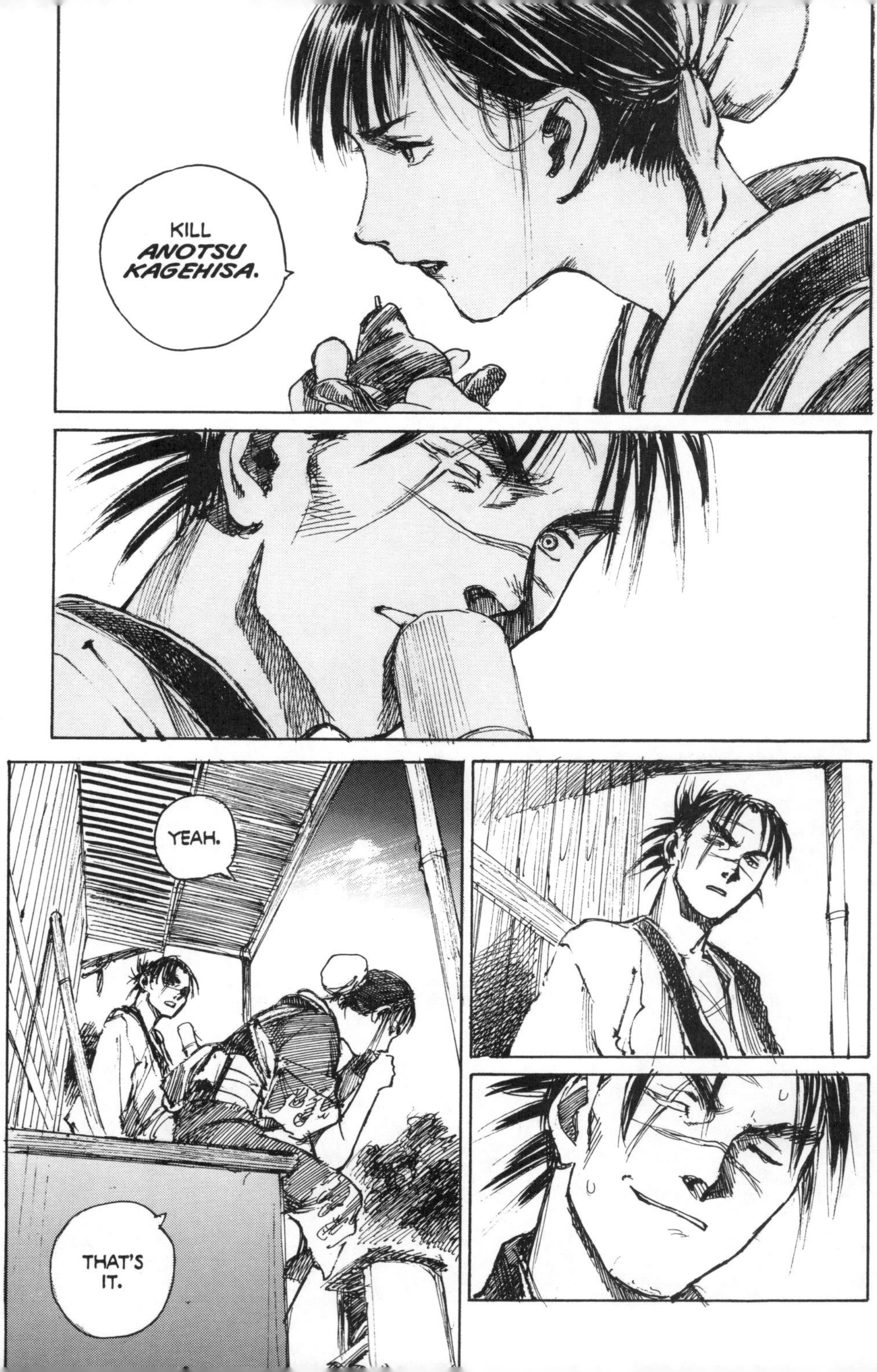
KILL *ANOTSU KAGEHISA.*
YEAH.
THAT'S IT.

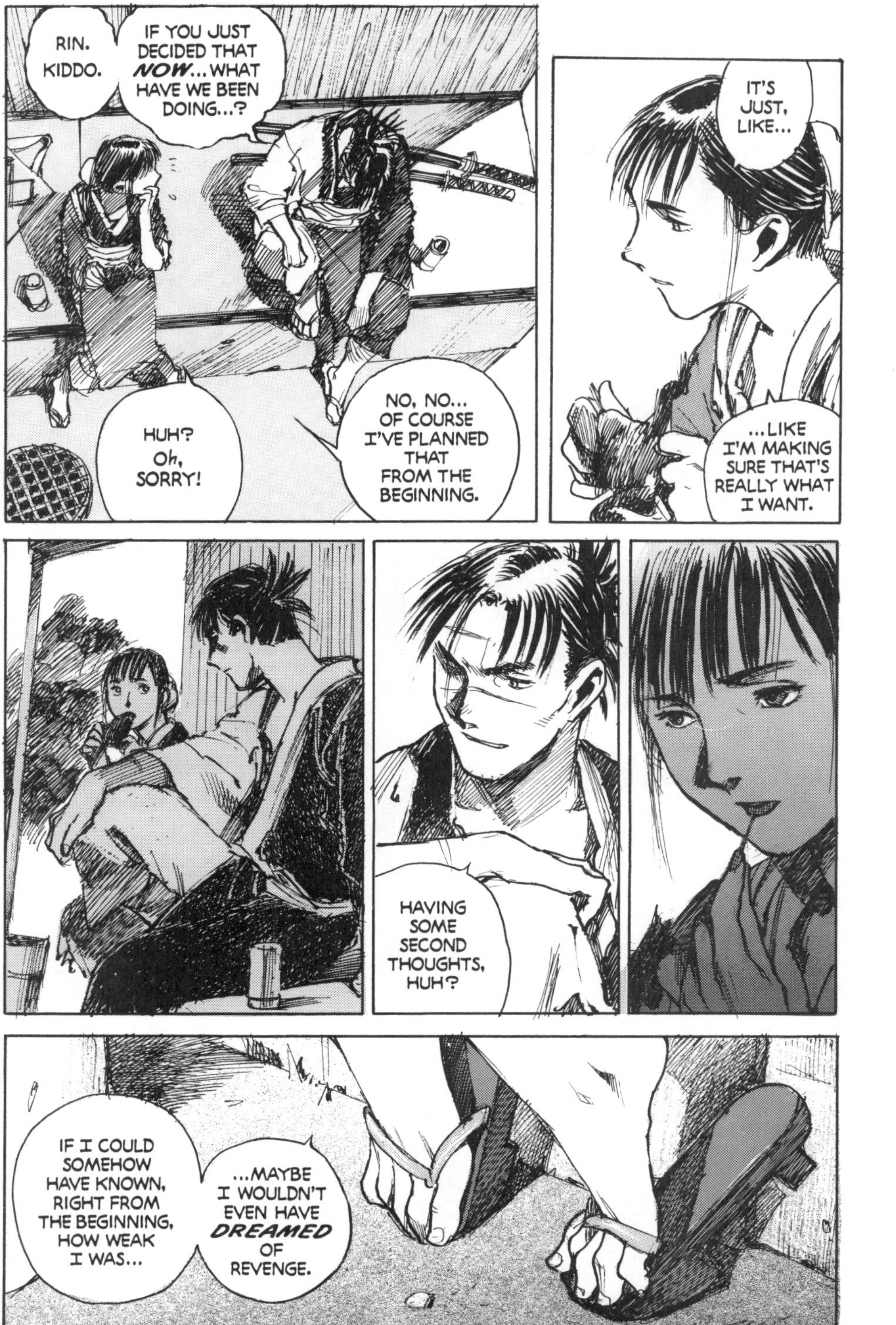
RIN. KIDDO.
IF YOU JUST DECIDED THAT *NOW*...WHAT HAVE WE BEEN DOING...?
HUH? Oh, SORRY!
NO, NO... OF COURSE I'VE PLANNED THAT FROM THE BEGINNING.
IT'S JUST, LIKE...
...LIKE I'M MAKING SURE THAT'S REALLY WHAT I WANT.
HAVING SOME SECOND THOUGHTS, HUH?
IF I COULD SOMEHOW HAVE KNOWN, RIGHT FROM THE BEGINNING, HOW WEAK I WAS...
...MAYBE I WOULDN'T EVEN HAVE *DREAMED* OF REVENGE.

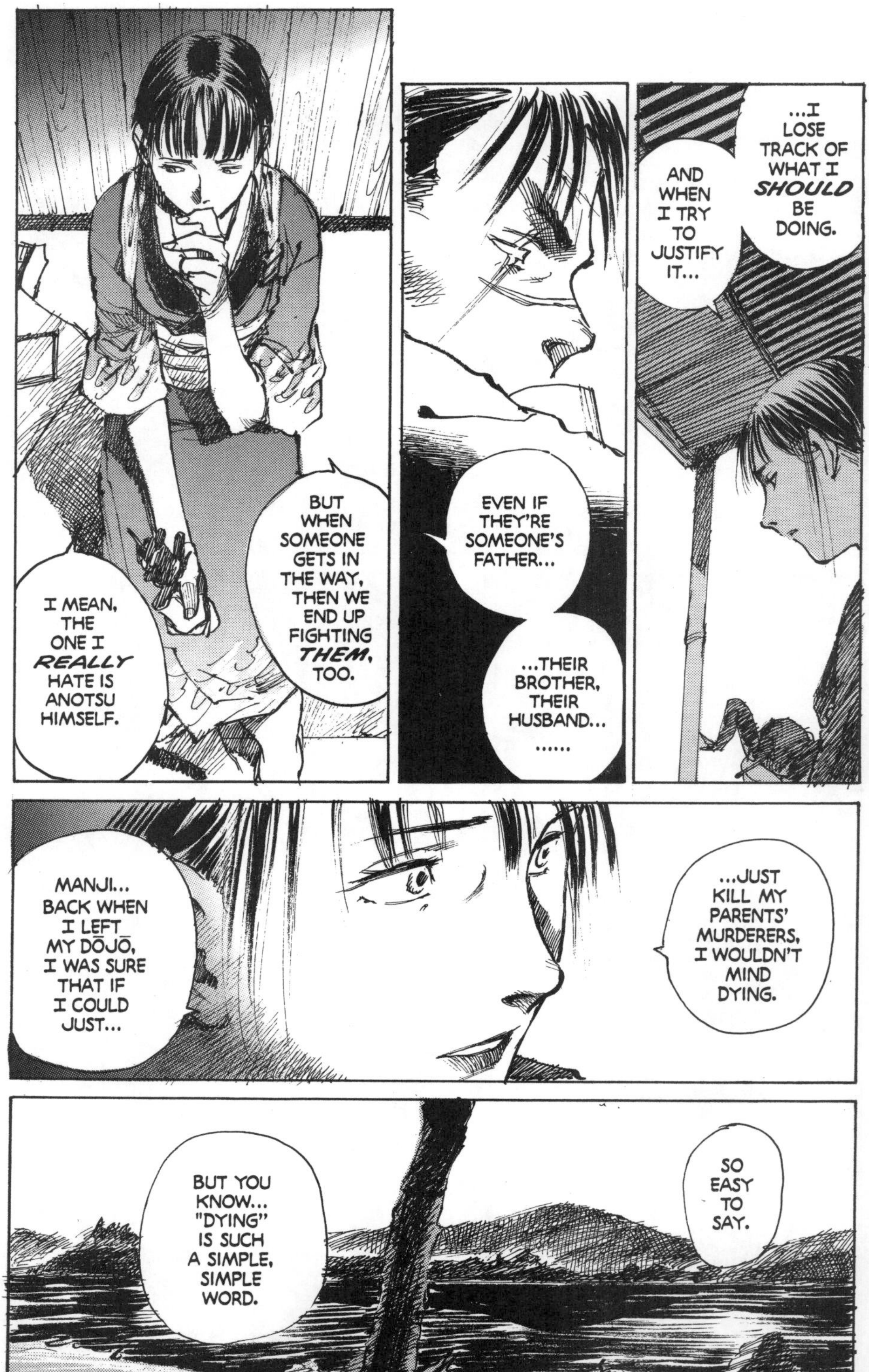
I MEAN, THE ONE I *REALLY* HATE IS ANOTSU HIMSELF.
BUT WHEN SOMEONE GETS IN THE WAY, THEN WE END UP FIGHTING *THEM*, TOO.
EVEN IF THEY'RE SOMEONE'S FATHER...
...THEIR BROTHER, THEIR HUSBAND... ......
AND WHEN I TRY TO JUSTIFY IT...
...I LOSE TRACK OF WHAT I *SHOULD* BE DOING.
MANJI... BACK WHEN I LEFT MY DŌJŌ, I WAS SURE THAT IF I COULD JUST...
...JUST KILL MY PARENTS' MURDERERS, I WOULDN'T MIND DYING.
BUT YOU KNOW... "DYING" IS SUCH A SIMPLE, SIMPLE WORD.
SO EASY TO SAY.

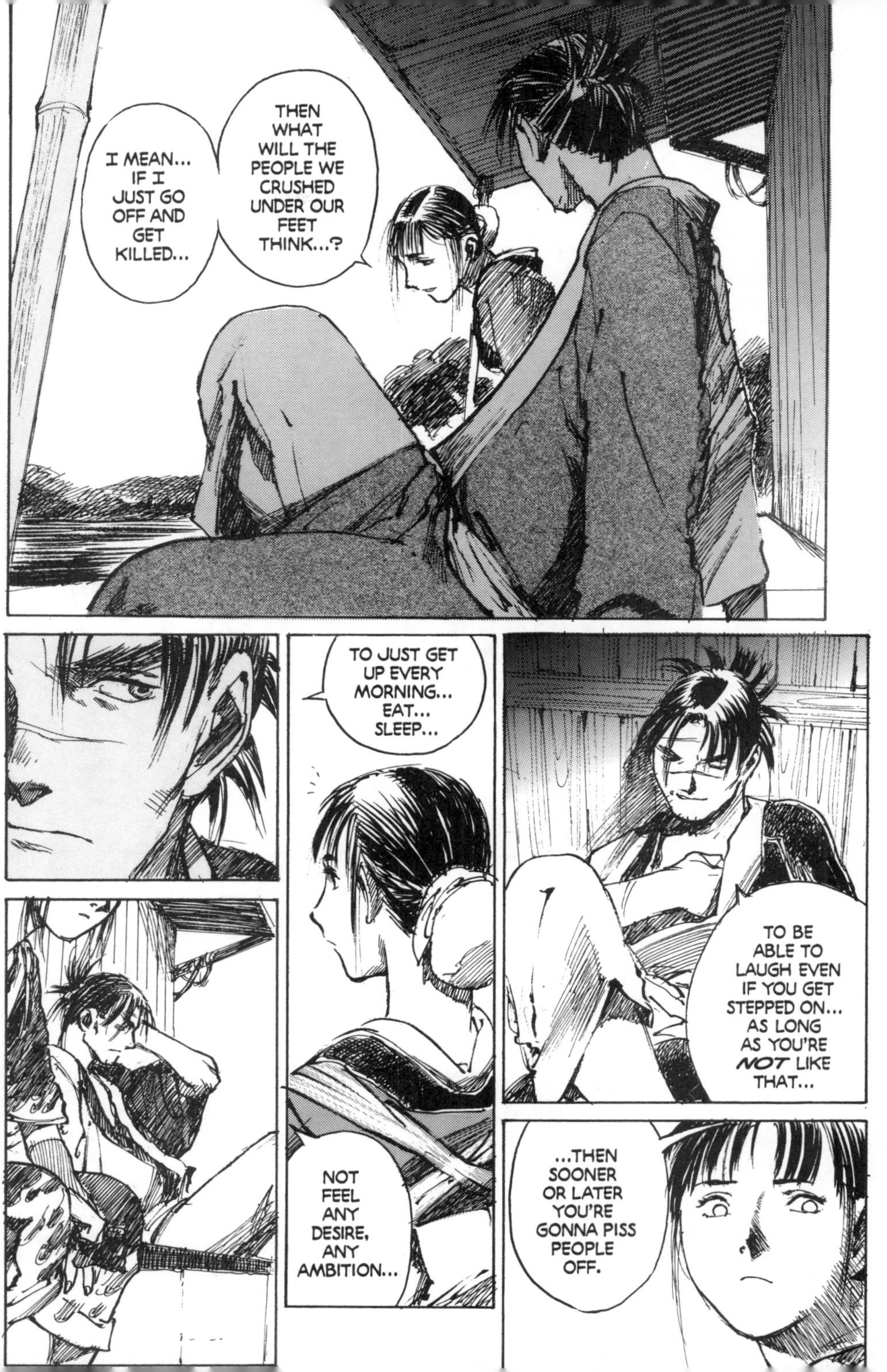
I MEAN... IF I JUST GO OFF AND GET KILLED...
THEN WHAT WILL THE PEOPLE WE CRUSHED UNDER OUR FEET THINK...?
TO JUST GET UP EVERY MORNING... EAT... SLEEP...
NOT FEEL ANY DESIRE, ANY AMBITION...
TO BE ABLE TO LAUGH EVEN IF YOU GET STEPPED ON... AS LONG AS YOU'RE NOT LIKE THAT...
...THEN SOONER OR LATER YOU'RE GONNA PISS PEOPLE OFF.

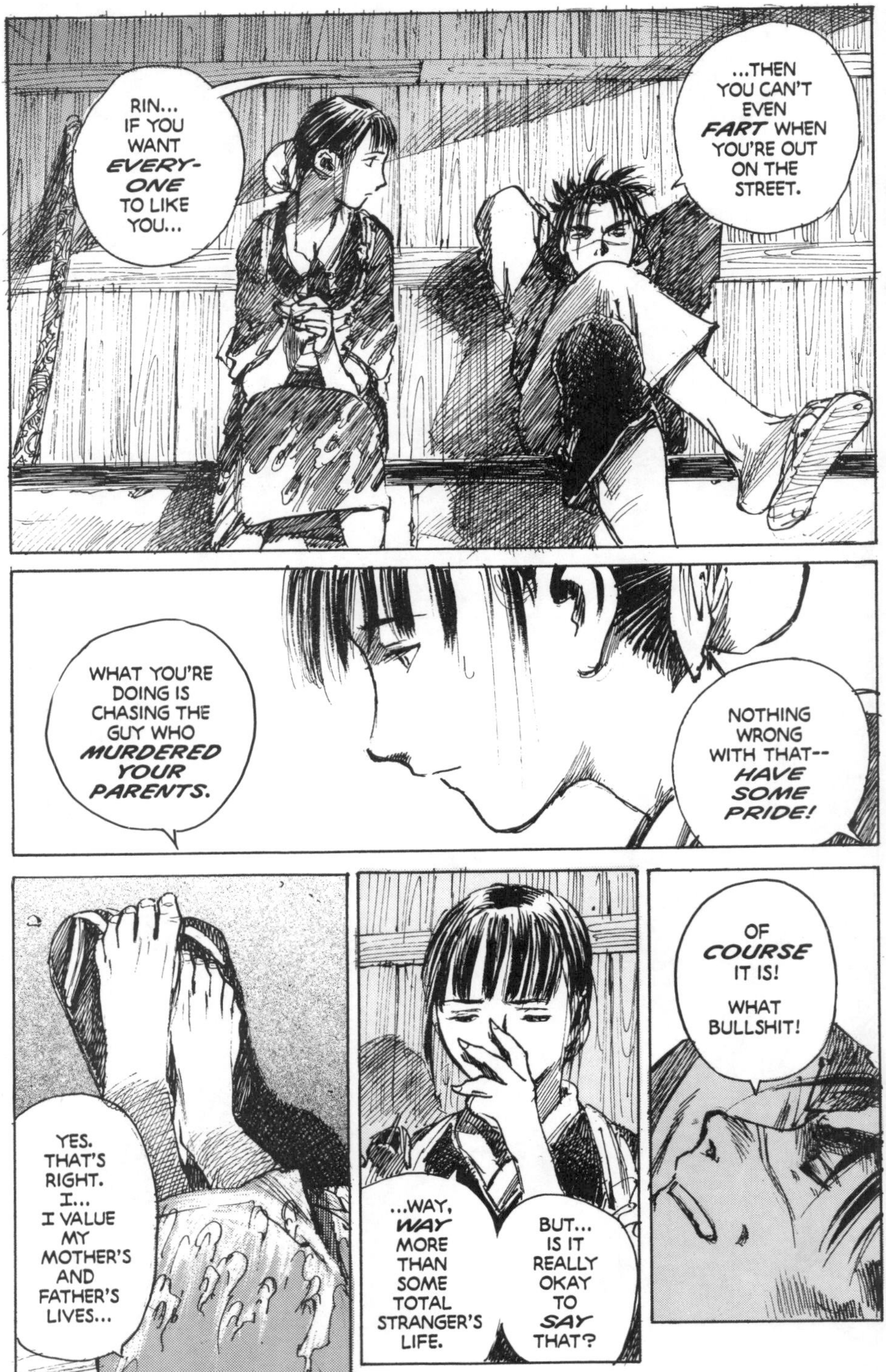
RIN... IF YOU WANT EVERY-ONE TO LIKE YOU...
...THEN YOU CAN'T EVEN FART WHEN YOU'RE OUT ON THE STREET.
WHAT YOU'RE DOING IS CHASING THE GUY WHO MURDERED YOUR PARENTS.
NOTHING WRONG WITH THAT-- HAVE SOME PRIDE!
YES. THAT'S RIGHT. I... I VALUE MY MOTHER'S AND FATHER'S LIVES...
...WAY, WAY MORE THAN SOME TOTAL STRANGER'S LIFE.
BUT... IS IT REALLY OKAY TO SAY THAT?
OF COURSE IT IS!
WHAT BULLSHIT!

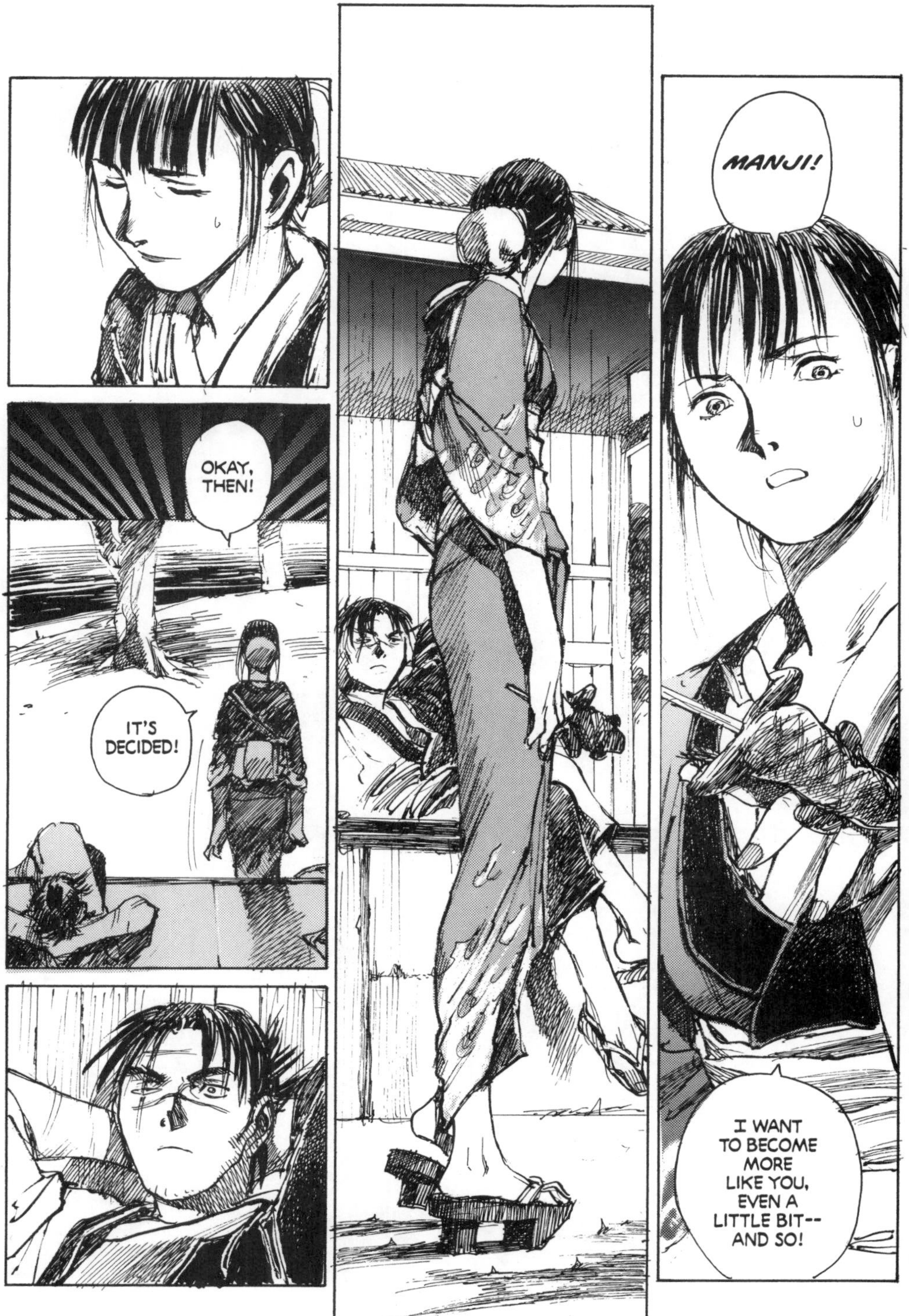
OKAY, THEN!
IT'S DECIDED!
MANJI!
I WANT TO BECOME MORE LIKE YOU, EVEN A LITTLE BIT-- AND SO!

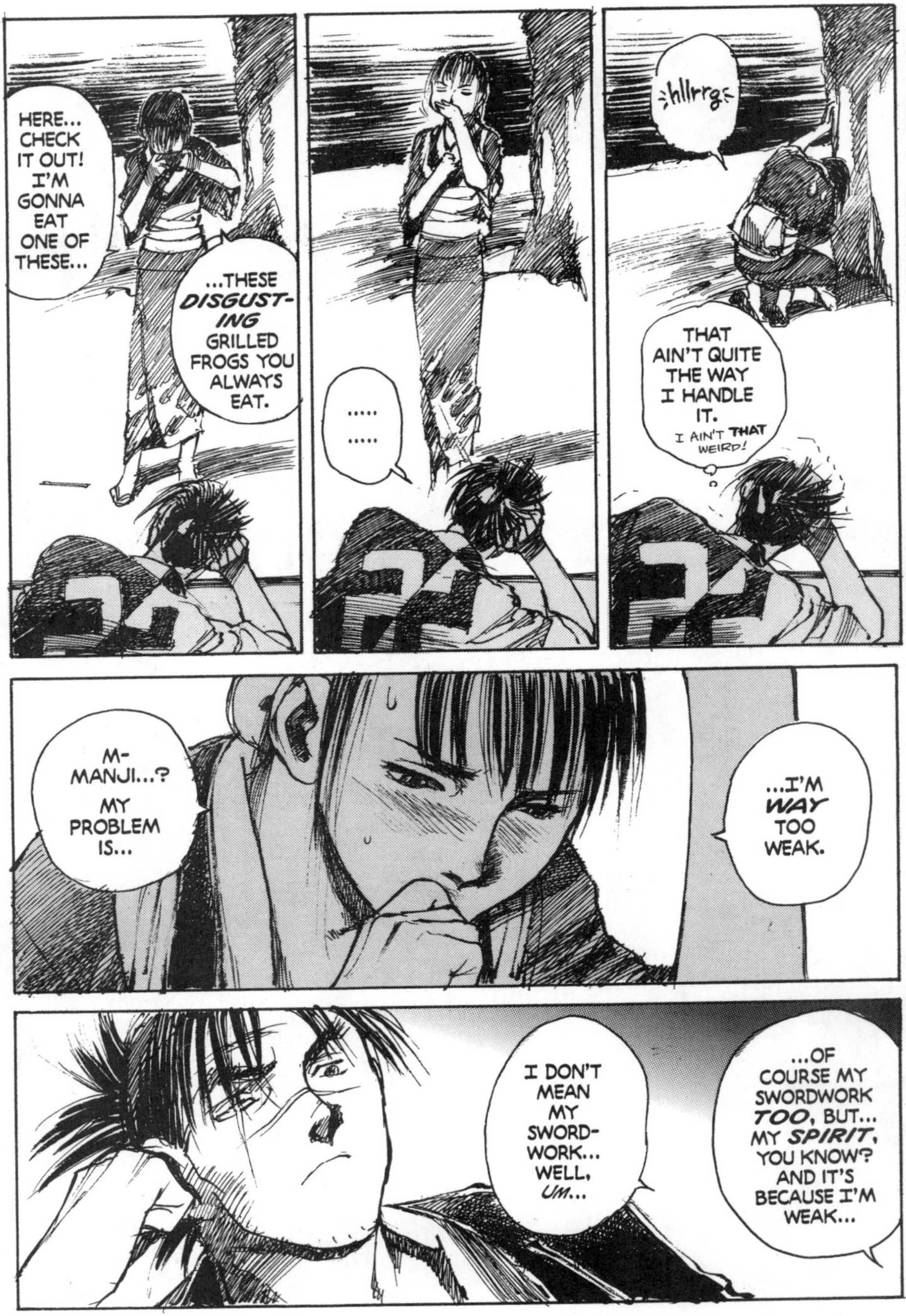
HERE... CHECK IT OUT! I'M GONNA EAT ONE OF THESE...
...THESE DISGUSTING GRILLED FROGS YOU ALWAYS EAT.
.....
.....
hllrrg
THAT AIN'T QUITE THE WAY I HANDLE IT.
I AIN'T THAT WEIRD!
M-MANJI...? MY PROBLEM IS...
...I'M WAY TOO WEAK.
I DON'T MEAN MY SWORD-WORK... WELL, UM...
...OF COURSE MY SWORDWORK TOO, BUT... MY SPIRIT, YOU KNOW? AND IT'S BECAUSE I'M WEAK...

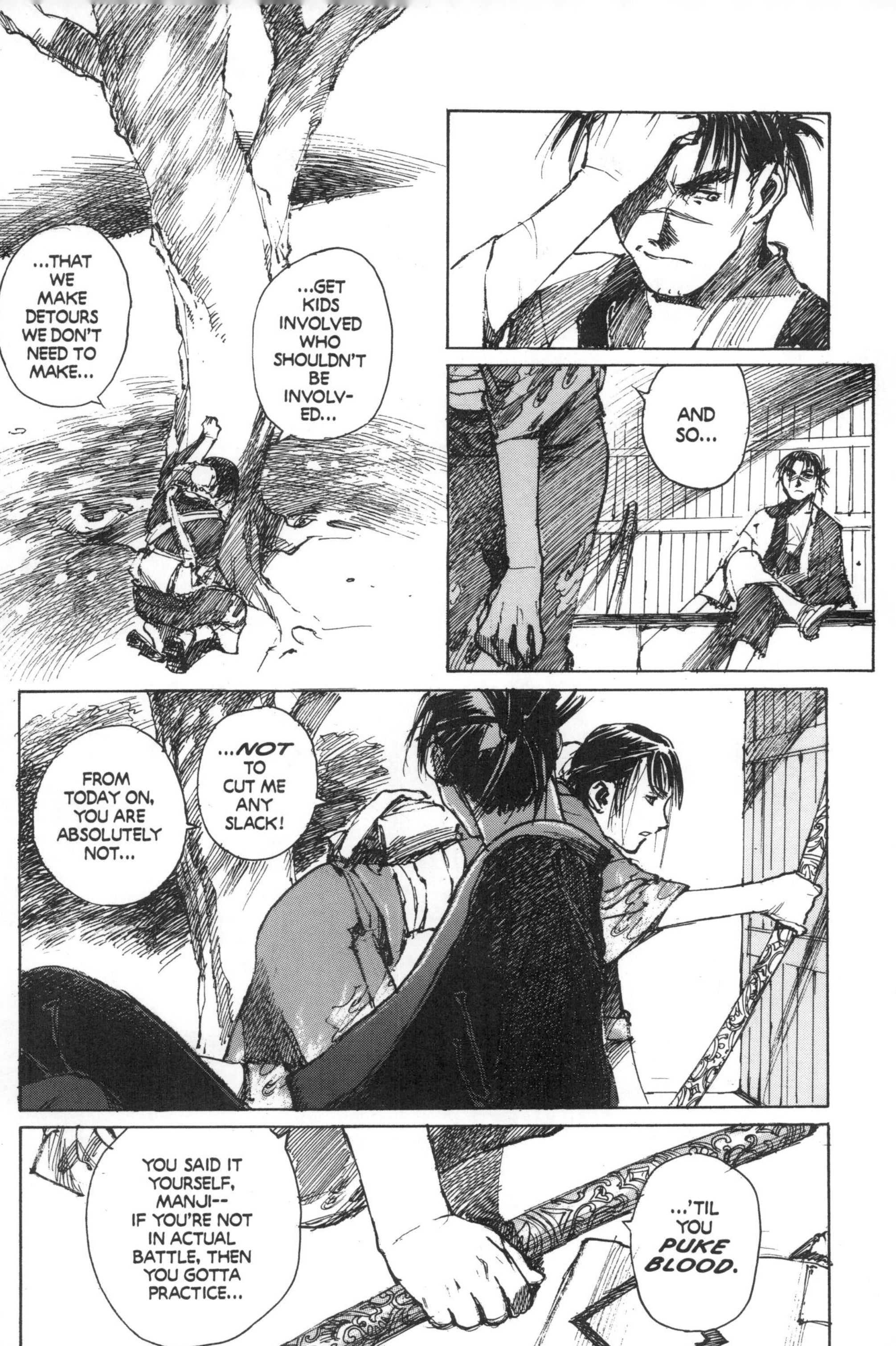
...THAT WE MAKE DETOURS WE DON'T NEED TO MAKE...
...GET KIDS INVOLVED WHO SHOULDN'T BE INVOLV-ED...
AND SO...
FROM TODAY ON, YOU ARE ABSOLUTELY NOT...
...*NOT* TO CUT ME ANY SLACK!
YOU SAID IT YOURSELF, MANJI-- IF YOU'RE NOT IN ACTUAL BATTLE, THEN YOU GOTTA PRACTICE...
...'TIL YOU ***PUKE BLOOD.***

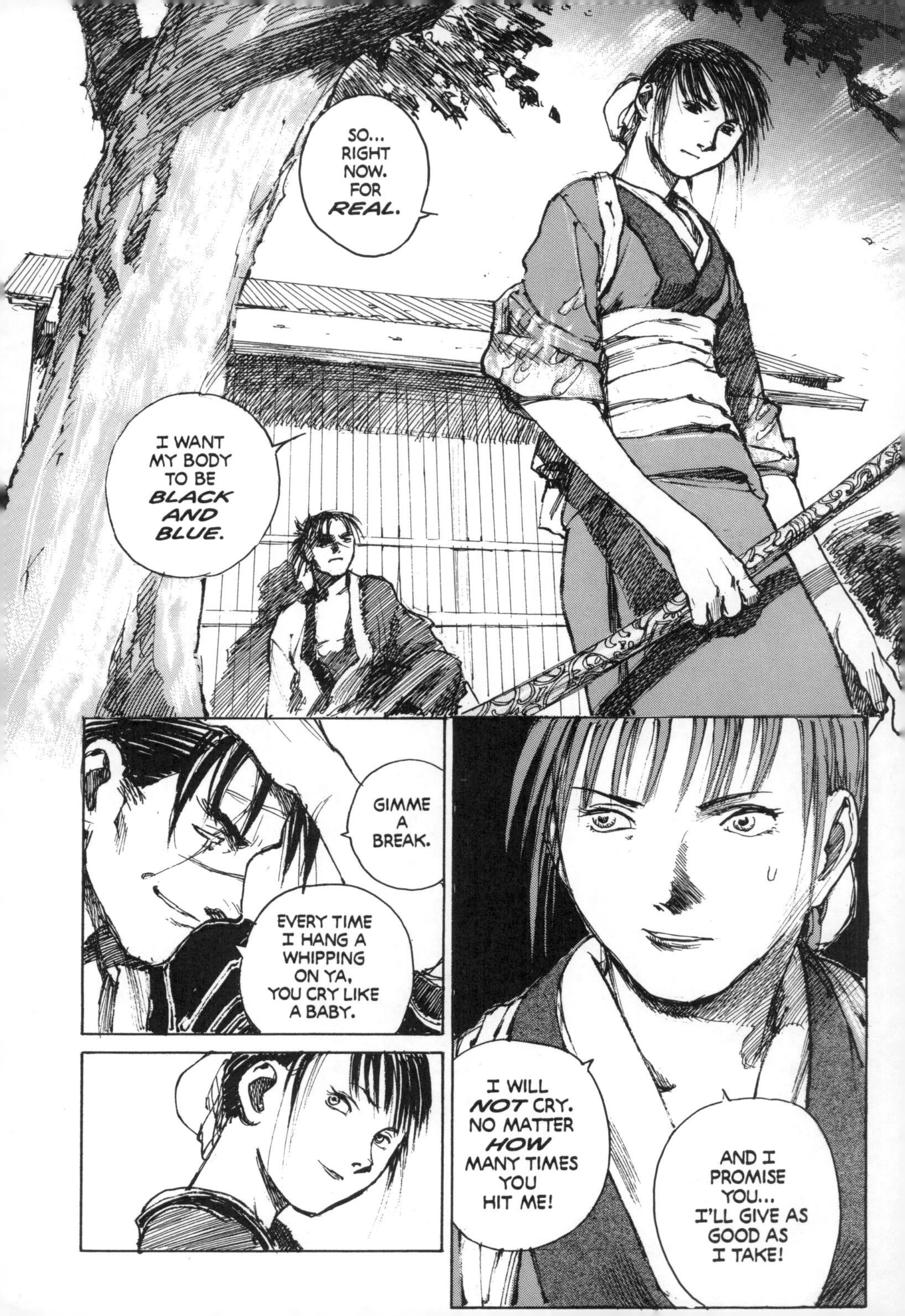
SO... RIGHT NOW. FOR *REAL.*
I WANT MY BODY TO BE *BLACK AND BLUE.*
GIMME A BREAK.
EVERY TIME I HANG A WHIPPING ON YA, YOU CRY LIKE A BABY.
I WILL *NOT* CRY. NO MATTER *HOW* MANY TIMES YOU HIT ME!
AND I PROMISE YOU... I'LL GIVE AS GOOD AS I TAKE!

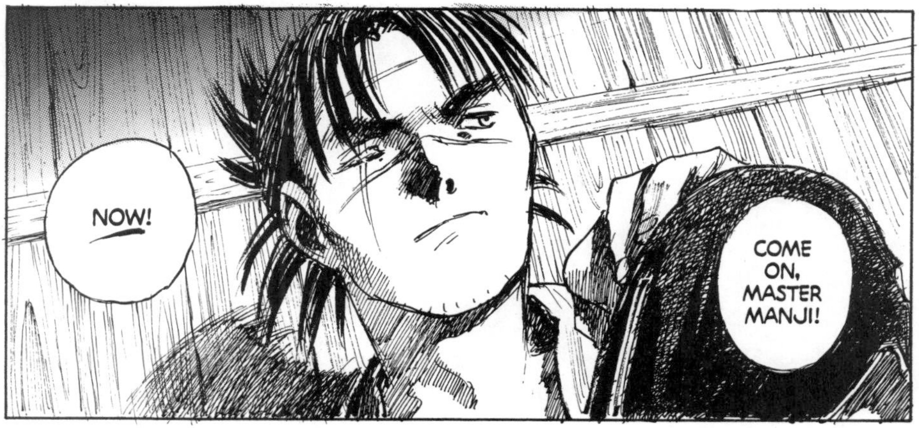
NOW!
COME ON, MASTER MANJI!

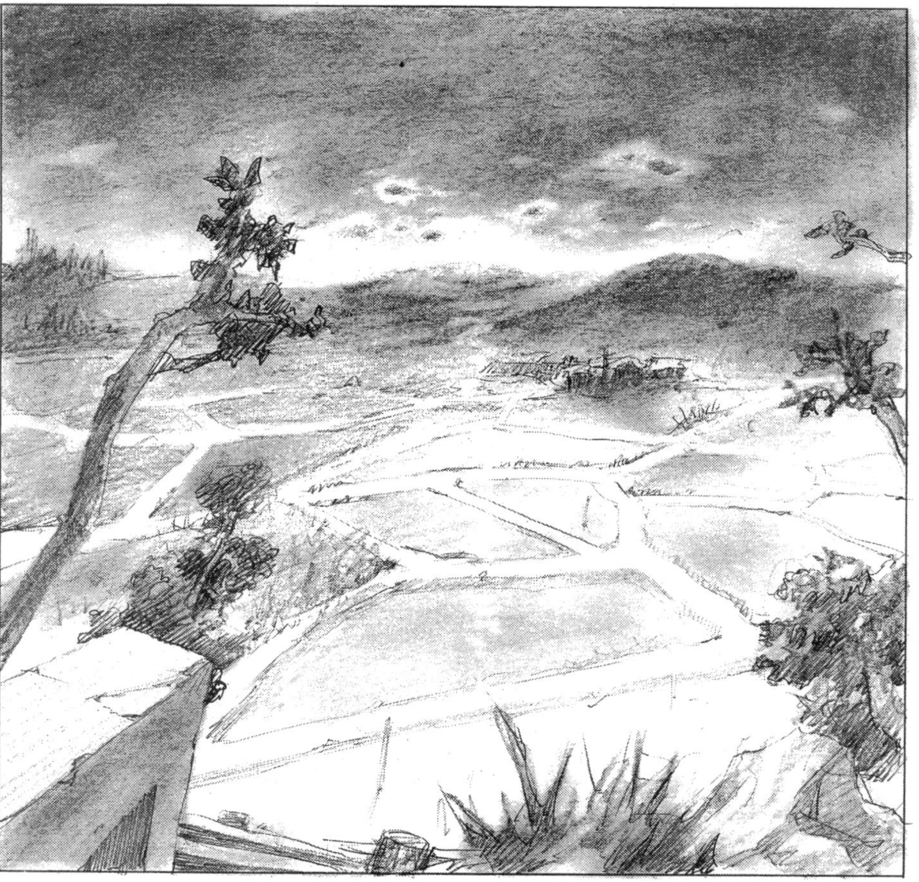

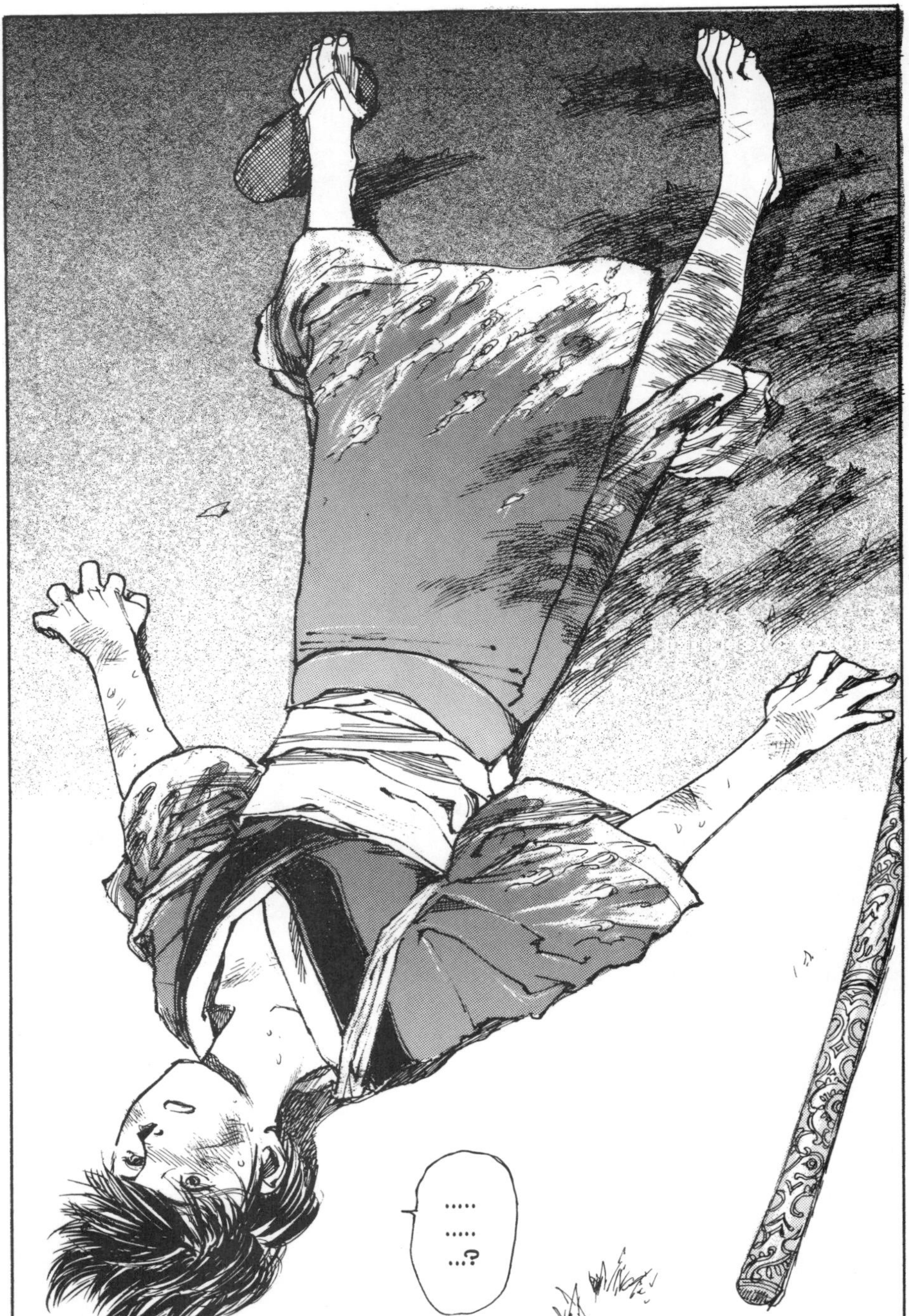
……
……
…?

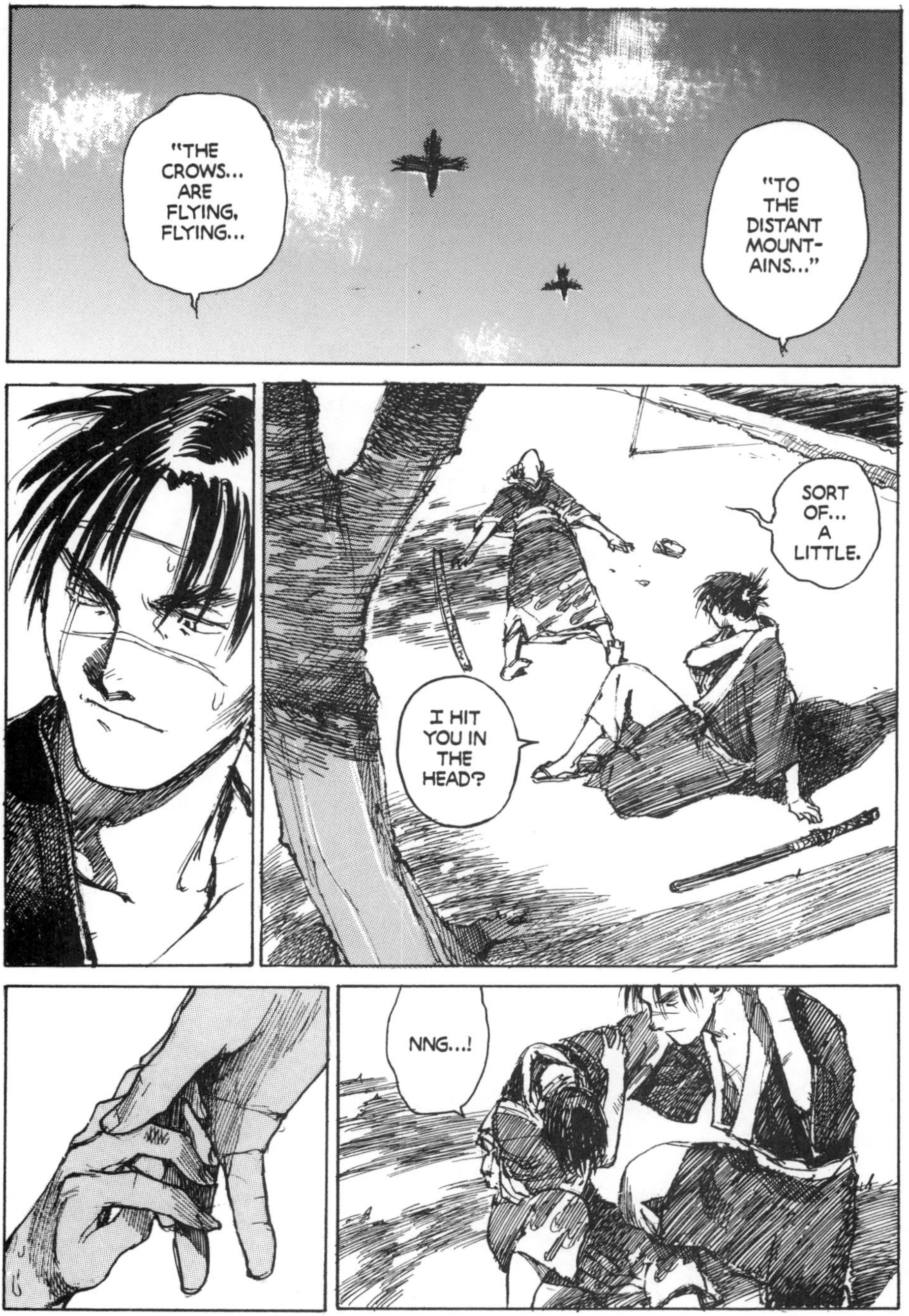
"THE CROWS... ARE FLYING, FLYING...
"TO THE DISTANT MOUNT-AINS..."
SORT OF... A LITTLE.
I HIT YOU IN THE HEAD?
NNG...!

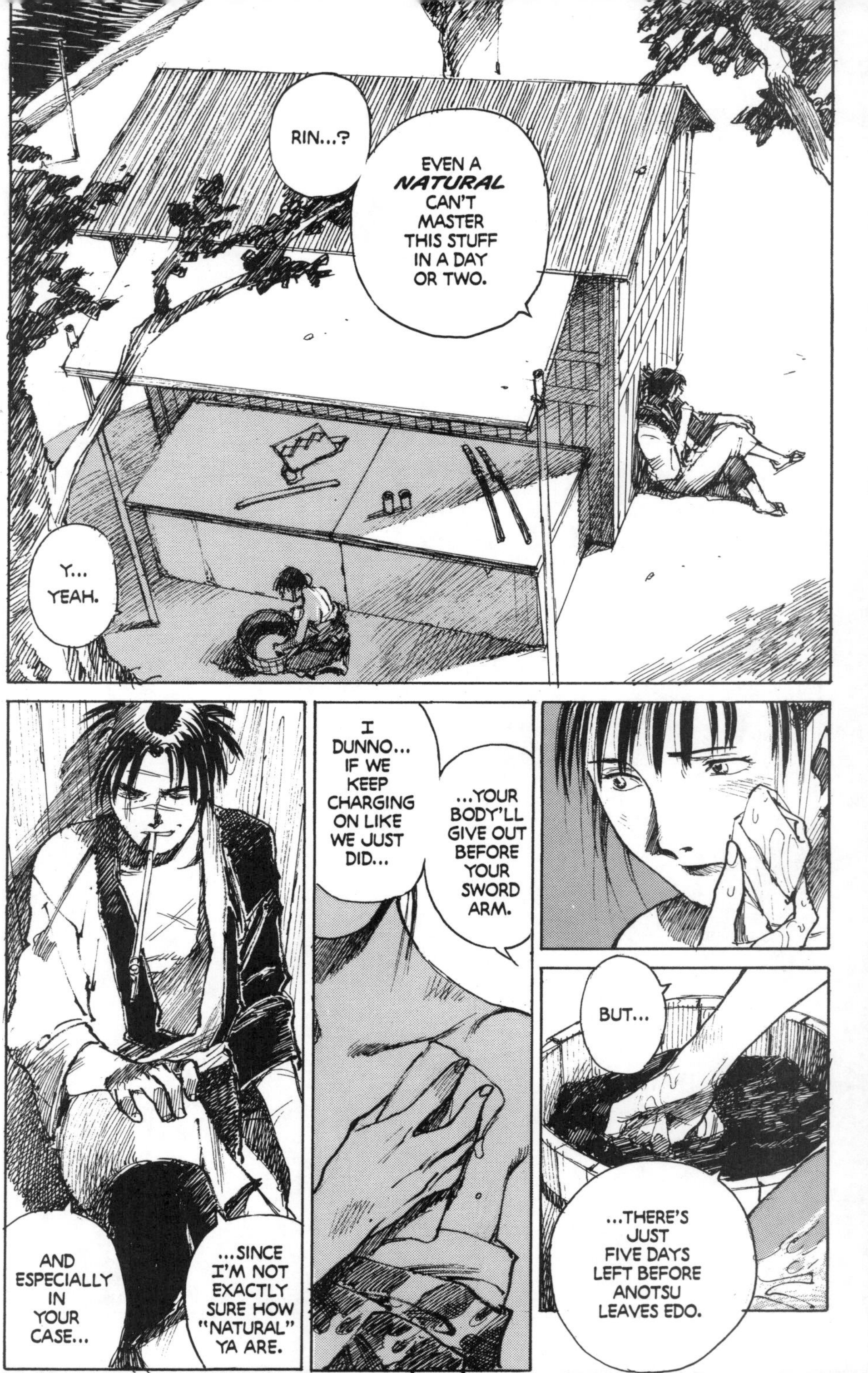
RIN...?
EVEN A NATURAL CAN'T MASTER THIS STUFF IN A DAY OR TWO.
Y... YEAH.
AND ESPECIALLY IN YOUR CASE...
...SINCE I'M NOT EXACTLY SURE HOW "NATURAL" YA ARE.
I DUNNO... IF WE KEEP CHARGING ON LIKE WE JUST DID...
...YOUR BODY'LL GIVE OUT BEFORE YOUR SWORD ARM.
BUT...
...THERE'S JUST FIVE DAYS LEFT BEFORE ANOTSU LEAVES EDO.

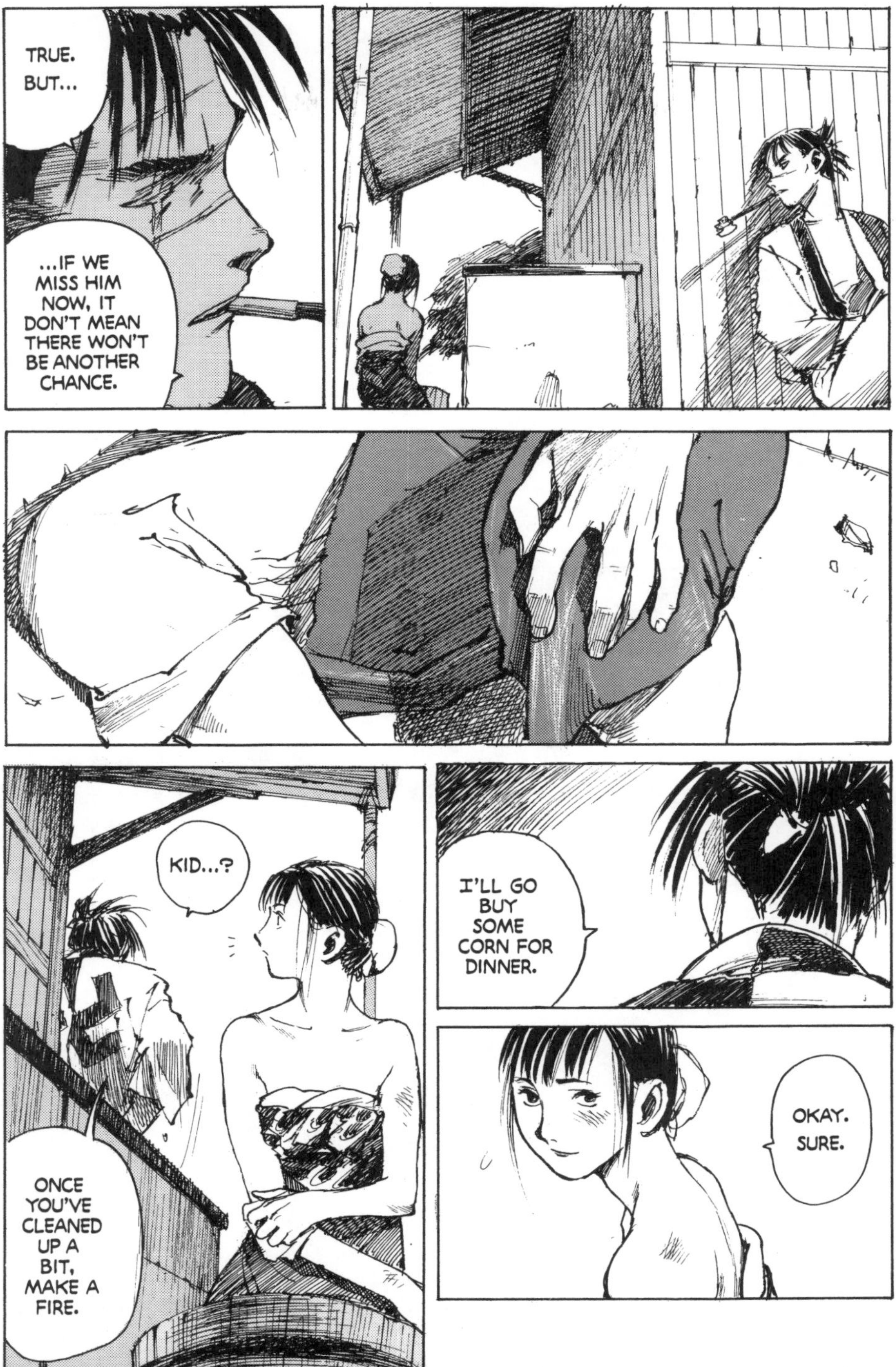
TRUE. BUT...
...IF WE MISS HIM NOW, IT DON'T MEAN THERE WON'T BE ANOTHER CHANCE.
KID...?
I'LL GO BUY SOME CORN FOR DINNER.
ONCE YOU'VE CLEANED UP A BIT, MAKE A FIRE.
OKAY. SURE.

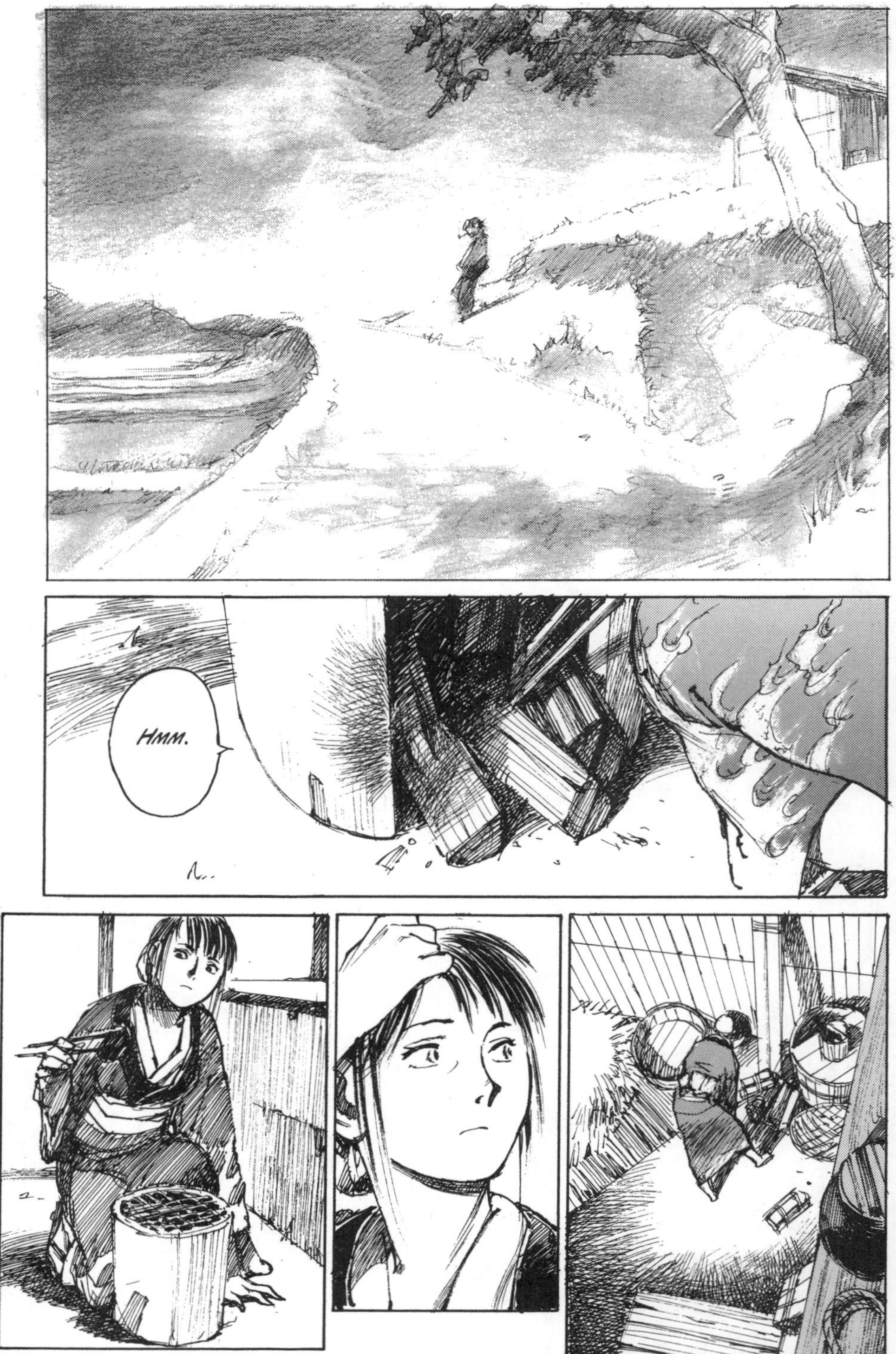
HMM.

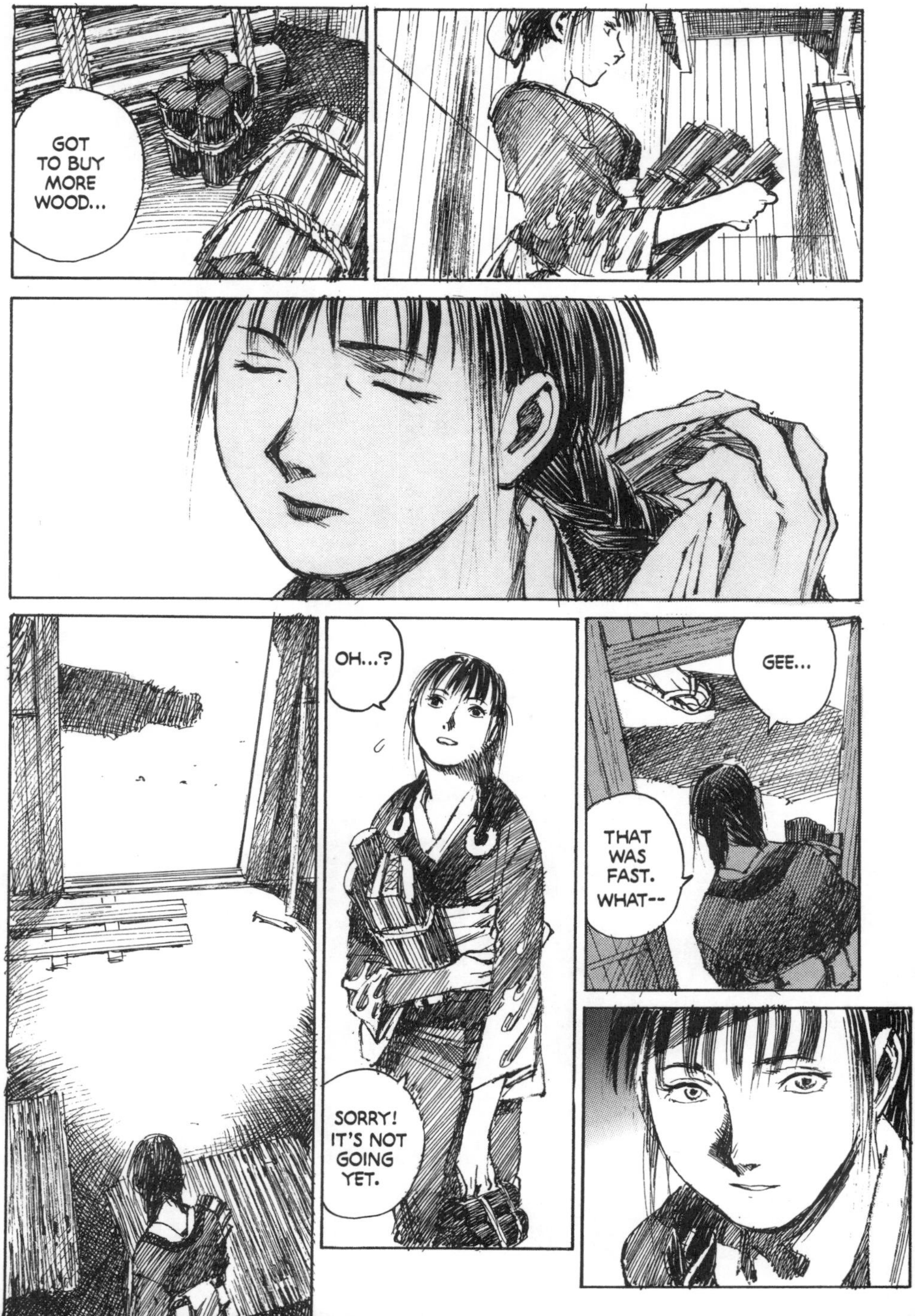
GOT TO BUY MORE WOOD...
OH...?
SORRY! IT'S NOT GOING YET.
GEE...
THAT WAS FAST. WHAT--

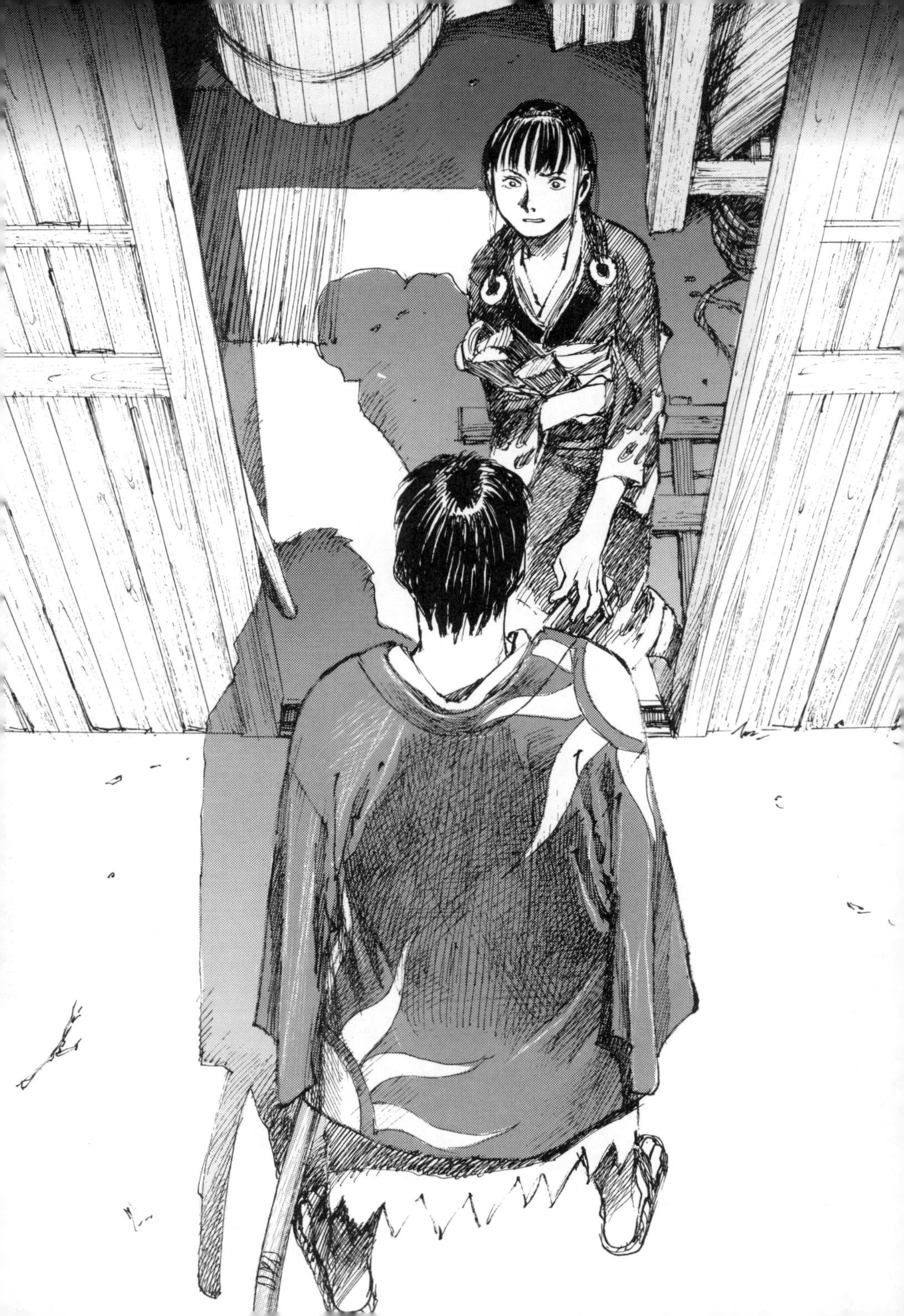

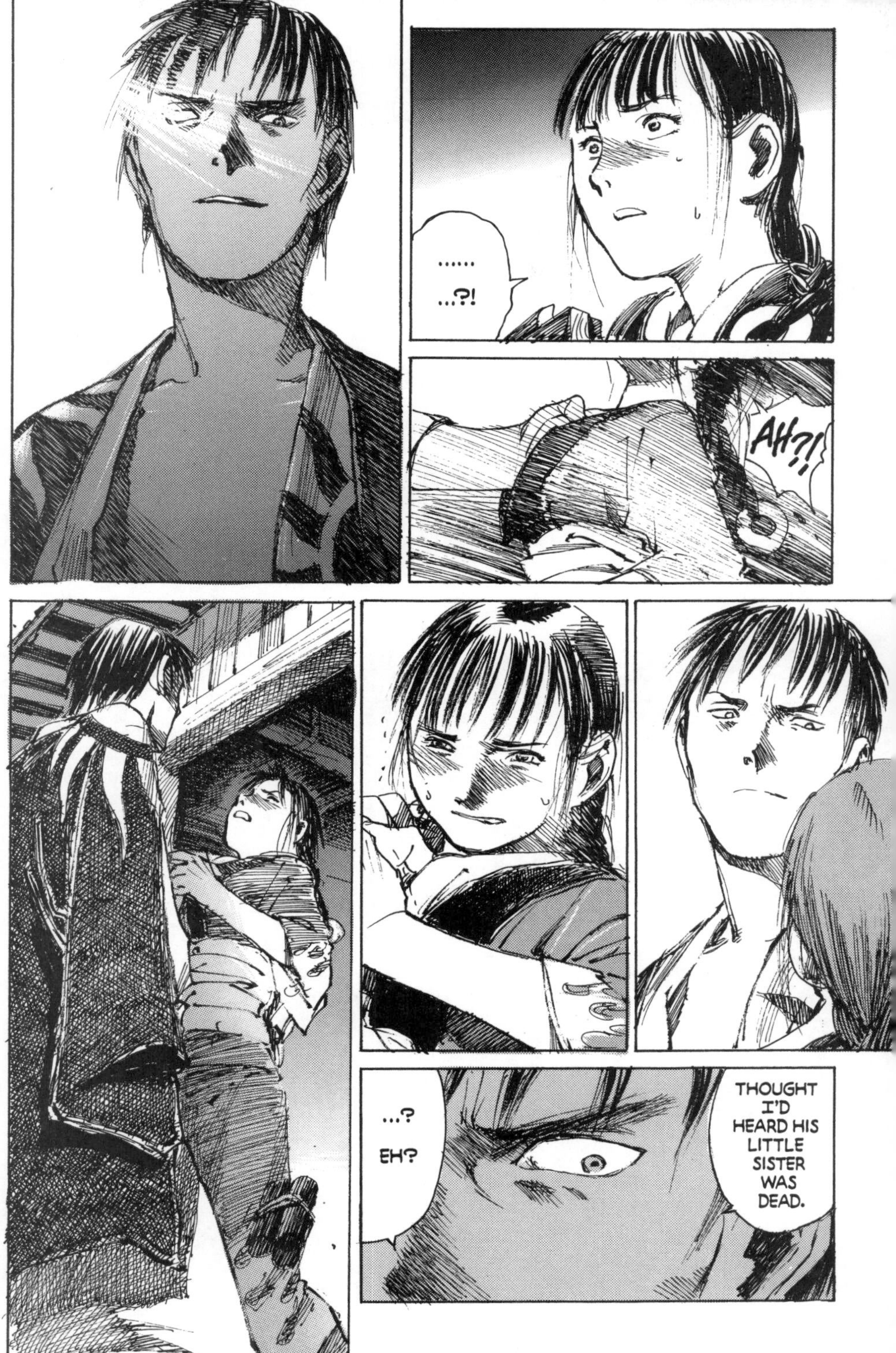
......
...?!
AH?!
...?
EH?
THOUGHT I'D HEARD HIS LITTLE SISTER WAS DEAD.

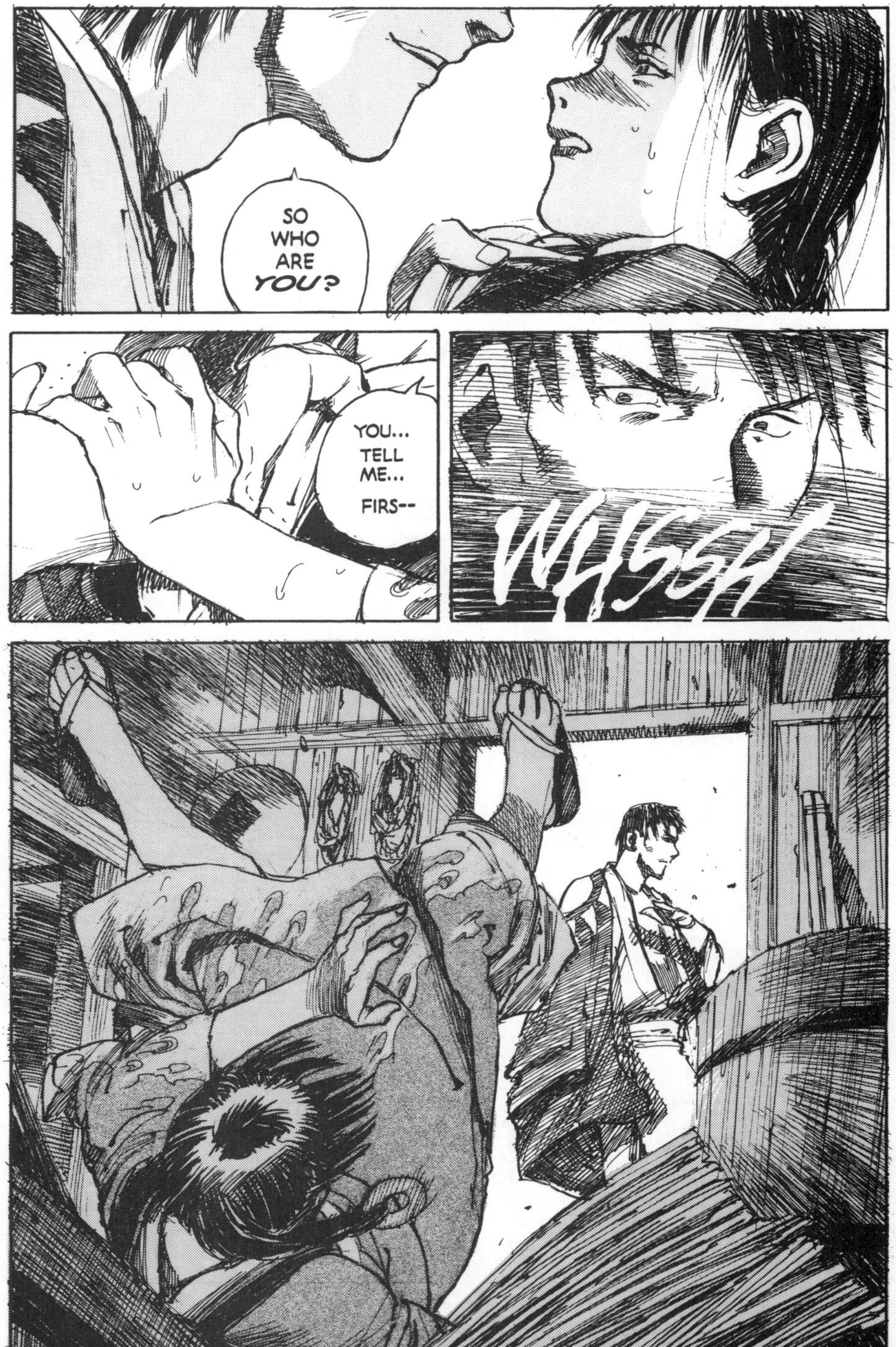
SO WHO ARE YOU?
YOU... TELL ME... FIRS--
WHSSH

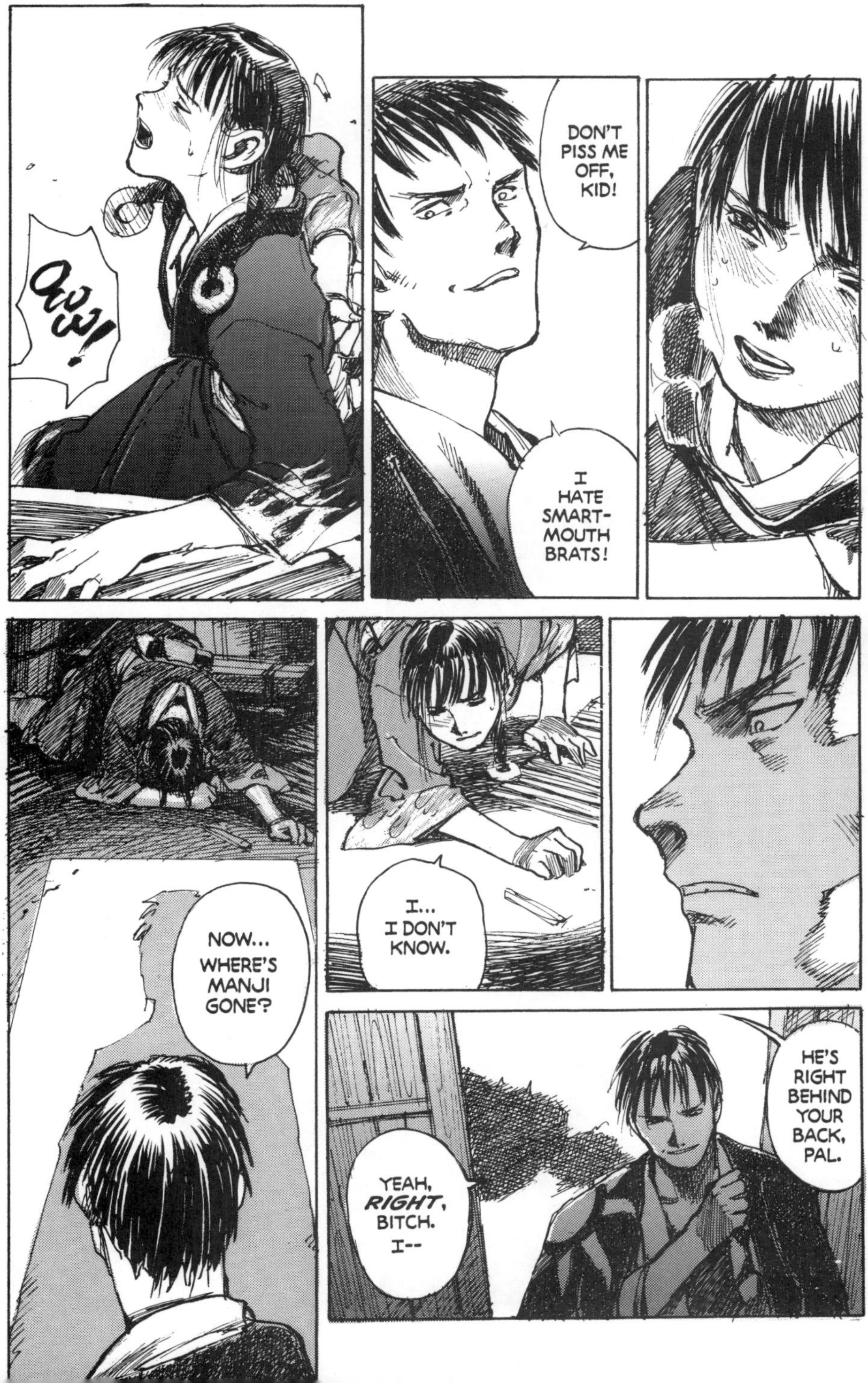
OUCH!
DON'T PISS ME OFF, KID!
I HATE SMART-MOUTH BRATS!
NOW... WHERE'S MANJI GONE?
I... I DON'T KNOW.
HE'S RIGHT BEHIND YOUR BACK, PAL.
YEAH, *RIGHT*, BITCH. I--

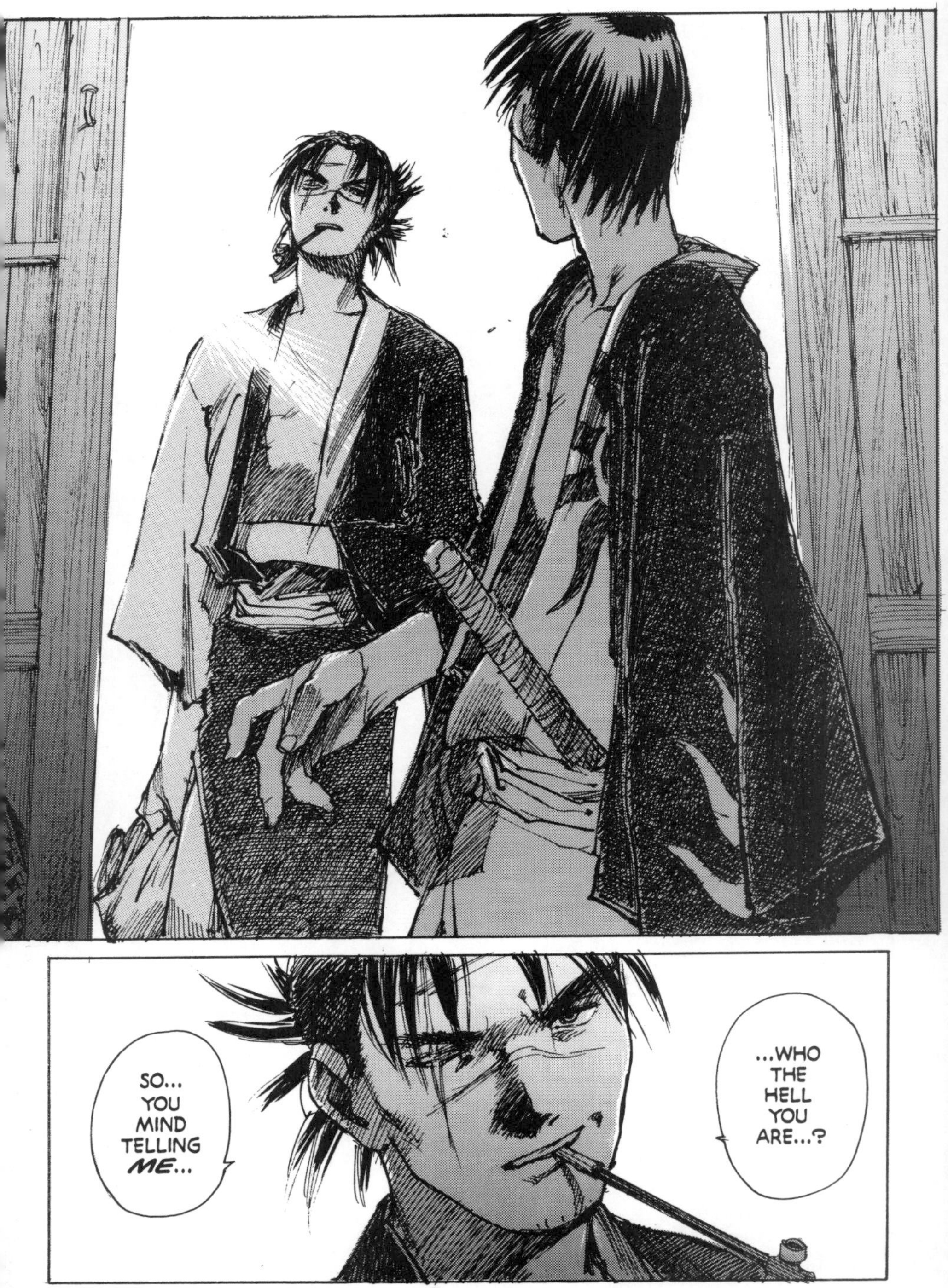
SO... YOU MIND TELLING *ME*...
...WHO THE HELL YOU ARE...?

FOOD

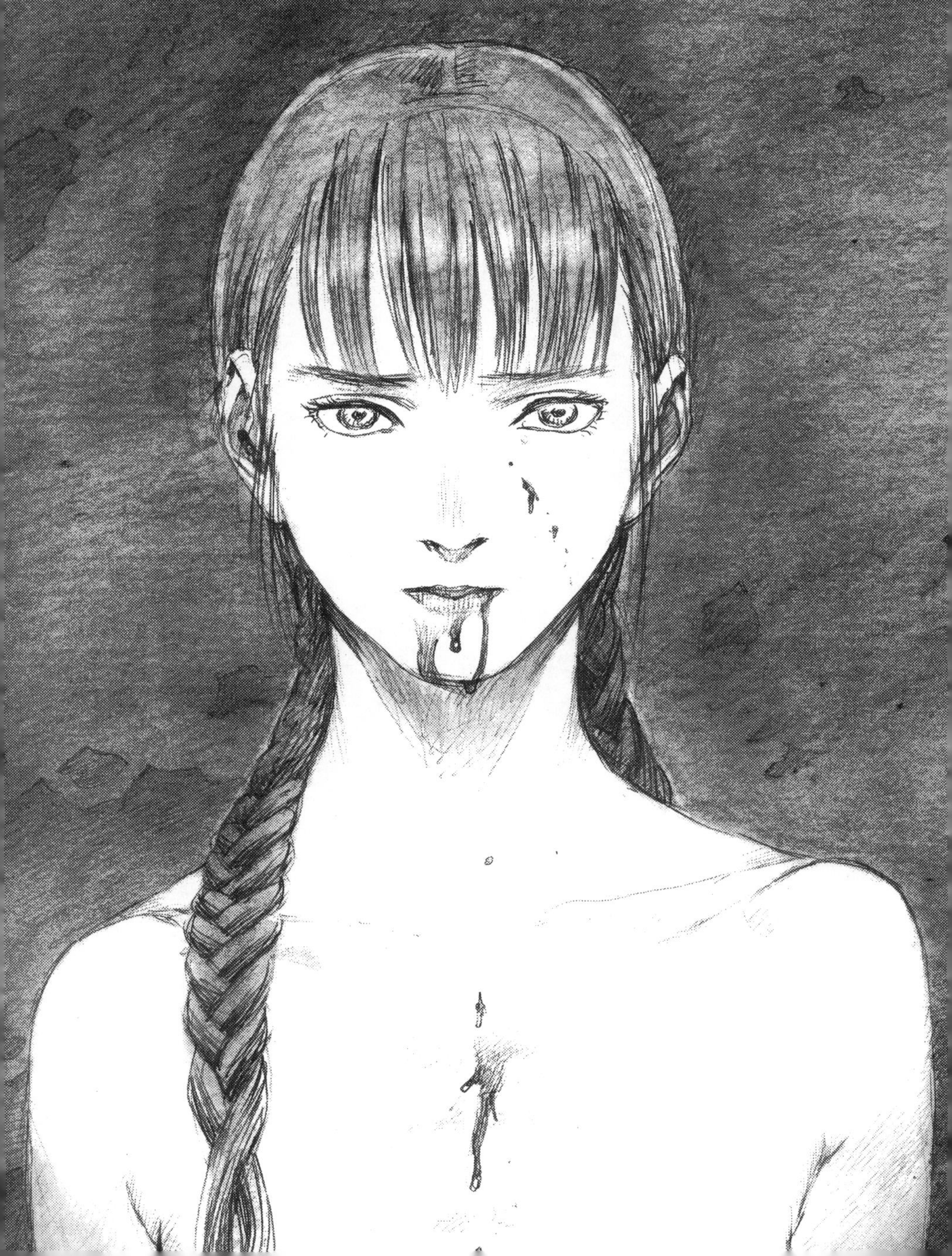

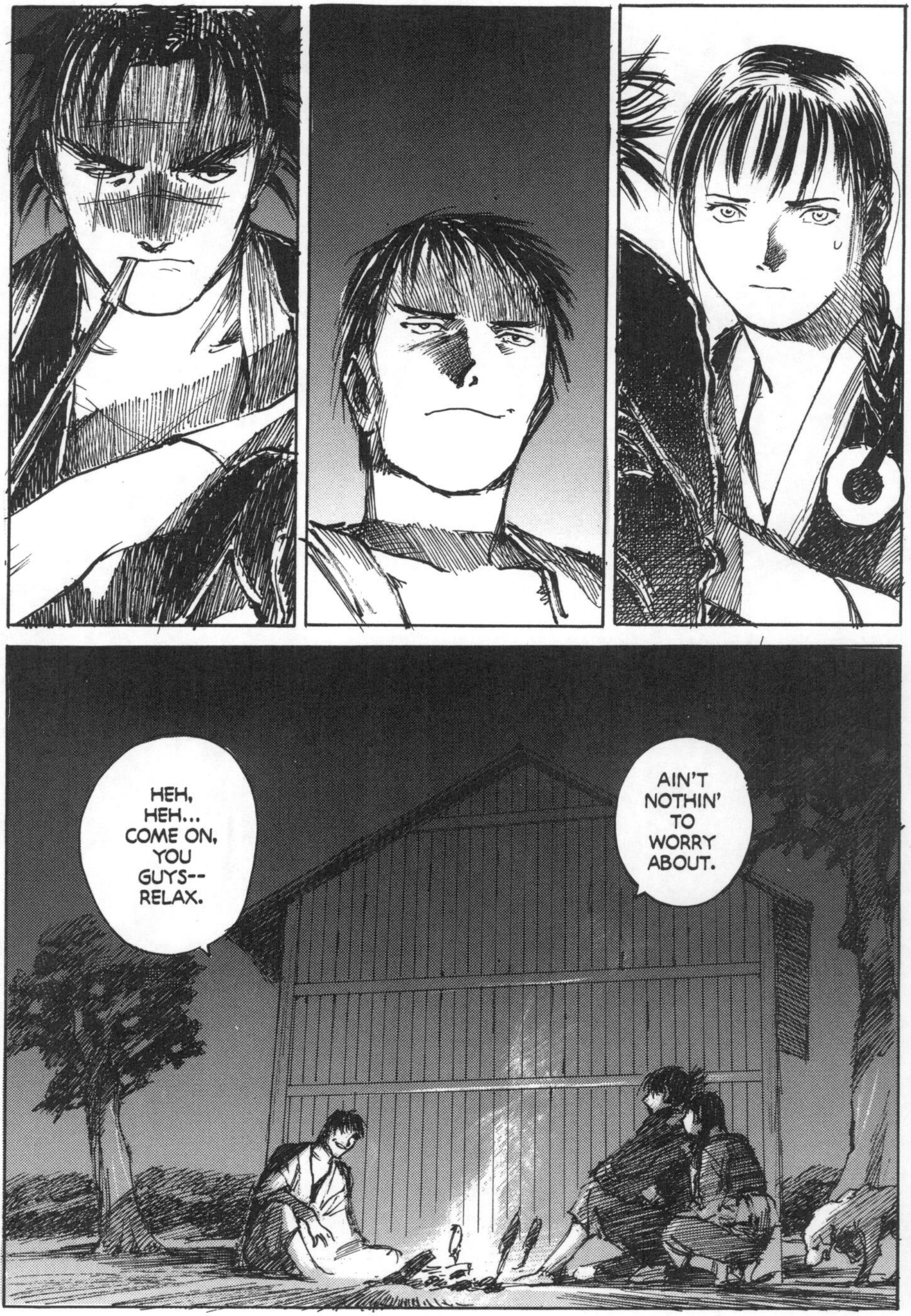
HEH, HEH... COME ON, YOU GUYS-- RELAX.
AIN'T NOTHIN' TO WORRY ABOUT.

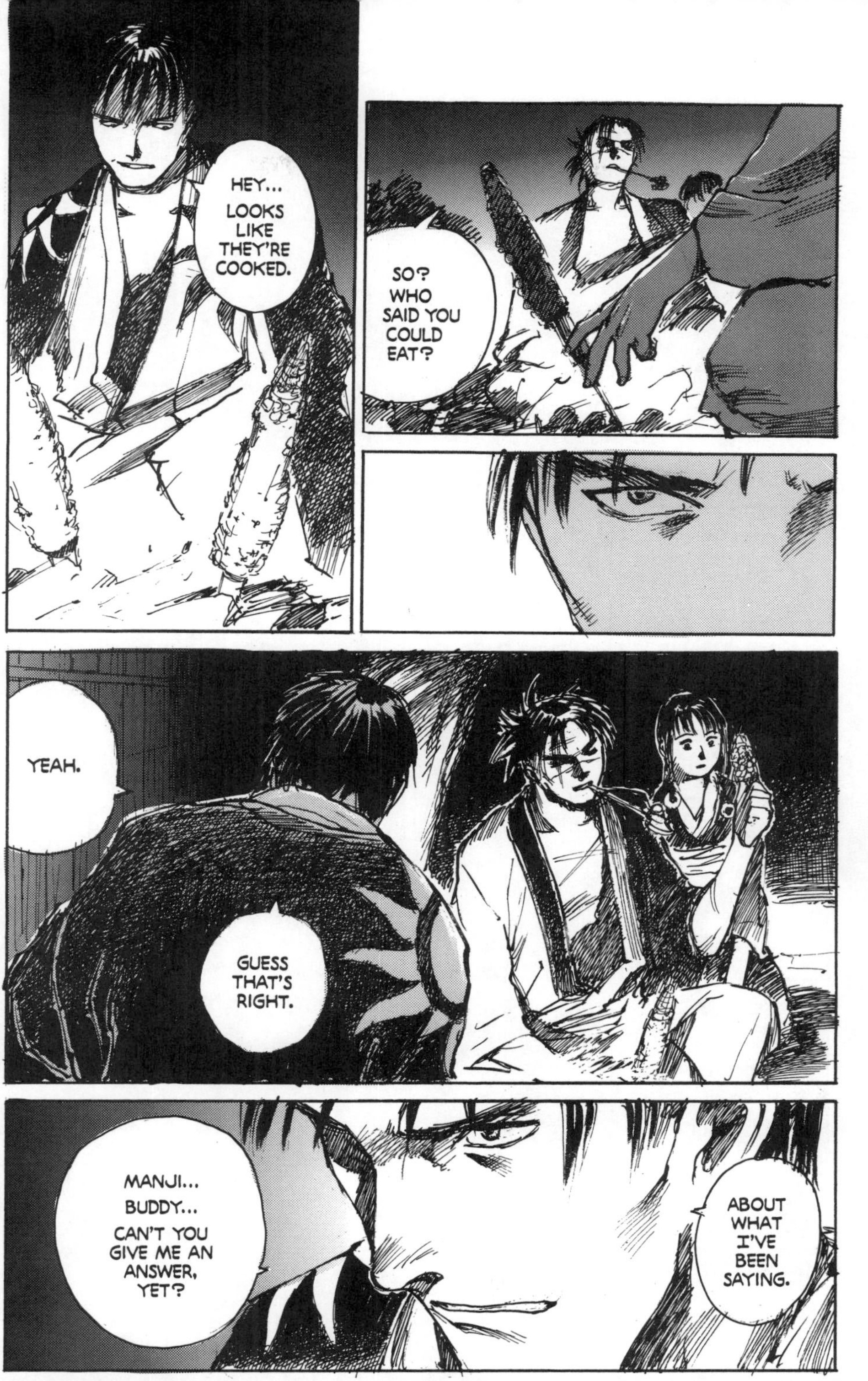
HEY... LOOKS LIKE THEY'RE COOKED.
SO? WHO SAID YOU COULD EAT?
YEAH.
GUESS THAT'S RIGHT.
MANJI... BUDDY... CAN'T YOU GIVE ME AN ANSWER, YET?
ABOUT WHAT I'VE BEEN SAYING.

YOUR SWORD SCHOOL.

MUGAI-RYU. THAT'S WHAT YOU CALLED IT, RIGHT?

I'LL TELL YOU STRAIGHT--

--I AIN'T NEVER HEARD OF IT.

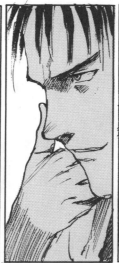

WE'RE A PISSANT LITTLE OUTFIT, JUST BORN YESTERDAY, PRACTICALLY.

SO HELL, AIN'T NO WONDER.

COUNTING ME, THERE'S ONLY EIGHT OF US.

SNAK

NAW, WAIT-- TWO OF 'EM CROAKED... SO MAKE IT SIX, HUH? HEH, HEH.

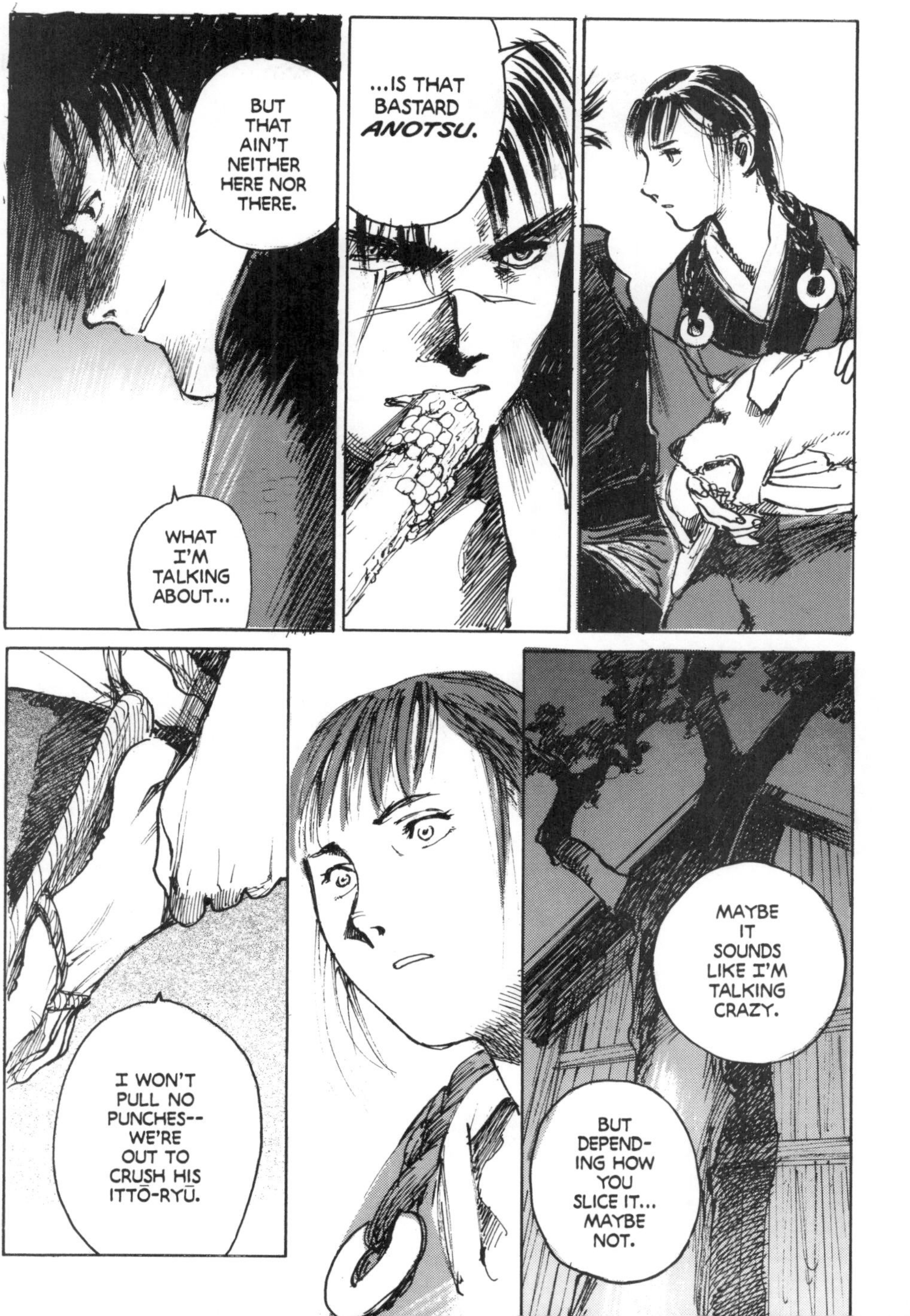
BUT THAT AIN'T NEITHER HERE NOR THERE.
WHAT I'M TALKING ABOUT...
...IS THAT BASTARD *ANOTSU.*
I WON'T PULL NO PUNCHES-- WE'RE OUT TO CRUSH HIS ITTŌ-RYŪ.
MAYBE IT SOUNDS LIKE I'M TALKING CRAZY.
BUT DEPEND-ING HOW YOU SLICE IT... MAYBE NOT.

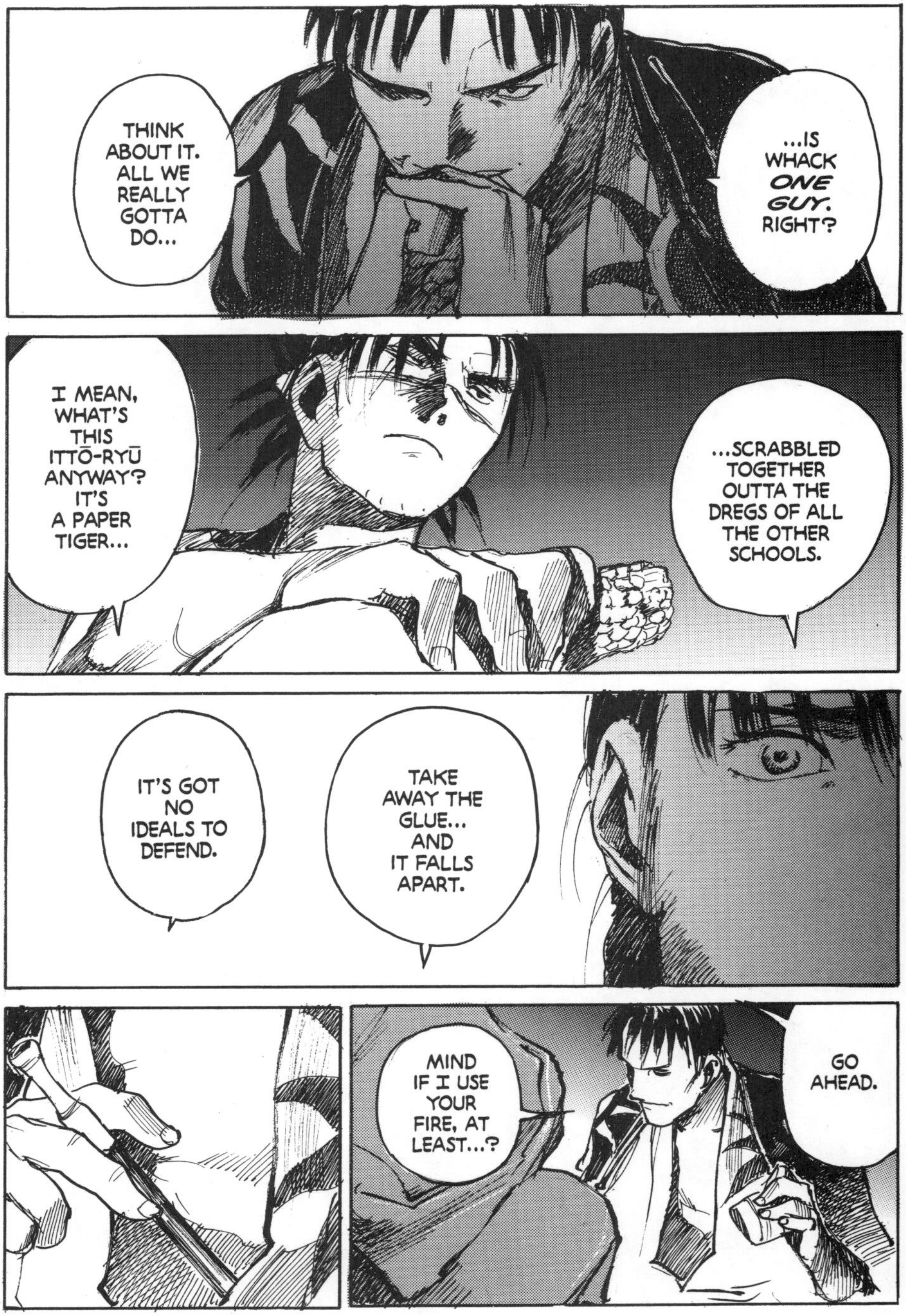
THINK ABOUT IT. ALL WE REALLY GOTTA DO...
...IS WHACK *ONE GUY*. RIGHT?
I MEAN, WHAT'S THIS ITTŌ-RYŪ ANYWAY? IT'S A PAPER TIGER...
...SCRABBLED TOGETHER OUTTA THE DREGS OF ALL THE OTHER SCHOOLS.
IT'S GOT NO IDEALS TO DEFEND.
TAKE AWAY THE GLUE... AND IT FALLS APART.
MIND IF I USE YOUR FIRE, AT LEAST...?
GO AHEAD.

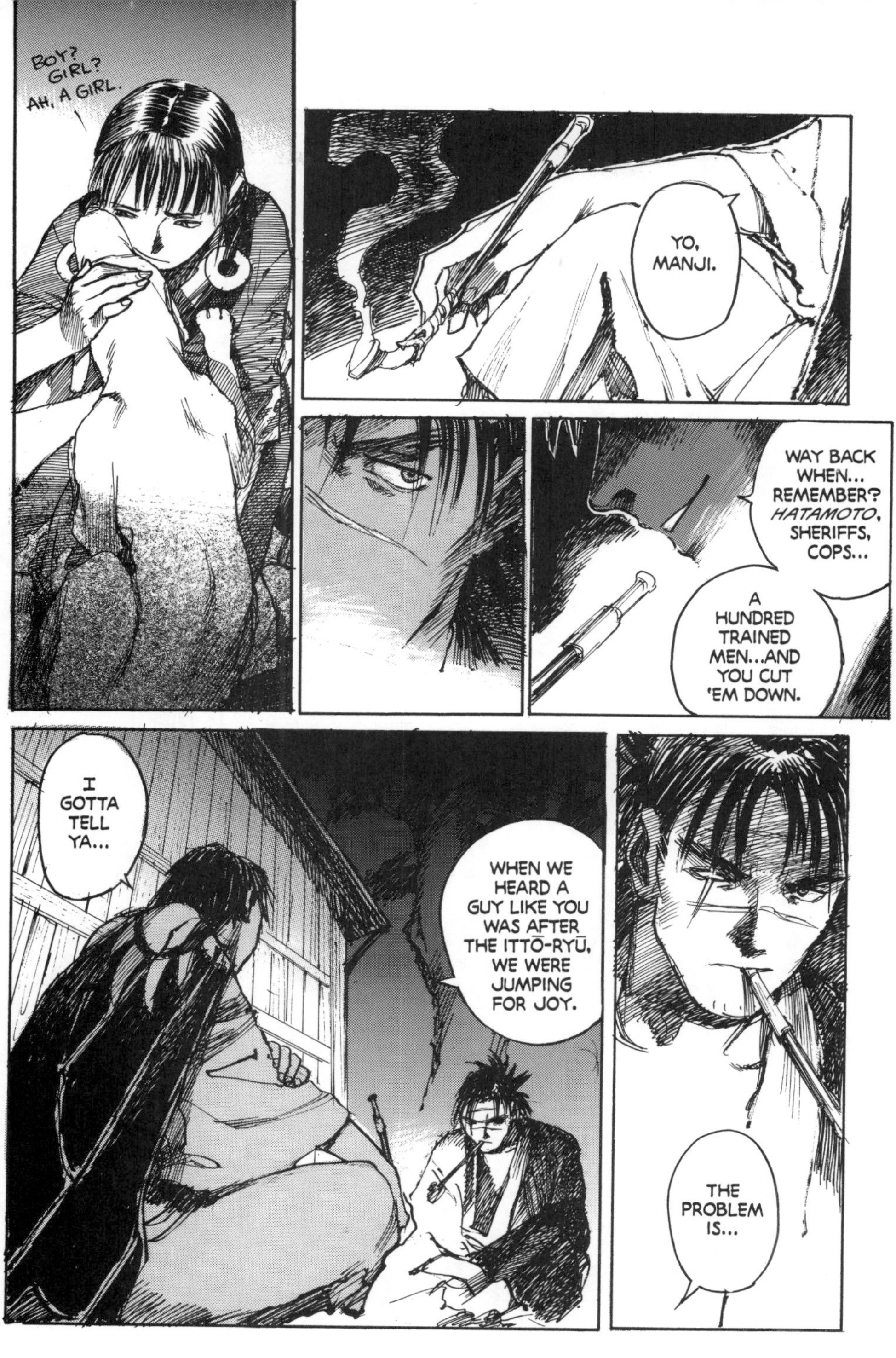

BOY? GIRL? AH, A GIRL.
YO, MANJI.
WAY BACK WHEN... REMEMBER? *HATAMOTO*, SHERIFFS, COPS...
A HUNDRED TRAINED MEN...AND YOU CUT 'EM DOWN.
I GOTTA TELL YA...
WHEN WE HEARD A GUY LIKE YOU WAS AFTER THE ITTŌ-RYŪ, WE WERE JUMPING FOR JOY.
THE PROBLEM IS...

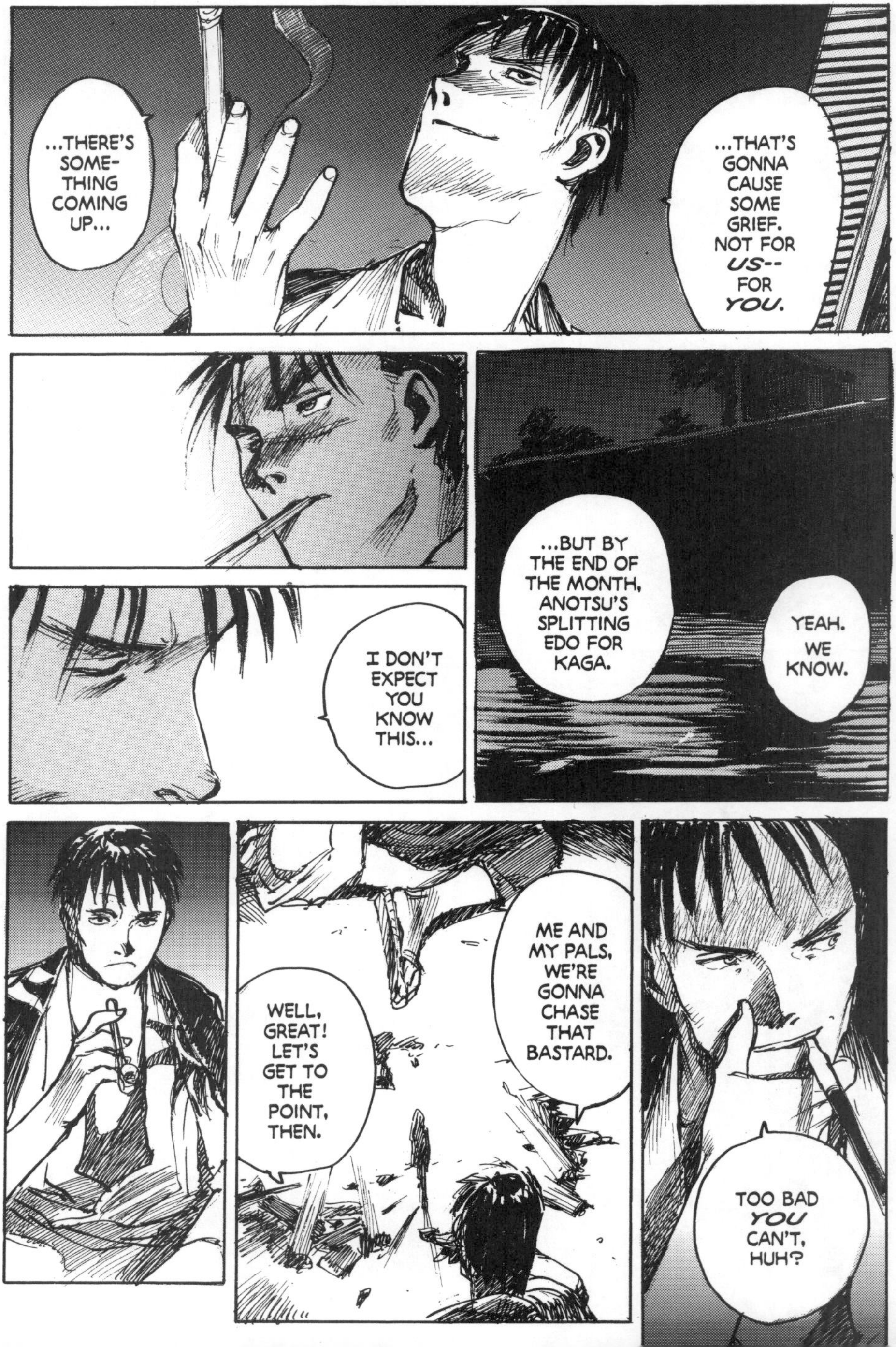
...THERE'S SOME-THING COMING UP...
...THAT'S GONNA CAUSE SOME GRIEF. NOT FOR *US*-- FOR *YOU*.
I DON'T EXPECT YOU KNOW THIS...
...BUT BY THE END OF THE MONTH, ANOTSU'S SPLITTING EDO FOR KAGA.
YEAH. WE KNOW.
WELL, GREAT! LET'S GET TO THE POINT, THEN.
ME AND MY PALS, WE'RE GONNA CHASE THAT BASTARD.
TOO BAD *YOU* CAN'T, HUH?

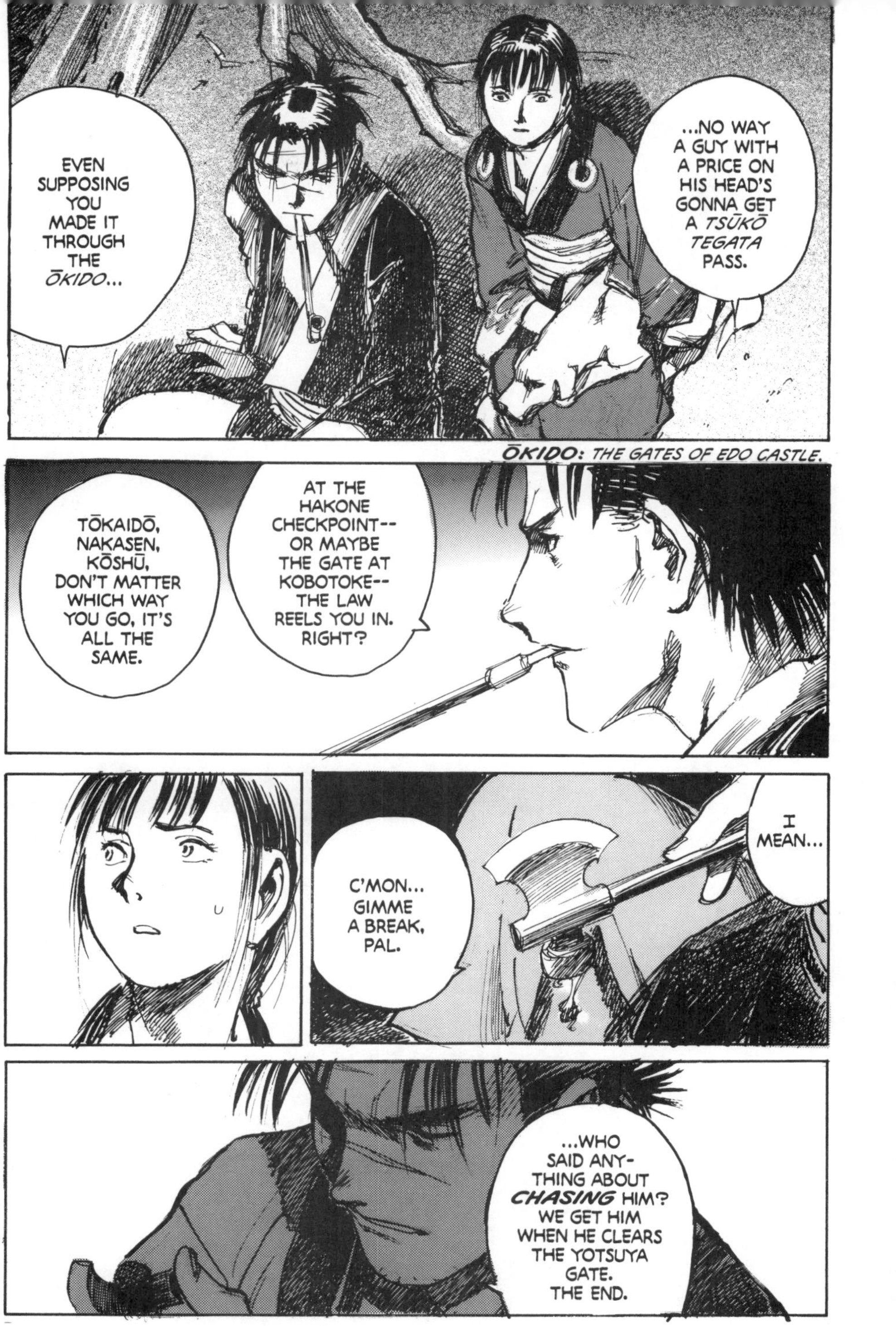
EVEN SUPPOSING YOU MADE IT THROUGH THE *ŌKIDO*...
...NO WAY A GUY WITH A PRICE ON HIS HEAD'S GONNA GET A *TSŪKŌ TEGATA* PASS.
ŌKIDO: THE GATES OF EDO CASTLE.
TŌKAIDŌ, NAKASEN, KŌSHŪ, DON'T MATTER WHICH WAY YOU GO, IT'S ALL THE SAME.
AT THE HAKONE CHECKPOINT-- OR MAYBE THE GATE AT KOBOTOKE-- THE LAW REELS YOU IN. RIGHT?
C'MON... GIMME A BREAK, PAL.
I MEAN...
...WHO SAID ANYTHING ABOUT ***CHASING*** HIM? WE GET HIM WHEN HE CLEARS THE YOTSUYA GATE. THE END.

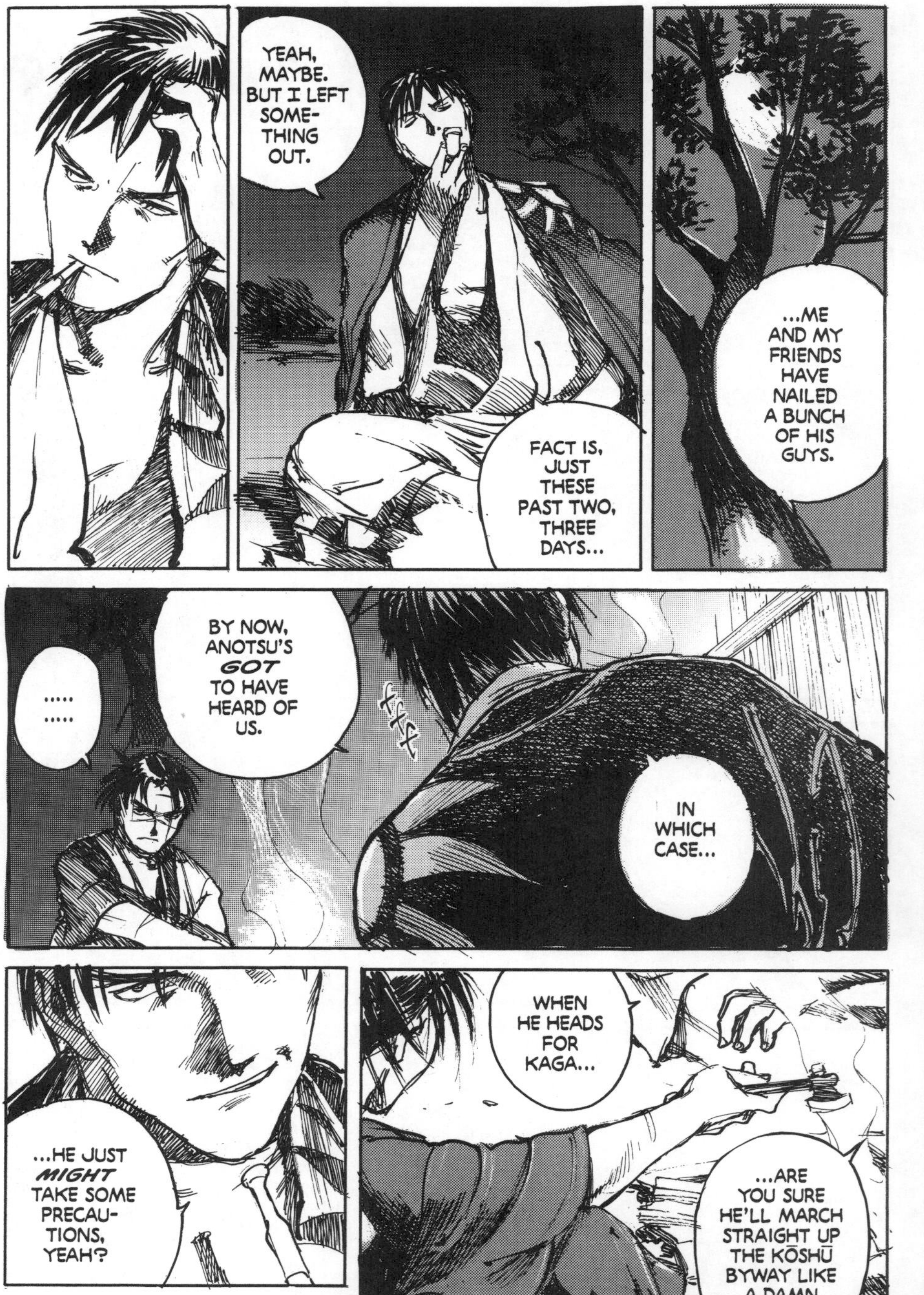
YEAH, MAYBE. BUT I LEFT SOME-THING OUT.
FACT IS, JUST THESE PAST TWO, THREE DAYS...
...ME AND MY FRIENDS HAVE NAILED A BUNCH OF HIS GUYS.
.....
.....
BY NOW, ANOTSU'S *GOT* TO HAVE HEARD OF US.
IN WHICH CASE...
...HE JUST *MIGHT* TAKE SOME PRECAU-TIONS, YEAH?
WHEN HE HEADS FOR KAGA...
...ARE YOU SURE HE'LL MARCH STRAIGHT UP THE KŌSHŪ BYWAY LIKE A DAMN FOOL?

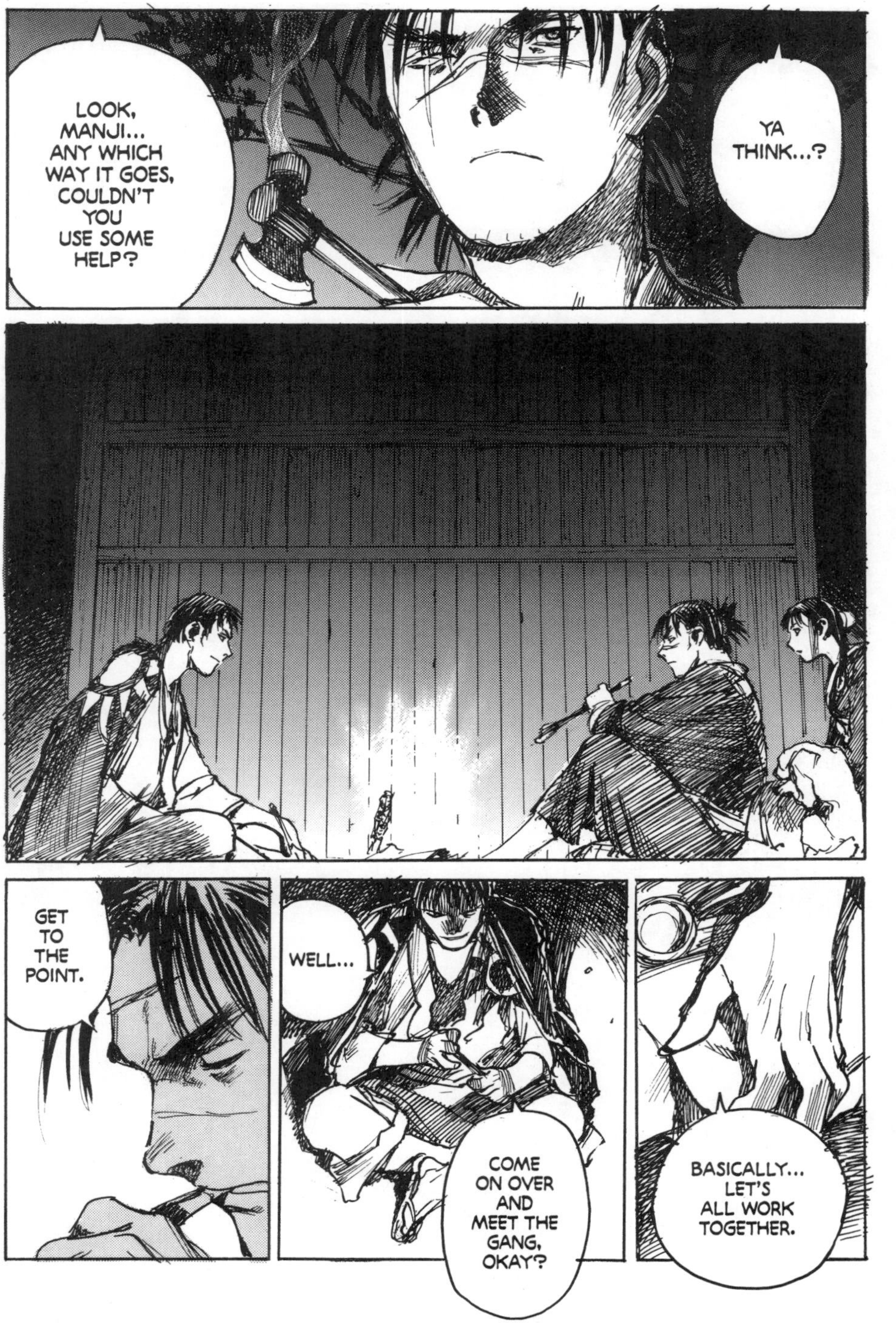

LOOK, MANJI... ANY WHICH WAY IT GOES, COULDN'T YOU USE SOME HELP?
YA THINK...?
GET TO THE POINT.
WELL...
COME ON OVER AND MEET THE GANG, OKAY?
BASICALLY... LET'S ALL WORK TOGETHER.

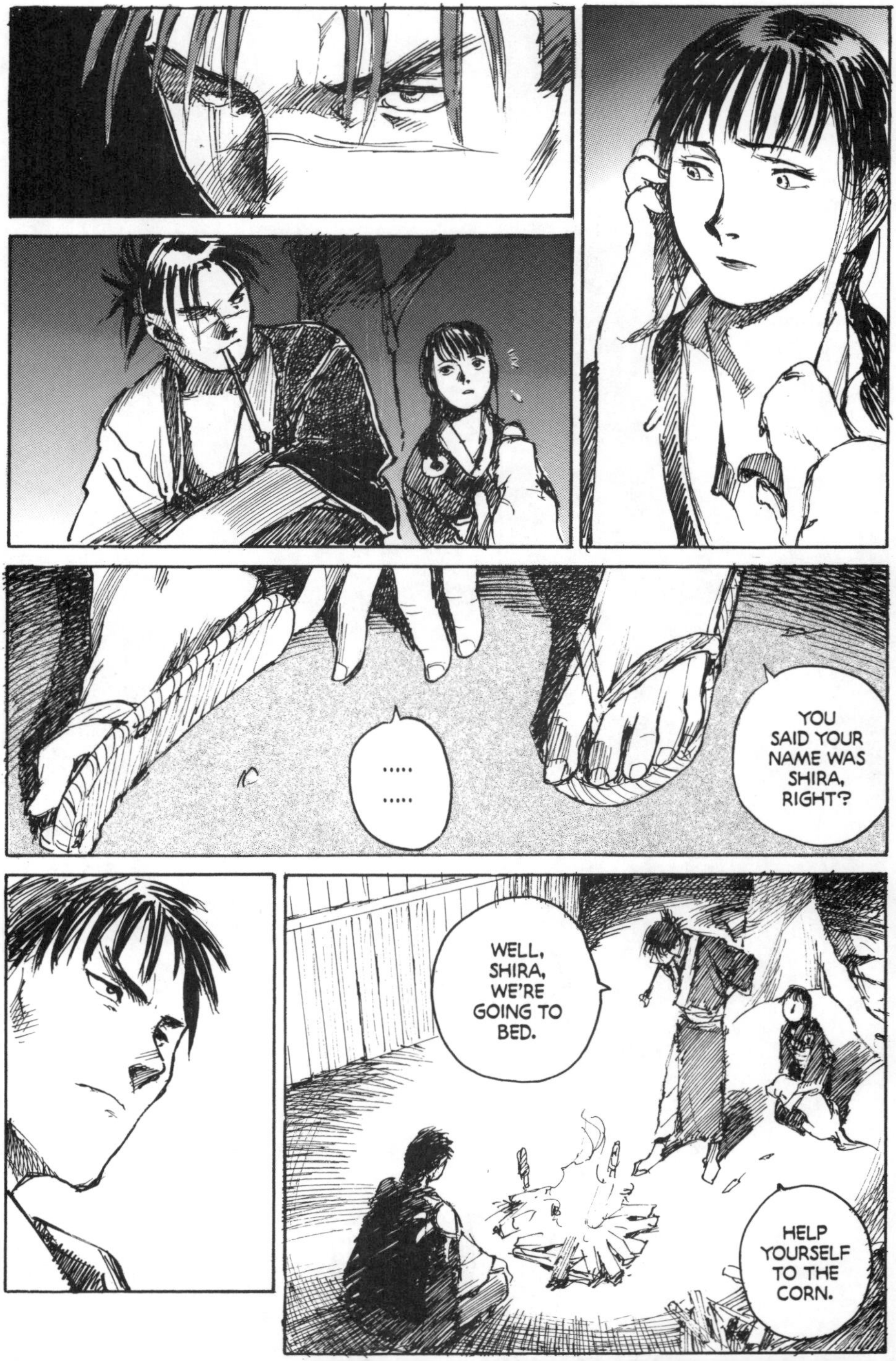
.....
.....
YOU SAID YOUR NAME WAS SHIRA, RIGHT?
WELL, SHIRA, WE'RE GOING TO BED.
HELP YOURSELF TO THE CORN.

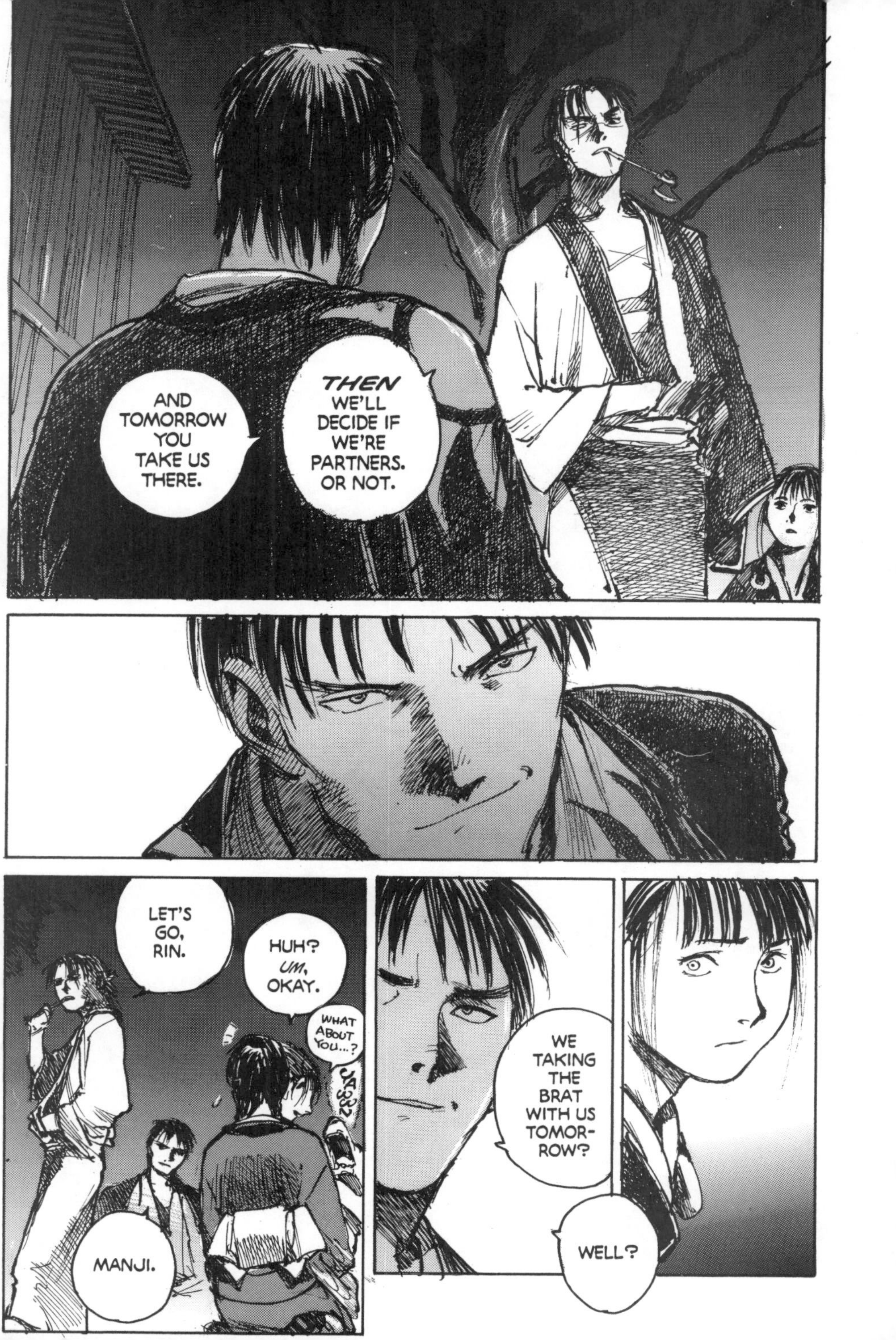
AND TOMORROW YOU TAKE US THERE.
THEN WE'LL DECIDE IF WE'RE PARTNERS. OR NOT.
LET'S GO, RIN.
HUH? *UM*, OKAY.
WHAT ABOUT YOU...?
MANJI.
WE TAKING THE BRAT WITH US TOMOR-ROW?
WELL?

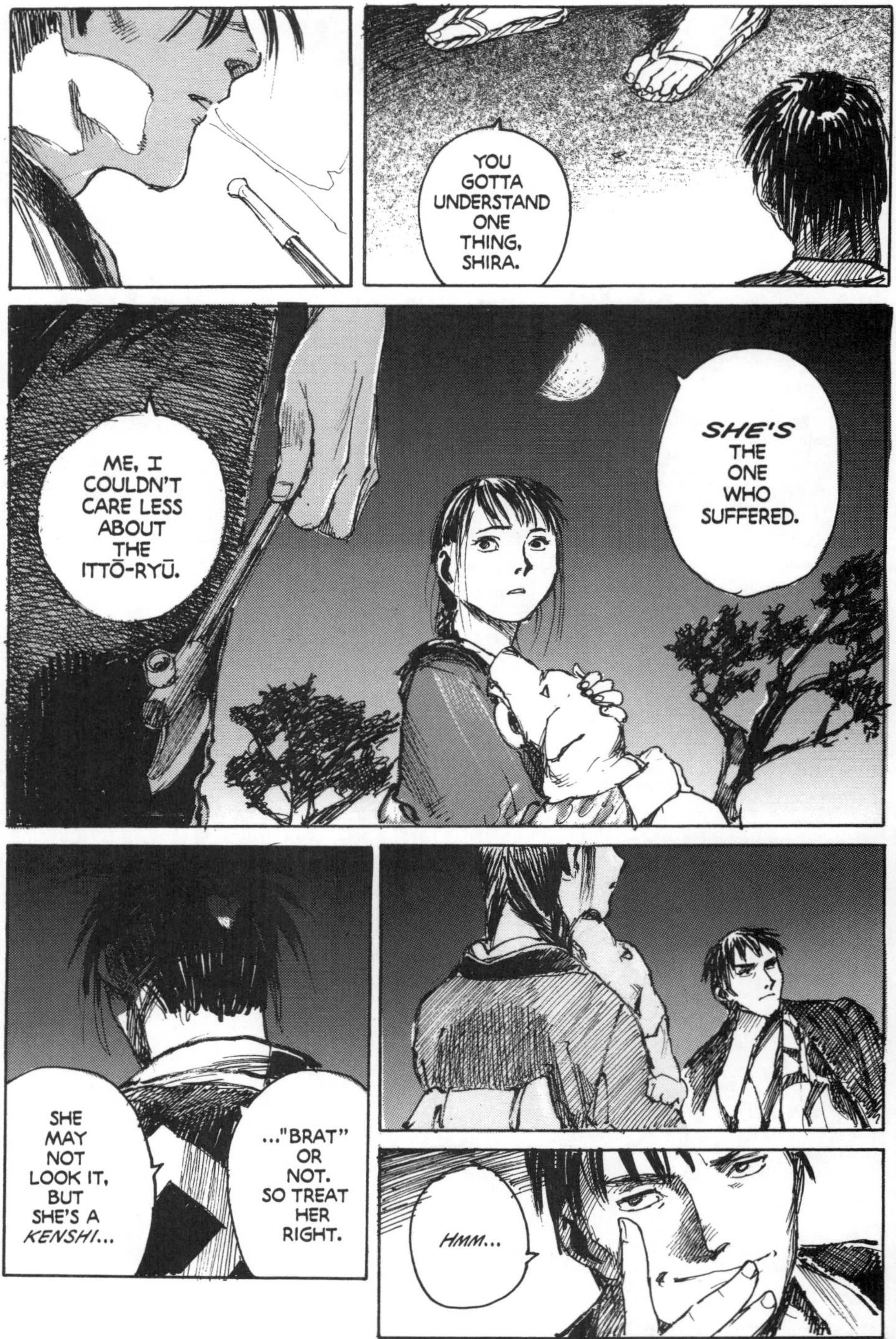
YOU GOTTA UNDERSTAND ONE THING, SHIRA.
ME, I COULDN'T CARE LESS ABOUT THE ITTŌ-RYŪ.
SHE'S THE ONE WHO SUFFERED.
SHE MAY NOT LOOK IT, BUT SHE'S A *KENSHI*...
..."BRAT" OR NOT. SO TREAT HER RIGHT.
HMM...

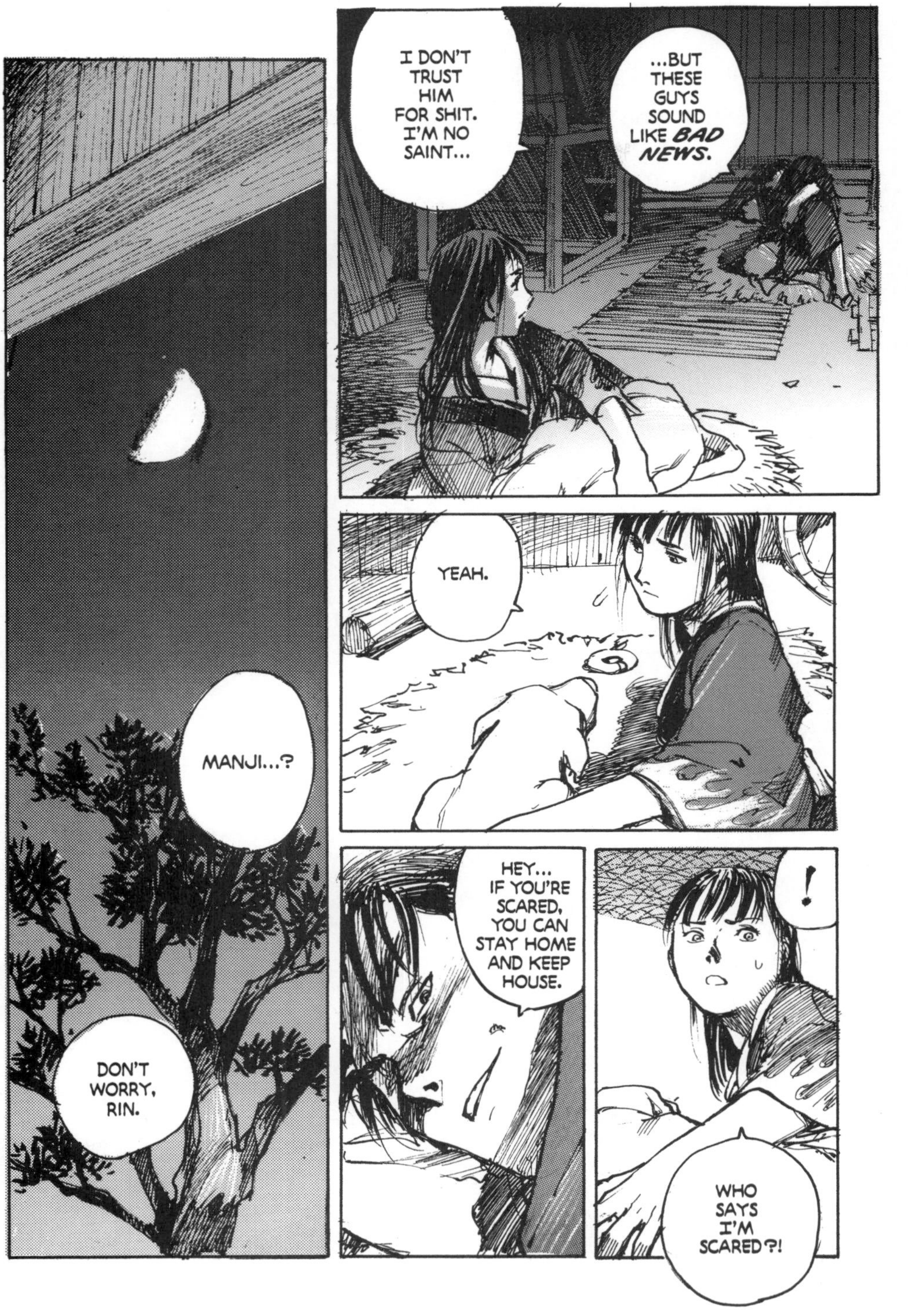
MANJI...?
DON'T WORRY, RIN.
I DON'T TRUST HIM FOR SHIT. I'M NO SAINT...
...BUT THESE GUYS SOUND LIKE BAD NEWS.
YEAH.
HEY... IF YOU'RE SCARED, YOU CAN STAY HOME AND KEEP HOUSE.
!
WHO SAYS I'M SCARED?!

IT'S JUST... THAT GUY. HIS EYES...

...THEY AREN'T... *NORMAL.*

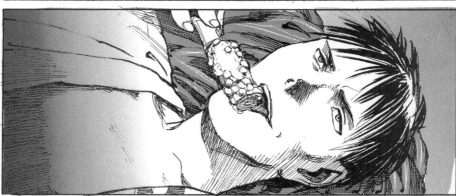

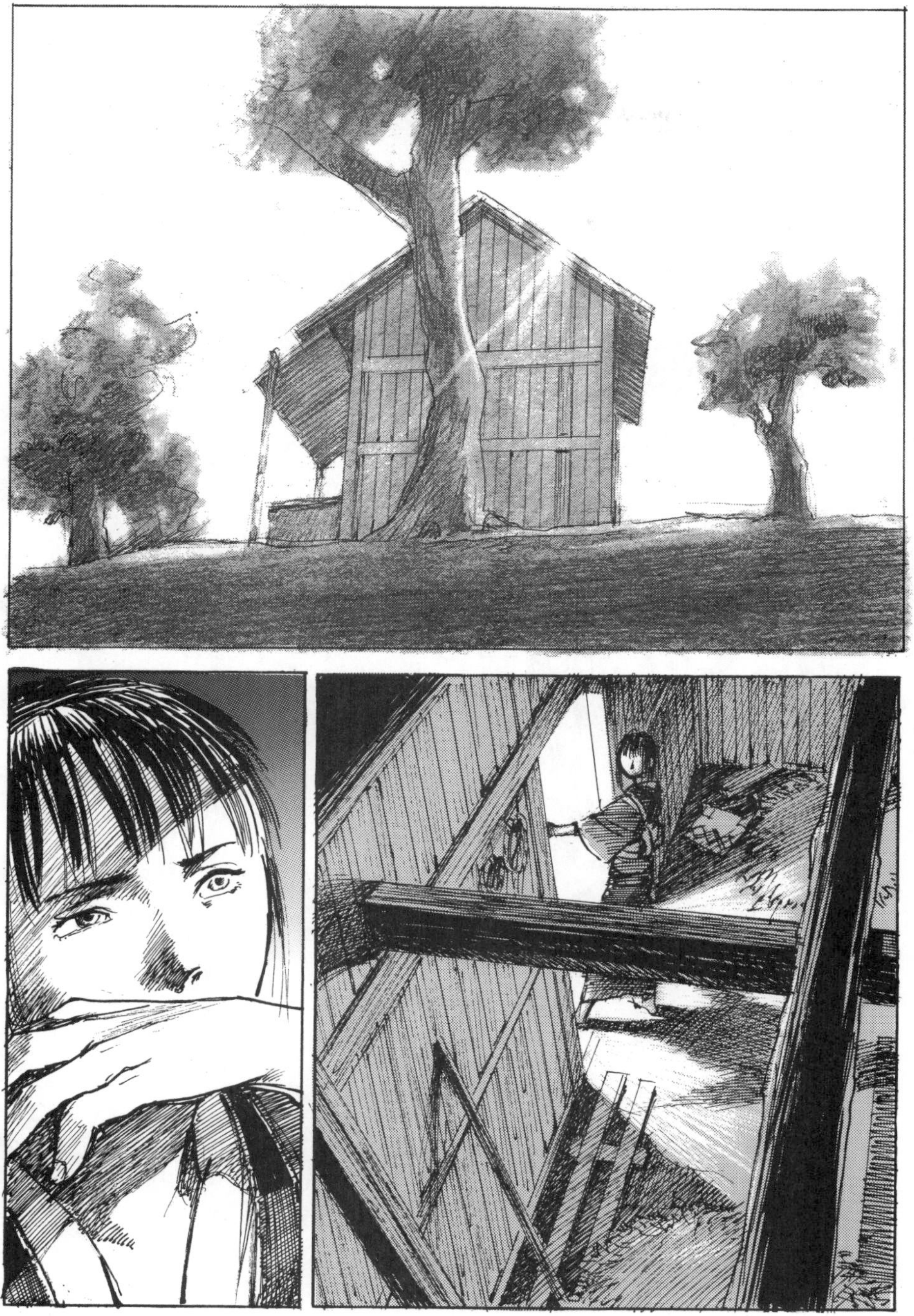

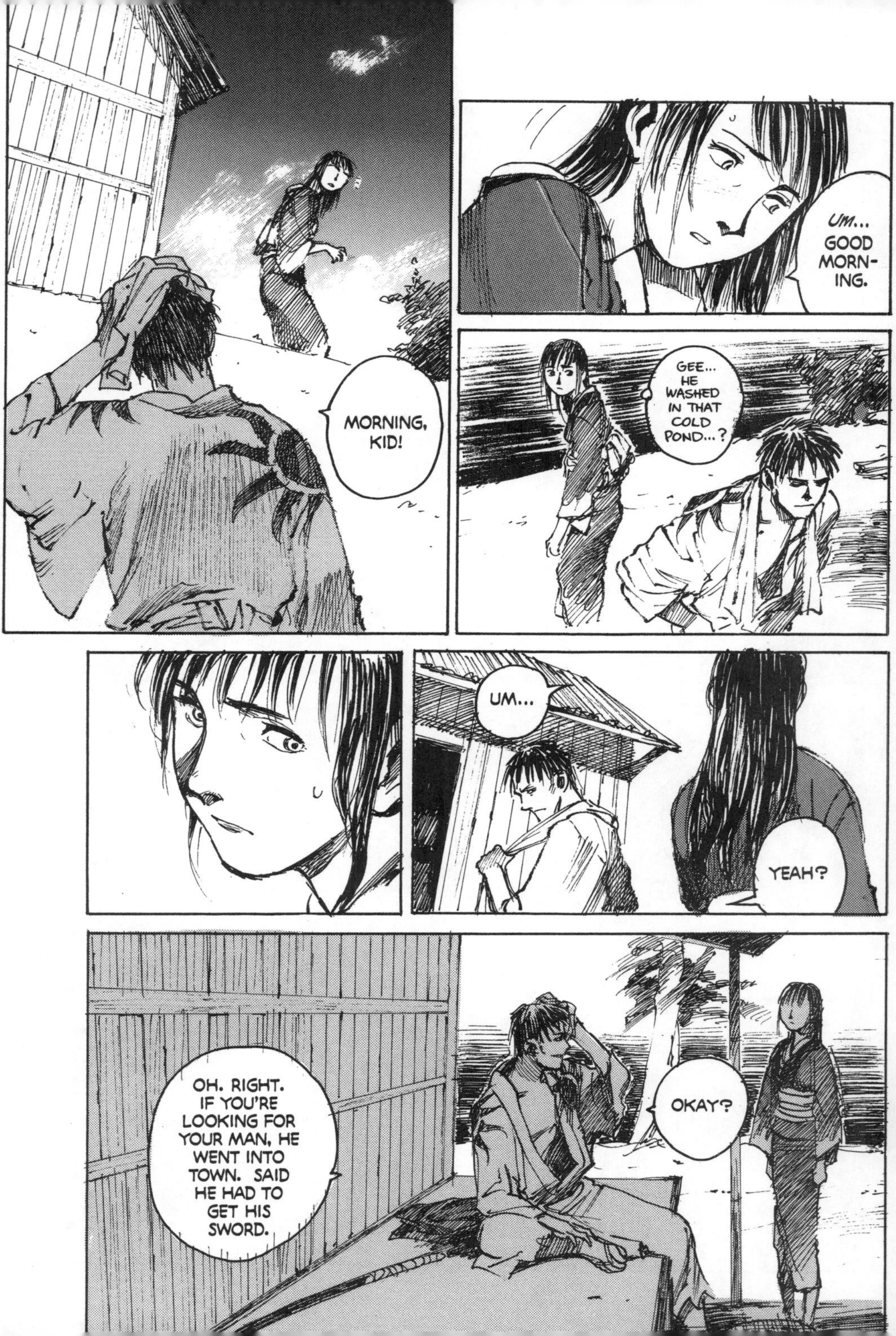
MORNING, KID!
UM... GOOD MORNING.
GEE... HE WASHED IN THAT COLD POND...?
UM...
YEAH?
OH. RIGHT. IF YOU'RE LOOKING FOR YOUR MAN, HE WENT INTO TOWN. SAID HE HAD TO GET HIS SWORD.
OKAY?

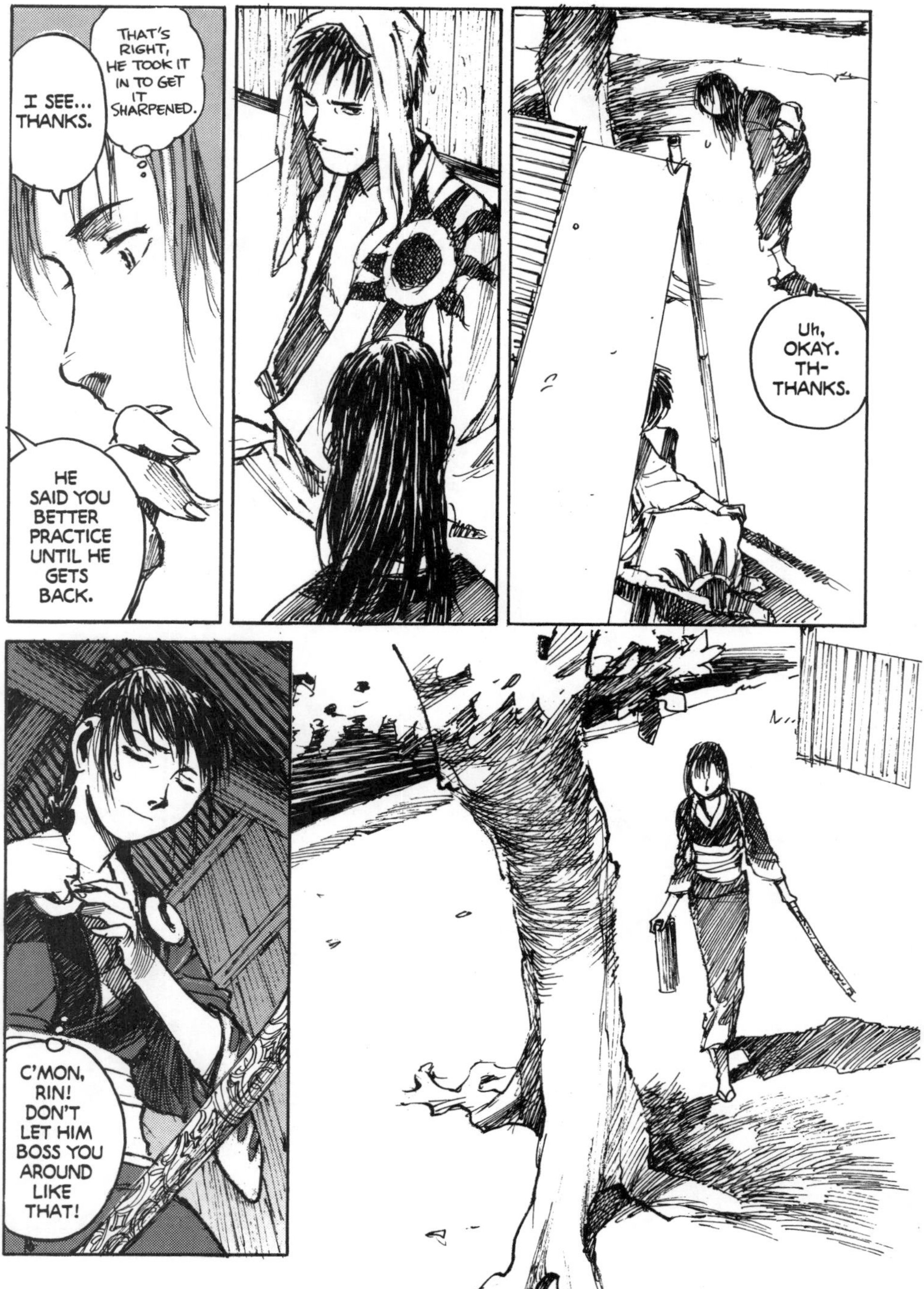
THAT'S RIGHT, HE TOOK IT IN TO GET IT SHARPENED.
I SEE... THANKS.
HE SAID YOU BETTER PRACTICE UNTIL HE GETS BACK.
Uh, OKAY. TH- THANKS.
C'MON, RIN! DON'T LET HIM BOSS YOU AROUND LIKE THAT!

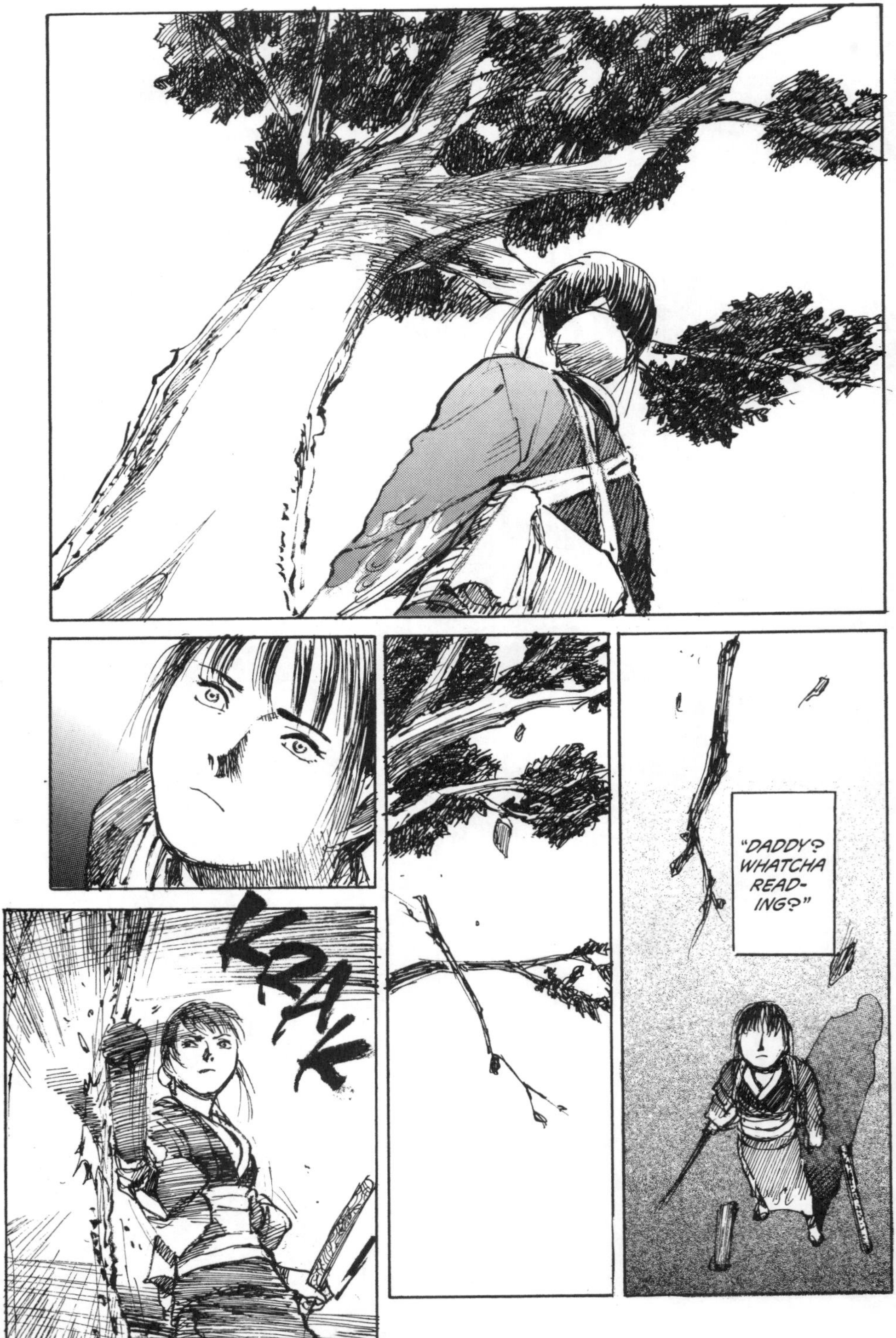
KRAK
"DADDY? WHATCHA READ-ING?"

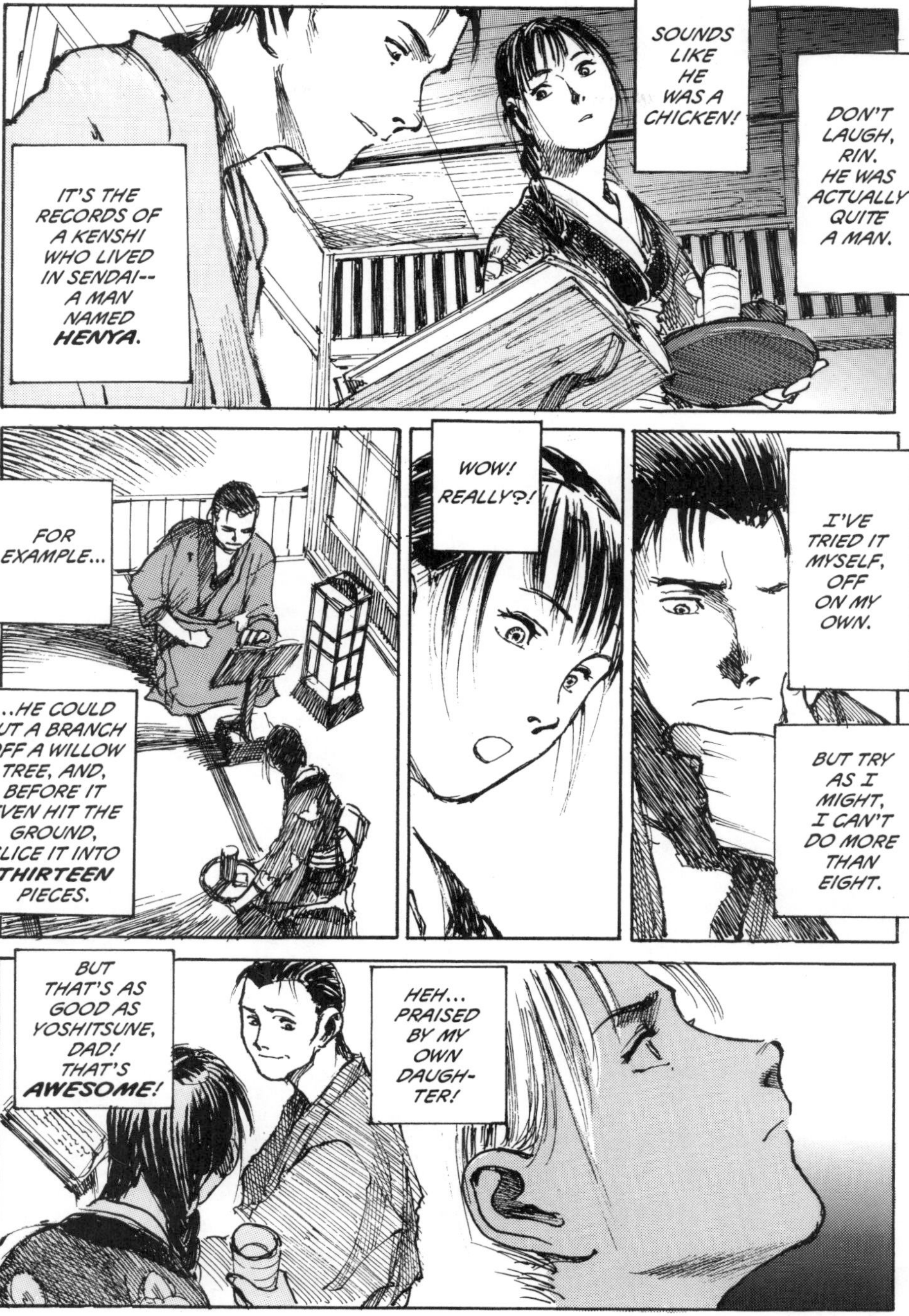
IT'S THE RECORDS OF A KENSHI WHO LIVED IN SENDAI--A MAN NAMED **HENYA**.
SOUNDS LIKE HE WAS A CHICKEN!
DON'T LAUGH, RIN. HE WAS ACTUALLY QUITE A MAN.
FOR EXAMPLE...
...HE COULD CUT A BRANCH OFF A WILLOW TREE, AND, BEFORE IT EVEN HIT THE GROUND, SLICE IT INTO **THIRTEEN** PIECES.
WOW! REALLY?!
I'VE TRIED IT MYSELF, OFF ON MY OWN.
BUT TRY AS I MIGHT, I CAN'T DO MORE THAN EIGHT.
BUT THAT'S AS GOOD AS YOSHITSUNE, DAD! THAT'S **AWESOME**!
HEH... PRAISED BY MY OWN DAUGHTER!

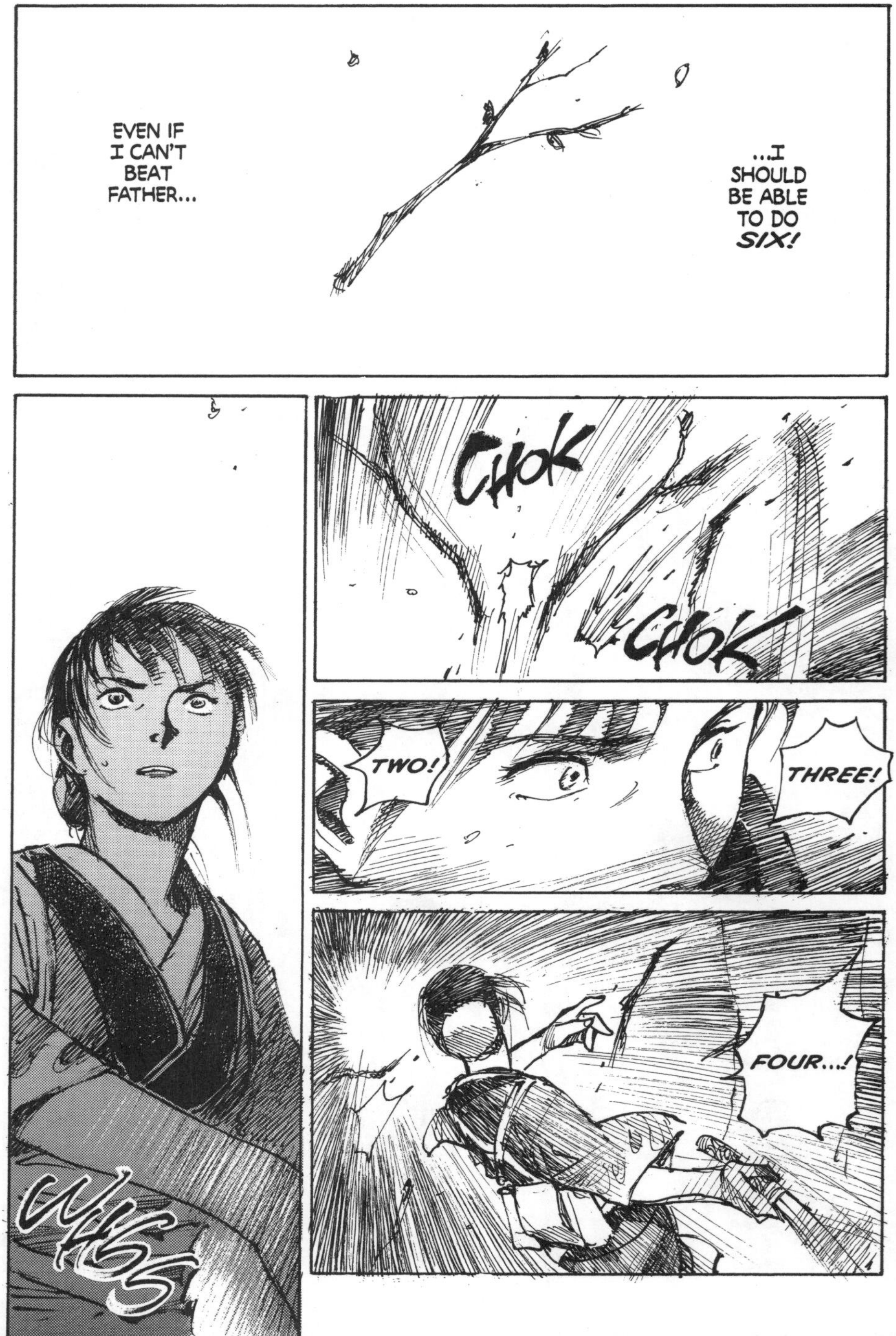
EVEN IF I CAN'T BEAT FATHER...
...I SHOULD BE ABLE TO DO SIX!
WHSS
CHOK
CHOK
TWO!
THREE!
FOUR...!

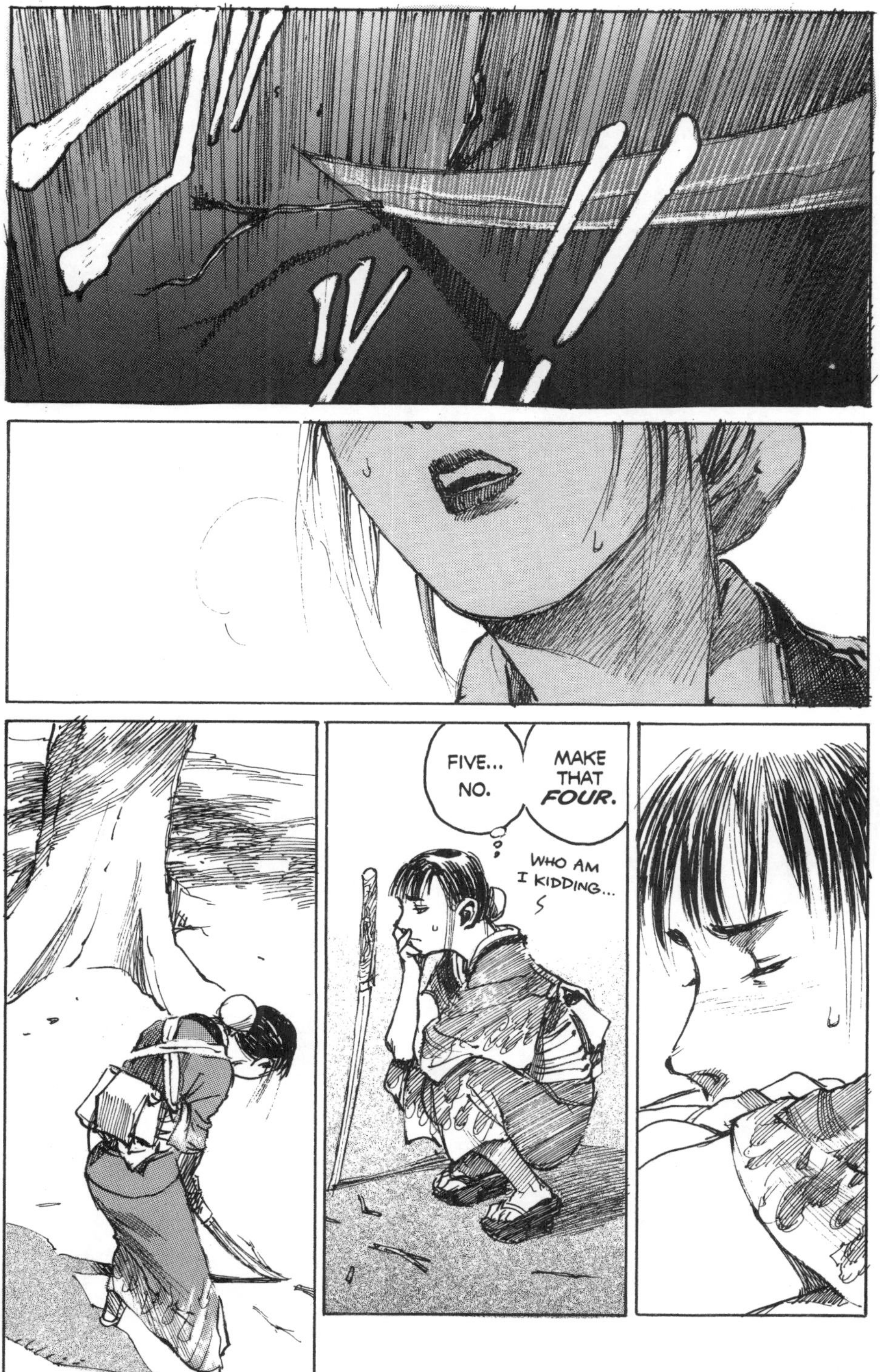
FIVE... NO.
MAKE THAT **FOUR**.
WHO AM I KIDDING...

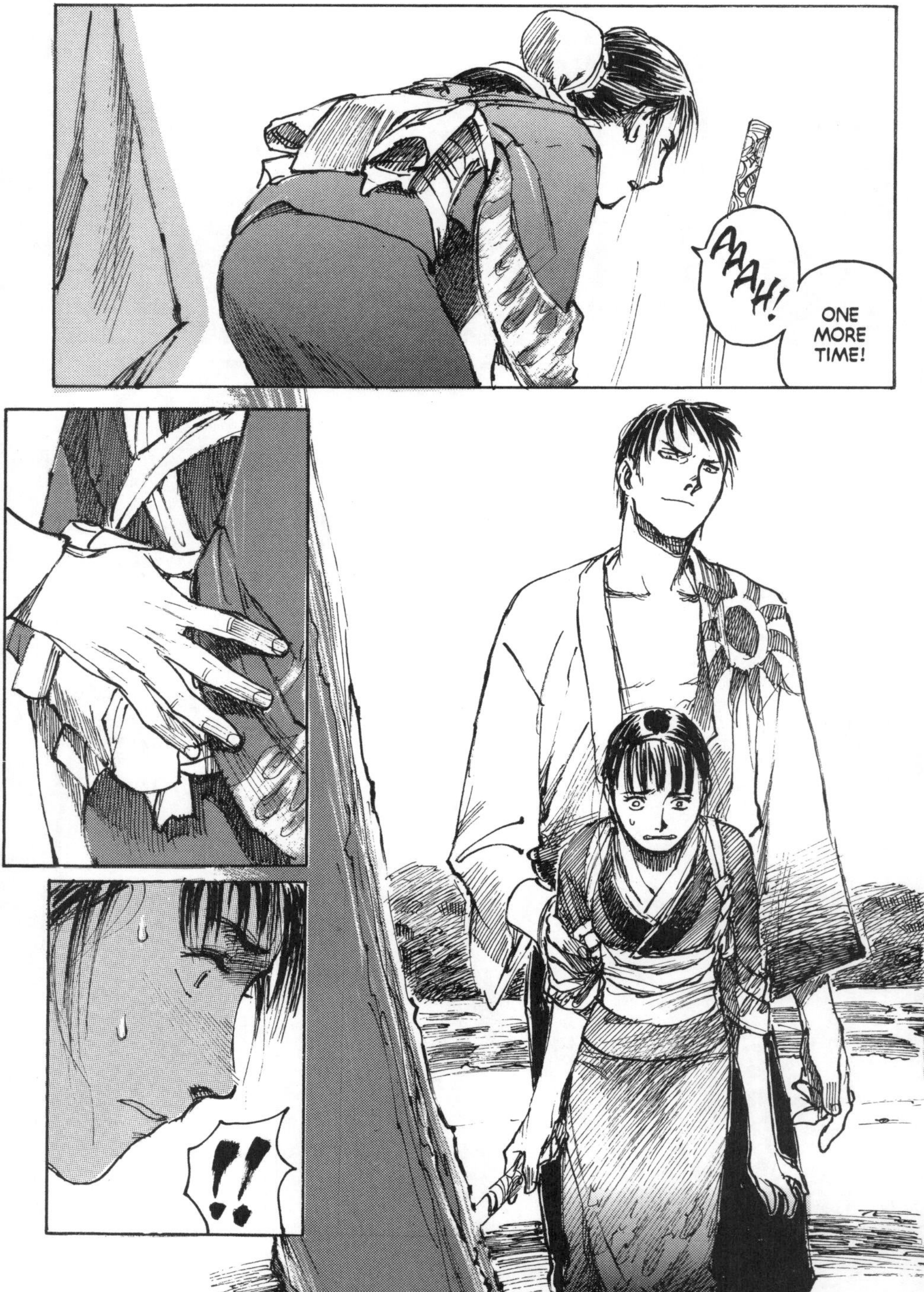
AAAH!
ONE MORE TIME!
!!

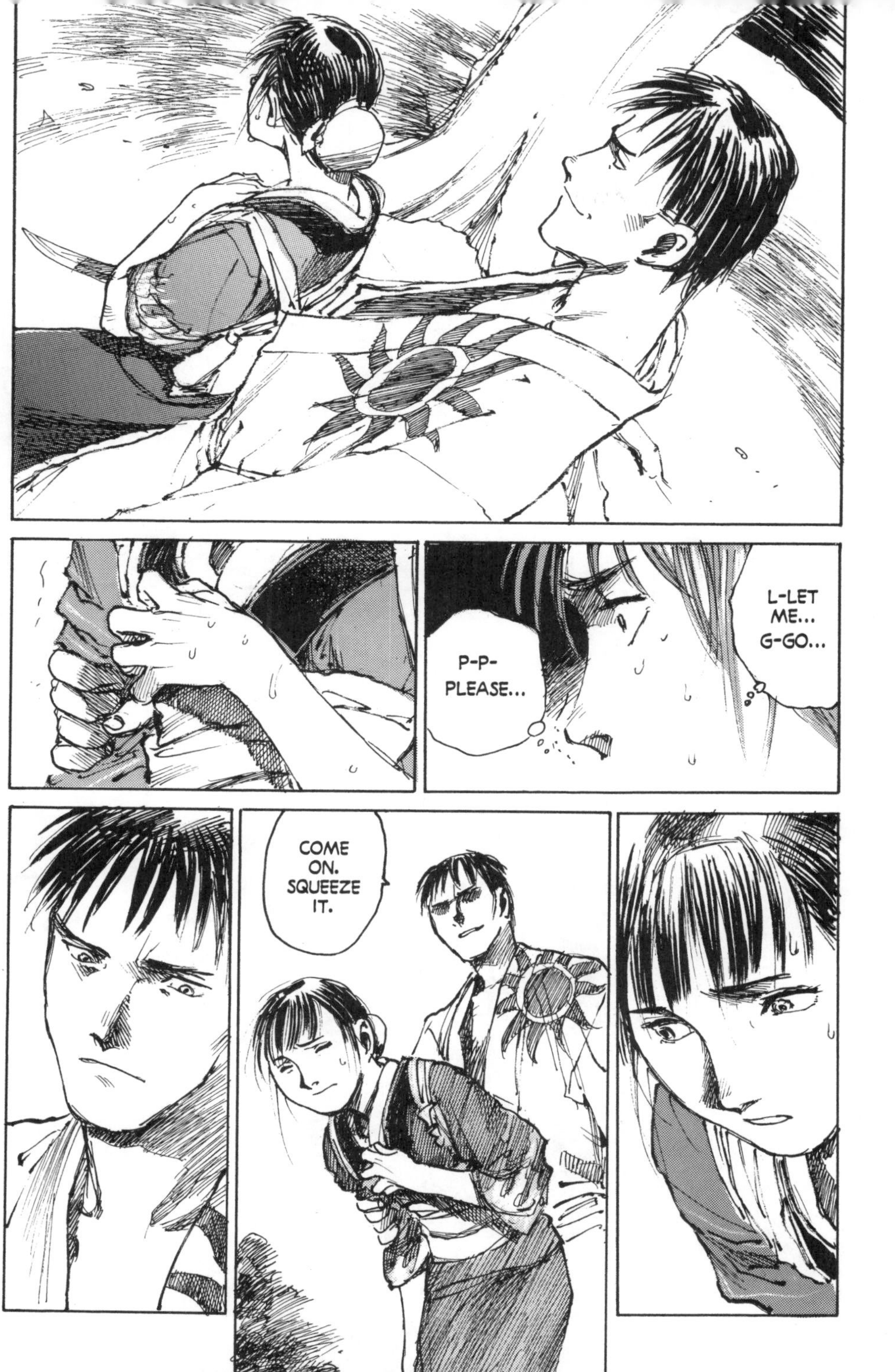
P-P-
PLEASE...
L-LET
ME...
G-GO...
COME
ON.
SQUEEZE
IT.

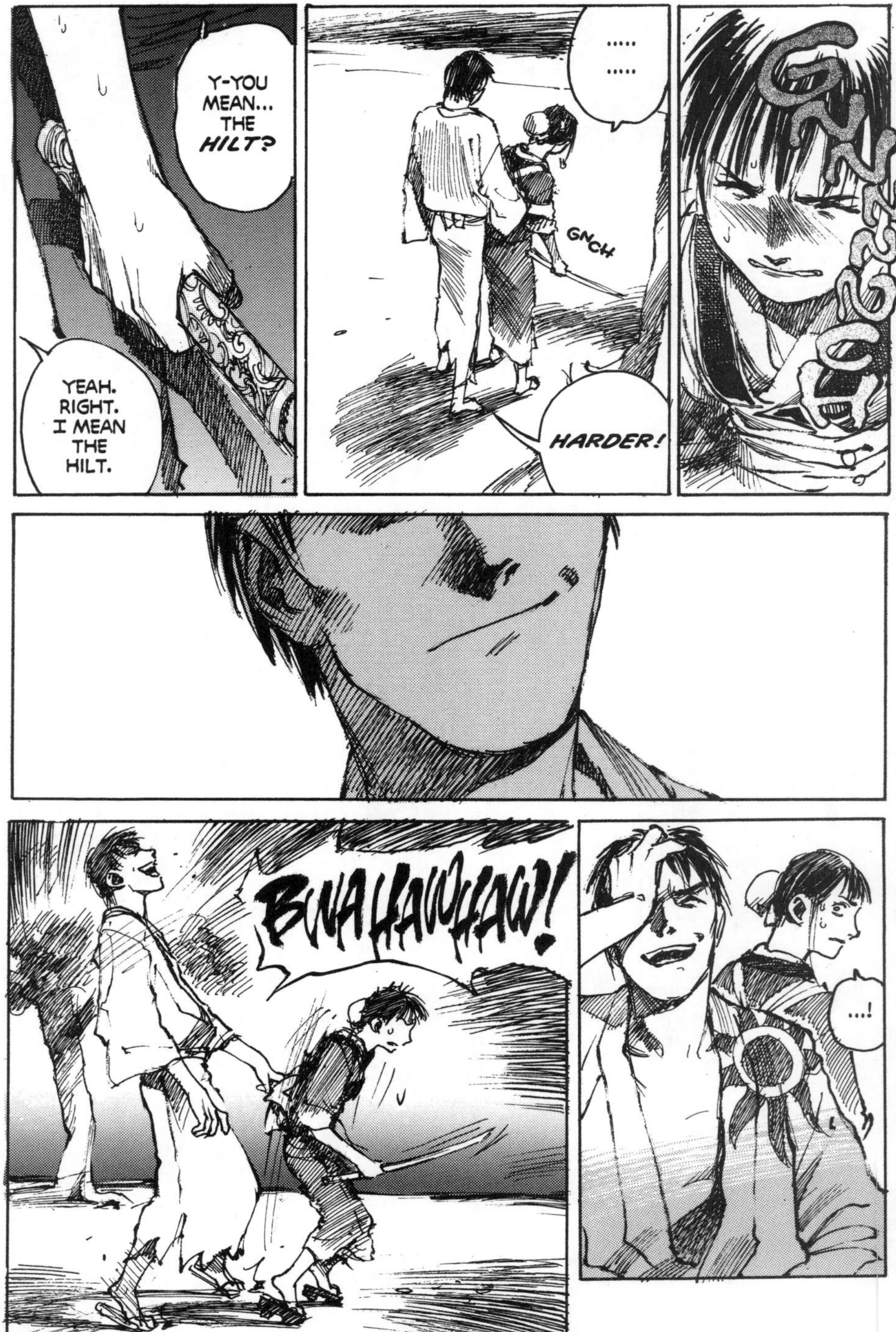
Y-YOU MEAN... THE HILT?
YEAH. RIGHT. I MEAN THE HILT.
.....
.....
GNCH
HARDER!
BWAHAWHAW!
...!

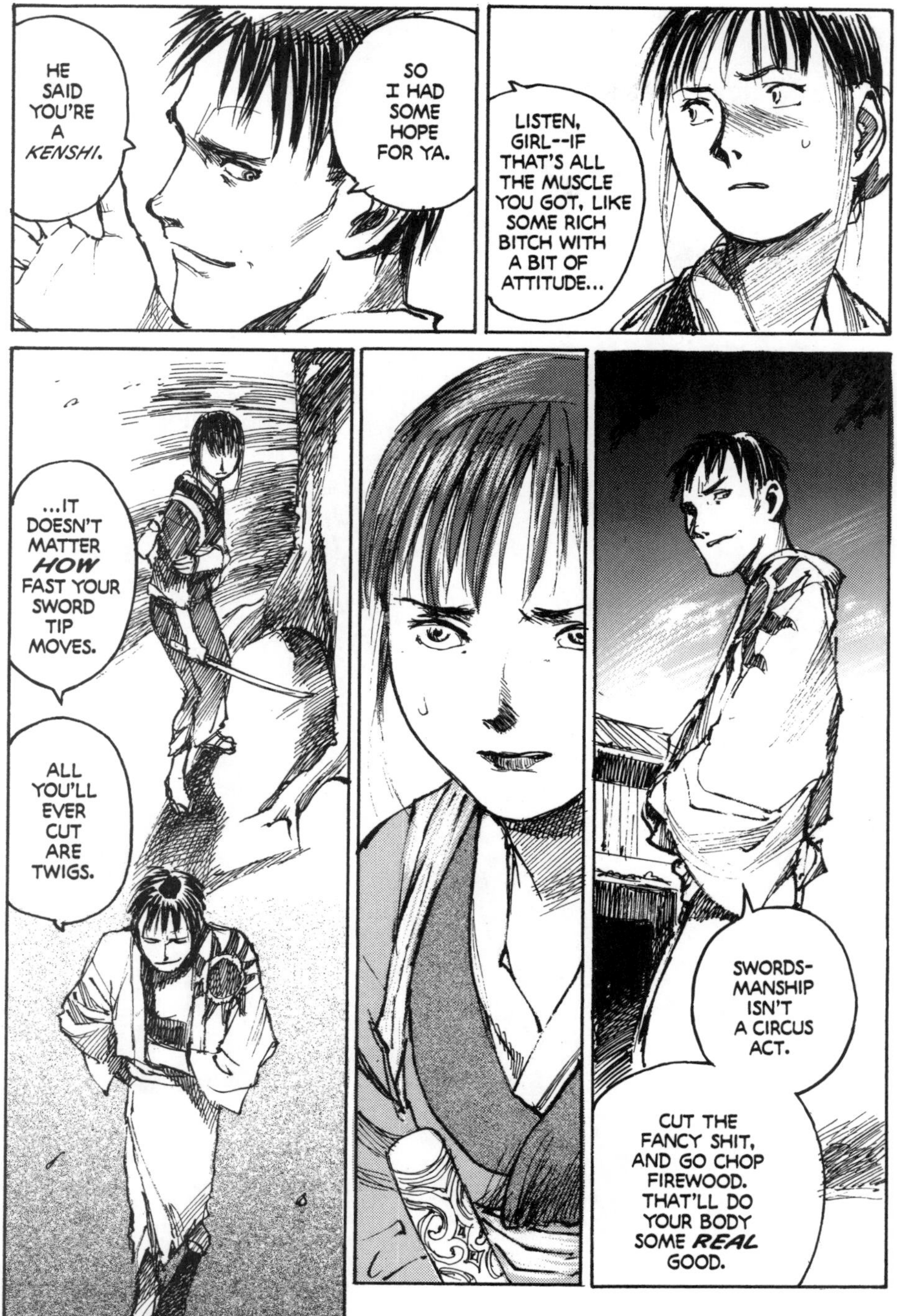
HE SAID YOU'RE A *KENSHI*.
SO I HAD SOME HOPE FOR YA.
LISTEN, GIRL--IF THAT'S ALL THE MUSCLE YOU GOT, LIKE SOME RICH BITCH WITH A BIT OF ATTITUDE...
...IT DOESN'T MATTER ***HOW*** FAST YOUR SWORD TIP MOVES.
ALL YOU'LL EVER CUT ARE TWIGS.
SWORDS-MANSHIP ISN'T A CIRCUS ACT.
CUT THE FANCY SHIT, AND GO CHOP FIREWOOD. THAT'LL DO YOUR BODY SOME ***REAL*** GOOD.

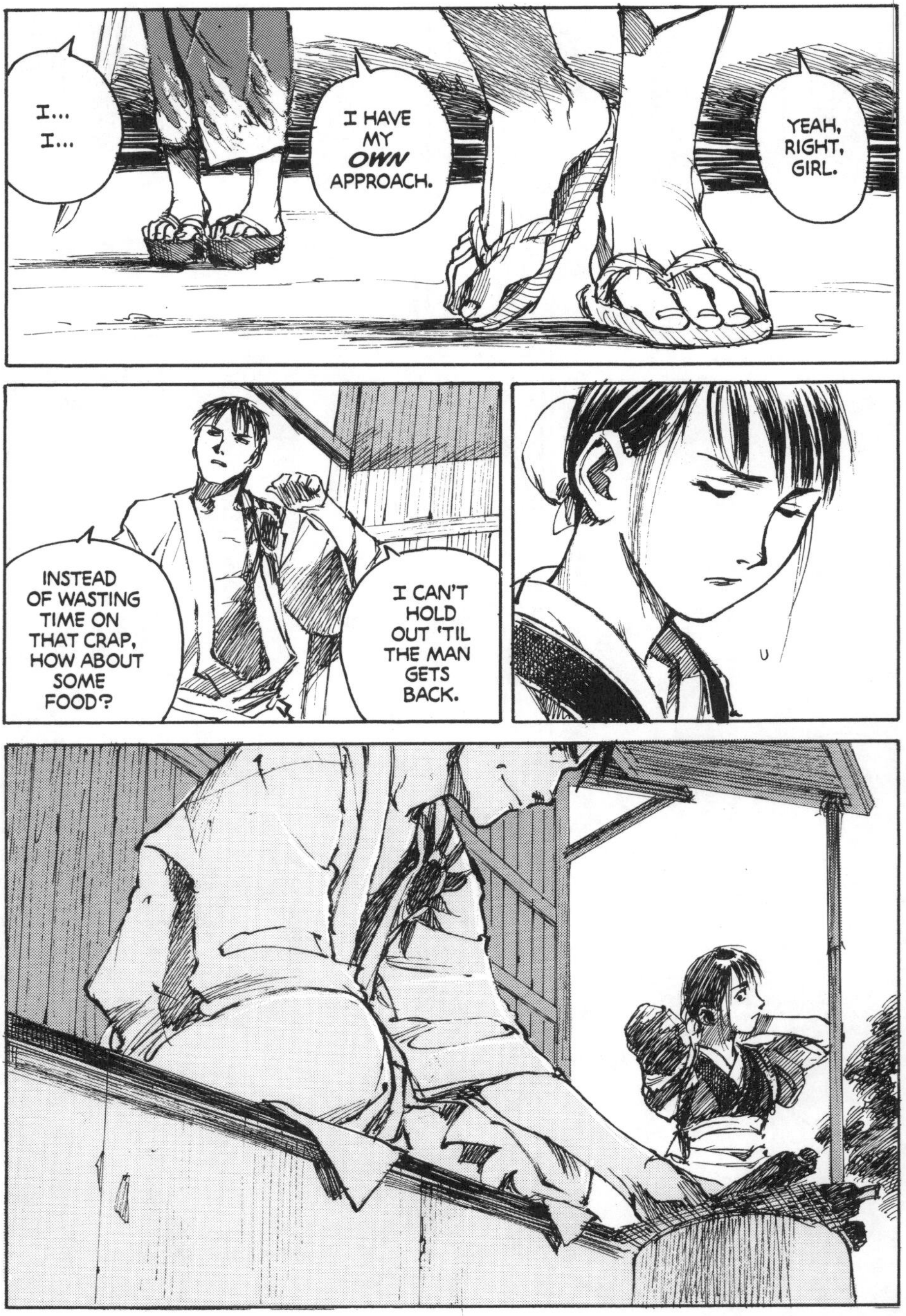
I... I...
I HAVE MY OWN APPROACH.
YEAH, RIGHT, GIRL.
INSTEAD OF WASTING TIME ON THAT CRAP, HOW ABOUT SOME FOOD?
I CAN'T HOLD OUT 'TIL THE MAN GETS BACK.

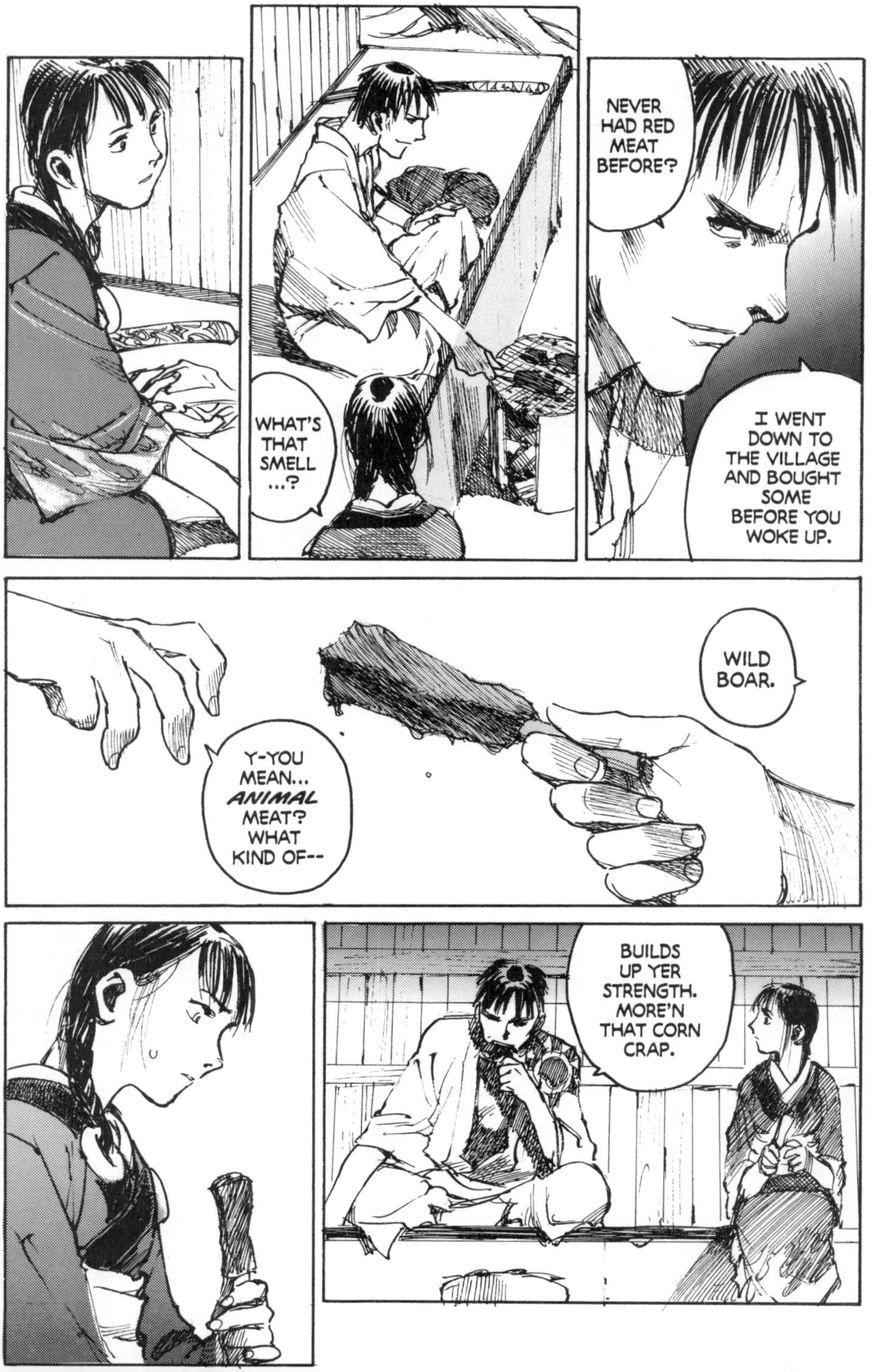
WHAT'S THAT SMELL ...?
NEVER HAD RED MEAT BEFORE?
I WENT DOWN TO THE VILLAGE AND BOUGHT SOME BEFORE YOU WOKE UP.
Y-YOU MEAN... *ANIMAL* MEAT? WHAT KIND OF--
WILD BOAR.
BUILDS UP YER STRENGTH. MORE'N THAT CORN CRAP.

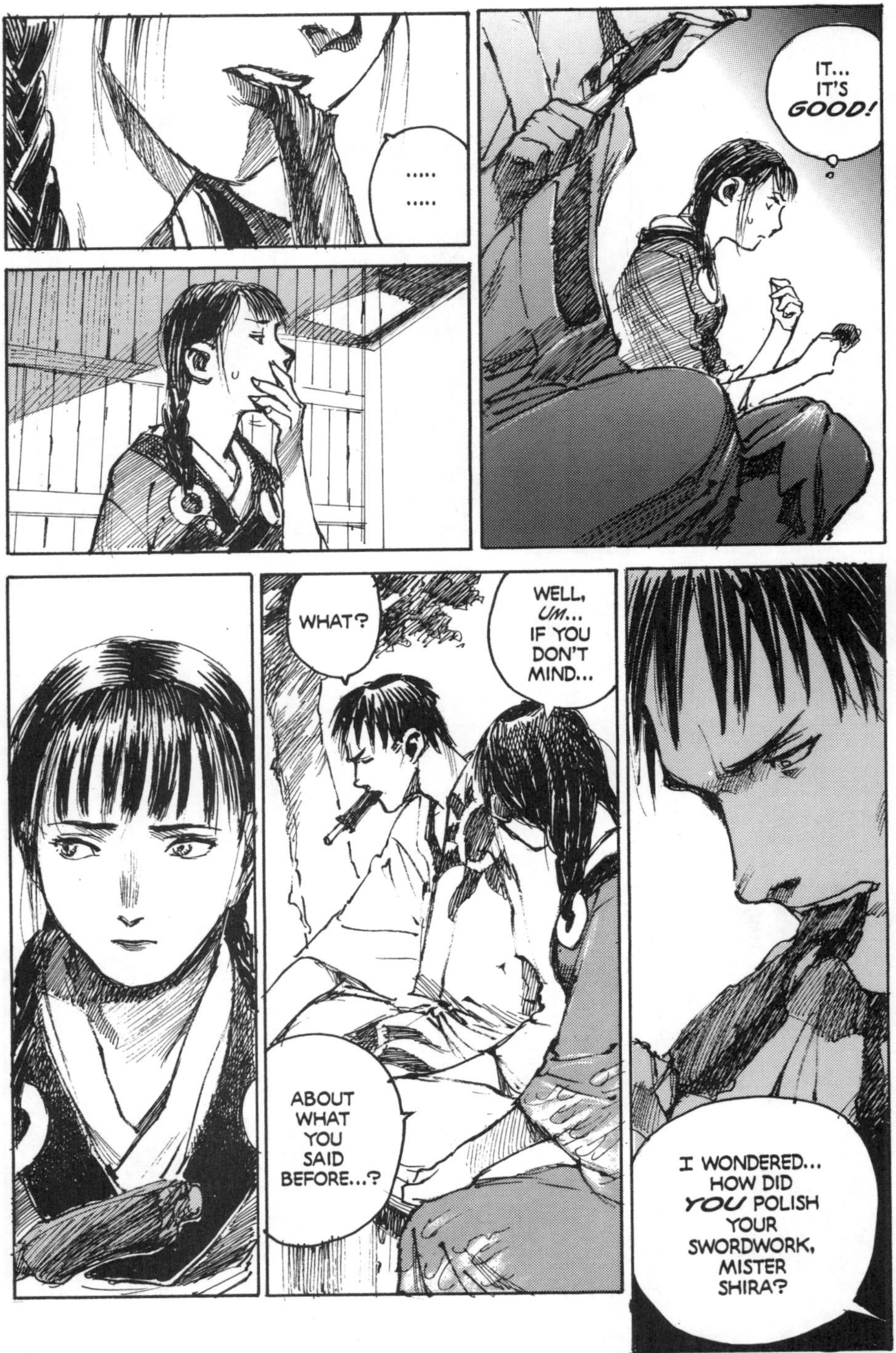
.....
.....
IT... IT'S *GOOD!*
WHAT?
WELL, *UM*... IF YOU DON'T MIND...
ABOUT WHAT YOU SAID BEFORE...?
I WONDERED... HOW DID *YOU* POLISH YOUR SWORDWORK, MISTER SHIRA?

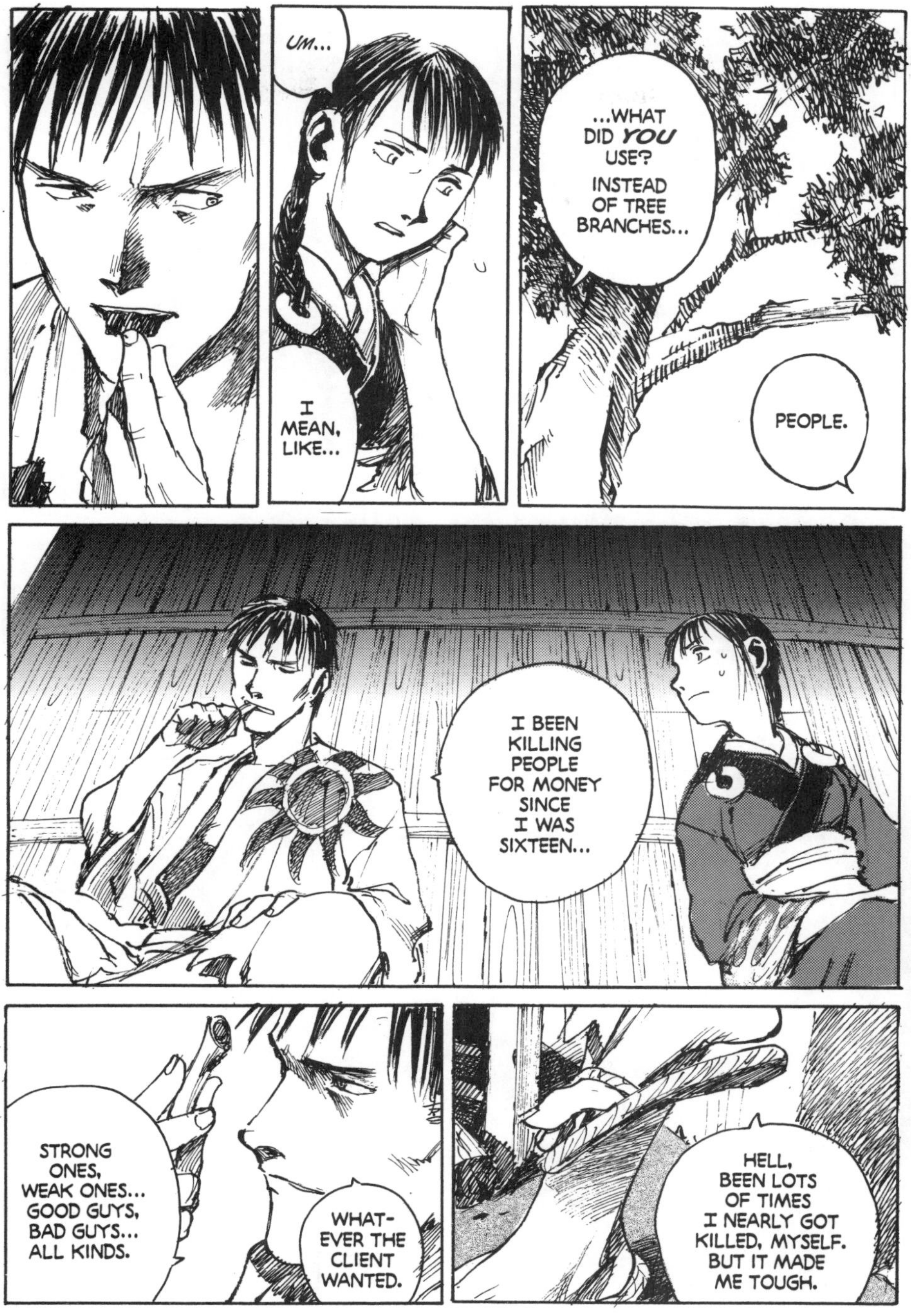
UM...
I MEAN, LIKE...
...WHAT DID *YOU* USE?
INSTEAD OF TREE BRANCHES...
PEOPLE.
I BEEN KILLING PEOPLE FOR MONEY SINCE I WAS SIXTEEN...
STRONG ONES, WEAK ONES... GOOD GUYS, BAD GUYS... ALL KINDS.
WHAT-EVER THE CLIENT WANTED.
HELL, BEEN LOTS OF TIMES I NEARLY GOT KILLED, MYSELF. BUT IT MADE ME TOUGH.

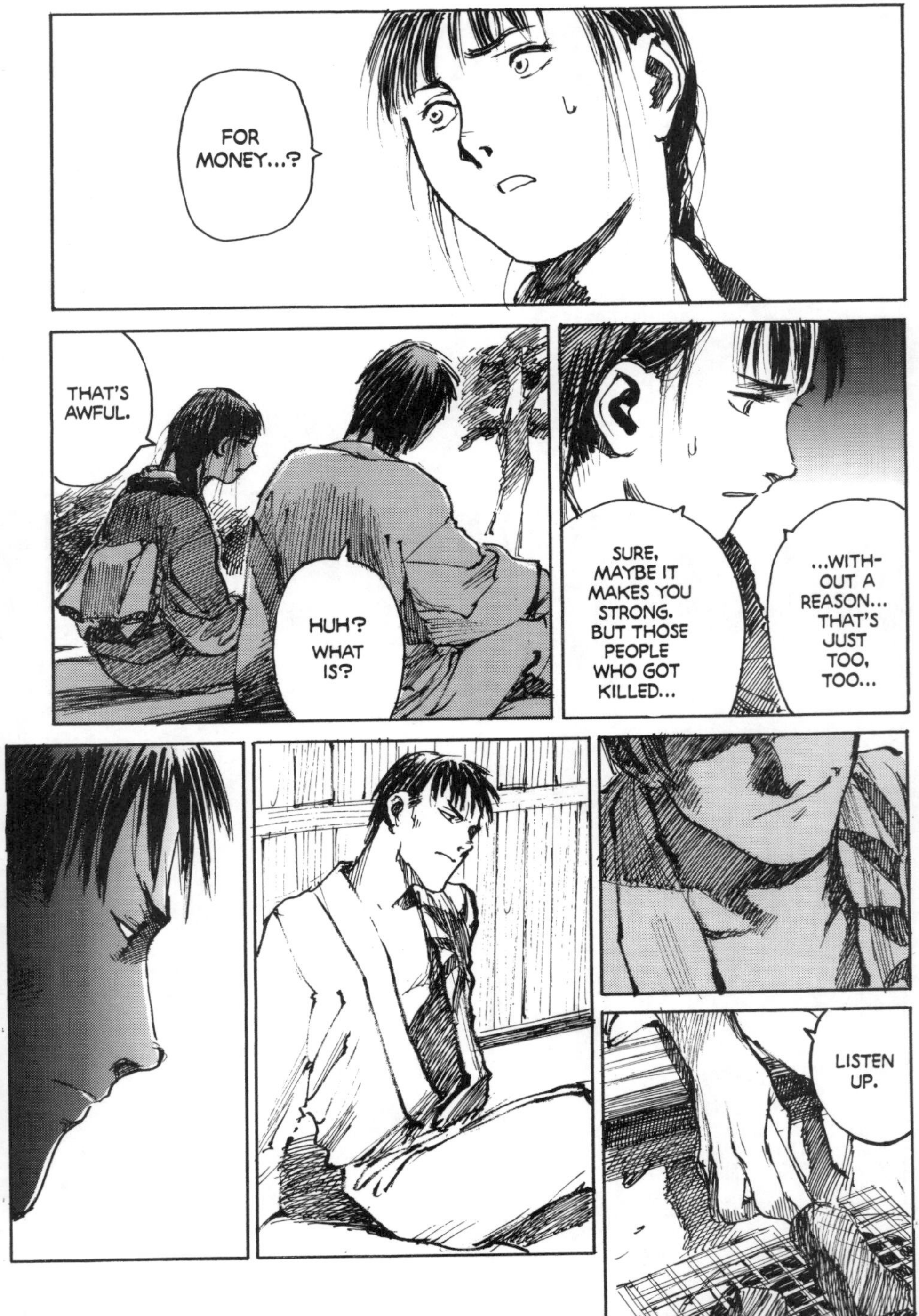
FOR MONEY...?
THAT'S AWFUL.
HUH? WHAT IS?
SURE, MAYBE IT MAKES YOU STRONG. BUT THOSE PEOPLE WHO GOT KILLED...
...WITH-OUT A REASON... THAT'S JUST TOO, TOO...
LISTEN UP.

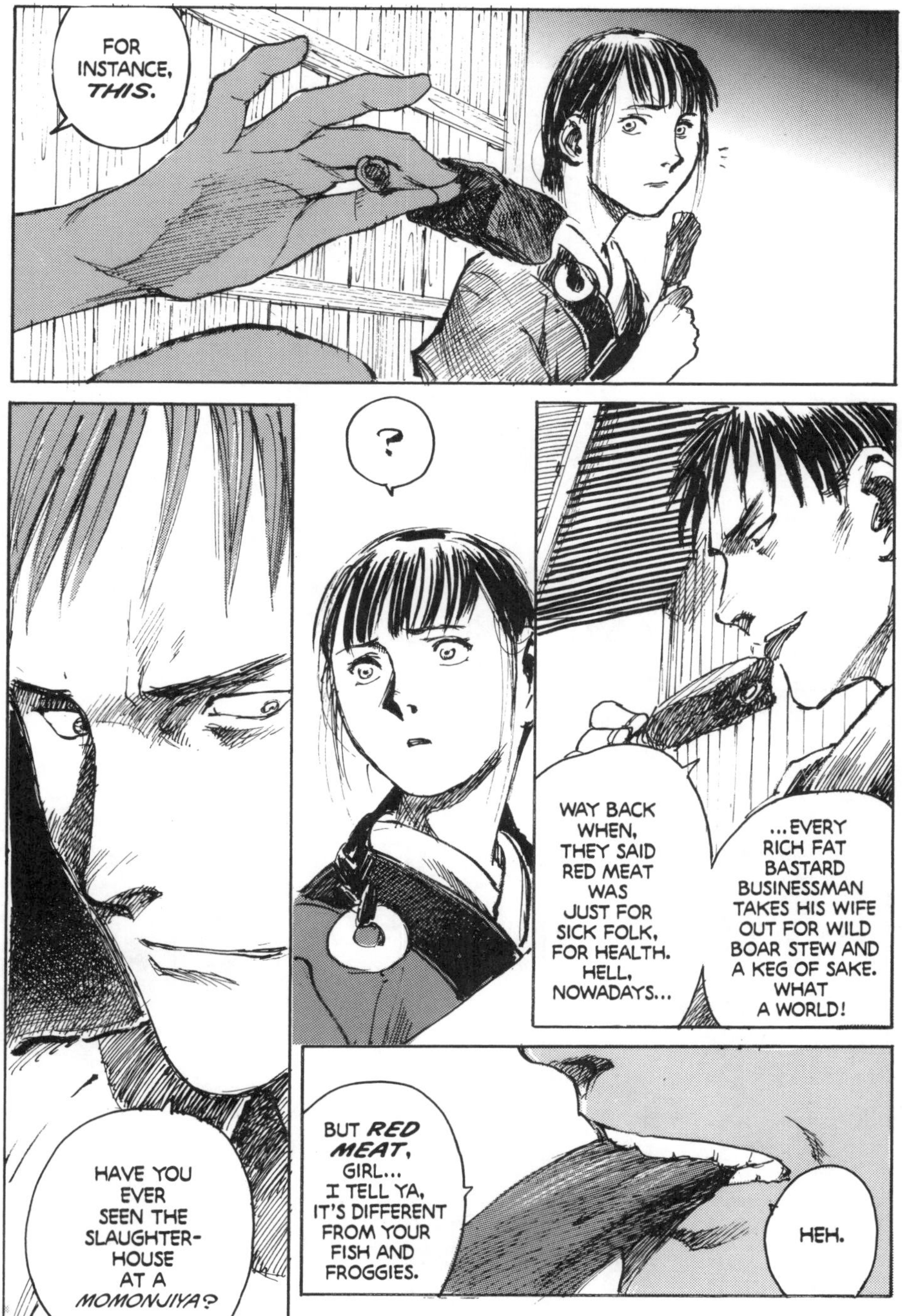
FOR INSTANCE, *THIS.*
HAVE YOU EVER SEEN THE SLAUGHTER-HOUSE AT A *MOMONJIYA?*
?
WAY BACK WHEN, THEY SAID RED MEAT WAS JUST FOR SICK FOLK, FOR HEALTH. HELL, NOWADAYS...
...EVERY RICH FAT BASTARD BUSINESSMAN TAKES HIS WIFE OUT FOR WILD BOAR STEW AND A KEG OF SAKE. WHAT A WORLD!
BUT *RED MEAT*, GIRL... I TELL YA, IT'S DIFFERENT FROM YOUR FISH AND FROGGIES.
HEH.

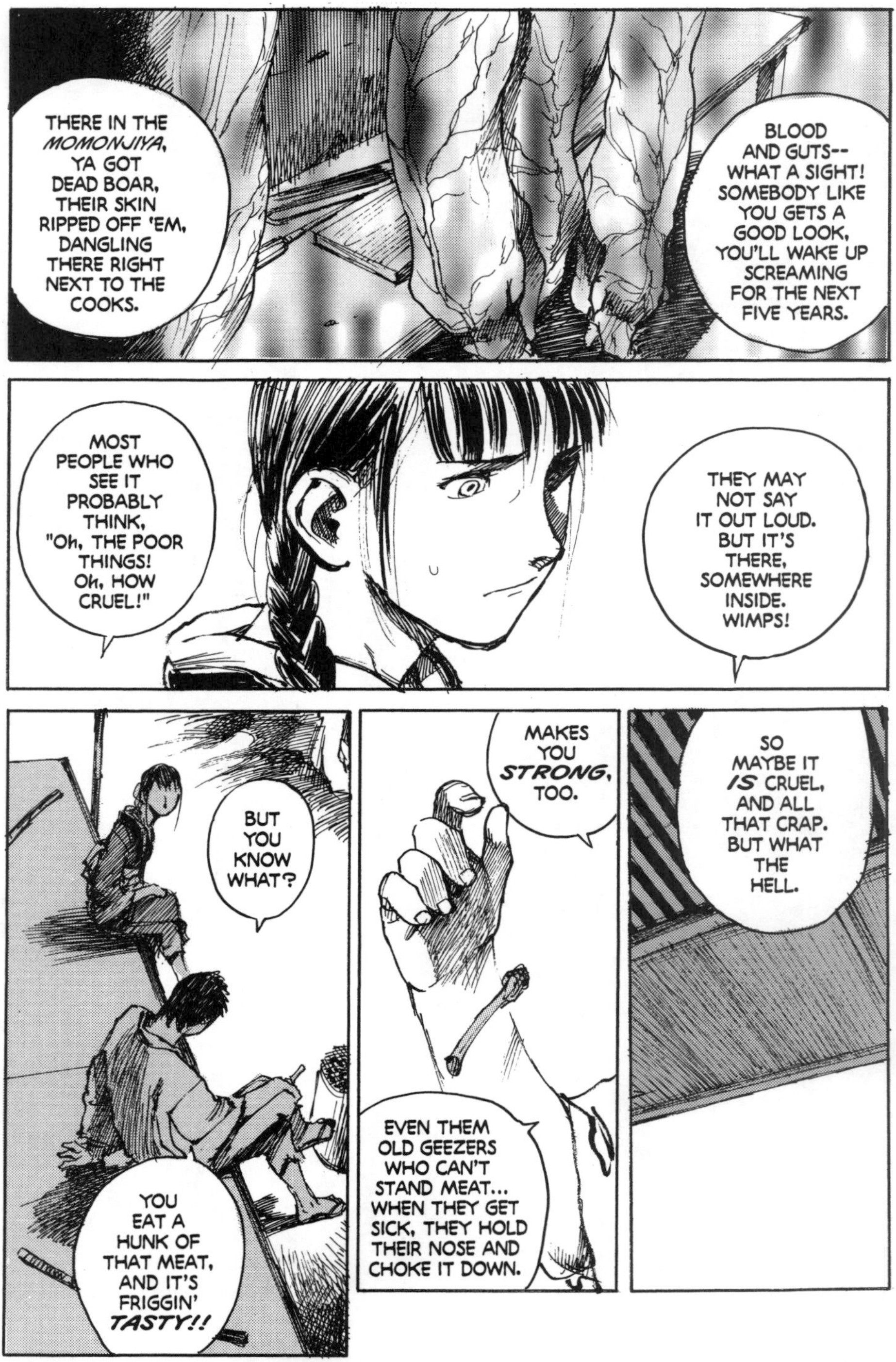
THERE IN THE *MOMONJIYA*, YA GOT DEAD BOAR, THEIR SKIN RIPPED OFF 'EM, DANGLING THERE RIGHT NEXT TO THE COOKS.
BLOOD AND GUTS-- WHAT A SIGHT! SOMEBODY LIKE YOU GETS A GOOD LOOK, YOU'LL WAKE UP SCREAMING FOR THE NEXT FIVE YEARS.
MOST PEOPLE WHO SEE IT PROBABLY THINK, "Oh, THE POOR THINGS! Oh, HOW CRUEL!"
THEY MAY NOT SAY IT OUT LOUD. BUT IT'S THERE, SOMEWHERE INSIDE. WIMPS!
BUT YOU KNOW WHAT?
YOU EAT A HUNK OF THAT MEAT, AND IT'S FRIGGIN' *TASTY!!*
MAKES YOU ***STRONG***, TOO.
EVEN THEM OLD GEEZERS WHO CAN'T STAND MEAT... WHEN THEY GET SICK, THEY HOLD THEIR NOSE AND CHOKE IT DOWN.
SO MAYBE IT ***IS*** CRUEL, AND ALL THAT CRAP. BUT WHAT THE HELL.

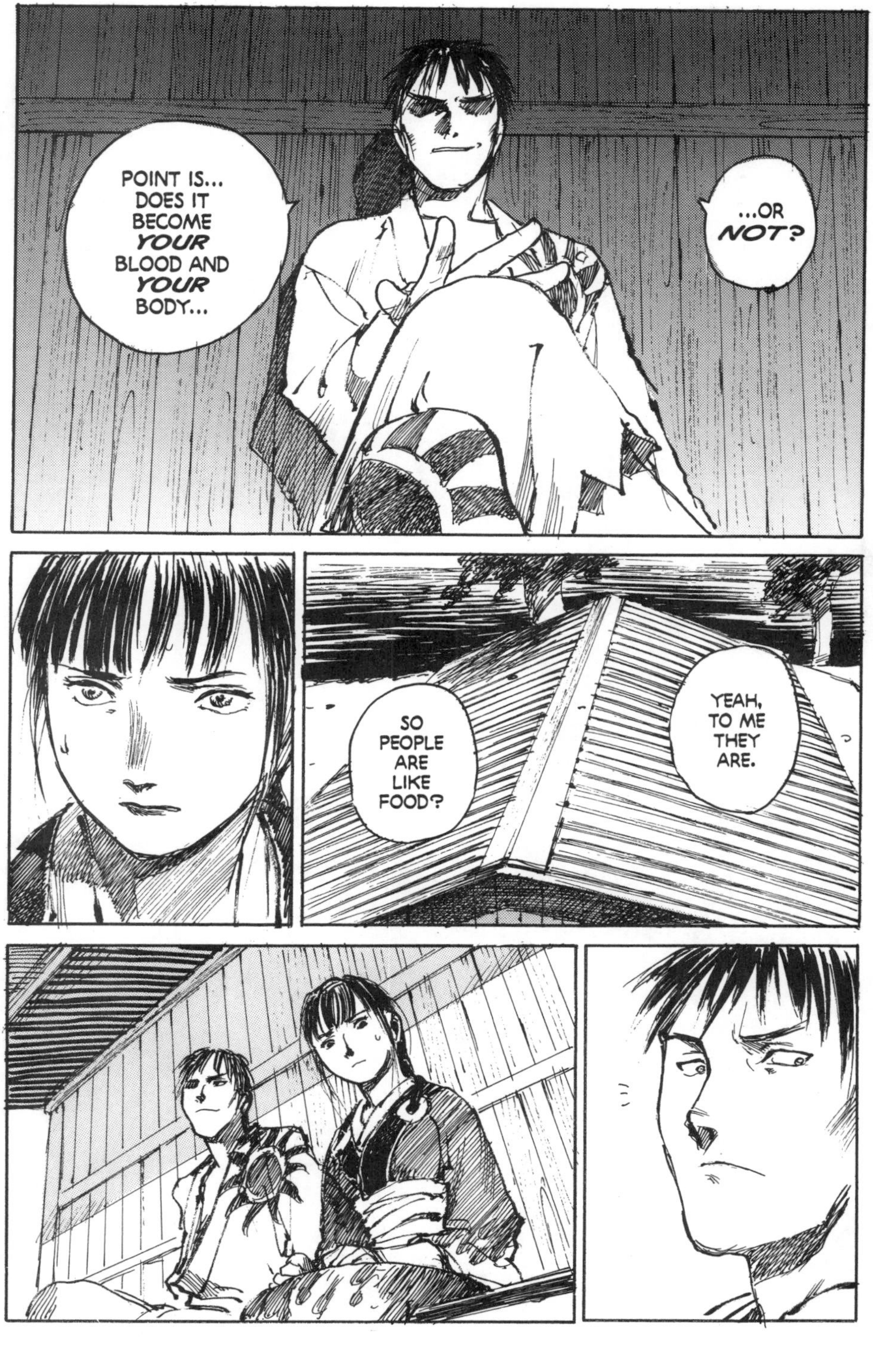
POINT IS... DOES IT BECOME *YOUR* BLOOD AND *YOUR* BODY...
...OR *NOT?*
SO PEOPLE ARE LIKE FOOD?
YEAH, TO ME THEY ARE.

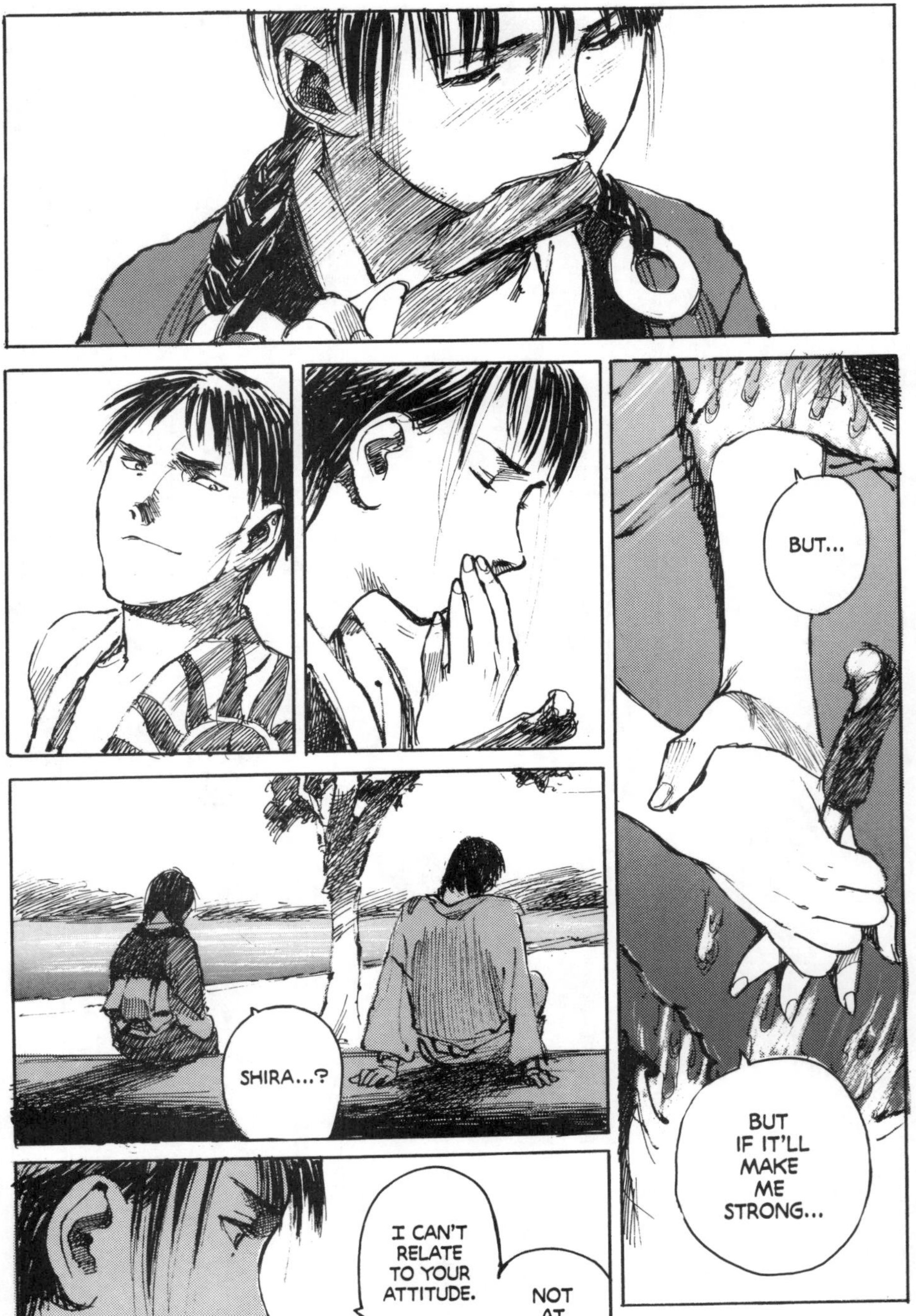
SHIRA...?
I CAN'T RELATE TO YOUR ATTITUDE.
NOT AT ALL.
BUT...
BUT IF IT'LL MAKE ME STRONG...

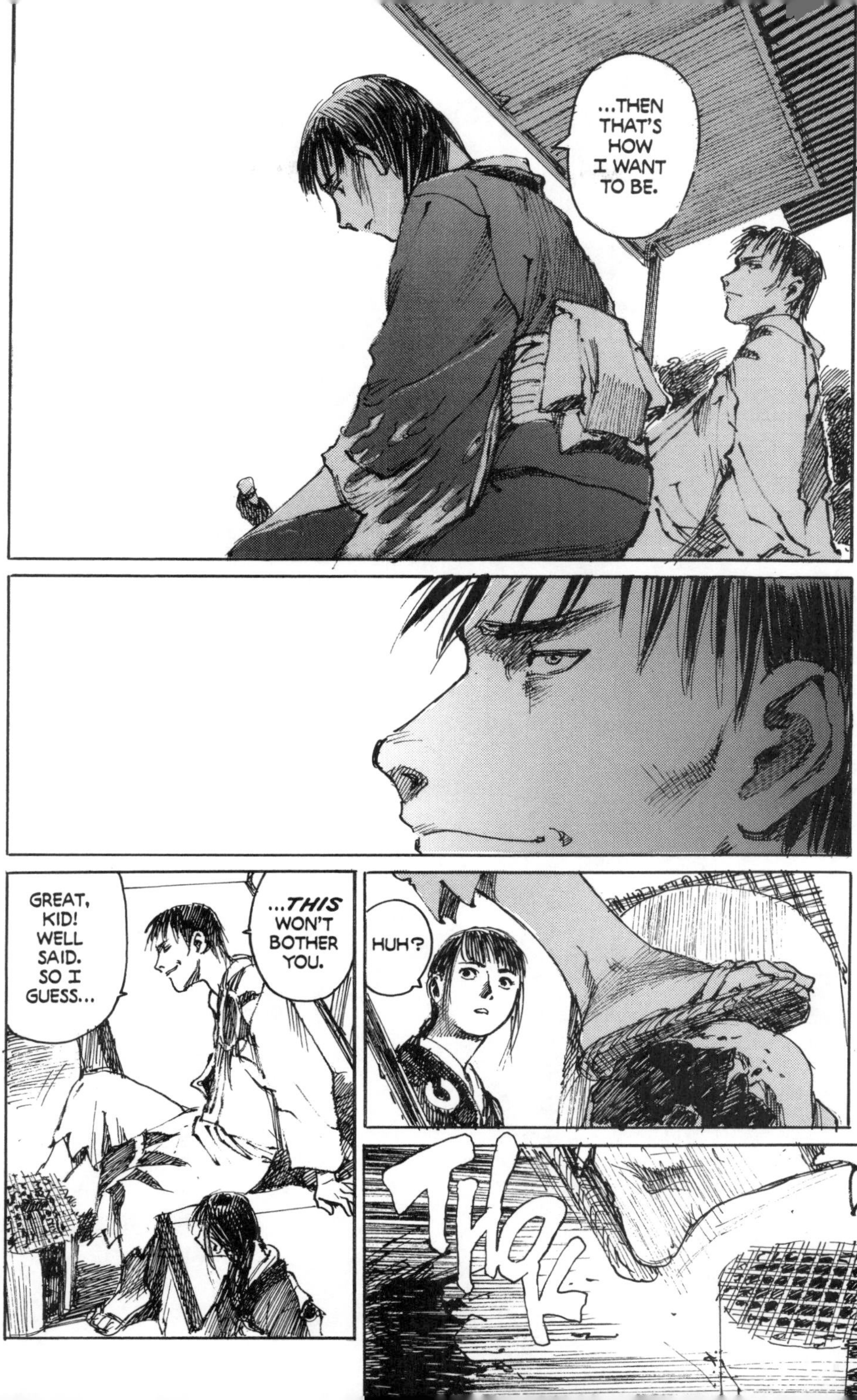
...THEN THAT'S HOW I WANT TO BE.
GREAT, KID! WELL SAID. SO I GUESS...
...THIS WON'T BOTHER YOU.
HUH?
THOK

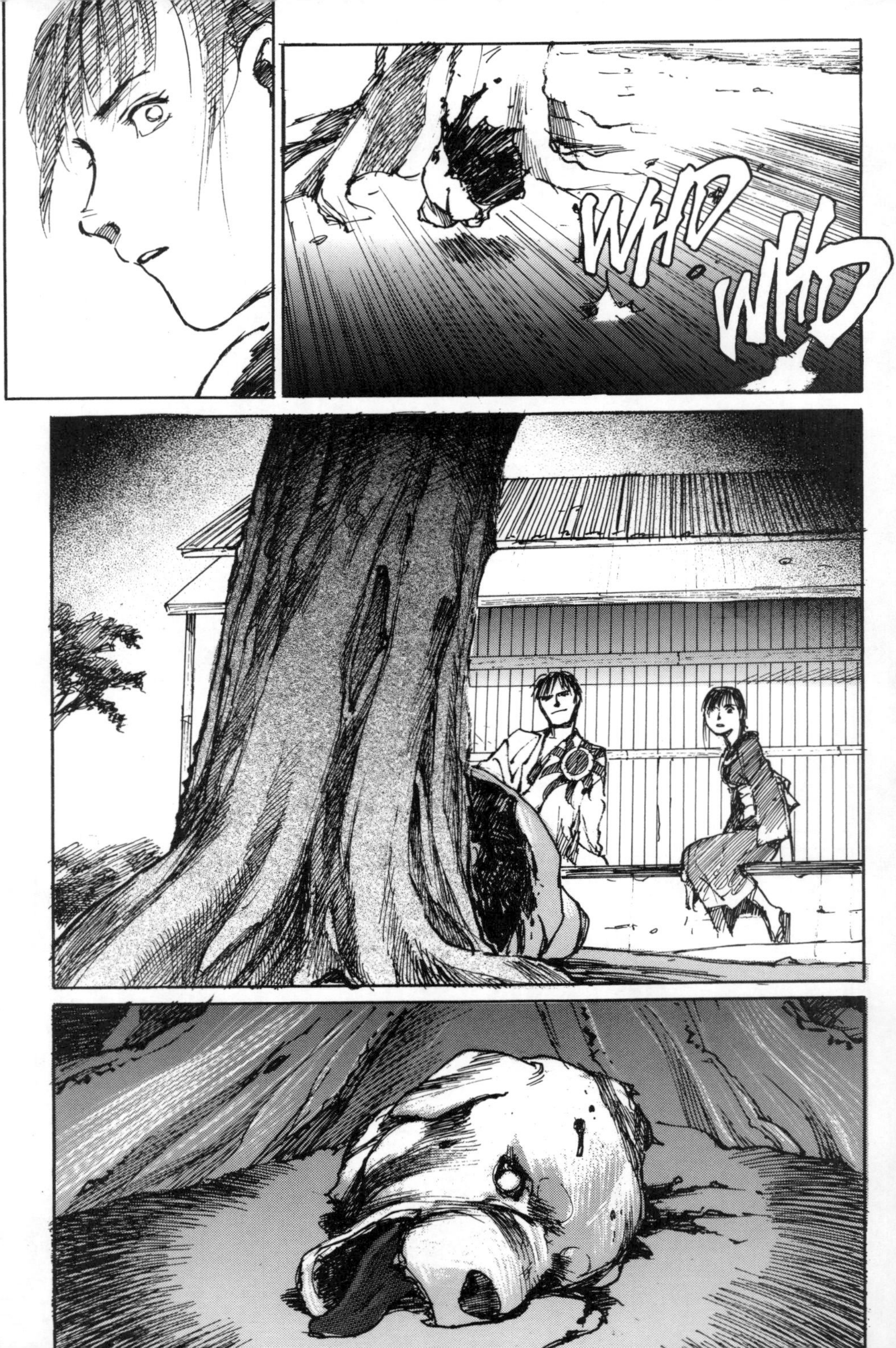
WHO
WHO

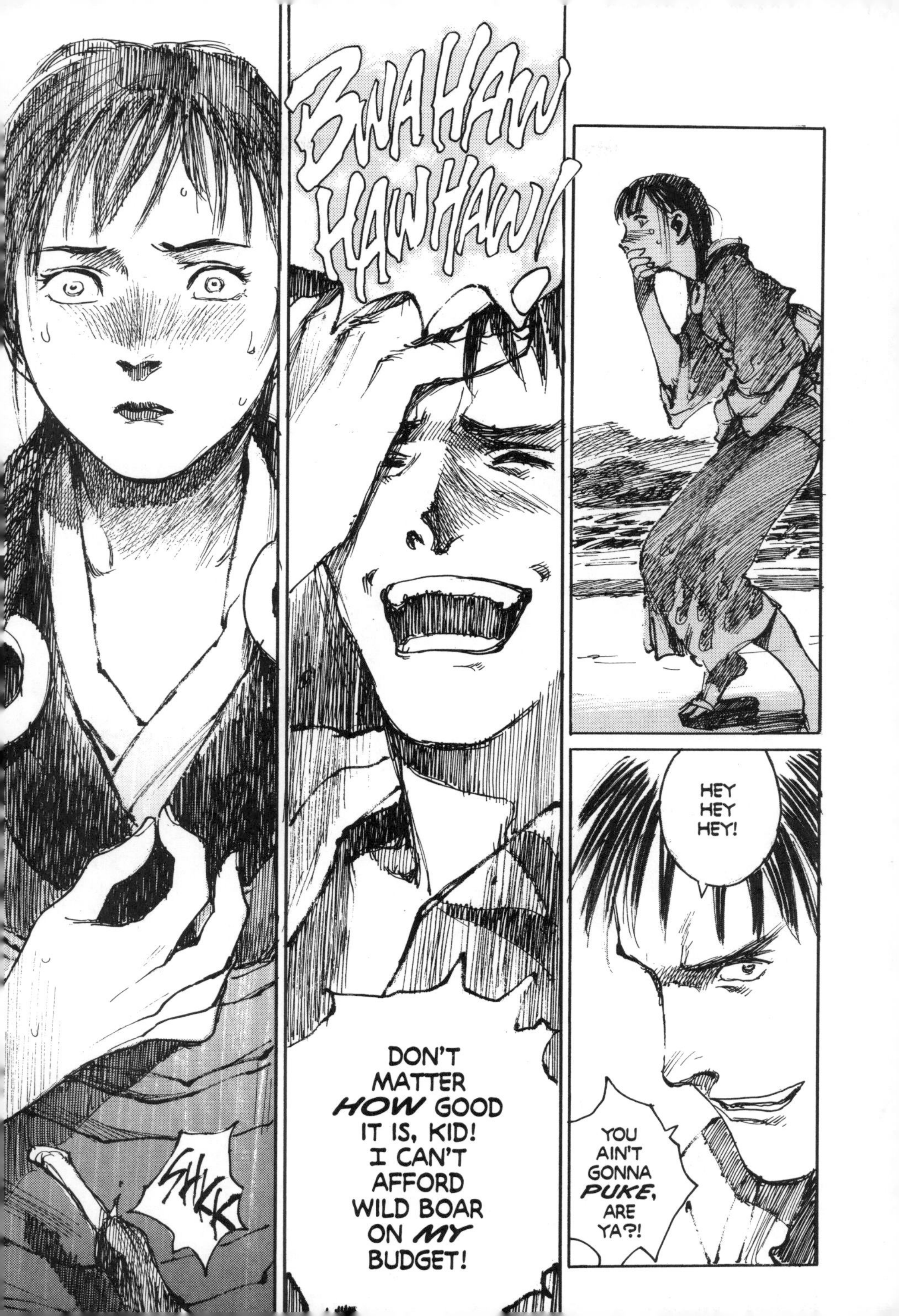
SHKK
BWAHAW HAWHAW!
DON'T MATTER *HOW* GOOD IT IS, KID! I CAN'T AFFORD WILD BOAR ON *MY* BUDGET!
HEY HEY HEY!
YOU AIN'T GONNA *PUKE*, ARE YA?!

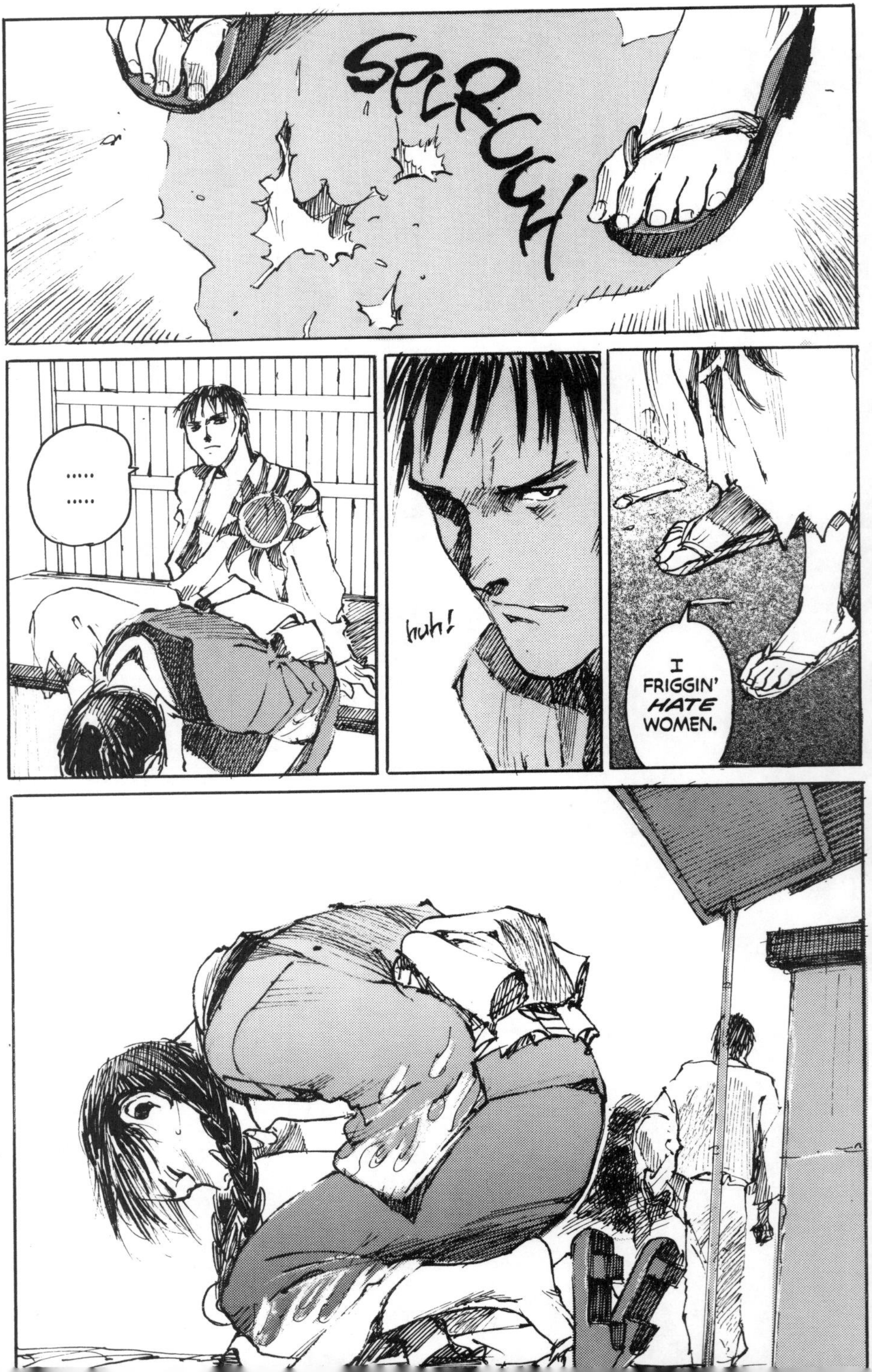
SPLRUCH
......
......
huh!
I FRIGGIN' *HATE* WOMEN.

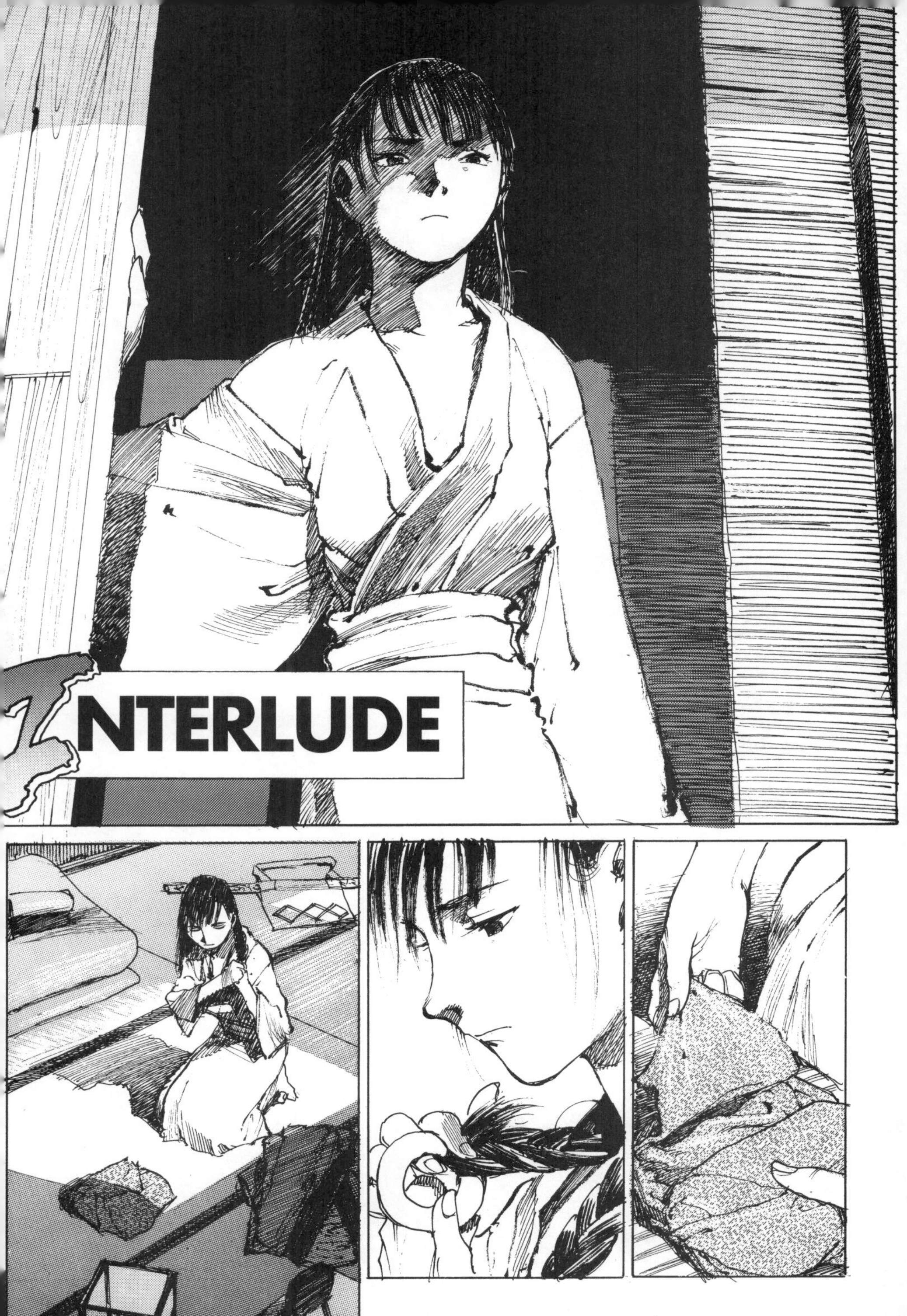
INTERLUDE

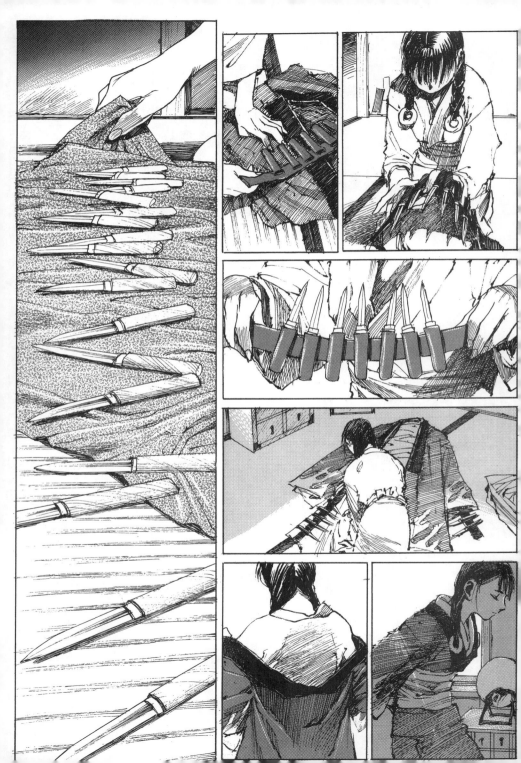

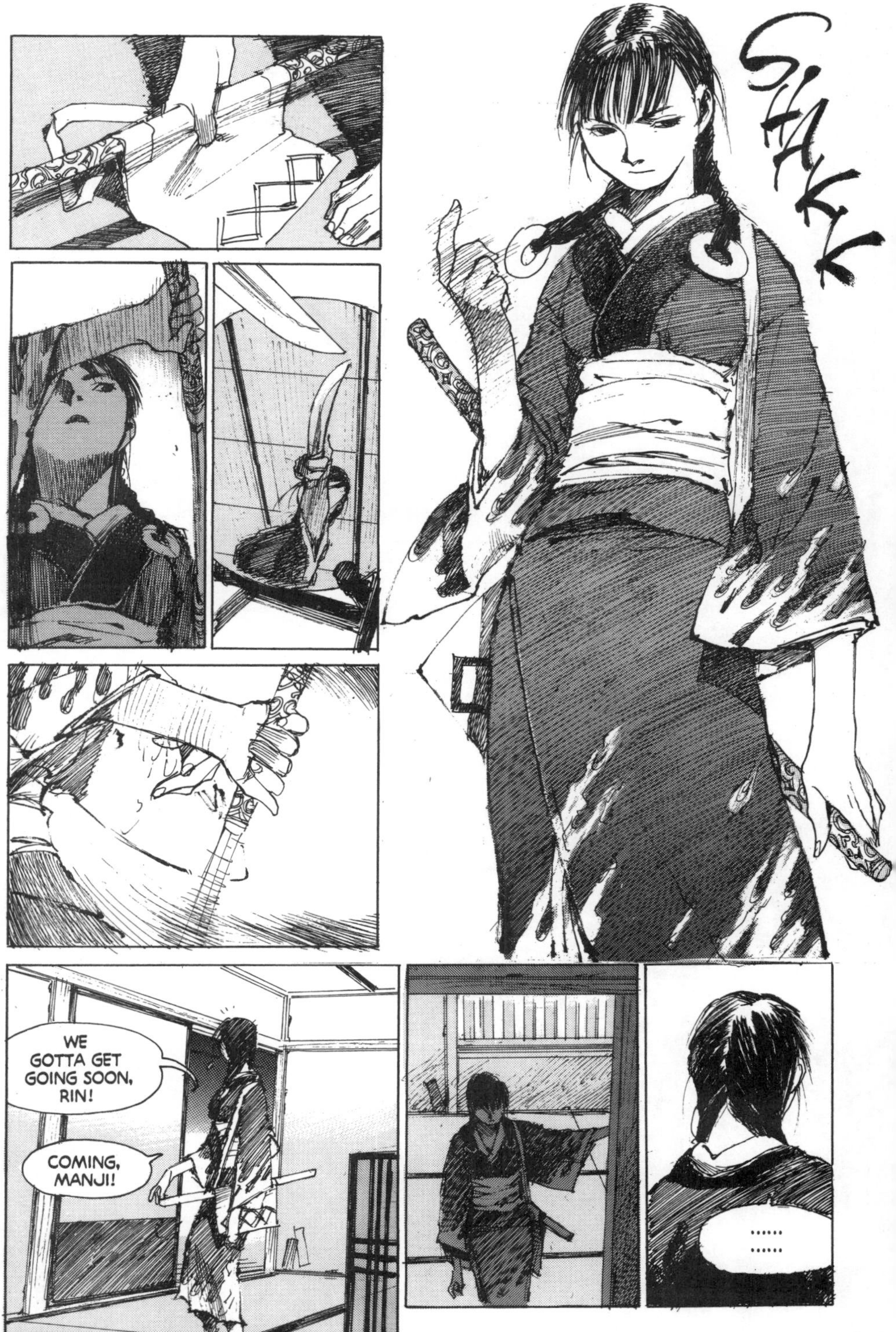
SHAKK
WE GOTTA GET GOING SOON, RIN!
COMING, MANJI!
....

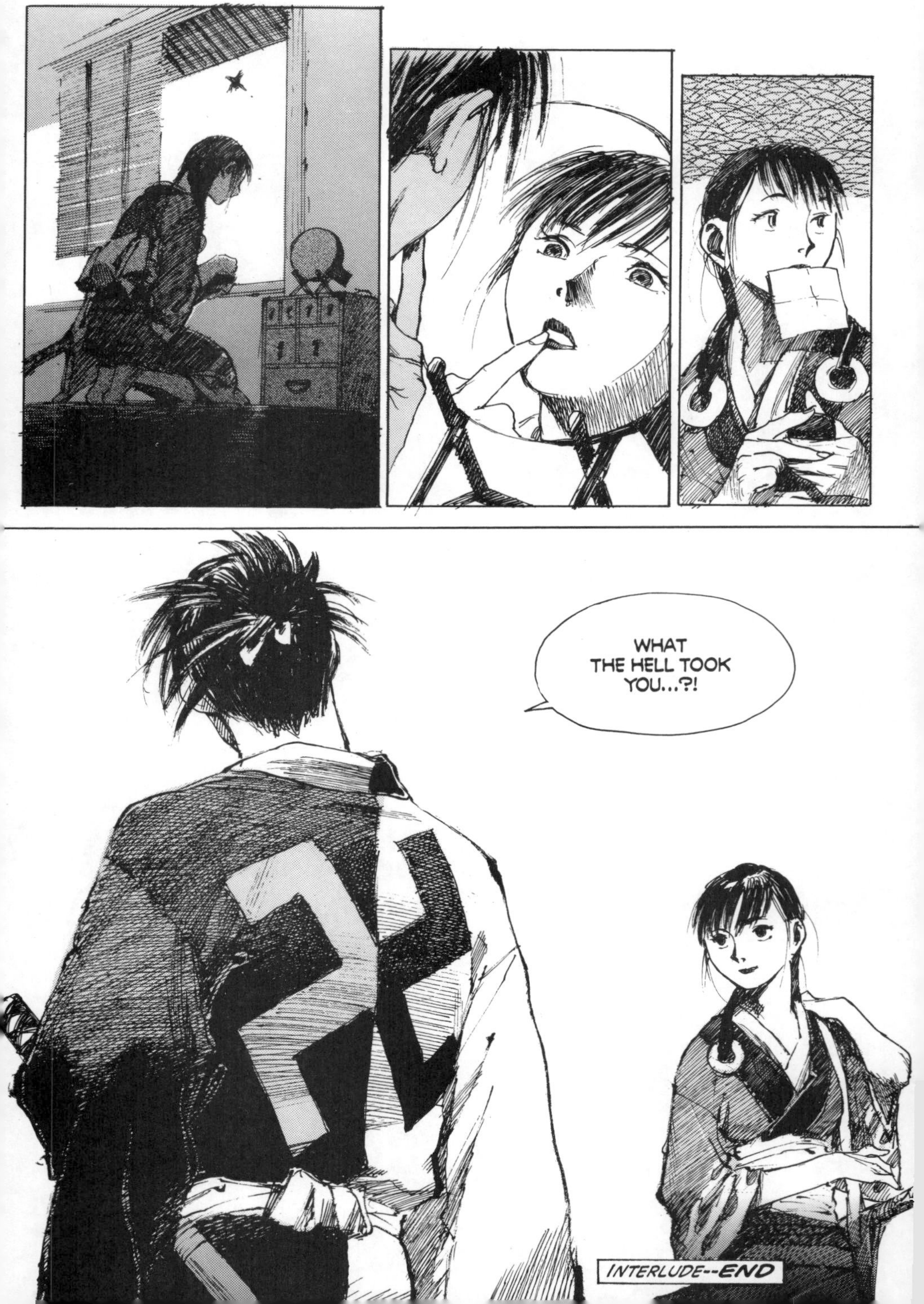
WHAT THE HELL TOOK YOU...?!
INTERLUDE--END

GLOSSARY

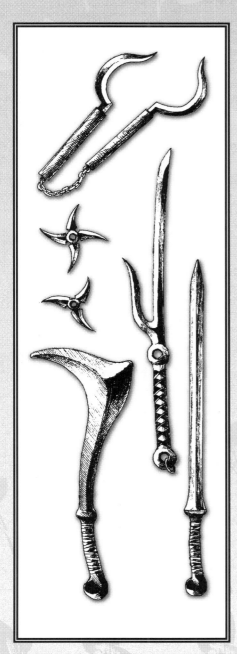

Bakufu: the central government, originally established in Edo, today's Tokyo, by the warlord Tokugawa Ieyasu

Banshū: officers serving under the Shogun, usually assigned to Edo Castle to defend the Shogun himself

Bushi: warriors; samurai

Daimyō: lords of provincial feudal fiefs known as han

Dōjō: a hall for martial arts training

Hatamoto: the inner circle of daimyō, or feudal lords. The Tokugawa Shogunate maintained uneasy central control over scores of han, independent feudal fiefs headed by daimyō lords with considerable local autonomy. The hatamoto daimyō were the most trustworthy of the daimyō feudal lords, and helped the Tokugawas keep more rebellious han under control.

Hakone, Kobotoke: the names of *seki* (checkpoints) along the major byways. Hakone in particular, guarding the mountain approaches to Edo from the south, was one of the most rigorous seki in feudal Japan.

Ittō-ryū: sword school of Anotsu Kagehisa

Kengō: a highly accomplished swordsman

Kenshi: swordsman (or swordswoman)

Momonji: literally, a "hundred beasts," but usually referring to wild boar, one of the few game animals eaten in pre-modern Japan, where there was a Buddhist prescription against eating animals that walked on four legs. A momonji-ya was a store offering wild boar, venison, and other game.

Mugai-ryū: sword school of the Akagi assassins; literally, "without form"

Ōkido: literally, "the great wood gate," the gates of Edo Castle. Edo Castle, seat of the Tokugawa Shogunate, was a sprawling fortification with inner and outer walls, with residential districts within the outer walls. The ōkido referred to here are gates in these outer walls, the place names of some of which still remain in modern Tokyo.

Rangaku: literally, "Dutch studies," the study of Western science, technology, arts, and society, entering Japan through the predominantly Dutch special economic zone of Dejima Island in Nagasaki harbor, southern Japan

Sagejū: a low-class Edo period call girl. Sagejū would deliver "sagejū" lunch boxes to their clients as a pretext for selling sexual favors.

Sankin gyōretsu: the procession of a feudal lord travelling to or from the capital. To maintain control over Japan's often rebellious fiefs, the Bakufu required feudal lords to alternate every several years between their home fiefs and the capital of Edo. When the lords returned to the provinces, wives or children would have to stay behind as hostages to the central government. This system was called Sankin. The task of relocating a whole household to Edo was colossal, and a Sankin gyōretsu procession could include hundreds of retainers, guards, and servants.

Shihan-dai: senior instructors; in a sword school, swordsmen skilled enough to teach the school's sword technique in place of the head of the school

Tōkaidō, Nakasen, Kōshū: the names of the main byways through Japan. The most famous, the Tōkaidō or eastern sea road, ran near the coast from Edo to Kyoto. The Nakasen and Kōshū byways ran through the mountainous interior of Japan.

Tsuji-kiri: literally, "to cut down at a corner," used to describe anonymous killers, who would attack people on the street. Often assassins, but sometimes obsessed swordsmen who would challenge passing samurai to combat as a way of testing their own skill.

Tsūkō tegata: wooden passes issued by the government to allow travelers to pass through the checkpoints along the major byways. Fearful of rebellion, the Tokugawa Shogunate restricted travel: religious pilgrims and common people could obtain the passes as well, but criminals on the run could not risk applying to the bureaucracy for a pass lest they be arrested on the spot.

Unohana: dried tailings left over from making tofu

Yoshitsune Minamoto: the near-mythical hero of the famous twelfth century war between the Taira and the Minamoto clans. While a real historical figure, Yoshitsune the folk legend was painted as a virtual superhero.

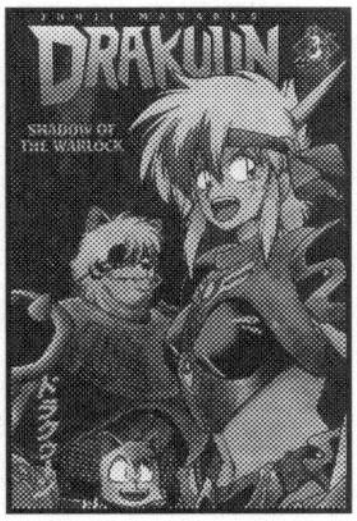
DRAKUUN
SHADOW OF THE WARLOCK

SHADOW OF THE WARLOCK
ISBN: 1-56971-406-1 $14.95

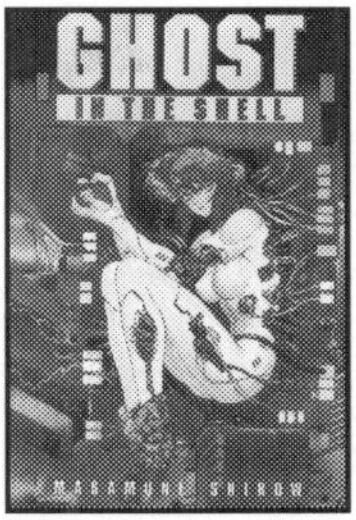
GHOST
IN THE SHELL
MASAMUNE SHIROW

GHOST IN THE SHELL
ISBN: 1-56971-081-3 $24.95

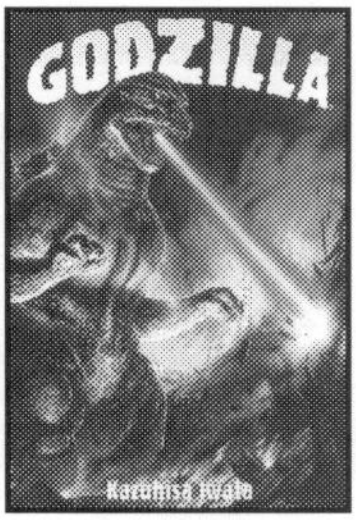
GODZILLA
Kazuhisa Iwata

GODZILLA
ISBN: 1-56971-063-5 $17.95

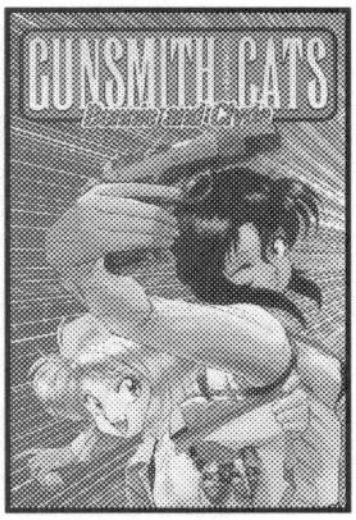
GUNSMITH CATS

BONNIE AND CLYDE
ISBN: 1-56971-215-8 $13.95

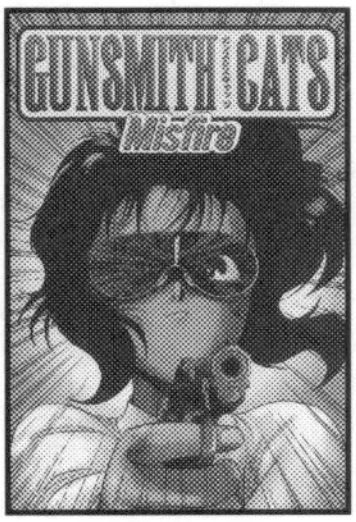
GUNSMITH CATS
Misfire

MISFIRE
ISBN: 1-56971-253-0 $14.95

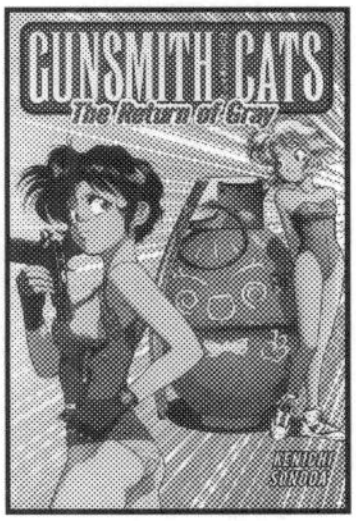
GUNSMITH CATS
The Return of Gray
KENICHI SONODA

THE RETURN OF GRAY
ISBN: 1-56971-299-9 $17.95

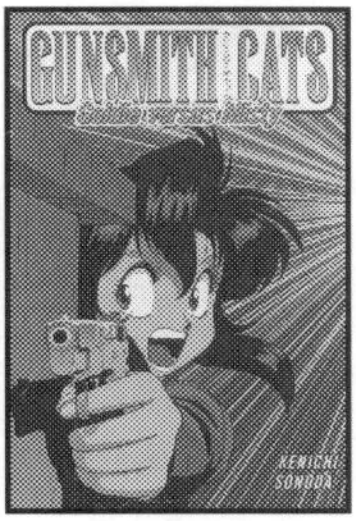
GUNSMITH CATS
KENICHI SONODA

GOLDIE VS. MISTY
ISBN: 1-56971-371-5 $15.95

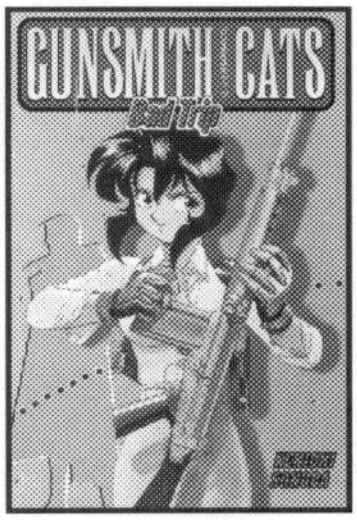
GUNSMITH CATS
Bad Trip

BAD TRIP
ISBN: 1-56971-442-8 $13.95

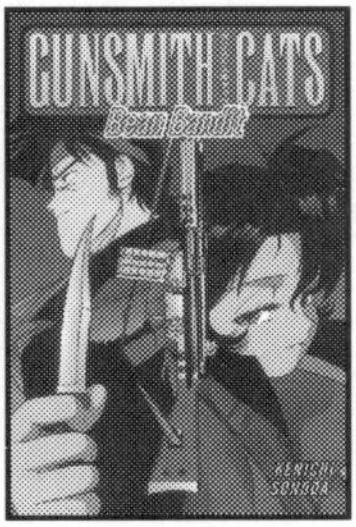
GUNSMITH CATS
Bean Bandit
KENICHI SONODA

BEAN BANDIT
ISBN: 1-56971-453-3 $16.95

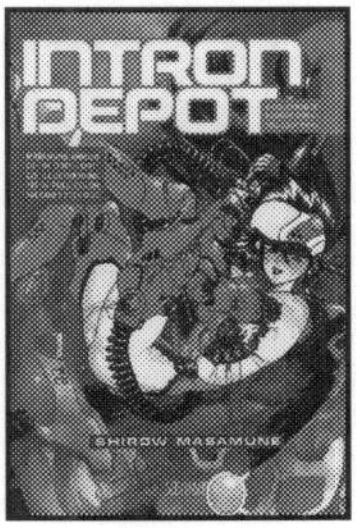
INTRON DEPOT
SHIROW MASAMUNE

INTRON DEPOT
ISBN: 1-56971-085-6 $39.95

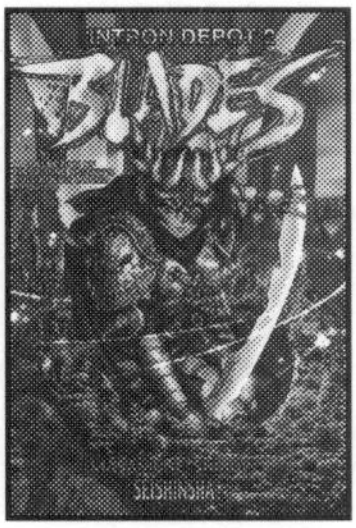
BLADES

INTRON DEPOT 2: BLADES
ISBN: 1-56971-382-0 $39.95

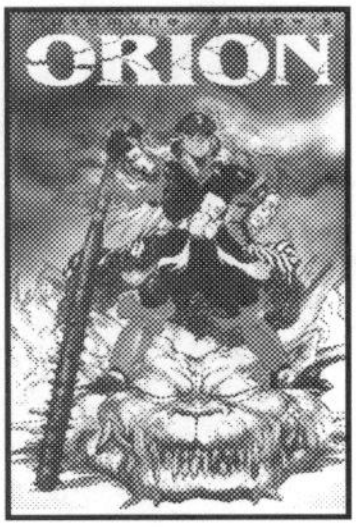
ORION

ORION
ISBN: 1-56971-148-8 $17.95

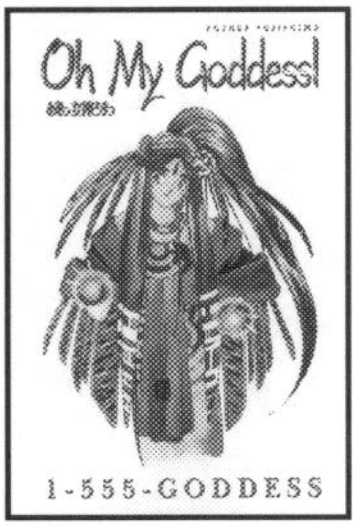
Oh My Goddess!
1-555-GODDESS

1-555-GODDESS
ISBN: 1-56971-207-7 $13.95

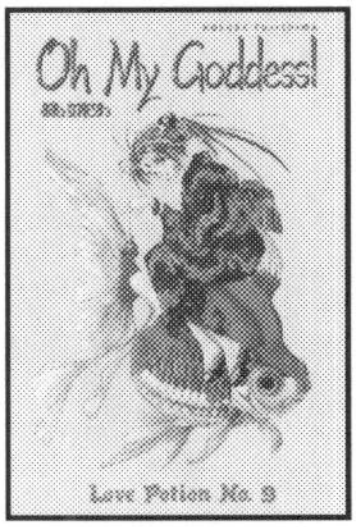
Oh My Goddess!
Love Potion No. 9

LOVE POTION NO. 9
ISBN: 1-56971-252-2 $14.95

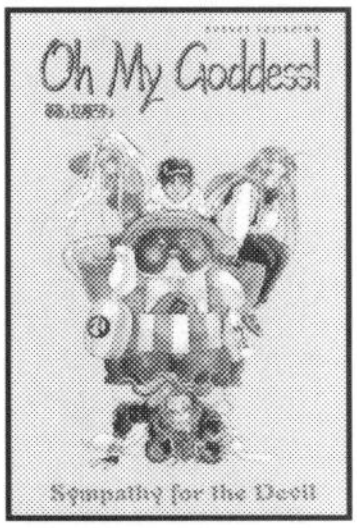
Oh My Goddess!
Sympathy for the Devil

SYMPATHY FOR THE DEVIL
ISBN: 1-56971-329-4 $13.95

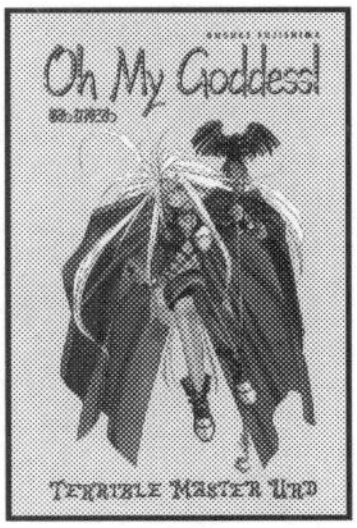
Oh My Goddess!
TERRIBLE MASTER URD

TERRIBLE MASTER URD
ISBN: 1-56971-369-3 $14.95

AVAILABLE AT YOUR LOCAL COMICS SHOP OR BOOKSTORE

To find a comics shop in your area, call 1-888-266-4226 • For more information or to order direct:
• On the web: www.darkhorse.com • E-mail: mailorder@darkhorse.com
• Phone: 1-800-862-0052 or (503) 652-9701 Mon.-Sat. 9 A.M. to 5 P.M. Pacific Time

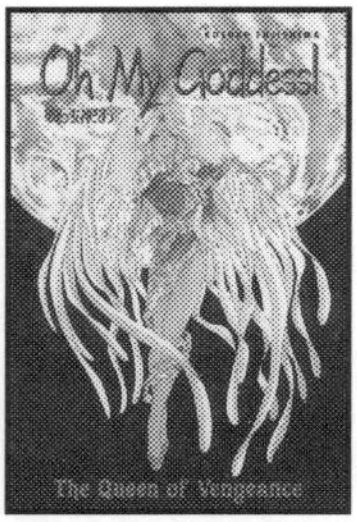
Oh My Goddess!
The Queen of Vengeance

THE QUEEN OF VENGEANCE
ISBN: 1-56971-431-2 $13.95

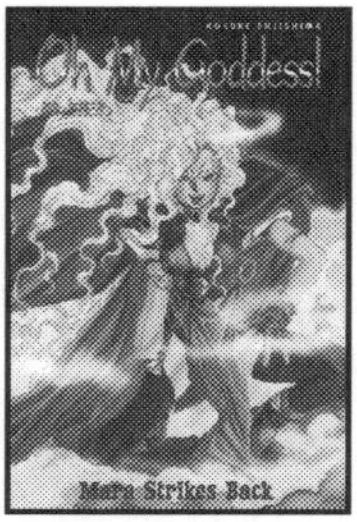
Oh My Goddess!
Mara Strikes Back

MARA STRIKES BACK
ISBN: 1-56971-449-5 $14.95

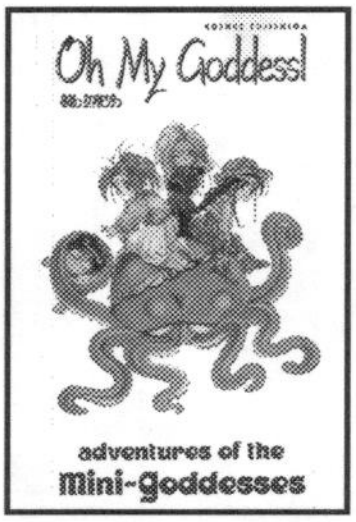
Oh My Goddess!
adventures of the
Mini-Goddesses

ADVENTURES OF THE MINI-GODDESSES
ISBN: 1-56971-421-5 $9.95

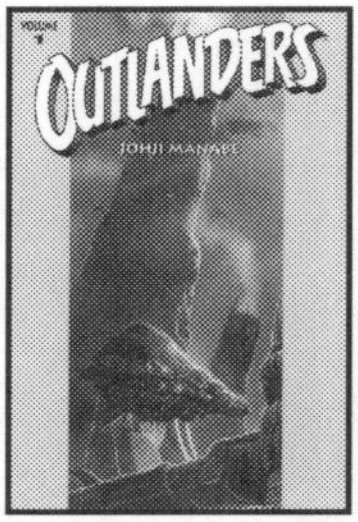
OUTLANDERS
JOHJI MANABE

VOLUME 1
ISBN: 1-56971-161-5 $13.95

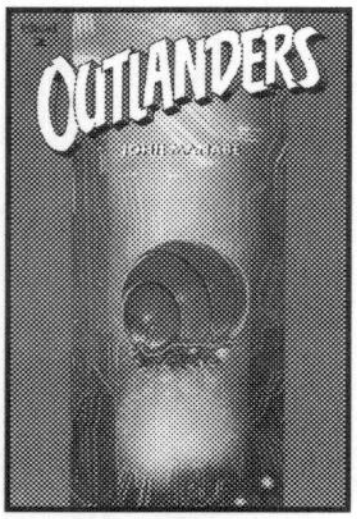
OUTLANDERS

VOLUME 2
ISBN: 1-56971-162-3 $13.95

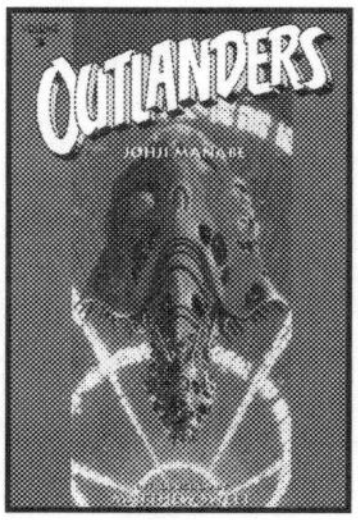
OUTLANDERS
JOHJI MANABE

VOLUME 3
ISBN: 1-56971-163-1 $13.95

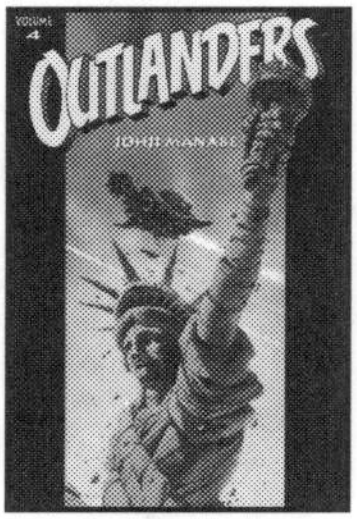
OUTLANDERS
JOHJI MANABE

VOLUME 4
ISBN: 1-56971-069-4 $12.95

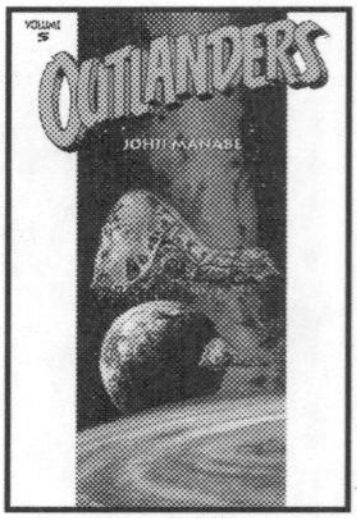
OUTLANDERS
JOHJI MANABE

VOLUME 5
ISBN: 1-56971-275-1 $14.95

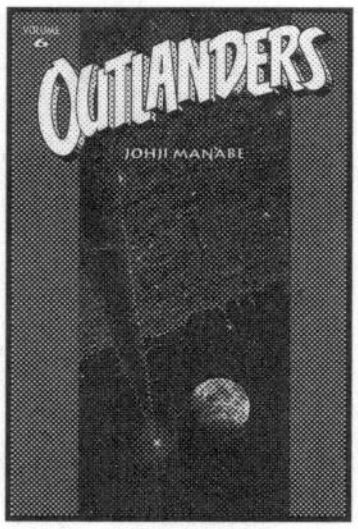
OUTLANDERS
JOHJI MANABE

VOLUME 6
ISBN: 1-56971-423-1 $14.95

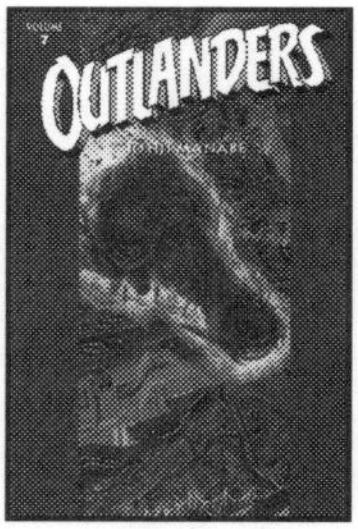
OUTLANDERS

VOLUME 7
ISBN: 1-56971-424-X $14.95

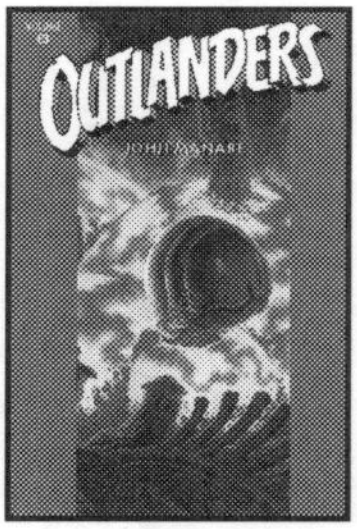
OUTLANDERS

VOLUME 8
ISBN: 1-56971-425-8 $14.95

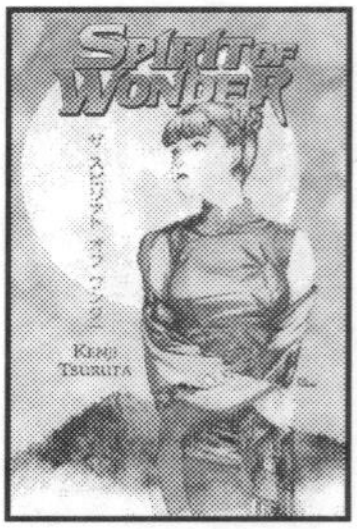
Spirit of Wonder
KENJI TSURUTA

SPIRIT OF WONDER
ISBN: 1-56971-288-3 $12.95

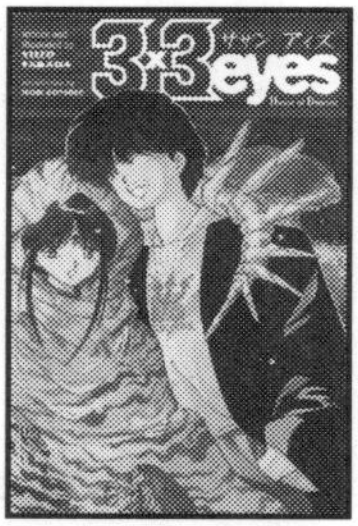
3×3 eyes

HOUSE OF DEMONS
ISBN: 1-56971-059-7 $12.95

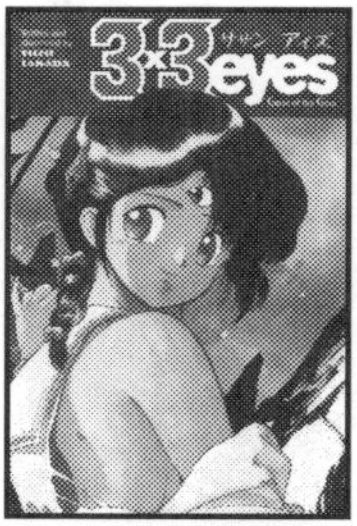
3×3 eyes

CURSE OF THE GESU
ISBN: 1-56971-175-5 $12.95

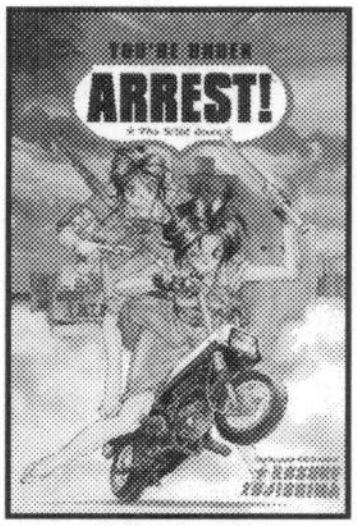
YOU'RE UNDER
ARREST!

THE WILD ONES
ISBN: 1-56971-319-7 $12.95

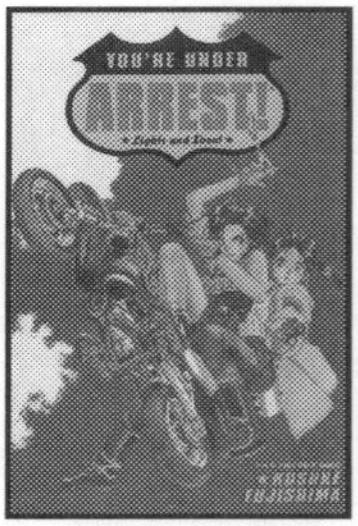
YOU'RE UNDER
ARREST!

LIGHTS AND SIREN
ISBN: 1-56971-432-0 $10.95